Helen Maria Williams
and the Age of Revolution

The Bucknell Studies in Eighteenth-Century Literature and Culture

The Bucknell Studies in Eighteenth-Century Literature and Culture aims to publish challenging, new eighteenth-century scholarship. Of particular interest is critical, historical, and interdisciplinary work that is interestingly and intelligently theorized, and that broadens and refines the conception of the field. At the same time, the series remains open to all theoretical perspectives and different kinds of scholarship. While the focus of the series is the literature, history, arts, and culture (including art, architecture, music, travel, and history of science, medicine, and law) of the long eighteenth century in Britain and Europe, the series is also interested in scholarship that establishes relationships with other geographies, literatures, and cultures of the period 1660–1830.

Titles in This Series

Helen Maria Williams and the Age of Revolution

Deborah Kennedy

Lewisburg
Bucknell University Press
London: Associated University Presses

Associated University Presses
440 Forsgate Drive
Cranbury, NJ 08512

Associated University Presses
16 Barter Street
London WC1A 2AH, England

Associated University Presses
P.O. Box 338, Port Credit
Mississauga, Ontario
Canada L5G 4L8

The paper used in this publication meets the requirements of the American National Standard for Permanence of Paper for Printed Library Materials Z39.48-1984.

Library of Congress Cataloging-in-Publication Data

Kennedy, Deborah, 1959–
    Helen Maria Williams and the Age of Revolution / Deborah Kennedy.
        p.   cm. — (Bucknell studies in eighteenth-century literature and culture)
    Includes bibliographical references and index.
    ISBN 0-8387-5511-9 (alk. paper)
    1. Williams, Helen Maria, 1762–1827.   2. Williams, Helen Maria, 1762–1827 —
Views on French revolution.   3. France — History — Revolution, 1789–1799 —
Historiography.   4. Women and literature — England — History — 18th century.
5. Women and literature — France — History — 19th century.   6. Poets, English —
18th century — Biography.   7. Poets, English — 19th century — Biography.
8. Historians — Great Britain — Biography.   9. British — France — History.
10. Paris (France) — Biography.   I. Title.   II. Series.
PR3765.W54 Z76   2002
821'.6 — dc21
[B]   2001052900

PRINTED IN THE UNITED STATES OF AMERICA

To my husband, my parents, and my sisters

Contents

List of Illustrations

9

Acknowledgements

I WOULD LIKE TO THANK THE MANY LIBRARIANS IN DIFFERENT PARTS of the world who have helped me to locate material related to the research for this book, including B. C. Barker-Benfield, Gayle Barkley, Frances Harris, and Madeleine de Terris. I am grateful for the financial assistance of the Social Sciences and Humanities Research Council of Canada, Saint Mary's University, and Mount Saint Vincent University. For permission to reproduce photographs, I would like to thank the Bibliothèque nationale de France, the Bodleian Library, the British Museum, and the National Portrait Gallery, London. Permission to quote from manuscript letters has kindly been granted by Lord Abinger, the British Library Board, the Huntington Library, John Rylands University Library of Manchester, Harris Manchester College Oxford, Princeton University Library, and University College London.

For assistance in a number of ways, I would like to give special thanks to Marie Bartoszewski, Flora Christie, C. Coquerel, Valerie Creelman, Lesley Crowe, John Dagger, Paul J. A. Fraser, Jack Fruchtman, Jr., Anthony Harding, John Kennedy, Nancy Kennedy, Lorraine Kennedy, William McCarthy, W. C. Pieterse, Allen Robertson, Janet Todd, Eleanor Ty, Lynette Wilkinson, and, most of all, my husband J. Russell Perkin.

Introduction

A FAMOUS BRITISH POET, HELEN MARIA WILLIAMS (1761–1827) GAINED an international reputation for her books on the French Revolution, becoming one of the only women of her era to write on contemporary political subjects. Her 45-year literary career began when she published her first poem in 1782. She soon established herself as a literary hostess in London in the 1780s, and then lived in Paris from the early 1790s until her death at the age of 66 in 1827. Her eight-volume *Letters from France* and subsequent works were based on her eyewitness accounts of the revolutionary changes that altered France and much of Europe during those important decades. Williams recalled having been accustomed from childhood to cherish the noble causes of humanity,[1] and her idealism was shaped by her deeply felt Presbyterian faith and the teachings of her Dissenting friends, who were active in London's reformist Whig circles.

When she moved to Paris, her family became prominent members of the French Protestant community, and she established a salon (or *conversazione*) frequented by eminent writers, politicians, and thinkers of the day, including J. P. Brissot, Madame Roland, Ruth and Joel Barlow, Henri Grégoire, and Alexander von Humboldt. Although Williams never married, she raised her two nephews, Athanase and Charles Coquerel, with the help of her family and her longtime friend, John Hurford Stone, a British reformer and entrepreneur. At the turn of the century, her liberal circle became disenchanted with Bonaparte, and Williams wrote little during his reign; however, she published several books in the post-Napoleonic period, and in her early 60s told a friend she would continue "scribbling" while "I can still hold my pen."[2] A woman formed by the enlightenment, Williams looked confidently towards the future and hoped that her books would "make a part of that marvellous story which the eighteenth century has to record to future times."[3]

Despite the importance and the influence of her books during her lifetime, they suffered from neglect after her death. With the exception of Lionel Woodward's biography in French, *Une anglaise amie de la révolution française: Hélène-Maria Williams et ses amis* (1930), little attention had

13

been paid to Williams until the advent of feminist literary criticism, when in the 1970s two facsimile reprints of Williams's work appeared, including Janet Todd's edition of the spectacular eight-volume *Letters from France* (1975). More recently, studies of the Revolution (invigorated by the 1989 bicentenary) and an increasing interest in early women writers have produced a climate in which work on Williams has flourished. A number of her writings have been anthologized and published in a variety of forms, ranging from a version of her *Letters from France* abridged for young readers to scholarly editions of her poetry and prose.[4]

The following study, which examines her work in chronological order, is interdisciplinary by necessity since Williams's books encompass the fields of British and European literature, history, and politics. It was not for nothing that Williams described herself as a "citizen of the world."[5] She demonstrated a great deal of courage and optimism during the course of her life, qualities epitomized in a comment made when she set out for her first trip to Paris in 1790: giving up a visit to Streatham, the home of her friend Hester Thrale Piozzi, she remarked that, "we have literary conversation, a fine library, charming music and sweet walks; but soothing as these enjoyments are, I must renounce them a little while for the sublimer delights of the French Revolution."[6] Helen Maria Williams's life and literary career show that much would be renounced but much would also be gained by a woman known as "a friend of liberty,"[7] living in the age of revolution.

List of Abbreviations

LF	*Letters from France*, eight volumes in two, introduction by Janet Todd (Delmar: Scholars' Facsimiles & Reprints, 1975). The abbreviation is used only in the notes. Parenthetical citations in the text are identified simply by the series number, the volume number, and the page number (e.g., 2.1.7).
Narrative	*A Narrative of the Events Which Have Taken Place in France from the Landing of Napoleon Bonaparte on the 1st of March, 1815, till the Restoration of Louis XVIII* (Cleveland: Burrows, 1895).
Poems	*Poems*, 2 vols. (London: Cadell, 1786).
Poems 1823	*Poems on Various Subjects. With Introductory Remarks on the Present State of Science and Literature in France* (London: Whittaker, 1823).
Restoration	*Letters on the Events Which Have Passed in France Since the Restoration in 1815* (London: Baldwin, Cradock, and Joy, 1819).
Sketches	*Sketches of the State of Manners and Opinions in the French Republic, towards the Close of the Eighteenth Century*, 2 vols. (London: Robinson, 1801).
Souvenirs	*Souvenirs de la révolution française*, translated by Charles Coquerel (Paris: Dondey-Dupré, 1827).
Tour	*A Tour in Switzerland; Or, A View of the Present State of the Governments and Manners of those Cantons: with Comparative Sketches of the Present State of Paris*, 2 vols. (London: Robinson, 1798).
Woodward	Lionel Woodward, *Une anglaise amie de la révolution française: Hélène-Maria Williams et ses amis* (Paris: Librairie Ancienne Honoré Champion, 1930; Geneva: Slatkine Reprints, 1977).

Chronology

1761   Helen Maria Williams born in London on 17 June 1761. Her parents, Helen Hay and Charles Williams, were married 1 June 1758.

1762   Charles Williams (father) dies.

n.d.   Resides in Berwick-upon-Tweed.

1781   Returns to London.

1782   *Edwin and Eltruda.*

1783   *An Ode on the Peace.*

1784   *Peru.*

1786   *Poems.*

1788   *A Poem on the Bill Lately Passed for Regulating the Slave Trade.* "The Morai. An Ode."

1790   *Julia, A Novel; Interspersed with Some Poetical Pieces.*
Travels to France, July 1790.
Returns to England, September 1790.
Letters written in France in the summer 1790; or *Letters from France* (first series) vol. 1.

1791   *A Farewell, for Two Years, to England. Poems* 2nd. ed.
Travels to France, August 1791

1792   *Letters from France* (first series) vol. 2.
Returns to England, June 1792.
Travels to France, August 1792.

1793   *Letters from France* (first series) vol. 3 and 4.
Imprisoned in Paris, October to November 1793.

1794   Cecilia Williams (sister) marries Marie-Martin-Athanase Coquerel, March 1794.
Travels to Switzerland, c. June to December 1794.

1795   Nephew Athanase Coquerel is born, August 1795.
Trans. *Paul and Virginia*, by J.H. Bernardin de Saint-Pierre.
Letters from France (second series) vol. 1 and 2.
Letters from France (second series) vol. 3.

1796   *Letters from France* (second series) vol. 4.
Poems included in *Poems. Moral, Elegant and Pathetic.*
"On the Death of the Rev. Dr. Kippis," *Gentleman's Magazine.*

1797 Nephew Charles Coquerel is born, April 1797.

1798 *A Tour in Switzerland.*
      Cecilia Coquerel (sister) dies, September 1798.

1799 Writes obituary for Charles B. Wadstrom, in *Decade Philosophique*
      and *Monthly Magazine.*

1801 *Sketches of the State of Manners and Opinions in the French Republic.*
      Publishes "Ode to Peace," in the *Morning Chronicle.*

1803 Edits *The Political and Confidential Correspondence of Lewis the Six-
      teenth*, 3 vols.

1809 *Verses Addressed by H. M. W. to Her Two Nephews on Saint Helen's
      Day.*

1812 Mrs. Helen Williams (mother) dies, April 1812.

1814 Trans. *Researches concerning . . . Inhabitants of America*, by Alexan-
      der von Humboldt.
      Trans. *Personal Narrative of Travels to . . . the New Continent*, by
      Alexander von Humboldt, 7 vols. 1814–1827.

1815 *A Narrative of the Events Which Have Taken Place in France from the
      Landing of Napoleon Bonaparte to the Restoration of Louis XVIII.*

1816 *On the Late Persecution of the Protestants.*

1817 Trans. *The Leper of the City of Aoste*, by Xavier de Maistre.
      Naturalized as French citizen.

1818 John Hurford Stone dies, May 1818.

1819 *Letters on the Events Which Have Passed in France Since the Restora-
      tion in 1815.*
      The Charter.

1823 *Poems on Various Subjects.*
      Moves to Amsterdam.
      Persis Williams (half-sister) dies, December 1823.

1827 Returns to Paris.
      Souvenirs de la révolution française, trans. Charles Coquerel.
      Helen Maria Williams dies, 15 December 1827, age 66.

Helen Maria Williams
and the Age of Revolution

1

The Poetry of Sensibility

In her *LETTERS FROM FRANCE*, HELEN MARIA WILLIAMS ONCE DEscribed herself as belonging to a "family of women" (2.1.7), which seems an appropriate way to characterize her early years, since her father died when she was only an infant, and she and her sister and half-sister grew up under the care of her mother. Little is known about the life of Williams before her rise to fame in the 1780s, but surviving records allow for at least the following account of her family background. She was born in London on 17 June 1761 to Charles and Helen Williams.[1] Charles Williams was a man of some property, who served as the Secretary for the island of Minorca. This was a second marriage for him; he was a widower with one child, named Persis after his first wife. It is likely that, before he went to Minorca, he was stationed with the army in Cork, Ireland, since his daughter was born there in 1743.[2] When Williams's parents married on 1 June 1758 in St. Martin-in-the-Fields, Westminster, Persis Williams was one of the witnesses who signed the marriage register, and she became a well-loved member of her father's new family.[3]

Helen Maria Williams's mother, Helen Hay, was 27 when she married Charles Williams. She was Scottish, christened in Kilmany, Fife, on 27 December 1730, and the daughter of George Hay and Mary Balfour,[4] whose own marriage had been recorded in 1713 in Errol, Perth, and Kingsbarns, Fife.[5] Helen Hay may have been introduced to Charles Williams by her brother, David Hay, who probably knew him in Minorca, where Hay served in Port-Mahon as secretary for Lieutenant-General William Blakeney (1672–1761), the Lieutenant-Governor of Minorca from 1748–1756.[6] When the British were forced to surrender Minorca to the French in 1756, David Hay brought with him from the island a Bible that was then passed down in the Williams family as the treasured "Bible de Minorca."[7]

Charles and Helen Williams had two children, but although we have been able to ascertain the date of Helen Maria Williams's birth, no birth records have been found for either her or her sister Cecilia, though it has been conjectured that Cecilia was the older sister. Just four years after his marriage, Charles Williams died in December 1762, when both girls were still infants; he was buried on 23 December 1762 in St. John the Evangelist Church, Westminster.[8] Identified in his will as then a resident of West Clandon, Surrey, he left an annuity of 50 pounds to his daughter Persis, and the remainder of his estate to his wife Helen and their children, with provisions for supporting his own mother.[9] His estate and his pension would provide the main source of income for the Williams family for several decades. A useful and succinct account of these circumstances is found in the diary of the British painter Joseph Farington, who visited Helen Maria Williams in 1802:

> Moore told me that Miss Williams's father was Coll. Williams who had a situation under the English Government being a Consul or Agent to some State in the Mediterranean. He had two Wives & by the second wife, Sister to Coll. [blank] had Miss Williams. Mrs Williams, the Widow, has a small pension and also Mrs Williams the daughter of the former wife abt. £90 a year.[10]

Farington's diary entry is one of the few extant references to Williams's father; she never mentioned him in her work, though she may have been alluding to his death when she wrote elsewhere of her "early sorrows" (Poems 1823, ix).[11]

Even though Williams and her sister Cecilia were too young to remember their father, they were taught to value his Welsh ancestry. The Williams children—Persis, Cecilia, and Helen—were raised to have a sense of pride in their family heritage. These loyalties were passed on to the next generation. Of the three daughters, Cecilia was the only one to marry and have children. She and her French husband, Marie-Martin-Athanase Coquerel, had two boys, Athanase and Charles Coquerel, who both took a keen interest in their British background. Cecilia's son Athanase recounted his parentage in the Preface to one of his own books, published in 1847:

> our grandfather, Mr. Ch. Williams, of Aberconway, Caernarvon, Wales, held a high station in the War Office; he was descended from a very old Welsh family; one of his ancestors having been John Williams of Aberconway, Archbishop of York, who succeeded Bacon as Keeper of the Seals. To one of the branches of the family belonged the celebrated dissenting divine, Daniel Williams, who married, in 1701, the daughter of a French refugee, and left to his trustees, for public use, the institution called Williams's library. Our grandmother was a Hay of Naughton, a direct descendant of one of the ardent supporters of religious liberty in Scotland, who took the

field for the Covenant in 1643; and I still preserve with due care his silken banner, blue and white.[12]

The Hay banner is preserved today, and a family history and Coquerel genealogy is on file at the Société de'l Histoire du Protestantisme Français, in Paris, an institution supported in its early years by Williams's nephew Athanase Coquerel and his son the liberal theologian Athanase Coquerel, Jr. (1820–75).[13]

Helen Maria Williams was raised in the Presbyterian tradition of her mother. Mrs. Williams's piety was legendary in the family; in an obituary for his uncle Charles Coquerel (the second of Cecilia's two children), Athanase Coquerel, Jr., mentioned that Mrs. Williams influenced the whole family with her "Scottish Presbyterian piety— fervent, grave, deep."[14] Members of the family were known as dedicated Protestants, who regarded the Bible as the most important book in the house; and, Williams once gave the following brief glimpse into her Protestant upbringing: "For myself, brought up in all the severity of dissenting principles, every impression of childhood, every remembered habit of early life, impel me to reverence the strict observance of the Sabbath."[15] Mrs. Williams and her children were members of the Reverend Dr. Andrew Kippis's congregation at the Princes Street Presbyterian Church in Westminster.[16] The well-liked Kippis (1725–1795) was minister at Princes Street from 1753 until his death in 1795. Helen Maria Williams wrote a memorial poem to Kippis, in which she recounts that he taught her "in the house of prayer" when she was a child, and then helped her to discover her literary vocation:

> My earliest teacher, and my latest guide.
> First, in the house of pray'r, his voice impress'd
> Celestial precepts on my infant breast;
> 'The hope that rests above,' my childhood taught,
> And lifted first to God my ductile thought.[17]

In his Preface to her first published poem, *Edwin and Eltruda. A Legendary Tale*, Kippis states that he had "long been intimate with the family," and that Williams moved from her "native" London to a "remote" region of England at an early age:

> The young lady who is the writer of the following Poem is a native of London, but was removed, with her Family, in very early life, to a remote part of the kingdom, where her sole instruction was derived from a virtuous, amiable, and sensible mother.[18]

It appears that some time after the death of Charles Williams, Mrs. Williams moved with her two children and her step-daughter to Berwick-upon-Tweed to be closer to her own Scottish relatives. Several years later, the clergyman Percival Stockdale recalled meeting Helen Maria Williams in Berwick-upon-Tweed in 1779. This was before she had become a published poet, but even then Stockdale (who later criticized her for her support of the Revolution) observed her "elegant literary taste" and the engaging earnestness for which she became known:

> HELEN MARIA WILLIAMS, at that time lived at BERWICK. The graces of her mind, were *then*, as attractive, and charming, as those of her person. She had a tenderness, and delicacy of soul; and was a sincere friend of all order, moral, civil, and religious.[19]

Having been valued at a young age for the "graces of her mind," not only for her beauty, probably helped Williams to gain the confidence to become, in Anna Seward's words, Britain's "lovely female bard."[20]

In summer 1781, Mrs. Williams brought her two daughters and her step-daughter back to London.[21] Helen Maria Williams, now 20 years old, had been writing verses from a young age. In her memorial poem to Kippis, she wrote that

> When first with timid hand I touch'd the lyre,
> And felt the youthful poet's proud desire;
> His lib'ral comment fann'd the dawning flame,
> His plaudit sooth'd me with a Poet's name.[22]

Once in London, Kippis helped her to publish her work. A literary man as well as a Presbyterian minister, Kippis wrote several pamphlets on political reform including *A Vindication of the Protestant Dissenting Ministers* (1772). He belonged to a number of Whig organizations such as the Club of Honest Whigs, a group made up mostly of Dissenters interested in politics and science, including Joseph Priestley, Richard Price, James Burgh, Samuel Vaughan, and Benjamin Franklin.[23] Known as an amiable man, Kippis was a contributor to the *Gentleman's Magazine* and an editor for the *New Annual Register* and the *Biographia Britannica*. His own connections as a respectable Presbyterian minister and man of letters enabled Williams to establish a place for herself in London's literary and Whig circles. By the time that she published her major two-volume collection *Poems* in 1786, she was well known as the author of three major poems: *Edwin and Eltruda* (1782), *An Ode on the Peace* (1783), and *Peru* (1784).

Andrew Kippis was a valuable mentor and father figure for Williams. He promoted her early work from the beginning. Not only did he write a preface for *Edwin and Eltruda*, but he printed an extract from it in the

New Annual Register (1783), and ensured that she was mentioned in that journal's essay on "Domestic Literature, of the Year 1782":

> A new female poet hath been introduced into the world, in the writer of "Edwin and Eltruda; a Legendary Tale." The author is a young lady of about twenty years of age, Miss Helen Williams. This production, though somewhat diffuse, affords many demonstrations of excellence, being highly pathetic, and abounding with strokes of genuine poetry. In the language there is a happy union of simplicity and elegance. The genius of Miss Williams, if properly cultivated and improved, will, in time, enable her to rank with the first poetic ladies of this country.[24]

Following convention, the title page of *Edwin and Eltruda* noted only that the poem was "By a Young Lady." But, in the *New Annual Register*, Kippis can with propriety identify Williams by name, and he uses glowing terms to usher into the world "a new female poet," whom he hoped would become one of the "first poetic ladies of this country."

Edwin and Eltruda was a promising start. Set during the War of the Roses, it owed much to the current interest in the ballad tradition and in literature of sensibility. A pacifist, Williams laments how war tears apart the families of Edwin and Eltruda, who fight on opposite sides. The poem ends with the tragic death of the young couple, who had been full of promise and exemplars of benevolence. The portrait of Eltruda is especially poignant because she is such a gentle young woman. Her actions epitomize the way a woman of feeling should live her life, caring for all around her:

> For the bruis'd insect on the waste,
> A sigh would heave her breast;
> And oft her careful hand replac'd
> The linnet's falling nest.
>
> . . . .
>
> Full oft with eager step she flies
> To cheer the roofless cot,
> Where the lone widow breathes her sighs,
> And wails her desp'rate lot.[25]

Eltruda's charity extends to the life of other creatures, not only to human beings. While some people would regard an interest in animal welfare as a ludicrous extension of the ethos of sensibility, it is in keeping with Williams's humane beliefs and was a concern of hers for all of her life, though it would be some time before the protection of animals became a topic of public debate. Both Edwin and Eltruda seem to have walked out of the pages of Thomas Gray's *Elegy Written in a Country*

Church-Yard) (1751), a poem that influences this one throughout. The young pair are uncorrupted by wealth and in their goodness they embody the "soothing dream / Of golden ages past" (*Poems* 1:72). But their story is tragic because of what Williams regards as a senseless war, and finally "the mournful muse" must wipe away "the tears that blot / The melancholy page" (*Poems* 1:93). Williams's first published poem, though conventional in some ways, demonstrates her willingness to deal with the ills of the world through the medium of the sympathetic heart, for which she became known.

By 1782, Kippis had introduced her to several writers of his acquaintance, including William Hayley (1745–1820), Joseph Warton (1722–1800), Thomas Warton (1728–90), and John Hoole (1727–1803), Johnson's good friend and the translator of Tasso and Ariosto. Frances Burney's sister Charlotte Burney recorded meeting Williams at a large party given by Hoole, which Kippis and the Wartons also attended in January 1782: "Miss Williams, author of Edwin and Eldrada [sic], a legendary tale, a pretty girl rather, but so superfinely affected that, tho' I had the honour of being introduced to her, I could n't think of conversing with her."[26] Although she found Williams "affected," she also noticed that many of the people at the party were interested in meeting her: "Mr. Blunt senior came took him [Mr. Mathias] off to introduce him to Miss Williams, and then I had scarce any more fun with him."[27] Charlotte Burney appears to be put off by Williams's ease in the company of men, but perhaps it was that very ease that made Williams suited to her eventual role as literary hostess (or salonnière). Furthermore, Williams's friendship with men like the influential Warton brothers was important to her becoming known in literary circles. The Wartons had, after all, helped to shape the literary tastes of the late eighteenth century. Thomas Warton, famous for his poem *The Pleasures of Melancholy* (1747) and his multi-volume *History of English Poetry* (1774–81), became Poet Laureate in 1785. His older brother, Joseph Warton, a member of Johnson's Literary Club, was the author of the controversial *Essay on Pope* (1756) and the head of Winchester School. He befriended many writers, among them "some of the leading literary women" of the age, and Williams included in a later book of poetry a piece written at his request: "Dulce Domum, an old Latin Ode, sung annually by the Winchester Boys" (*Poems 1823*, 219).[28]

William Hayley, another popular poet and friend of Kippis, also encouraged Williams to pursue her literary work. Hayley's biographer explains that he helped the "learned and benevolent Dr. Kippis" with his work on the *Biographia Britannica*, and later, as a progressive liberal, Hayley shared Williams's enthusiasm for the French Revolution.[29] His letters provide useful information about this early phase of Williams's career, revealing how she herself was emerging as both a poet and a literary hostess. On 17 January 1783, he wrote that he was "engaged to drink tea with Mrs. Bates, (the exquisite singer) on Thursday next, at the house of the young Muse, (Miss Williams,) who is also musical."[30] It is possible that he may have introduced Williams to Charlotte Smith since it is believed that the two women knew each other, and it was around this time that Joseph Warton and Charlotte Smith visited Hayley at his country home.[31]

Williams was also becoming acquainted with Elizabeth Montagu, the famous bluestocking, known as the Queen of the Blues. As Stuart Curran has observed, "an entire school of poets—women poets—" owed a debt of gratitude to "the intellectual energy of the bluestocking circle of Elizabeth Carter and Elizabeth Montagu."[32] Hayley's letters reveal that by January 1783, Williams was already making plans to dedicate one of her poems to the formidable Montagu (it would be *Peru*):

> On my calling yesterday morning on the young Muse, (Helen Maria Williams,) she told me she had an intention of dedicating her *Poem* to Mrs. Montagu, who has indeed behaved with the most friendly politeness to her; and upon my expressing the highest approbation of her design, she produced a letter from Mrs. Montagu to her on the subject, which contained the portrait I have mentioned. She had dined with her patroness the preceding day, and her manuscript is now in Portman-square.[33]

Williams made several visits to Portman Square, discussing her poetry with Montagu, who, in turn, discussed it with others, as Hayley reports:

> From Gibbon, I proceeded to the great Mrs. Montagu, and was honoured with a *tete-à-tete* in her magnificent mansion. Our whole discourse turned on the poem of the young Muse, which she criticised with infinite spirit and judgement and with the most friendly severity.[34]

Elizabeth Montagu's own literary fame rested on her reputation as a critic following the publication of her *Essay on the Writings and Genius of Shakespeare* (1769). Montagu was regarded by some as "the best female critic, ever produced in any country," and it would have been a compliment for Williams to be the recipient of her "friendly severity."[35]

When the *Ode on the Peace* was published in 1783, the title page again omitted Williams's name, referring to her only as the author of *Edwin and Eltruda*. The poem had no dedication, but it did include complimentary passages on both Hayley and Montagu. Andrew Kippis himself had written a pamphlet on the peace between Britain and America, and he and his Whig friends had argued in favour of American independence for years, so he may have encouraged Williams to write a poem on the subject.[36] In the patriotic rhetoric of the *Ode*, the state of peace is celebrated as a fitting condition for a noble and enlightened nation. Peace is a nation's glory, as are its scientific and artistic achievements. Surveying some of the leading figures of her age (many of whom she knew personally), Williams mentions George Romney's paintings (*Poems* 1:51, note); William Hayley's poetry ("Hayley wakes the magic string," *Poems* 1:52); the historical writing of Hayley's friend Edward Gibbon (the "historic Muse," *Poems* 1:53); the work of the astronomer William Herschel, who discovered the planet Uranus in 1781 (*Poems* 1:54); and the "eloquence and wit" of Elizabeth Montagu (*Poems* 1:55). Williams depicts war as a stain on the image of a civilized nation that prided itself on its progressive institutions and culture. Her treatment of this theme was particularly commended in Kippis's *New Annual Register*, which printed two sonnets and extracts from her *Ode* in 1784:

> Now we are speaking of odes, we must not omit one upon the peace, for which the public is indebted to Miss Helen Williams, author of the elegant and pathetic legendary tale, Edwin and Eltruda. The restoration of the peace was a proper subject for the Muse, though being a political event, it was scarcely popular enough to excite much attention. Miss Williams's Ode upon it has not detracted from, but added to her reputation. The thoughts are well adapted to the occasion, the images truly poetical, the versification sweetly harmonious, and, towards the conclusion, where the author describes the advancement of art and science, she rises to no small degree of sublimity.[37]

The reviewer acknowledges some surprise in Williams choosing to write on a "political" event, but no mention is made of it being an inappropriate subject for a woman; in fact, the poem is regarded as one that would strengthen "her reputation" as a writer.[38]

In the late eighteenth century, the atmosphere of acceptance for women poets owed a great deal to earlier writers, bluestocking hostesses, and male mentors. Among the last group, perhaps the most important was Samuel Johnson, who encouraged so many women in their intellectual and literary pursuits.[39] By the time that Williams met Johnson in 1784, she was known as a "poetess." Charlotte Burney again lists her among the guests at John Hoole's in January 1784: "There was an immense party between dinner and supper, thirty five people, among them were Romney the painter, . . . Dr. Kippis, *Miss Williams, the poetess*, Captain Romney, Mr. Romney's brother, the Kirwins, Captain Phillips."[40] It was at another party of John Hoole's on 30 May 1784 that Kippis introduced her to Samuel Johnson, who complimented her *Ode on the Peace*, an incident recounted in Boswell's *Life of Johnson*:

He had dined that day at Mr. Hoole's, and Miss Helen Maria Williams being expected in the evening, Mr. Hoole put into his hands her beautiful "Ode on the Peace;" Johnson read it over, and when this amiable, elegant, and accomplished young lady was presented to him, he took her by the hand in the most courteous manner, and repeated the finest stanza of her poem; this was the most delicate and pleasing compliment he could pay. Her respectable friend, Dr. Kippis, from whom I had this anecdote, was standing by, and was not a little gratified. Miss Williams told me, that the only other time she was fortunate enough to be in Dr. Johnson's company, he asked her to sit down by him, which she did, and upon her inquiring how he was, he answered, 'I am very ill indeed, Madam. I am very ill even when you are near me; what should I be were you at a distance.'[41]

Johnson died on 13 December 1784; Williams met him only twice, but their acquaintance was important to her, and she frequently and with great fondness alludes to his work in her own books.

In 1784, Williams began her custom of publishing with her name on the title page, showing a confidence that set her apart from other women writers who were still cautious about putting themselves forward in the public eye. Williams's name first appeared on *Peru*, a major poem in six cantos, which was prominently reviewed. An ambitious work (to be discussed later), it was preceded by a dedicatory poem to Elizabeth Montagu, dated 24 April 1784 (*Poems* 2:51). Williams honors Montagu for her intellectual achievements, for her charity, and for being a model to other women: "woman, pointing to thy finished page, / Claims from imperious man the critic wreathe" (*Poems* 2:50). The dedication, entitled "To Mrs. Montagu," was discussed in bluestocking circles, as Mary Hamilton recounts in her diary:

Sunday, May 23 [1784] . . . Mr. Pepys read aloud a dedication to Mrs. [Elizabeth] Montagu, prefix'd to a Poem just published by Miss Williams . . . extremely pretty . . . 10 (p.m.) I went to Mrs. Montagu's she had a large Assembly of People of Fashion . . . I told Mrs. Montagu that I had just heard Miss Williams' dedication read, & how well I was pleased with it.[42]

Williams's poetry was being read in first-rate literary company. After being in London for only three years, she had achieved a noteworthy and respectable position as a young poet.

It was around this time that Williams became friends with another woman writer, Anna Seward (1742–1809), whom she had complimented in the *Ode on the Peace* (*Poems* 1:40–41). Seward's father the Reverend Thomas Seward (1708–90) was rector of Lichfield, and a poet and member of Erasmus Darwin's Lunar Society. He had written for Dodsley's *Collection* (1748) the anonymous piece called "The Female

Right to Literature," and his daughter Anna began publishing poetry in the late 1770s, receiving some acclaim for her *Elegy on Captain Cook* (1780) and other works.[43] Though Anna Seward could be a harsh critic, she was helpful to Williams, taking her under her wing when they met in 1785, introducing her to a number of literary people, and offering advice on her work. Seward prepared her own letters for posthumous publication, and they include several to Helen Maria Williams. One dated 25 August 1785 begins affectionately, "I write to you, dear Helen."[44] They became intimate friends, as one of Seward's biographers confirms: "In May [1786] Anna Seward . . . made one of her rare visits to London . . . She was much with her friend Helen Maria Williams, the poet."[45] Seward's letter of 5 June 1786 shows how much Williams was beginning to establish herself as a literary hostess in London: "Shall I talk to you of our animated literary breakfasting, at the house of Miss Helen Williams, Mr. Mathias, &c.; of the belle esprits of both sexes, whose genius, wit, and knowledge, made those little meetings so brilliant?"[46] Herself a strong-minded single woman, Seward thrived on intelligent company and especially enjoyed her time at Williams's because of the camaraderie among "the belle esprits of both sexes."

Of the half-a-dozen or so poems written about Helen Maria Williams during her lifetime, one of the most interesting is a poem by Seward published in February 1785 in *London Magazine*. Laudatory verses addressed by one poet to another were common in the eighteenth century among both male and female poets.[47] In her sonnet, Seward praises Williams for taking on the challenge of an epic poem, or, in her words, seizing "the epic lyre—with art divine":

Sonnet to Miss Williams,
On her Epic Poem PERU.

Poetic Sister, who, with daring hand,
  Ere thy fourth lustre's last soft year is flown,
Hast seiz'd the epic lyre—with art divine;
  Wak'd on its golden strings each spirit bland!
  Or bade its deep sonorous tones expand.
Shalt thou the claim to glory's meed resign,
Call other strains, less silver sweet than thine,
  To hymn the fate of a disastrous land?
  See, at that call, Peru's wild genius flies,
To Thespian bow'rs!—there, as Urania strays,
Grasps her bright robe, and thus impatient cries,
  With bending knee and supplicating gaze:
  "Be mine alone the lovely female bard,
'O from obtrusive lyres my well-sung story guard!"[48]

This sonnet is especially important as a tribute from one "poetic sister" to another, with Seward praising Williams as if what she had done in the six-canto *Peru* is good for all women poets. By using the phrases "poetic sister" and "lovely female bard," she also asserts a positive and empowering identity for women poets, demonstrating a solidarity between them. In other words, bards do not only have to be men, there can be "female bard[s]" as well, and women can assert a collective right to poetry in all its forms, including the most elevated classical form of the "epic lyre."

As James Averill has put it, "Poetesses were in vogue in the eighties."[49] This was apparent in the popularity of serious poets like Seward, Smith, More, and Williams, as well as women associated with the more eccentric Della Cruscan circle, which was formed by Robert Merry, Hester Thrale Piozzi, William Parsons, and Bertie Greatheed who had all collaborated in 1785 on the *Florence Miscellany*, a collection of about 80 poems, written for amusement during their stay in Florence.[50] Afterward, although people like William Gifford in his *Baviad* ridiculed the Della Cruscans, Merry engaged in an exchange of poems with the poet Hannah Cowley, who used the pen name Anna Matilda to conduct a literary correspondence with Merry in the press. Although these poems did not have the seriousness of Williams's writing, they contributed to what was a unique atmosphere in the 1780s when female poets were given a significant level of acceptance. That did not mean that there were no caricatures, criticisms, or rivalries, however, as shown in this private letter from Horace Walpole to Lady Ossory, dated 4 November 1786:

> Miss Hannah More is the best of our numerous Calliopes; and her heart is worth all Pindus. Misses Seward and Williams and half-a-dozen more of those harmonious virgins, have no imagination, no novelty. Their thoughts and phrases are like their gowns, old remnants cut and turned.[51]

Horace Walpole was certainly the master of the cutting remark, and in this passage he attacks women poets where they were most vulnerable: the question of their femininity. Exempting only his friend Hannah More, Walpole denigrates the female poets of his day en masse. His use of the analogy that compares their thoughts to their "old" gowns was especially pointed since a woman's appearance—her neatness and mode of dress—were so essential to her respectability. According to this formulation, only a woman who is unfeminine would try to be a poet; and a female poet is by definition slovenly and unclean. However amusing his sartorial comparison may be, Walpole's comment is a reminder of the animosity that women still faced despite the climate of acceptance in the 1780s.

Still, Helen Maria Williams was fortunate to have many influential friends. Around 1784, she met Dr. John Moore, who would become an important mentor, second only to Andrew Kippis. Moore (1729–1802) was a medical doctor from Glasgow who had moved to London in 1778, after spending five years travelling on the continent as tutor to the Scottish nobleman the young Douglas, 8th Duke of Hamilton. A literary man as well as a physician, Moore published several novels; two popular travel books, *A View of Society and Manners in France, Switzerland, and Germany* (1779) and *A View of Society and Manners in Italy* (1781); and two books on the French Revolution, *A Journal during a Residence in France* (1793) and *A View of the Causes and Progress of the French Revolution* (1795).[52] He and Williams developed an affectionate friendship, nourished no doubt by their shared Scottish background.[53] Moore took the opposite view of Horace Walpole by respecting Williams's literary vocation. In his admiration of her for caring more about the life of the mind and spirit than the body, he recalls the admonitions of Mary Astell in *A Serious Proposal to the Ladies* (1694) and the speech of Clarissa in Pope's *The Rape of the Lock* (1717). In one playful poem, Moore did tease Williams about her appearance, but he felt free to do so because he thought she was "remarkably pretty," and so she could take the jest:

> For *you* never can think—you're too much refined—
> That your body is *you*—you's entirely your mind.
> And when yr sweet genius so gracefully flows,
> In melodious verse or poetical prose,
> Who thinks of your chin or the turn of yr toes?
> For you, my dear Helen, have proved by your works
> That women have souls, in the teeth of the Turks.[54]

While Moore's humour might not be to everyone's taste, his verse does reveal how Williams's friends perceived her as being very earnest in her literary pursuits. Unlike many of her peers, she was not primarily interested in fashion and appearance.

Williams included in her *Poems* of 1786 a long poem in Moore's honor, entitled "Epistle to Dr. Moore, Author of A View of Society and Manners in France, Switzerland, and Germany" (*Poems* 2:3–20). Somewhat reminiscent of Pope's praise of Dr. Arbuthnot in his *Epistle* of 1736, Williams's "Epistle to Dr. Moore" commends his gifts as a doctor and as a man of letters, who encouraged her own interest in the life of the mind. Moore's travel books enabled her vicariously to roam "the foreign paths" of Europe (*Poems* 2:8), and she admired his tolerance and acceptance of others, in contrast to those who through "Europe range,/ And deem all bad, because 'tis strange" (*Poems* 2:19). The literary associations of some of his destinations also appealed to her, including his visit to Virgil's tomb:

> I feel how oft his magic powers
> Shed pleasure on my lonely hours.
> Tho' hid from me the classic tongue,
> In which his heavenly strain was sung,
> In *Dryden*'s tuneful lines, I pierce
> The shaded beauties of his verse.
>
> (*Poems* 2:16–17)

This passage illustrates Williams's fascination with the world at large, with a world of history and literature beyond London, beyond Berwick-upon-Tweed. Her own interest in the intellectual wealth of the world is evident in her gratitude to Dryden for his English translation of Virgil. In her "Epistle to Dr. Moore" Williams appears as a young woman who does not fear to proclaim her interests in the wider world, but instead stands eager to learn, full of energy, with a traveller's curiosity and an open mind. This is the Helen Maria Williams who would one day host a vibrant Parisian salon.

As mentioned earlier, in 1786 Williams published a major two-volume collection, entitled simply *Poems*. The fact that she had such an enormous list of subscribers—around 1,500—shows how popular she had become. One of the 1786 subscribers was the Dissenter and London businessman John Hurford Stone (1763–1818), who would become an intimate friend of the Williams family in the years ahead. A second edition of the *Poems* was issued with some revisions and additions in 1791.[55] In her prefatory dedication to Queen Charlotte (dated 25 April 1786), Williams acknowledged the great number of people who supported her in her efforts as a poet: "When I survey such an evidence of the zeal of my friends to serve me, as the following honourable and extensive list affords, I have cause for exultation in having published this work by subscription" (*Poems* Preface n. p.). One man who worked tirelessly on her behalf collecting subscriptions was the lawyer and literary man George Hardinge (1743–1816), the anonymous benefactor thanked in her Preface along with Dr. Kippis.[56] What comes as a surprise in light of Williams's political views is that George Hardinge (a friend of the Tory Prime Minister William Pitt) also attempted to get Williams a position at court like Frances Burney's, as Anna Seward reports in a letter to Mrs. Granville dated 3 October 1786:

> Mr. Hardinge tells me he has been straining every nerve to get the amiable Helen Williams a little place at Court of the *same nature* as Miss Burney's,

but as yet he has not succeeded; however, he avows a resolution not to rest till he does something materially and permanently conducive to her interest.[57]

One can only wonder how Williams's life might have been different if she had been given a position at court. Though Frances Burney certainly did not enjoy the grueling work of the second mistress of the wardrobe, she was a royalist and, through her close contact with the King and Queen she developed sincere affection for them. If Helen Maria Williams had worked at court in the late 1780s, one wonders if she would have been as interested in the politics of France. Instead, the end of the decade proved to be a time of fervent activity for her Dissenting friends, and she became equally absorbed in the issues that engrossed them.

Williams's literary reputation was firmly established by her *Poems* of 1786, which brought together new work and revised versions of her already published pieces.[58] Two poems included in the collection were later set to music: one, a hymn "While Thee I Seek Protecting Power," can still be found in Protestant hymnals; and the second, a short romantic ballad "A Song" or "No Riches from His Scanty Store," was set to music by Robert Cooke.[59] The collection very much represents the interests of the age, a time when several "Paraphrases from Scripture" could sit comfortably next to a popular gothic poem about the Tower of London, entitled "An Irregular Fragment." The frontispiece of the book is a drawing by the popular young artist Maria Cosway (1759–1838) that illustrates the section from the latter poem on the fifteenth-century murder of the young King Edward V and his brother.[60] With her characteristic discourse of sensibility, Williams describes the story of the ill-fated "Princes in the Tower":

> Look where a royal infant kneels,
>   Shrieking, and agonized with fear,
> He sees the dagger pointed near
>   A much-lov'd brother's breast.
>
> (*Poems* 2:33)

Using this scene for the only picture in the book draws attention to Williams's treatment of historical subject matter. Her interest in the turbulent history of her own country demonstrates her affinity for the political issues that would later absorb her during the period of the French Revolution and its aftermath. Nonetheless, it can certainly be said that the murdered British King Edward V was clearly an object of pathos, whereas Louis XVI's regicide evoked more mixed emotions, occurring as it did in the midst of the Revolution.

The second half of the eighteenth century is often called the Age of

Sensibility, a time when individual and collective emotional responses were validated rather than ignored. It became more acceptable to express how one was moved by an experience: be it one's own or another's; be it one of joy or one of sorrow. In his poem *The Seasons*, James Thomson, one of Williams's favorite authors, told his readers that if they thought about human suffering, "The Conscious heart of Charity would warm, / And her wide wish Benevolence dilate; / The social tear would rise, the social sigh."[61] Sympathizing with others became an important sign of one's humanity, and this led to a climate in which the subjects of charity and injustice could be more freely explored. In the Dissenting community (to which Williams's family belonged), there was a general interest in social and political reform, and this was aptly matched by the new literary and "sentimental interest in the deprived," documented by Janet Todd.[62] Helen Maria Williams's work shows clearly the link between literature of sensibility, politics, and religion, and as M. Ray Adams has noted, her "sentimentalism was deeply rooted in a religious nature."[63] For Williams, it was the most natural thing to be concerned about human suffering; her faith and her religious conscience demanded it.

Even a brief survey of the *Poems* of 1786 enables one to identify key recurring topics in Williams's poetry. For example, three narrative poems in the collection all speak out against the devastating effects of war. *Edwin and Eltruda*, as mentioned earlier, is set in the period of the War of the Roses; *An American Tale* concerns the American War of Independence; and *Peru* deals with the Spanish massacre of the Incas. In the first two poems, the female protagonist is unable to do anything to avert the tragedy that ensues when her lover and her father take opposite sides in a military conflict. The repercussions of war are felt by those left behind, their domestic lives shattered. In the 1,500-line *Peru*, the story of the conquest of the Incas throws a different light on the problem of human suffering by providing a critique of the violence of imperialism. In the course of her poem, Williams cites several learned sources, including William Robertson's *The History of America* (1777). The subject had recently been treated by Jean-François Marmontel in his *Les Incas, ou la destruction de l'empire du Pérou* (1777), and would again be popularized by the German playwright August von Kotzebue's *Die Spanier in Peru* (1796), a work translated into English by Anne Plumptre and then adapted by Richard Sheridan for his play *Pizarro* (1799).[64] Williams's poem, first published in 1784, opens with a glowing description of Peru that appeals primarily to readers' sympathy and secondarily to contemporary fascination with exotic locales. She presents the grim story of the massacre of the Incas, by concentrating on several prominent families. Heroic in their martyrdom, they possess a strength of character that their brutal attackers lack. As if to embody the responses of readers, the figure of Sensibility herself comes to weep for the Incas. Tears are not enough, though. In a note, Williams cites the political uprisings of the 1780s, stating that, "there is much reason to hope, that these injured nations may recover the liberty of which they have been so cruelly deprived" (*Poems* 2:176). This note implicitly reminds readers that the sympathy they feel for the Incas of centuries ago must be applied to those people who are suffering injustice now. The whole poem urges one to sympathize with the plight of the Peruvian natives, and the feelings that result must be directed towards the real world.

This is partly where the dangers of sensibility lie. If one felt too much for others' suffering, one would have to be advocating for change. The conservative writer Hannah More recognized these implications and was quick in her own qualified tribute to sensibility to caution that it should be applied only to life in the home and not lead people, women especially, to venture to consider issues beyond the private domain.[65] But Helen Maria Williams found sensibility compatible with her Dissenting commitment to reform. Her poem "To Sensibility" is a confident and earnest treatment of the subject, which takes into account some of the criticisms leveled against sensibility, as seen in Frances Greville's poem of 1759, "A Prayer for Indifference."[66] For Williams, to be "indifferent" would be to lack a vital part of being human, to lose the "sacred power to weep" (*Poems* 1:26). To feel for others is not just a passing fancy but brings with it a moral responsibility. While it had long been acknowledged that women were more emotionally sensitive than men, this was usually held against them as a sign of their irrationality, but in the late eighteenth century, it became more acceptable for both men and women to examine their feelings. This was a moment in history when a traditionally feminine characteristic became valued at large.

Some critics complained that Williams's work was too emotional— "*tears*, and *love*, and *sounds of woe*, &c. &c. those eternal topics of female poetry, are rather too predominant in Miss Williams's poetry."[67] However, the man who would become the greatest poet of his age—William Wordsworth—had great respect for Williams's work. It is easy to see how the future author of the Lucy poems would have been moved by a poet like Williams, who had compared her gentle Eltruda to a "lonely flower" that "smiles in the desert vale" (*Poems* 1:65):

> So liv'd in solitude, unseen,
>   This lovely, peerless maid;
> So grac'd the wild, sequester'd scene,
>   And blossom'd in the shade.

>   (*Poems* 1:66)

The young William Wordsworth addressed his first published poem to Williams, and it appeared under the pseudonym "Axiologus,"in March 1787 in the *European Magazine*: "Sonnet on Seeing Miss Helen Maria Williams Weep at a Tale of Distress." The title of Wordsworth's poem creates a reified portrait of Williams in the act of weeping, so that she becomes the very type of the emotive woman. But this is not a sign of weakness, since her tears reveal her own compassion and exert power over her readers by compelling them to take some form of action to alleviate the "distress[es]" of others:

> *Sonnet on Seeing Miss Helen Maria Williams*
> *Weep at a Tale of Distress.*
>
> She wept.—Life's purple tide began to flow
> In languid streams through every thrilling vein;
> Dim were my swimming eyes—my pulse beat slow,
> And my full heart was swell'd to dear delicious pain.
> Life left my loaded heart, and closing eye;
> A sigh recall'd the wanderer to my breast;
> Dear was the pause of life, and dear the sigh
> That call'd the wanderer home, and home to rest.
> That tear proclaims—in thee each virtue dwells,
> And bright will shine in misery's midnight hour;
> As the soft star of dewy evening tells
> What radiant fires were drown'd by day's malignant pow'r,
> That only wait the darkness of the night
> To cheer the wand'ring wretch with hospitable light.[68]

Wordsworth illustrates the nature of the discourse of sensibility here as his poem luxuriates in the bodily effects of a deeply felt emotion. But he also regards this as part of a moral response: the tear is a sign of "virtue," just as, to use his metaphor, a star in the night sky brings comfort after a long day. In a sense, Wordsworth's sonnet enacts the conflicts of sensibility, where emotional responses sometimes threaten to become divorced from any practical action to alleviate "misery's midnight hour." As Esther Schor has observed, Wordsworth foreshadows the compassionate concerns of his own poetry, when he forces himself outside of himself in order "To cheer the wand'ring wretch with hospitable light."[69] Parallel to Wordsworth's concern for the poor, Helen Maria Williams spoke out against injustice in the many books that she wrote throughout her life. The poetry in Williams's collection of 1786 anticipates her own future involvement in issues of social and political change. In one of her paraphrases from scripture, she writes of how the world should be changed for the better, imagining a time when "No more the powerful would the weak oppress" (*Poems* 1:113). Her belief in that scriptural message was a guiding force in her life's work.

In the years before the French Revolution would change her direction as a writer, Williams continued to concentrate diligently on her poetry and to widen the circle of her literary acquaintances. In 1787, under the auspices of John Moore, who was a relative of Mrs. Dunlop, one of Robert Burns's good friends,[70] she began corresponding with Burns, who, of all the poets she knew in these early days, has attained the most lasting place in the British literary canon. Burns, who had just taken the nation by storm with his *Poems, Chiefly in the Scottish Dialect* (1786), wrote to Moore about Williams's work on 15 February 1787:

> I had never before heard of her; but the other day I got her Poems, which for several reasons, some belonging to the head, and others the offspring of the heart, give me a great deal of pleasure. I have little pretensions to critic lore; there are, I think, two characteristic features in her poetry—the unfettered wild flight of native genius, and querulous, *sombre* tenderness of "time-settled sorrow." I only know what pleases me without being able to tell why.[71]

Williams was only too happy to have Robert Burns reading her poetry, whatever his lack of "pretensions to critic lore."

Burns's very status as a poet was caught up in the eighteenth-century debate on unlettered poets, a debate on nature versus art, that took up the phenomenon of women writers too. While Burns himself was being heralded as a "native genius," he used the same terminology to praise what he called Helen Maria Williams's "unfettered wild flight of native genius." In her "Sonnet on Reading Burns's 'Mountain Daisy,'" published in the 1791 second edition of her *Poems* and later reprinted, Williams described Burns as being nursed "By Genius in her native vigour" (*Poems* 1823, 205). The phrase "native genius" tended to be a euphemism used to show approval for the talents of someone who lacked a formal education. It was usually applied to laboring class poets, dating back to 1730 when the "thresher-poet" Stephen Duck enjoyed the patronage of the learned Queen Caroline of Anspach, consort of George II. It was also used for women poets of the working class, such as the "washer-woman" poet, Mary Collier, and Burns's contemporary Ann Yearsley, known as the Bristol milkwoman, whose *Poems* were published in 1785. Since Helen Maria Williams was staunchly middle class, she would have regarded herself as different from laboring class poets like Burns and Yearsley. But she appears to have taken to heart Thomas Gray's remarks honoring the potential talents of the poor in his famous *Elegy Written in a Country Church-Yard*. Where Gray describes the "Chill Penury"[72] that oppressed the villagers, Williams praises Burns for becoming a poet in spite of "penury's bare soil and bitter gale" (*Poems* 1823, 205). Furthermore, having grown up in the isolated region of Berwick-upon-Tweed, Williams could probably identify with Burns in ways that most of London's literati could not.

One surviving letter from Williams to Burns (dated 20 June 1787) is especially interesting for revealing how she attempted to overcome the deficiencies of her eduction by being a keen student of poetry and finding her heroes among the great poets of the age.

Sir,[73]

Your friend Dr. Moore having a complaint in his eyes, has desired me to become his secretary, and thank you, in his name, for your very humorous poem, entitled, Auld Willie's Prayer, which he had from Mr. Creech.

I am happy in this opportunity of expressing my obligations to you for the pleasure your poems have given me. I am sensible enough that my suffrage in their favour is of little value, yet it is natural for me to tell you, that, as far as I am capable of feeling poetical excellence, I have felt the power of your genius. I believe no one has yet read oftener than myself your Vision, your Cotten's Evening, the Address to the Mouse, and many of your other poems. My mother's family is Scotch, and the dialect has been familiar to me from my infancy; I was, therefore, qualified to taste the charm of your native poetry, and, as I feel the strongest attachment for Scotland, I share the triumph of your country in producing your laurels.

I know the enclosed poems, which were addressed to me by Dr. Moore, will give you pleasure, and shall, therefore, risque incurring the imputation of vanity by sending them. I own that I gratify my own pride by so doing. You know enough of his character not to wonder that I am proud of his friendship, and you will not be surprised that he who can give so many graces of wit and originality to prose, should be able to please in verse, when he turns his thoughts that way. One of these poems was sent to me last summer from Hamilton House; the other is so local that you must take the trouble to read a little history before you can understand it. My mother removed lately to the house of a Captain Jacques, in Southampton Row, Bloomsbury Square. What endeared this situation not a little to my imagination, was the recollection that Gray, the poet, had resided in it. I told Dr. Moore that I had very solid reason to think that Gray had lived in this very house, and had composed the Bard in my little study; there were but fifty chances to one against it, and what is that in poetical calculation? I added, that I was convinced our landlord was a lineal descendant of Shakespeare's Jacques. Dr. Moore laughed, as he has often occasion to do, at my folly; but the fabric which my fancy had reared upon the firm substantial air, soon tottered; for it became a matter of doubt if our habitation was in Southampton Row, or in King Street, which runs in a line with it. In the mean time, Dr. Moore called upon me, and left the enclosed verses on my table.

It will give me great pleasure, Sir, to hear that you find your present

retirement agreeable, for, indeed, I am much interested in your happiness. If I only considered the satisfaction I should derive from your acquaintance, I should wish that your fortune had led you towards London; but I am persuaded that you have had the wisdom to chuse the situation most congenial to the Muses.—I am, Sir, with great esteem, your most obedient servant,
    H. M. Williams

This letter to Burns shows Williams's deep appreciation of her Scottish roots. Having a special bond with him because of her own strong "attachment for Scotland," Williams read his work carefully, enjoying his use of dialect, because as she told him: "My mother's family is Scotch, and the dialect has been familiar to me from my infancy." Beyond that, Burns has already commented favorably on her own poems, and poetry was a special link between her and Burns.

Williams frequently remarked on a sense of kinship with certain other poets, something that also occurs in this letter when she mentions the house her family was renting in Bloomsbury. Hearing that Thomas Gray had once lived there, she wants to believe it was true, and even pictures him composing "The Bard" in the "little study" she uses. Imaginatively, she can project herself into the world of the male poet. She was a friend of Thomas Warton, appointed Poet Laureate in 1785; and, clearly, her family encouraged her by letting her use the study as a place to write. Of all Gray's poems, "The Bard" is the one that most strikingly proclaims the national importance of poets. Her choice of "The Bard" indicates her own fascination with the idea of poetic lineage and tradition, and it implies that she wants to see herself as in some way connected to that world; her being a woman does not preclude her identification with other poets.

While Burns found Scotland "congenial to the Muses," as Williams said in her letter, she continued to find London as "congenial" for herself. In 1787, her literary soirées were highly regarded, and her long list of friends and acquaintances continued to grow. Anna Seward arranged for her to meet the literary Colonel Henry Barry in October 1787 and the Anglican priest and writer Thomas Whalley in December of that year.[74] The Reverend Dr. Andrew Kippis introduced her to his former student from the Dissenting Academy at Hackney, the poet and banker Samuel Rogers, noting in a letter dated 14 November 1787: "Miss Helen Williams desires his company at tea on Monday next. She lives at St. Jacques's, the first house in Southampton Row, Bloomsbury, opposite Russell Street."[75] It was at the instigation of Kippis that Williams wrote her next poem, "The Morai: An Ode," included in an appendix in Kippis's 1788 biography of the explorer Captain James Cook.[76] The poem is in keeping with Williams's other work since it combines pathos and exotic descriptions while touching on public concerns, in a manner by now familiar to her readers.

In "The Morai," Williams imagines the beauty of Tahiti (known then as Otaheite), describing the island before proceeding to an elaborate account of the local funeral rites, amid the island's "fragrant bowers" (213). Only after this does she mention Captain Cook, who died several years after his trip to Tahiti, when he was murdered by natives in Hawaii. After learning of the funeral rites of the Morai, the reader is all the more moved by the fact that Cook—the "friend of human race" (217)—did not receive any type of proper funeral. The widow in Tahiti is more fortunate than Cook's widow, who does not have the comfort of visiting her husband's grave: she can only sigh in thoughts of the "wild abyss" where lie his bones (218). Nonetheless, Cook is treated like a hero around the world, and in England he will be memorialized by "the marble tomb, the trophied bust" (218). Cook was widely honored because he set an example by acting more humanely than other explorers: "Not like that murd'rous band he came, / Who stain'd with blood the new-found West" (217). Ultimately, this poem reveals not only Williams's attachment to her nation's heroes, but also her respect for a culture totally different from her own. In this last regard, it can be linked to her lifelong work against slavery, which began with the poem she wrote after "The Morai."

Williams's *A Poem on the Bill Lately Passed for Regulating the Slave Trade* (1788) involved her directly in a topical political and social issue: the British campaign to abolish the slave trade. The campaign had its roots in early Quaker opposition to slavery, dating from the establishment of the Royal African Company of Slave Traders in 1660, but it was not until the late eighteenth century that opposition to slavery and the slave trade became a major public issue. From its start in the 1780s, the nation-wide campaign involved women, and their work in the anti-slavery movement as it continued into the nineteenth century has long been recognized.[77] Women participated in local petitions and boycotts of West-Indian sugar,[78] and many women writers gave their support to the cause, with Helen Maria Williams, Hannah More, and Ann Yearsley all publishing long poems against the slave trade in 1788, a key year in the legislative struggle. In the case of both Williams and More, this exemplified the way that women collaborated with men who held key positions of political influence, since More was asked by William Wilberforce (the leader of the parliamentary campaign) to write her poem. She expressed some anxiety when she was working on it in December 1787, that it might not be published in time for the debates.[79] It is likely that Andrew Kippis encouraged Williams to write her poem, since he had been elected to the London Committee for abolition in

April 1788.[80] Williams would have had encouragement from her friend William Smith as well, since he was, after Wilberforce, one of the most active Members of Parliament working for abolition.[81]

The parliamentary campaign represented the interests of the Society for Effecting the Abolition of the Slave Trade, which had been founded in 1787 by a diverse group that included Joseph Woods, other members of the Quaker community, and Anglicans like Thomas Clarkson.[82] Led by its London Committee, the Society sought to end Britain's involvement in the international slave trade, and conducted a highly successful petition campaign throughout Britain, lobbying politicians in their home constituencies and in London. William Pitt introduced a motion to make the slave trade a topic of formal debate in the House of Commons. That same summer a bill was passed to improve conditions on the slave ships. Sir William Dolben's Bill on Slave Limitation to regulate the size of slave ships on the Middle Passage was passed in both Houses of Parliament after debates on 13 May and 24 June 1788.[83] Known as the Slave Trade Regulation Act, it became law on 11 July 1788.[84] Helen Maria Williams's poem was written in direct response to the passage of Dolben's bill and was part of a larger effort to continue working for further gains in abolition.

Along with the many pamphlets, poems, and books printed during the height of the movement from 1788 to 1792, there were two visual designs that Clarkson's Society began to use in 1788 as part of its promotional campaign: one was the image of the slave in chains with the heading "Am I not A Man and A Brother," designed by Josiah Wedgwood's company; and the other was a diagram or plan of a typical slave ship. The Wedgwood design was used not only on prints but also on medals fitted onto snuff-boxes and on the fashionable jasper-ware cameos, both of which were valuable gifts for abolitionists to use to promote their cause.[85] The illustration of the slave ship, which was based on the *Brookes* of Liverpool, was originally designed in December 1788 for the Plymouth Abolition Committee, which distributed thousands of copies in the spring of 1789. The London Committee, which entitled it *Description of a Slave Ship*, revised the print, adding more diagrams and more explanatory text, and sent copies to all members of the House of Commons and the House of Lords.[86] J. R. Oldfield notes that pictures of the slave ship were posted in the streets of Edinburgh; Quakers were known to frame them for displaying on their walls; and they became one of the "most arresting of all anti-slavery images": "As propaganda the print was shocking, yet neither sentimental nor unduly graphic. Here, in diagrammatic form, were human beings reduced to the level of inhuman objects, treated as so much merchandise and stowed on board ship in the most appalling conditions."[87] These illustrations were used in an international campaign as well, and Thomas Clarkson distributed copies of the plan on his visit to members of the Société des Amis des Noirs, in France in August 1789. It so shocked Mirabeau that he made "a wooden model of it," which was passed on to the French abolitionist Henri Grégoire, who showed it to Lady Morgan in 1817.[88]

Williams recounts in her *Souvenirs* that she took several copies of the *Description of a Slave Ship* and a number of Wedgwood cameos to France in 1790: "I distributed, on my first visit to Paris, several engravings of the plan of the slave ships, and several of the small Wedgwood cameos, which represent the black man on his knees, pleading his cause and showing his chains" (*Souvenirs* 197).[89] It is indicative of Williams's own serious commitment to the campaign that she distributed both the more sober plans as well as the attractive cameos. The consumerist and fashionable appeal of the latter is, however, an important symbol of the way that women could safely take part in this debate: wearing the cameos demonstrated their own commitment to abolition, but in an aesthetically pleasing way.

There were dozens of literary works that contributed to the abolitionist campaign as well. Williams's mentor Andrew Kippis was one of many people who subscribed to the 1789 *Interesting Narrative*, the popular autobiography of Olaudah Equiano, a former slave living in England.[90] The British poet whose name was most associated with abolition was William Cowper, who had already written against slavery in Book Two of *The Task* (1785), and produced several other poems on the subject, his most famous being "The Negro's Complaint." This powerful ballad-style poem was often reprinted in illustrated editions including one to celebrate the end of the British slave trade in 1807, where it was accompanied by a specially commissioned painting by Henry Fuseli, *The Negro Revenged*.[91] Fuseli's painting shows a triumphant freed slave, who stands proudly, raising his hands in victory, as he looks out to sea. He is embraced by a woman in a white dress, who, while probably an allegorical figure of liberty, could represent the many white British women who worked for the abolition.

Among the poems written by women on the subject were (in addition to Williams's *A Poem on the Bill Lately Passed for Regulating the Slave Trade*): Hannah More's *Slavery: A Poem* (1788); Ann Yearsley's *A Poem on the Inhumanity of the Slave Trade* (1788); and Anna Laetitia Barbauld's *Epistle to William Wilberforce, Esq., on the Rejection of the Bill for Abolishing the Slave Trade* (1791) — all of which were well-received generally. In summer 1789, Robert Burns sent Williams a detailed critique of her poem, to which she replied with gratitude.[92] Anna Seward (who had herself been asked by Josiah Wedgwood to write a poem on slavery but declined)[93] disliked Williams's choice of metre (tetrameter, rather than pentameter), but thought highly of the poem overall, discussing it with her friend Mary Scott (1752–93), the author of *The Female Advocate* (1774), and telling Williams that "Your charming poem on the Slave Trade is a most welcome present."[94]

In a sense, abolition was a safe political subject for women to write about because women could be seen as naturally responding with the sympathetic heart, as is suggested by the title of Ann Yearsley's piece *A Poem on the Inhumanity of the Slave Trade*. One reviewer, commenting on Helen Maria Williams's poem, regarded it as advantageous that women were, in his view, not distracted by the political and economic issues of the trade:

> The accounts lately given to the Public respecting the *Slave Trade*, were horrid enough to call into vigorous exercise the amiable sensibility of the female breast. By the ladies, this subject has been contemplated through the pure medium of virtuous pity, unmixed with those political, commercial, and selfish considerations which operated in steeling the hearts of some men against the pleadings of humanity: to find THEM, [women], therefore, writing on it, by no means excites wonder. Though among the last, Miss Williams is not the least deserving of notice.[95]

Still, if women were "feeling" the pain and sorrow of the enslaved African—and Moria Ferguson has argued that women's own lack of freedom in society made them identify with those who were enslaved—their literary discourse was often presented as part of a political campaign to persuade the public and members of parliament to support bills concerning the slave trade.[96]

Williams's poem on the successful passage of Dolben's bill praises the government for its humane reforms and for being the "first of Europe's polish'd lands, / To ease the Captive's iron bands."[97] But Dolben's bill was just the first step in a process to abolish the slave trade altogether, and Williams thus urges legislators to continue their good work:

> Britain! the noble, blest decree
> That sooths despair, is fram'd by Thee!
> Thy powerful arm has interpos'd,
> And *one* dire scene for ever clos'd.
>
> (*Slave Trade* 31–34)

The Slave Trade Regulation Act addressed exclusively the problem of overcrowding, limiting the number of slaves allowed on a ship (relative to the ship's tonnage).[98] Williams's poem begins with a description of the agony of a slave "bound in hopeless chains," held captive below decks, where the air is "suffocating" and "tainted" (*Slave Trade* 6; 13;

22). The regulations will make this a thing of the past—it is "*one* dire scene for ever clos'd"—but her emphasis on the word "one" makes it clear that she regards this improvement as only a beginning.

Much of her poem is devoted to gaining sympathy for the slaves and appealing to the conscience of her readers in order to persuade them of the evils of the slave trade. She shows how those involved in the trade have become so unfeeling that they even begrudge giving the slaves a few more inches to move during the long trip. The opponents to Dolben's bill asked why slaves should be given

> The boon of larger space to breathe,
> While coop'd that hollow deck beneath?
> A lengthened plank, on which to throw
> Their shackled limbs, while fiercely glow
> The beams direct, that on each head
> The fury of contagion shed? —
>
> (*Slave Trade* 103–8)

The references to the planks and the beams indicate that Williams had likely read some of the information about conditions on the ships, which was widely available. As Dale H. Porter notes, Sir William Dolben upset other members of the House when he "recounted in detail the horrors of the 'middle passage' across the Atlantic. He dwelt at length on the filthy, poorly ventilated ships, packed so tightly that slaves could hardly stand up."[99] Graphic accounts of the conditions of transportation, such as the following, were printed with the illustrated *Description of A Slave Ship*: "The slaves are never allowed the least bedding, either sick or well; but are stowed on the bare boards, from the friction of which, occasioned by the motion of the ship, and their chains, they are frequently much bruised, and in some cases the flesh is rubbed off their shoulders, elbows and hips."[100]

In her poem, Williams calls attention to the human costs of the slave trade, depicting the grief and despair felt by those forced to leave their homeland. By showing the slaves to be fathers and mothers and people with families like anyone else, she not only gains sympathy for them, but aims to chastise the traders for lacking humanity. Moira Ferguson points out that maternal and familial images were often used in abolitionist literature to demonstrate the "humanity of the Africans."[101] By contrast, it was the investors, traders, and slave-owners who became less than human. It was common to use images depicting the baseness of the trade, and in perhaps the most well-chosen phrase in the poem, Helen Maria Williams describes their business as a "barb'rous commerce" (*Slave Trade* 228). Overall, though, she aims to persuade her readers through an encouraging tone, thanking those sailors who refuse to work on slave ships, and depicting Britain as a stronger nation for having passed the Dolben bill.[102] The sense of national pride is important: abolitionist writings frequently emphasized that British honor was at stake on this issue. J. R. Oldfield quotes one pamphlet that declared that the slave trade was in violation of "that inherent love of freedom which characterizes" the nation.[103]

Unfortunately, the women and men who joined forces in opposing the slave trade in 1788 were divided on other issues that arose, especially after the French Revolution broke out the next year. A good example of this fracture can be seen in an argument that Hannah More had with Horace Walpole about a poem by Helen Maria Williams's friend Anna Laetitia Barbauld. When Hannah More praised Barbauld's abolitionist *Epistle to William Wilberforce* (1791), she urged Walpole to "forgive [Barbauld's] politics for the sake of her poetry."[104] Walpole reprimanded More for being naive, and insisted that Barbauld's Dissenting loyalties and support of the French Revolution tainted her sympathy for the slaves.[105] Such sentiments illustrate why the abolition movement failed during the 1790s, when differences of opinion about the French Revolution and fears about its effects in England led those who had previously found common ground on the subject of slavery to regard each other with suspicion and animosity. The political world of 1788 with its proliferation of abolitionist poems, tracts, and cameos has an appearance of innocence and optimism that the next year's events would irrevocably change. Nonetheless, Helen Maria Williams remained a lifelong abolitionist, writing against the slave trade and slavery in virtually every book that she published.

Unlike Williams's poem on the slave trade, her novel *Julia* (1790), though written in 1789, did not deal directly with the politics of the day, yet it still reflects her commitment to progressive change. Troubling realities impinge on the polite world of *Julia*, and the longer form of the novel enables Williams to develop at more length those elements that defined her poetry. The lives of the main characters, Julia Clifford and her cousin Charlotte, create the novel's ethos, while the love triangle, based on their love of the same man, Frederick Seymour, shapes the plot—and links it to major works like Richardson's *Sir Charles Grandison*, Rousseau's *Julie, or the New Heloise*, and Goethe's *Werther*. This domestic tension is mirrored in the allusions to political upheaval, relevant to the novel's setting. Published in March 1790, when the world was watching the revolution in France and just months before Williams made her historic trip to Paris, the novel is set in England during the period of the American Revolution, but it includes a visionary poem on the Bastille. These hints at the world of politics are not essential to the story, but they show how Williams's interests inevitably extend beyond the domestic sphere.

In many ways, *Julia* exemplifies what by the end of the eighteenth century had become a form of the novel acceptable for female readers: the polite novel, which Nancy Armstrong defines as having "the virtue of dramatizing the same principles sketched out in the conduct books."[106] Williams's book conforms to the expectations of a conduct book because the interest in reading, in music, and in benevolent works, which sets Julia and Charlotte apart from the other characters, is to be emulated by female readers. At the beginning of the novel, the distinguished Clifford family are in difficult financial circumstances, but Julia's uncle brings a fortune back from India, providing money for Captain Clifford and Julia, and allowing their return to the old family estate in the north of England (a location reminiscent of Williams's Berwick-upon-Tweed). The Cliffords are known for their benevolence, and, though Julia's and Charlotte's mothers are deceased, their fathers—the Clifford brothers—are noble and kind men who take after their own father, the patriarch of the family. It was Julia's grandfather who taught her some of the lessons "of humanity," and she regards her newfound fortune as a means for showing charity to others.[107] A whole series of actions illustrate Julia's benevolence, which extends even to showing "tenderness to animals," something she learned from her grandfather, who quoted the passage from scripture on the value of every sparrow (*Julia* 1:105). Julia's maid saves a linnet from a cat (*Julia* 1: 69); a cottage girl rescues flies from drowning in a bowl of water (*Julia* 1:104); and Julia herself, who is known to move worms out of the pathways (*Julia* 1:105), tries to save a wounded thrush from the pranks of a boy (*Julia* 2:26).

Concern for the suffering of others is one sign of sensibility; another is writing poetry, and one of the first things that we are told about Julia is that she "discovered at a very early age a particular sensibility to poetry" (*Julia* 1:13). Williams seems to be thinking back to her own childhood when she describes with affectionate humor Julia's first appointment with the muses:

> When she was eight years old she composed a poem on the departure of one of her young companions, in which she displayed, with great diligence, her whole stock of classical knowledge; and obliged all the heathen gods and goddesses, whose names she had been taught, to pass in succession, like the shades of Banquo's line. (*Julia* 1.13)

With energy and determination, Julia made the most of a little girl's scanty education, and in this she was not alone. Book-loving, poetry-

writing heroines were the norm in many novels of the late eighteenth
century, especially those of Charlotte Smith and (somewhat later) Ann
Radcliffe, who, like Williams, interspersed their stories with the verses
of their heroines. Female readers would find their own interest in writing and in education validated when they saw that a "good" person like
Julia found such pleasure in poetry. In Williams's novel, it is the frivolous characters who are ridiculed for preferring cards over books. This
is one way in which her work differs from the satirical treatment of
literary women that we see, for instance, in Henry Fielding's Lady Di
Western from *Tom Jones*, and in the novels of Frances Burney, whose
intellectual or literary characters are sometimes mocked either by other
characters (the scholarly Eugenia in *Camilla*) or by the narrator herself
(Elinor in *The Wanderer*, or Mrs. Selwyn in *Evelina*). Similarly, Jane
Austen takes up the question of "proper" reading in her own fiction,
as illustrated by the treatment of Marianne in *Sense and Sensibility*, and
Catherine Morland in *Northanger Abbey*. Unlike these satirized characters, Julia is presented as a model of dignity and modesty. She read not
for excitement but for edification and comfort, and her favourite poets
were (the same as Williams's) "Pope and Thomson" (*Julia* 1:224; *Poems*
1823, xxxv).

As an idealized woman of feeling, Julia is also drawn to the beauties
of the natural world, such as Thomson describes in the *Seasons*.[108] Her
rural upbringing gives her a moral strength unknown to those
immersed in the dissipation of London, like Charlotte's frivolous aunt,
Mrs. Melbourne. Julia, who has known a simpler, peaceful life in a
remote part of England, prefers living in the country where she can
contemplate the beauty of the natural world:

> It is in such moments as these that the soul becomes conscious of her native
> dignity: we seem to be brought nearer to the Deity; we feel the sense of his
> sacred presence; the low-minded cares of earth vanish; we view all nature
> beaming with benignity, and with beauty; and we repose with divine confi-
> dence on him, who has thus embellished his creation. (*Julia* 1:80–81)

With these serious reflections, Williams joins the long line of eighteenth-century authors who have written on the virtues of rural life,
from Anne Finch, in her meditative "Petition for an Absolute Retreat,"
to William Cowper, with his famous remark in *The Task* that, "God
made the country, and man made the town."[109]

Along with the landscape meditations characteristic of the literature
of sensibility, Julia's kindness to others is evident at every turn: she
"usually spent two hours every day in teaching the children of the cot-
tagers to read" (*Julia* 1:103), and she gives money to an old friend of

her grandfather so that he will not have to go to the poorhouse. Early in the story, the Clifford family's return to the family mansion, with adoring servants all around, is an exemplary tableau of sensibility:

> The women brought their infants in their arms to receive his blessing, and the old men crawled to the side of the chaise as well as they could, and blessed God that they had lived to see their old master again.— . . . Amidst blessings and acclamations, this welcome retinue reached the family-seat. The tenants were feasted in the hall; the ale flowed liberally; nothing was heard but the voice of rejoicing: and the Vicar of Wakefield, who had a taste for happy human faces, would have found this a charming spectacle. (*Julia* 1.74)

The reference to Goldsmith's novel *The Vicar of Wakefield* illustrates Williams's confidence that her readers share her fondness for the Vicar, and that they have come to expect "a charming spectacle" of benevolence between master and servants. By drawing attention to the scene as a literary device, Williams shows that whatever artifice is used in constructing a fictional tale, readers still have a profound need for the scenes of benevolence produced by the culture of sensibility.

Julia's goodness shines the more in contrast to the selfishness and superficiality of Charlotte's relatives. G. J. Barker-Benfield has pointed out how other writers have used a female character's preference for "solitude and books" to contrast those who spend their time in "trifling amusements," a comment that applies well to this novel.[110] The vanity and vices of the fashionable set, including the Melbournes, are exposed and satirized throughout the novel. Julia is puzzled by Miss Melbourne's fascination with ribbons at the milliners; Mrs. Chartres cannot understand why Julia and Charlotte like "conversation better than cards" (*Julia* 2:25); and Mrs. Melbourne dislikes the "frequent reading parties at Mr. Clifford's" (*Julia* 1:209). Similarly, Julia is generous to the poor, while Mrs. Melbourne "could hear the complaints of misery with indifference" (*Julia* 1:99). Williams had already spoken out against "indifference" in her poem on sensibility. Now she speaks more directly about social disparity and injustice, using language inspired by the French Revolution: "The human heart revolts against oppression" (*Julia* 1:208). As the exemplary heroine, Julia has a heart that "throbbed with indignation at the oppressor, and melted with compassion for the oppressed" (*Julia* 2:78). In contrast, Miss Melbourne merely feigns an interested and melancholic pose:

> her conversation frequently wandered from a roasted duck to Minerva's owl, or Jove's eagle. She could not hear an Italian air without weeping; she pitied the miseries of the poor in very pathetic language; and [she] lamented

being obliged . . . to spend much more than she wished upon dress. (*Julia* 1:30)

In making a distinction between genuine and false sensibility, including a satirical reference to a book called *The Pangs of Sensibility* recommended by Mrs. Chartres (*Julia* 2:48), Williams presents a more cynical view of her society than she had in her poetry of the 1780s, which upheld a naive belief in the virtue of sympathy and did not take into account fashionable affectations.

The novel privileges rational and charitable pursuits for women, but still presents women's lives as inevitably complicated by the web of romantic relationships and marital matches. While Williams can promote charity and benevolence through the actions of her two heroines, she uses a male intermediary to refer to events outside of the domestic domain. It is through the character of Mr. F. (Julia's rejected though deserving suitor) that she introduces her poem "The Bastille, A Vision" (*Julia* 2:218–23), said to have been written by a friend of his who had been imprisoned in the notorious French prison. Along with a sentimental description of the prisoner, the poem contains his prophetic dream of the destruction of the Bastille, when "millions with according mind / [would] claim the rights of human kind" (*Julia* 2:221). When the Fall of the Bastille occurred there was general agreement that this was a significant moment in human history, and Williams, like many writers of her day, compared it to the "Roman page sublime" (*Julia* 2:222), as we shall see in Chapter Two.

Although, in some ways, the poem on the Bastille seems an odd intrusion on the main story, it also reflects the imprisoning and torturous condition of the novel's love triangle. Williams explores the suffering of each character, including Charlotte, who realizes that her husband loves Julia. Frederick's obvious attachment to Julia betrays a weakness in his character that the novel warns its readers against. On several occasions, Williams uses political metaphors to illustrate the inadvisability of unruly passions. Terms like "the land of despotism" and "arbitrary tyrant" would have had a special resonance for readers in 1790 (*Julia* 2:18). The triangle is resolved when Frederick dies, but Julia never marries, and the narrator acknowledges her unspoken attachment to Frederick. Despite this one "unconquerable weakness" of the heart, Julia remains an admirable woman, who finds fulfilment in a single life, as Eleanor Ty observes in her analysis of the novel (*Julia* 2:245).[111] Williams gave Julia many of the characteristics which she valued, and in viewing Helen Maria Williams's own life we can see that she too would find "consolation in the duties of religion, the exercise of benevolence, and the society of persons of understanding and merit"

(*Julia* 2:244). But Williams also led an active and public life and left behind the safer domestic world where Julia resided and where a woman could practice sensibility with approbation.

This novel stands as a transitional work in many ways, marking a dividing line between Williams's career as a poet and as a prose writer. *Julia*, her only novel, was published in the spring of 1790, before the summertime trip to Paris that would change the course of her life and literary career. The novel itself demonstrates that transition by implicitly revealing that Williams had reached the limitations of what she could do in the genre of the literature of sensibility. While Julia, her exemplary woman of feeling, was caring for injured birds or reading to the poor, a whole new way of dealing with suffering and injustice was being proposed by the revolution in France. Williams alluded to it in the poem on the Fall of the Bastille, wedged uncomfortably into the novel's plot. History itself—in the form of the new politics of France— was responding to the concerns and tears of men and women of feeling: the age of revolution was ready to take over the age of sensibility.

2

Citizen of the World, 1789–1792

By THE TIME THE FRENCH REVOLUTION BEGAN IN 1789, WILLIAMS HAD gained a place of some prominence in the Dissenting and Whig circles to which she had been introduced by her mentor, the Reverend Dr. Andrew Kippis. She held regular literary soirées at her home, and counted among her friends such writers as Edward Jerningham, Hester Thrale Piozzi, and Anna Laetitia Barbauld, and such liberal Members of Parliament as William Smith and Benjamin Vaughan.[1] Her guests included several of Kippis's students from the Dissenting academies at Hoxton and Hackney, some of whom became prominent writers themselves, including William Godwin, who was "a very constant visitor at the house of Miss Helen Maria Williams, where many literary people congregated almost every night at tea-time."[2]

Political topics would have been as common as literary ones in the late 1780s, when Williams's friends were involved in the campaign against the slave trade and the campaign to repeal the Test Act (1673) and Corporation Act (1661), which forbade non-Anglicans from holding civic, military, and elected offices, though some Dissenters got around those restrictions through "occasional conformity."[3] The year 1788 was also significant as the centenary anniversary of the Glorious Revolution of 1688. For 100 years the Revolution Society had met annually on 4 November, the birthday of William III.[4] It is a measure of Andrew Kippis's prominence in the Whig community that he gave the featured address at the annual meeting of the Revolution Society in the centenary year.[5] As Albert Goodwin explains in his book *The Friends of Liberty*, when Kippis gave his speech, the Revolution Society addressed "a comprehensive list of desirable reforms, including 'the repeal of all religious tests and penal laws regarding religion,' the total abolition of the slave trade, the reform of the code of criminal law, the abolition of press gangs and the revision of game laws."[6] The concerns of the Revolution Society in 1788 are comparable to the types of injustices that Williams drew attention to in her poems of sensibility.

A year later, the French Revolution absorbed everyone's attention, and the following comment by Samuel Romilly is often taken as representative of the generally positive British response. It is from a letter of 28 July 1789 by Romilly, a reformer associated with the Society for Constitutional Information (SCI), a group founded in 1780, whose members overlapped with those in the Revolution Society.[7] Romilly was writing to his Genevan friend Etienne Dumont, himself a member of an international circle of writers and activists who met at Bowood, the Wiltshire estate of the reformist Lord Lansdowne:[8]

> I think myself happy that [the Revolution] has happened when I am of an age at which I may reasonably hope to live to see some of the consequences produced. It will perhaps surprise you, but it is certainly true, that the Revolution has produced a very sincere and very general joy here. It is the subject of all conversations; and even all the newspapers, without one exception, though they are not conducted by the most liberal or most philosophical of men, join in sounding forth the praises of the Parisians, and in rejoicing at an event so important for mankind.[9]

Since the English had long complained of the despotic Ancien Régime, praise was widespread for the early phase of the Revolution. The events of 1789 seemed important not only for France, but, as Romilly wrote, for "mankind." While the Revolution Society sent congratulations to the National Assembly,[10] in the House of Commons, the Whig leader Charles James Fox championed the Fall of the Bastille. For its annual meeting on 4 November 1789, the Revolution Society accorded the honor they had given Kippis the previous year to another Dissenting minister Dr. Richard Price, whose speech "Discourse on the Love of Our Country" would make history as a seminal British text celebrating the French Revolution, best known for having moved Edmund Burke to write his response, *Reflections on the Revolution in France* (1790). Price's speech would undoubtedly have been discussed at the home of Helen Maria Williams, especially since the meeting of the Revolution Society took place on 4 November 1789, and two weeks later, on 17 November 1789, Godwin, who had attended the meeting,[11] "drank tea with Holcroft at Miss Williams's."[12]

The French Revolution occurred at a fortuitous time for the reform movement in England, especially for the Dissenters' campaign to repeal the Test and Corporation Acts. Although Parliament voted strongly against the Dissenters in 1787, optimism grew when the votes were much closer in May 1789.[13] Then, having been galvanized by the events of July 1789 across the channel, Dissenters met heavy disappointment when in the next year, on 2 March 1790, the third bill to repeal the Test and Corporation Acts was overwhelmingly defeated.[14] The day after this campaign failed, Williams's friend Anna Laetitia Barbauld wrote a pamphlet, entitled *Address to the Opposers of the Repeal of the Corporation and Test Acts*, admonishing the legislators for their intransigence.[15] Godwin records in an undated diary entry for 1790 that he had supper with the "Anti-Tests," a group of men that included Charles James Fox, Benjamin Vaughan, and John Hurford Stone.[16] Whether at this time John Hurford Stone ever joined Godwin and others around the Williamses' tea-table we do not know, but he soon became a close friend of the family. Anna Laetitia Barbauld (1743–1825) visited shortly after her pamphlet appeared. In a letter to Hester Thrale Piozzi, dated 27 February 1790, Williams invited Thrale Piozzi to meet the Barbaulds at her home on 11 March 1790: "Mr. & Mrs. Barbauld will drink tea with me, & I *hope* you are not engaged, or that if you are, you will at least gratify me with your company part of the evening—for Mrs. Barbauld lives at Hampstead, & I cannot often obtain a visit from her, & have ventured to favor her that satisfaction of meeting you."[17]

For Dissenting families like the Williamses and the Barbaulds, the accelerated change in France seemed just short of miraculous. The French National Assembly had voted in favor of the principle of freedom of religion, had adopted the Declaration of the Rights of Man (both in August 1789), and had passed decrees against several aspects of aristocratic privilege.[18] Williams discussed these changes with her friends, and it was common knowledge that she regarded the National Assembly with "devout admiration" (Woodward 32). Her own heightened rhetoric resembled that of Kippis's friends from the Revolution Society, such as Charles Stanhope, who wrote in his published letter to Edmund Burke,

> The Revolution in France is one of the most striking and memorable pages in History; and no political event was, perhaps, ever more pregnant with good consequences to future ages. That great and glorious Revolution will, in time, disseminate throughout Europe, liberality of sentiment, and a just regard for Political, Civil, and Religious Liberty.[19]

Lord Stanhope's claims for the future effects of the Revolution would be echoed by Williams in her private correspondence and in her published work.

By June 1790, Williams was excitedly planning her first visit to France. She and her mother and her sister Cecilia (and probably her half-sister Persis) went to stay with their friends Monsieur and Madame du Fossé at their chateau near Rouen. Cecilia Williams departed first, and on 25 June 1790, Helen Maria Williams wrote to her friend Colonel Barry:

The French family which my sister is gone to visit in Normandy, have some thoughts of going to see the solemnities of the 14th of July. You are too well acquainted with my devout admiration of the National Assembly to wonder that I, who think myself happy in living when such an assembly exists, intend to set off for Normandy next week, in the blessed expectation of this glorious spectacle at Paris. (Woodward 32)

Williams's excitement about going to France is based on her recognition of the French Revolution as a significant historical moment and the National Assembly as an unprecedented vehicle for political change. She wants to participate in "this glorious spectacle," even before she has been to France and witnessed the celebratory atmosphere of dancing peasants, tricolor pennants, and parading women in white, which she will describe in the travel letters that made up her first and most cited book on the Revolution, *Letters written in France, in the Summer 1790, to a Friend in England; containing Various Anecdotes relative to the French Revolution; and Memoirs of Mons. and Madame du F— —.*[20]

This book of *Letters* would become one of the eight volumes, known collectively as the *Letters from France*. A second volume would appear in 1792; two more in 1793; three volumes in 1795; and a last volume in 1796. In this multi-volume work, Williams combined the informal narrative of travel writing with the charm of the epistolary form. Letter writing had been regarded in the eighteenth century as a legitimate literary form, and it was one in which women were thought to excel. Lady Mary Wortley Montagu's posthumous *Embassy Letters* (1763), based on her travels in Turkey, were regarded as models of the genre, and as Cynthia Lowenthal notes, it would become a "common observation that the grace and elegance of women's correspondence make it infinitely superior to men's."[21] Williams's engaging *Letters* directed to an unnamed recipient, tell her readers of her adventures—and that they were—in France with a thrilling sense of one witnessing history in the making. She would probably have agreed with William Wordsworth who said of these years, "Bliss was it in that dawn to be alive, / But to be young was very heaven!"[22]

The first volume of *Letters from France* describes her summertime visit from July to September 1790, and it clearly endorses the politics of the Revolution Society, with which she was associated as the protegé of Andrew Kippis. In the famous speech *A Discourse on the Love of Our Country*, Kippis's friend the Reverend Dr. Richard Price described the Revolution as an event "in which every friend to mankind is now exulting," which, like the Glorious Revolution of 1688, was a victory not only for the people of its own nation, but for the larger effort to, in Price's words, "enlighten the world."[23] Price explained that it was not unpatriotic for the English to applaud events in France, because they should love their country

> ardently but not exclusively. We ought to seek its good, by all the means that our different circumstances and abilities will allow, but at the same time we ought to consider ourselves as *citizens of the world*, and take care to maintain a just regard to the rights of other countries.[24]

Williams echoed Price, and in the following statement lies the key to understanding how, as a British woman of letters, she could welcome the Revolution in France:

> You will not suspect that I was an indifferent witness of such a scene. Oh, no! this was not a time in which the distinctions of country were remembered. It was the triumph of human kind; it was man asserting the noblest privilege of his nature; and it required but the common feelings of humanity, to become in that moment a *citizen of the world*. (1.1.13–14; italics mine)

Terms like "human kind," "humanity," and "citizen of the world" illustrate Williams's internationalist position: she observes, without national prejudice, the improvements for humanity in another country. The essence of her experience in France in 1790 is not one of foreignness, but one of belonging, so that her political agreement with revolutionary ideals acts as a bond between her and the people around her. Williams also implicitly asserts her own right to take an interest in this political event of global importance. Although the phrase "citizen of the world" was not an uncommon one, women would not have had occasion to use it since it implied a freedom of thought and outlook enjoyed by men alone. The terms "Citoyen" and "citoyenne" had yet to emerge in France, but they would represent the brief period when the question of women's citizenship became an issue of some prominence in that country. By calling herself a "citizen of the world," Williams in a sense anticipates the claim that French women would make—however briefly—to the hopeful title of "citoyenne."[25] Witnessing the changes in France made Williams excited about the possibilities of what she could become and what her nation and world could become, but, at the same time, her readers would not likely have been threatened by her claiming the conventionally masculine title "citizen of the world," since its occurrence in the context of her rapturous travel narrative defuses its potentially radical implications.

While the *Letters from France* reflect the politics—and the excitement—of the Revolution Society, it had a popular appeal that the Society's political tracts did not have. Her book was a mixed genre: in the form of travel literature and familiar letters, it also anticipated and

influenced future historians of the Revolution in its selection of material. In one sense, her book is a "tour" through revolutionary France in
1790, but she says little about quotidian matters of food and lodging.
Instead, she takes her readers to important events and shows them significant signs of revolutionary activity and spirit, using scenes of public
splendour and tableaux of private benevolence. Mary Favret has rightly
pointed out that Williams offers "discrete, packaged moments calculated to entertain and *move* her British audience, as she has been
moved."[26]

Fortuitously arriving in time for the Festival of the Federation in
Paris in 1790, Williams opens her book with a panegyric to "the most
sublime spectacle, which, perhaps, was ever represented on the theatre
of this earth" (1.1.2). Her view was consistent with that of others, as
Mona Ozouf points out: "Everybody, indeed, seems to have sensed the
unmistakeably festive nature of the proceedings; the unanimity of the
contemporary accounts is too strong to imagine that it was a matter of
chroniclers looking back through rose-tinted spectacles."[27] Williams
emphasizes the democratic nature of the preparations for the Festival:
"the distinctions of rank were forgotten" and even "ladies" helped to
dig the earth to build the amphitheatre (1.1.6). After a long list of the
different groups in the procession through the Champs de Mars
(1.1.10–11), she describes the public's response: "In the streets, at the
windows, and on the roofs of the houses, the people, transported with
joy, shouted and wept as the procession passed" (1.1.9). The excitement
builds and the emotional pitch reaches its height at the moment when
the King and six hundred thousand spectators said the national oath
together, and the sun "burst forth," like a blessing from above (1.1.13).

The words "spectacle" and "theatre" in Williams's description constitute part of the rhetoric of drama that she and many others used to
describe the Festival and these early revolutionary events in France. It
was as if what was occurring in France was a huge theatrical production and the rest of the world was the audience. It would not be until
the period of the Reign of Terror that Williams's celebratory tone would
change; however, even in 1790, for opponents of the Revolution, its
"spectacles" already had the horror of a nightmare, and no one articulated this more famously than Edmund Burke in his *Reflections on the
Revolution in France*.

It is useful to compare Burke and Williams because their contemporary accounts are representative of contrasting British views of the Revolution. Where Williams found a "sublime spectacle" (1.1.2) in the
scenes of the Revolution, Burke found an "atrocious spectacle."[28] As
well, the narratives of both writers depend on appeals to pathos, making use of what Stephen Cox has called "sensibility as argument:" "the

assumption is that strong feeling is equivalent to argumentative author-ity."[29] Both shed tears over the events in France, but their emotional responses and the values and politics implied by them were diametri-cally opposed; tears of sorrow for Burke; tears of joy for Williams; or as Anna Seward put it, Williams showed her "the sunny side of the prospect" but Burke's book convinced her that "the boasted liberty of France [was] degenerating into coercive anarchy."[30]

Seward was quite right to contrast Williams's "sunny" Revolution with Burke's anarchic one. Each used details and anecdotes that illus-trated their perception of the Revolution. To convey her enthusiasm, Williams concentrated on pleasing social scenes, downplaying the inci-dents of violence, which were central to Burke. Their views of the march on Versailles of 5–6 October 1789 provide a noteworthy exam-ple. In the following passage, Burke attacks Richard Price for celebrat-ing the forced return of the Royal Family from Versailles to Paris. In his rebuttal, Price insisted that he was *not* celebrating October 6, 1789, but 14 July 1789.[31] Burke fused the events, condemning

> the most horrid, atrocious, and afflicting spectacle, that perhaps ever was exhibited to the pity and indignation of mankind. . . . Several English were the stupefied and indignant spectators of that triumph. It was (unless we have been strangely deceived) a spectacle more resembling a procession of American savages, entering into Onondaga, after some of their murders called victories, and leading into hovels hung around with scalps, their cap-tives, overpowered with the scoffs and buffets of women as ferocious as themselves, much more than it resembled the triumphal pomp of a civilized martial nation.[32]

Here the spectacle is all savagery, as Burke invokes tales of North American aboriginal violence to describe the male rioters and their equally "ferocious" female counterparts. He defends having written so much about "this atrocious spectacle" by arguing that "it is *natural* I should . . . because in events like these our passions instruct our rea-son."[33] Many liberal critics attacked Burke for his appeal to pathos, including Mary Wollstonecraft, who ridiculed his "gust of passion" and instructed him to "learn to respect the sovereignty of reason."[34]

In contrast, Williams offers only a brief and subdued account of the October 1789 procession from Versailles to Paris, quickly ending with the happy comment that the outcome was good, since "The King is now extremely popular, and the people sing in the streets" (1.1.86). Only at one point is she not far from Burke, and that is her description of the mob taunting the Queen at Versailles:

> All the bread which could be procured in the town of Versailles, was distrib-uted among the *Poissardes*; who, with savage ferocity, held up their morsels

of bread on their bloody pikes, towards the balcony where the Queen stood, crying, in a tone of defiance, "Nous avons du pain!" (1.1.84)

Although both Williams and Burke use terms like "savage" and "ferocious," in Williams's case such language registers her disapproval of the acts of violence, but she cannot risk being too critical because she supported the goals of the militant action. Burke, on the other hand, after his description of the attack on the Queen's bedchamber, presents not "bread" on pikes but the heads of two of the men massacred,[35] which demonstrates again that records of the Revolution depend very much on the political alliances of the recorder.

There is only one other incident in this first volume of *Letters* where Williams takes note of any revolutionary bloodshed:

> As we came out of La Maison de Ville, we were shewn, immediately opposite, the far-famed lanterne, at which, for want of a gallows, the first victims of popular fury were sacrificed. I own that the sight of *la lanterne* chilled the blood within my veins. At that moment, for the first time, I lamented the revolution. . . . It is for ever to be regretted, that so dark a shade of ferocious revenge was thrown across the glories of the revolution. But alas! where do the records of history point out a revolution unstained by some actions of barbarity? (1.1.80–81)

Even this visit to a real site of revolutionary violence is not at odds with the rest of her discourse, because she was "shewn" the lantern, as if, already, it were an item on a guided tour to the Revolution, and she places it on the map by telling readers where it is. Nonetheless, this demonstrates how Williams's eyewitness position gives added value to her narration. For instance, Catharine Macaulay mentioned the lamppost murders, but, not having been to France, she cannot describe the scene to her reader, as Williams can. Macaulay admits that "The punishment of the lamp-post, it must be owned, strikes terror to the mind, and calls forth an immediate effusion of *sympathy* to the sufferer,"[36] but both she and Williams dismiss these acts of violence as unfortunate but inevitable in a revolution, and Williams shows that the danger has been removed since she can visit the lamppost herself. For Burke, however, such arguments illustrated the way that supporters of the Revolution excused violence: he deplored the "scales hung in a shop of horrors" where "the crimes of new democracy [would be] posted as in a ledger against the crimes of old despotism."[37]

Nothing symbolized "the crimes of old despotism" more than the Bastille, the most famous site of early revolutionary violence—and, triumph. The Bastille had long been a universal symbol of the arbitrary power of kings to imprison their subjects and had gripped the imagination of writers in England and around the world. In his book *The Shadow of the Guillotine*, written for the British Museum's bicentenary exhibition on British responses to the Revolution, David Bindman cites several writers who alluded to the Bastille in works prior to 1789.[38] William Cowper, for instance, eloquently exposed the Bastille's legendary status in a passage from his long poem *The Task*, which deplored its "cages of despair" and claimed "There's not an English heart that would not leap / To hear that ye were fall'n at last."[39] Cowper was close to being prophetic here, because most hearts seemed to have leapt with joy at the Fall of the Bastille, a thrilling event for people in England and all over Europe.[40] The many poems, pamphlets, and pictures of the fall of the Bastille were largely favorable representations, and Williams herself praised the "courage of the besiegers" (1.1.26). Her own discourse of sensibility is mirrored in a painting by Henry Singleton, the brother of Joseph Singleton, who engraved her portrait in 1792. Completed in the same year, Henry Singleton's painting *The Destruction of the Bastille* (1792) can be seen as a visual counterpart to Williams's work, since, as David Bindman points out, Singleton emphasized "the rich humanity of the common people," foregrounding "ardent young men, women of tender feeling, and gallant elderly gentlemen."[41] At the very center of the painting, and away from the pointing spears, are two women of sensibility, looking with concern at a wounded man. They appear like ministering angels with soft, clean, white dresses, and the Bastille looks like a dark presence in the background. The fall of the Bastille was so important and romanticized an event that the anniversary celebrations in 1790 were especially euphoric on the site of the former prison. Williams attests that "the spectacle of all others the most interesting to my feelings, was the rejoicings at the Bastille" (1.1.21):

> Here the minds of the people took a higher note of exultation than in the other scenes of festivity. Their mutual congratulations, their reflections on the horror of the past, their sense of present felicity, their cries of "Vive la Nation," still ring in my ear! I too, though but a sojourner in their land, rejoiced in their happiness, joined the universal voice, and repeated with all my heart and soul, "Vive la nation!" (1.1.21)

Without any embarrassment, Williams participates in "the universal voice," drawing on the energy of the crowd, as she too repeats the words "Vive la Nation."

The predominant tone of the *Letters* is spirited, as Williams shows her readers how the Revolution has imprinted itself on French society, but the following examples also show how those incidents were inflected by her political vantage point: peasants march with national ribbons on their tools (1.1.61); a souvenir snuff box pokes fun at the Church: "you touch a spring, open the lid of the snuff-box, and the Abbé jumps up" (1.1.53); and the phrase "c'est une aristocratie" (1.1.74) describes something unpleasant. Along with these signs of the altered social land-scape, Williams's *Letters* contain severe criticism of the monarchy and the Roman Catholic Church. On these subjects, her tone is often scorn-ful, as in the following account of her visit to the City Hall in Paris:

> The walls are hung round with pictures of Kings and Dukes, which I looked at with much less respect than at the chair on which Mons. Bailly sits. If his picture should ever be placed in this apartment, I fancy that, in the estima-tion of posterity, it will obtain precedency over all the Princes in the collec-tion. (1.1.80)

Showing more respect for the untitled Monsieur Bailly than for the Kings of France, Williams tries her hand at some republican humour. While British anti-gallicism had long made sport of the Ancien Régime, such a joke would lose its lustre after the trial and execution of Louis XVI—for others, it would have been in bad taste even in November 1790, a year after the march on Versailles.

In many ways, Williams's views mark her as a product of the Age of Enlightenment, with its emphasis on individual rights, human progress, political reform, and religious freedom. Echoing the views of other Dis-senters, she regarded royalist and Roman Catholic traditions as archaic structures and superstitions that required subverting. Williams was rather unforgiving when it came to the entrenchment of royal or reli-gious prerogative. She had little patience for Catholicism—"a sad stum-bling block to reason" (1.1.113)—and was especially critical of convents, monasteries, and the rule of celibacy. Like Richard Price, she often compared "Popish countries" to regions of darkness.[42] Enlighten-ment progress meant ridding the world of superstitions and welcoming change. When Williams wrote, "it is not what is *ancient* but what is *mod-ern*, that most powerfully engages attention" (1.1.104), she was echoing the forward-looking enlightenment philosophy of Joseph Priestley and Thomas Jefferson who had corresponded on the subject in the 1780s.[43] Theirs was the very position that Burke would attack in the *Reflections*, where he defended the established order against "new" forms of gov-ernment.[44] Next to Williams's comment we could oppose Burke's remark that "With them it is a sufficient motive to destroy an old scheme of things, because it is an old one."[45] Indeed, Williams once said of a new nationalist banner exhibited in a church that, "Nothing in this fine old cathedral interested me so much as the consecrated banner" (1.1.104).

Williams was keenly aware that her readers might deem it unpatriotic for her to be so interested in the Revolution in France. She deals with this directly at several points, commenting at the end of Letter Eight *"you* are not one of those who will suspect that I am not all the while a good English woman" (1.1.65) and opening the next letter with a similar comment:

> Yesterday I received your letter; in which you accuse me of describing with too much enthusiasm the public rejoicings in France, and prophecy that I shall return to my own country a fierce republican. In answer to these accusations, I shall observe, that it is very difficult, with common sensibility, to avoid sympathizing in general happiness. (1.1.66)

Williams attempts to disarm her critics by implying that any of them — anyone "with common sensibility" — would respond as she did. While she jokingly imagines how they might caricature her, it would actually become a serious matter when the tide of public opinion turned against the Revolution; then her critics would revile her as a "fierce republican," because her enthusiasm would be seen as unnatural and unacceptable in a woman. Williams then levels more serious accusations at her would-be critics, asking why they would begrudge the French the happiness of liberty. Here, she echoes her friend Anna Laetitia Barbauld, who in her pamphlet on the Test Acts (March 1790) wondered if those English observers who did not applaud the Revolution were simply too proud to accept that France was superseding them in carrying the torch of liberty: "England who has held the torch for [France] is mortified to see it blaze brighter in her hands."[46] Like Barbauld, Williams accuses English critics of the Revolution of being jealous that "the French have gone too far, because they have gone farther than ourselves" (1.1.68), implying that it is hypocritical for her "own good countrymen" to "speak with contempt of the French for having imbibed the noble lesson which England has taught" the world since 1688 (1.1.69). The reviewer in *Gentleman's Magazine* sarcastically quoted Williams's words back at her: "We must be allowed to fear that 'the French have gone too far,' not 'because they have gone farther than ourselves,' but because they have gone beyond every principle and axiom of practical government."[47] The same reviewer also questioned Williams's francophilia: "With this good lady there is no country, no language in the world, equal to that of France."[48] This charge of disloyalty was one that would be levelled against Williams for years to come.

On her trip home from France in September 1790, Williams was shocked to find that many of the other passengers did not share her exuberant support of the Revolution. At the end of the book, she mocks the objectors as ill-informed and also defends herself against the rebukes of those who view supporters of the Revolution as "barbarous levellers" (1.1.219). Indignantly, she asks, "Must I be told, that my mind is perverted, that I am become dead to all sensations of sympathy, because I do not weep" for the rich? (1.1.218). The second half of her comment is effective because it would be difficult for any critic to say that the eminent Englishwoman of sensibility was "dead to all sensations of sympathy." She tries to explain how it was her "heart" that made her interested in the Revolution:

> my political creed is entirely an affair of the heart; for I have not been so absurd as to consult my head upon matters of which it is so incapable of judging. (1.1.66)

This is a memorable line in the *Letters*, but it was not the first or last time that a woman would make such a statement in a published work. A self-deprecatory stance was a common strategy for women writers, and would probably have seemed especially necessary for one who published on a political topic, since there was a longstanding tradition of excluding women from political discussion. As Henry Fielding's Squire Western remarked to his sister, "You know I don't love to hear you talk about politics; they belong to us, and petticoats should not meddle."[49] Women writers needed to defend themselves from critics who thought it unfeminine to put themselves forward as thinkers, intellectuals, or literary persons. Catharine Macaulay, for instance, confronted the issue directly in the first volume of her *History of England*, when she anticipated "the invidious censures which may ensue from striking into a path of literature rarely trodden by my sex."[50] While later in her career Williams will write with an earned confidence in her abilities as a writer and reporter, in this first book on the Revolution, she needs a defensive strategy and, to some extent, she may have been speaking the truth in acknowledging her ignorance of political matters. However, Williams's poetry was of a political kind, on the American War of Independence, the Spanish massacres in Peru, and on the abolition of the slave trade, so in reality it was not such a great leap to write on French politics, except for the fact that the reading public would have different expectations of a female poet than they would have of a female political commentator. Genre made a difference, since the acceptance that had been granted to women writing poetry had not as yet been extended to women writing non-fiction prose. Williams had to show her readers that the heart-felt responses that had made her poems of sensibility acceptable would also enable her to write about the Revolution without sacrificing her femininity.

Though she may deprecate her abilities, Williams was establishing an identity, in this book, as a vocal and committed reformer, albeit using the power of her "heart." Even Edmund Burke argued that "the true lawgiver ought to have an heart full of sensibility,"[51] though he accused the leaders of the Revolution of lacking just that.[52] Stephen Cox points out that the argument of sensibility is based on "the power to display or elicit emotional susceptibility."[53] It was a power which was, according to Williams, understood by revolutionary politicians who knew the heart or emotions of the people must be engaged to create change:

> The leaders of the French revolution are men well acquainted with the human heart. They have not trusted merely to the force of reason, but have studied to interest in their cause the most powerful passions of human nature, by the appointment of solemnities perfectly calculated to awaken that general sympathy which is caught from heart to heart with irresistible energy, fills every eye with tears, and throbs in every bosom. (1.1.61–62)

This passage exhibits Williams's keen analysis of a political terrain in which she is both observer and participant: first of all, her own heartfelt response is legitimized by the revolutionary leaders' acknowledgement of the value of the heart; secondly, she associates herself with the French people by describing a "general sympathy," binding everyone there; and thirdly, she outlines a process of propaganda in which the leaders are manipulating the passions of the people through particular public events or "solemnities" in order to achieve a political end. After this passage, she gives an example of a procession of 500 women dressed in white, leading newly freed prisoners to church—a "perfectly calculated" spectacle, in which stereotypical female charms are used in service to the state, or as Williams puts it, anticipating advertisers of our own century, "Thus have the leaders of the revolution engaged beauty as one of their auxiliaries; justly concluding, that, to the gallantry and sensibility of Frenchmen, no argument would be found more efficacious than that of a pretty face" (1.1.62–63). It is hard to gauge Williams's tone here: she seems to give her approval and even imply that this is an appropriate form of quasi-political activity for women, whose beauty can be used in service to the state.

Another spectacle of sorts in 1790 was the sight of women in the National Assembly watching the debates. Williams may defensively claim that she is motivated by her heart and not her head, but that argument wears thin. Is it, after all, a matter of the "heart" or the "head" that led Williams and her sister Cecilia to desire admission to both Westminster Hall in London and the National Assembly in Paris? Only in Paris were they successful, obtaining excellent seats, which reminded them, Williams wrote, that their "struggles to attain the same situation in Westminster Hall" had failed (1.1.42). In the eighteenth century, women were allowed admission to London's Westminster Hall, but we know this more from stories of fainting female spectators at the trial of Warren Hastings than from serious records of their attendance.[54] Still, the Hall was revered by Whigs because it was the site of important state trials, while, as Roland Quinault points out, Whigs had "less affection for the old House of Commons, which had long been under Tory control."[55] Williams's mention of the Hall rather than the House of Commons may have been for more practical reasons and not due simply to her Whig loyalties, since it would have been much harder for her to attempt to gain entrance to the House of Commons. Throughout the eighteenth century, women were occasionally allowed into the visitors or "strangers" gallery in the British House of Commons, most notably women of rank, but an incident on 2 February 1778 led to an unofficial ban on female spectators, even though some women still bribed their way in, only to find themselves usually seated in the attic peering through a ventilator hole.[56] That the Williams sisters sought admission at least to Westminster Hall, even if unsuccessfully, does, however, undercut Williams's comments about being uninterested in public life. One has to wonder, then, if the following statement about not being formerly interested in politics is meant ironically: "Did you expect that I should ever dip my pen in politics, who used to take so small an interest in public affairs" (1.1.108). If her interest in public affairs was "small" before, it may have been because there seemed to be no potential for growth, nowhere to go beyond writing a poem on the slave trade. But in France she was in the middle of something unprecedented, and it was revolutionary for Williams, and for any woman, to find herself sitting (albeit in the visitors' gallery) in a national legislature.

It was hard for anyone in France in 1790 not to be conscious of the new involvement of women in public life. In 1789, many women had been present at the storming of the Bastille in July. A group of affluent women had donated their jewellery to the state in September; and in October 1789 the protest of market women over the cost of bread led to the famous siege on Versailles. Historians Darline Gay Levy and Harriet Applewhite describe the period from 1789 to 1793 as one where "women assumed political identities as *citoyennes*," participating in a range of activities that included those mentioned above, plus submitting petitions to the government, taking part in the meetings of political clubs, and in 1792 seeking entry to the military.[57] When Williams arrived in Paris in 1790, members of the National Assembly had discussed Condorcet's famous article on women's rights, "Sur l'admission des femmes au droit de cité," which had been published on 2 July

1790.[58] Although it would be several months before Olympe de Gouges and Etta Palm d'Alders would emerge as leaders, Théroigne de Méricourt was a well-known female activist at this time. She and Gilbert Romme had established a political club, Société des amis de la loi, open to men and women, which lasted from January to March 1790, and Méricourt had attended in February 1790 "the solemn session at which the deputies swore the civic oath in the presence of the King."[59] While political clubs for women-only were established somewhat later, many clubs welcomed women at least as spectators, if not members. For example, in January 1790 Condorcet helped to found the Confédération des amis de la vérité, which as Joan Landes explains, "was especially devoted to improving women's conditions."[60] Over the next two years, women's political involvement would increase even more dramatically.[61]

In her first volume of *Letters*, Williams recorded several signs of the politicization of women which she observed or which others told her about while she was in France in 1790. She had seen and heard enough to declare that "The women have certainly had a considerable share in the French revolution" (1.1.37). This included women of all classes: she praised the courage of the women who showed "a spirit worthy of Roman matrons" (1.1.28) by helping at the siege of the Bastille, bringing food, nursing the injured, and even standing guard;[62] and she was delighted to see women of her own class participating, even if only in a token manner, in the preparations for the Festival of the Federation, where, as Catherine Marand-Fouquet states, all observers commented on the sight of women pushing wheelbarrows[63]: "Ladies took the instruments of labour in their hands, and removed a little of the earth, that they might be able to boast that they also had assisted in the preparations at the Champ de Mars" (1.1.6–7). Williams was intrigued by the incident of the "don patriotique" which occurred in September 1789, when, in imitation of Roman matrons, French women donated their jewels to help Minister Necker pay the national debt (1.1.37;55).[64] The artists' renderings of this incident show how much it gripped people's imagination because of its symbolic value. If things that were so important to women's beauty and comfort could be given up, then it suggested times were revolutionary indeed, something that Williams herself clearly recognized when she remarked on the fact that "even the personal ornaments, so dear to female vanity," could be sacrificed "for the common cause" (1.1.37).

The first time she refers to the "don patriotique" is in her fifth letter, which describes her acquaintance with the well-known educationalist, Madame de Genlis (also known as Madame Sillery and Madame Brulart) (1.1.33–41), who would become a long-time acquaintance and sometimes friend. Williams remarked on Genlis's expensive "Liberty" medallion, which was made with a polished stone from the Bastille and adorned with diamonds (1.1.38). This beautiful medallion was but one example of the way that the Revolution was being commodified, with souvenirs appearing everywhere, and stones from the Bastille selling by the pound.[65] But it also can be categorized with the incident of September 1789 to show that by donating their traditional jewellery and buying "revolutionary" jewellery to help the nation, women were finding a way to make their feminine world serviceable to the state. One of the only discordant notes about this new activism concerns the women's march on Versailles in October 1789, referred to earlier,[66] when "the *Poissardes* . . . with savage ferocity, held up their morsels of bread on their bloody pikes" (1.1.84). Williams would understandably have been more comfortable with the idea of women proffering jewels rather than bloodstained bread. The incident illustrates the class divide as well as the conflict between the domestic and the political roles of women. The image of the unruly poissardes jarred against Williams's own view of a compassionate female identity, as she strove to define an acceptable form of female heroism.

Williams's visit to the National Assembly was especially important because witnessing the debates and watching laws in the making was an experience women were usually denied. Although she continued to deprecate her abilities, saying, she was "so little qualified to judge of oratory" (1.1.45), contending with this self-effacement was her desire to convey to her readers the excitement of being present at a national legislature: "all seem more inclined to talk than to listen; and sometimes the President in vain rings a bell . . . But one ceases to wonder that the meetings of the National Assembly are tumultuous, on reflecting how important are the objects of its deliberations" (1.1.44). In another reference to the Assembly, Williams recounts the story of an eldest son who begs the representatives to pass a bill overturning the right of primogeniture because he wants to share his wealth with his siblings. It is her attitude to this young man that is so interesting. Williams declares that she is "violently in love with him" (1.1.60)—a self-parodic comment that plays on her own position as a single woman. Perhaps the defining cultural image for the summer of 1790 would be women swooning over revolutionary politicians. Williams's point was that this man's behaviour was exactly the kind that should be found attractive. It gave male readers a model for how to behave and female readers a model for what to expect or demand in a suitor, showing, in Julie Ellison's words "the erotic appeal of a figure who combines attractive manhood with emotional intensity and an unselfish commitment to social justice."[67] Furthermore, the playful avowal of sexual interest reflects something of

Williams's own personality, for she must have been a woman whom men found attractive. Already a hostess of literary soirées in London, she established a salon in Paris frequented by many of the leading intellectuals, politicians, and writers of her day. Since she was confident in the company of important men, it is not surprising that she gained a sense of empowerment from attending the debates in the National Assembly.

The excitement that Williams conveys about visiting the Assembly and about so many other incidents described in the *Letters* adds a heightened tone and a keen level of interest to the narrative. However, it was the long story of her friends the du Fossés that most seized her readers' imagination. The story of the du Fossés is like a work of fiction, bearing all the signs of an adventurous love story: a tyrant father dividing class-crossed young lovers, a secret marriage, exile, poverty, imprisonment, evil brothers, escape, and restitution. Williams was already adept at writing poems about family love and loss, but this true story had all the right elements, so much so, that, as Robert Mayo indicates, it was reprinted many times, and once appeared under the title, "Family Pride and Parental Cruelty."[68] Later, William Wordsworth used the story in his own poetic account of star-crossed lovers, "Vaudracour and Julia."[69] Williams explained that what happened to the du Fossés illustrated the need for the Revolution:

> I am glad you think that a friend's having been persecuted, imprisoned, maimed, and almost murdered, under the ancient government of France, is a good excuse for loving the revolution. What, indeed, but friendship, could have led my attention from the annals of imagination to the records of politics; from the poetry to the prose of human life? (1.1.195)

Williams safeguards her reputation by implying that it was not personal ambition which led her to write about politics, simply a response of the heart:

> In vain might Aristocrates have explained to me the rights of kings, and Democrates have descanted on the rights of the people. How many fine-spun threads of reasoning would my wandering thoughts have broken; and how difficult should I have found it to arrange arguments and inferences in the cells of my brain! But, however dull the faculties of my head, I can assure you, that when a proposition is addressed to my heart, I have some quickness of perception. I can then decide, in one moment, points upon which philosophers and legislators have differed in all ages: nor could I be more convinced of the truth of any demonstration in Euclid, than I am, that, that system of politics must be the best, by which those I love are made happy. (1.1.195–96)

Once again, Williams admits that she does not understand all of the legal arguments about the change in government in France. But she says this without shame (after all she is acknowledging that women are not given a proper education, something for which she cannot be blamed); and she asserts with an almost fierce pride that the understanding of her heart compensates for the factual knowledge she lacks. When she writes "however dull the faculties of my head," she is invoking the usual comments made about women's intellectual inferiority, and, if her critics are unwilling to acknowledge the possibility that her "head" could be anything but "dull," she challenges them at least to grant her the ability to judge by feeling. Women are accorded that power and a natural "quickness of perception"—if little else.

A brief review of the plot of the du Fossé story will illustrate how it functions as a paradigmatic revolutionary narrative. The villain of Williams's *Letters from France*, the Baron du Fossé ruled his feudal properties "with a rod of iron" (1.1.124) and he opposed his son's marriage to Monique Coquerel, because her father was a farmer with only distant links to nobility. Some months after a secret marriage, Monique was escorted by her brothers to Caen where she gave birth to a son, but when the Baron found out about the marriage, he tried to get a lettre de cachet against Monique (1.1.131), so the couple left their child in Caen (where he eventually died) and traveled through Switzerland, Germany and Holland, arriving in London in spring 1775. There, Monique gave birth to a girl, but by this time they were destitute. Their story is so awful that it makes Williams cry as she is writing it down: "my mind is overwhelmed with its own sensations.—The paper is blotted by my tears—and I can hold my pen no longer" (1.1.135). Williams's admission allows for an intimacy between her and her readers, and the apparent spontaneity of her weeping authenticates her role as a model of sensibility. Stephen Cox quotes an interesting example from Edmund Burke which parallels this. In a letter of 20 February 1790 Burke explained that "the abominable" attack on Versailles horribly contrasted with his recollection of seeing the Queen in her "brilliancy, splendour, and beauty" in 1774: the contrast "did draw Tears from me and wetted my Paper."[70] Once more we see how Williams and Burke use their emotional responses as a means to authorize their politics, except that Williams weeps for what the du Fossés suffered under the Ancien Régime, and Burke weeps for how the Ancien Régime is being destroyed.

At the center of the du Fossé story is the failure of a father, the Baron du Fossé, to love his son: "The endearing name of father conveyed no transport to *his* heart" (1.1.123). Lynn Hunt has shown how the rupture of the father-son relationship can be viewed as an allegory for the

French Revolution itself, with Louis XVI as the father of France who failed his people. Although Hunt does not refer to the du Fossé story, it perfectly mirrors the allegory she constructs. She explains first of all that in the eighteenth century "the ideal of the good father" emerged through the rise of the novel: "A stern, repressive father was incompatible with the new model of the family as emotional center for the nurturing of children and the new model of the individual as an autonomous self."[71] The Baron du Fossé's use of lettres de cachet against his family is a glaring mark against him. As Hunt explains, even before the Revolution, the King's ministers attempted to "put a stop to misuse of lettres de cachet."[72] Hunt's analysis in *The Family Romance of the French Revolution* confirms what Williams's story of the du Fossés implies, namely, that familial tyranny and royal tyranny were mirror images.

In the story of the Du Fossés, their "oppressed virtue" and the "glowing . . . benevolence" of those who help them is set against the "malignity" of the Baron (1.1.141). The force of Williams's rhetoric as she demonizes the Baron is a measure of her antipathy towards unjust authority figures. The Baron becomes for her the emblem of the institutions she opposed. If the Baron emphatically rejects any sentimental role of "father," Williams sketches a hero in the young du Fossé, who provides a model of both responsibility and affection. The scenes where he parts from his daughter and his wife are conventional tableaux of sensibility: "He pressed the child for a long while to his bosom, and bathed it with his tears" (1.1.143). After he arrives in Normandy in June 1778, it is not long before his father has him imprisoned. Again Williams pauses to confer with her reader about the unnaturalness of the Baron's actions:

> Is it not difficult to believe that these sufferings were inflicted by a father? A father!—that name which I cannot trace without emotion; which conveys all the ideas of protection, of security, of tenderness; that dear relation to which, in general, children owe their prosperity, their enjoyments, and even their virtues! (1.1.156)

Here Williams outlines the qualities expected in the ideal father, and few could argue with the "ideas of protection, of security, of tenderness". One need look no further than this for confirmation of Lynn Hunt's argument, which is also supported by Janet Todd's assertion that the "kindly parent" became a favorite figure in eighteenth-century literature.[73]

After a decade of promoting family tableaux of sensibility, Williams argues passionately for what a father should be; fortunately, she can present the Baron's antithesis in "the small, loving nuclear family" of

Monsieur and Madame du Fossé.[74] Du Fossé finally escapes and makes a heroic trip to London, reuniting with Monique after an absence of three years (1.1.187). A few years later, in 1785, Williams met the du Fossés, when Monique was recommended as a French teacher. On 7 October 1787 (1.1.186) the Baron died; but, due to legal wrangling with his brothers, du Fossé delayed returning to France until, as it happened, 15 July 1789, the day after the fall of the Bastille, a coincidence that makes for a nice ending. Williams again draws attention to the fictional quality of their story: "Has it not the air of romance? and are you not glad that the dénouement is happy? — Does not the old Baron die exactly in the right place; at the very page one would choose?" (1.1.193). Here the boundary between fact and fiction is blurred, leaving Williams in the unenviable position of having confessed her delight in the death of the real-life Baron, though she apologizes for it later.

In the concluding section of the *Letters*, Williams's visit to the du Fossés ends with a private theatrical performance put on at their chateau. Her sister Cecilia had a part in "La Fédération, ou La Famille Patriotique," and Williams agreed to serve as the statue of Liberty, allowing herself to be adorned appropriately and draped with the national riband. For Williams to publish this anecdote in her book suggests that she wanted the English public to see just how committed she was to the idea of liberty, so much so, that she would devote her own person to its cause, in this case in a performance, but also in her very life's work. She was proud to be identified with the very image of liberty in the mind of her readers. The day's celebrations were an apotheosis for Williams, as she and her sister Cecilia (who was being courted by Madame du Fossé's nephew Marie-Martin-Athanase Coquerel (1767–1825), whom she would marry in 1794), experienced the freedom to celebrate political change. The importance of that day is registered by the "tears of luxury" they evoked:

A more joyous scene, or a set of happier countenances, my eyes never beheld. When I recollected the former situation of my friends, the spectacle before me seemed an enchanting vision: I could not forbear, the whole evening, comparing the past with the present; and, while I meant to be exceedingly merry, I felt that tears, which would not be suppressed, were gushing from my eyes — but they were tears of luxury. (1.1.207)

The picture of her crying is meant to influence her readers, to have a power over them as her emotions have overpowered her body, so that heart and mind and body together reveal her approval of the Revolution that has produced such family happiness. Near the end of the book Williams emphasizes the scenes of sensibility that represent for her the

France of 1790 which she came to know and love: "We must leave the charming society at the *château*—we must leave the peasants dance under the shade of the old elms, while the setting sun pours streams of liquid gold through the foliage" (1.1.213). Finally, she closes one letter with the explicit statement: "I may as well explain myself in one line—I am sorry to leave France!" (1.1.214).

Although not everyone shared her enthusiasm, Williams's first volume of *Letters* was a critical and popular success, appearing at a time when British support of the Revolution was still at its peak. Nonetheless, the book found more favor in Whig- than Tory-leaning journals, mirroring Williams's own political alliances, a pattern that would continue throughout her career. The liberal *Analytical Review* was especially warm in their praise:

> The interesting unaffected letters which this pleasing writer has now presented to the public, revived these reflections, and gave new force to them, at the same time that they confirmed the very favourable opinion we have entertained of the goodness of the writer's heart. . . . As the destruction of the Bastille was an event that affected every heart—even hearts not accustomed to the melting mood, it was natural to suppose that it would particularly touch a tender one—and every page of Miss W.'s book tells us, in an unequivocal tone, that her's is true to every soft emotion.[75]

Almost more important than the compliments paid to the *Letters* in this effusive review is the tribute paid to Williams's character. The emphasis on the "goodness" of her heart was especially important since some readers might regard with apprehension a book in which a woman took up a political subject, however much it was couched in romantic stories or festive anecdotes. As if to deflect any possible criticism of this sort, the reviewer presents the book as an extension of Williams's work as a poet of sensibility. If every heart is moved by the fall of the Bastille, then surely her response would be the most pathetic and eloquent since she understands the "melting mood," the "tender" and "soft" emotions. Thus, her rhetoric of feeling legitimates even the quasi-political *Letters*. When the *Gentleman's Magazine* gave a flippant review of the *Letters*, one reader wrote in to defend her with a chivalry that would have made Burke proud, had he not been in the opposite political camp. Her anonymous champion declared that, "I think I scarcely ever saw, in equal compass, more happy expression of just and elegant sentiments enhanced by the sweetness of feminine grace."[76] In 1790, Williams had an enamored readership who came to her defence, finding her all "sweetness" and "feminine grace"—even when she wrote about the Revolution.

In the vast literature that comprises contemporary British responses to the Revolution, Williams's book was one of the key early texts to present a favourable perspective. Her book was published only two weeks after Burke's *Reflections*, though it was not a response to Burke's, since she had finished writing it a short time before his appeared. Nonetheless, because both books appeared around the same time, hers was categorized with other books published in favor of the Revolution, including those that *were* direct replies to Burke. One indication of her celebrity is that she was featured in a satirical print published on 1 December 1790: *Don Dismallo Running the Literary Gantlet*.[77] The "Don Dismallo" of the title is Edmund Burke, who is being attacked by his political opponents. Burke was regularly featured in political cartoons, as Nicholas Robinson documents in his book *Edmund Burke: A Life in Caricature*.[78] Since the British public greeted the Revolution favorably at this early stage, many political cartoons ridiculed Burke for reacting against it. In this caricature, he is running a gantlet, where his political opponents (whose names are stated on the print) wait to flog him with cat-o-nine-tails: Helen Maria Williams, Richard Price, Anna Laetitia Barbauld, Richard Sheridan, John Horne Tooke, and Catharine Graham Macaulay. Depicting Williams, Barbauld, and Macaulay, this is one of the few prints to feature women writers who took part in the Revolutionary debates. Their identity is revealed not only by the names at the foot of the page, but also by the "dialogue" attributed to each figure. Williams is quoted as using the phrase "shivering lances" from the conclusion to her *Letters* (1.1.219): "Though I decline shivering lances in this glorious cause, I think I have made him feel the full force of a Cat-o-nine-tails." The caption for Barbauld, whose pamphlet *Address to the Opposers of the Repeal of the Corporation and Test Acts* (1790) alludes to the French Revolution, refers to the "urchins" in her school. Macaulay (identified by her married name, Mrs. Graham) is shown defending her Whig *History of England* (her reply to Burke was not published until late December). Richard Price accuses Burke of being a Jesuit, while Burke pleads for mercy from Sheridan, and the figure of Justice points a sword at him. "Liberty" with her back to Burke helps an old prisoner from the Bastille, who carries a flag decorated with scenes related to the history of the prison. Burke is dressed like a clown, while the others are dressed in normal eighteenth-century fashions, the women very similar to one another, without any distinguishing features.

The somewhat anonymous or general appearance of the female figures is, perhaps, in keeping with the history of eighteenth-century satirical prints, since it was not common to depict individual women by name, except in cases of well-known (famous or notorious) personages, as in the unflattering caricatures of Queen Charlotte, or the sexually provocative depictions of royal mistresses like Mary "Perdita" Robinson and Dorothy Jordan.[79] More relevant to the three women writers is the case of Georgiana Cavendish, Duchess of Devonshire, who was an active supporter of Whig causes. Cavendish was caricatured in a number of prints when she became involved in the election of 1784. As Linda Colley notes, prints issued in the Duchess's defence did little to offset the negative effects of those that ridiculed her as an unnatural woman because of her interest in politics.[80] Remarkably, the depiction of Williams, Barbauld, and Macaulay has none of the hostility found in the prints of Cavendish. Rather, along with the evident humour of the print, there is an air of propriety in regards to the three women chastising Burke. In this rare moment in British political history, readers were encouraged to side with women on a political issue, and the print offers in a visual form evidence of the legitimization—however tenuous—that these women writers achieved.

What Williams thought of the print we do not know, but she was pleased by a flattering poem written about her *Letters from France*, in which she is also depicted as an opponent of Edmund Burke.[81] In Edward Jerningham's poem, entitled "On reading 'Letters written from France in the summer 1790, to a Friend in England, by Helen Maria Williams,'" public opinion on the Revolution becomes a disputed terrain, and Williams and Burke vie for readers' approval. It is a battle of the sexes in which the sweet appeal of Williams wins out over the masculine power of Burke:

> While Burke, equip'd for daring fight
> Steps forth a literary Knight,
> In folds of ancient armour drest,
> And boldly rears his feudal crest;
> Waves high in air his brandish'd lance,
> And his huge gauntlet throws at France;
> Near the stern Chief, a lovely Maid
> Comes in simplicity array'd:
> The flowing robe in which she moves
> Wove by the Graces and the Loves;
> She tries no formal refutation
> Of his elab'rate speculation,
> Nor raves of Governments and Laws,
> For she to Nature trusts her cause;
> Makes to the heart her strong appeal,
> Which all who have a heart must feel;
> Bids the quick tear of pity roll,
> And seizes on the vanquish'd soul.[82]

Though Burke is an accomplished adversary with extensive parliamentary experience—"equip'd for daring fight"—Williams can win over the

British public because she "comes in simplicity array'd" and "makes to the heart her strong appeal." According to Jerningham, Williams does not engage in those verbal battles about "Governments and Laws" more suited to a man, but uses her natural feminine compassion to reach her audience.

After Williams published her *Letters* in mid-November 1790,[83] two women did publish responses to Burke's *Reflections*, Mary Wollstone-craft in November and Catharine Macaulay in December 1790. Since Thomas Paine's famous reply *Rights of Man* had yet to appear, a reviewer in the *Analytical Review* was quite right to comment on the fact that two women were among the first to fight back at Burke: "how deeply must it wound the feelings of a *chivalrous knight* . . . to perceive that two of the boldest of his adversaries are women!"[84] As would be expected from a woman of her stature, Catharine Macaulay, whose multi-volume *History of England* (1763–83) met with a favorable response,[85] printed her name on the title page of *Observations on the Reflections of the Right Hon. Edmund Burke, on the Revolution in France, In a letter to the Right Hon. Earl of Stanhope.* Mary Wollstonecraft's *Vindication of the Rights of Men*, a direct response to Burke, was first published anon-ymously on 27 November 1790, but it sold well, establishing her reputa-tion as a serious writer,[86] and she added her name to the second edition, published on 18 December. Upon discovering that the author of the book was a woman, the *Critical Review* complained about her assuming "the disguise of a man."[87] Wollstonecraft deliberately used a male per-sona in order to take on Burke anonymously, without having to worry about defending her right as an unknown woman to do so. Her amazon-like persona was praised by William Roscoe in his own radical poem called *The Life, Death, and Wonderful Atchievements of Edmund Burke: A New Ballad* (1791). The frontispiece features a drawing by Roscoe of Burke dressed like a knight in the House of Commons, with Fox weeping at Burke's supposed apostasy. In his poem, Roscoe depicts Wollstonecraft as an "Amazon" who pounds Burke's feeble "coat of rusty steel" with her "vigorous strokes," before Thomas Paine is left to finish the job.[88] With her physical strength and sturdy weapon, Roscoe's Wollstonecraft is the polar opposite of Jerningham's feminine Williams. Wollstone-craft's more aggressive rhetorical style, though admired by Roscoe and others, was very different from Williams's style and persona. The images in the two poems make a useful contrast between Wollstone-craft's outspokenness, which looks ahead to the feminists of later gener-ations, and Williams's propriety, which partakes more of the decorum of the eighteenth-century woman of letters or bluestocking.

The publication of the *Letters from France* (1790) brought Williams to the height of her popularity. As she continued to write about the progress of the French Revolution in the 1790s, she remained a famous woman of letters, though her reputation suffered as Burke's counter-revolutionary position took hold in England. This change is best illustrated by the alteration in Williams's relationship with Hester Thrale Piozzi, a close friend from 1789 to 1793. Thrale Piozzi's journals and correspondence provide valuable information about Williams's life, her social circle, and her reputation as a woman of letters. At the very time when the *Don Dismallo* print was published, Williams had been one of Thrale Piozzi's guests for 10 days at Streatham Park, a place she often praised for its "dear Library" and "attic breakfasts."[89] On one visit her friend Penelope Weston (later Pennington; 1752–1827) was also a guest. Escorted to Streatham by their mutual friend Colonel Barry, she alluded to Burke's already famous assertion that "the age of chivalry is gone," by joking with Barry that "notwithstanding the alarming decay of chivalry, Miss W— — is so persuaded that Colonel Barry still possesses a portion of that gallant spirit, that she ventures to ask him to put off his excursion till the second of December, when she would be happy to go under his protection."[90] Thrale Piozzi herself refers to this humorous allusion, but she also praises Burke's book: "Colonel Barry, Miss Weston, and Miss Williams have been our ten Days Guests. . . . So some Chivalry *is* left in the World notwithstanding Mr. Burke. His Book is the greatest Performance in Literature that has appeared for a long Time. Helena Williams will please you however."[91]

Although it would be some time before choosing sides in the revolutionary debates would become a more serious matter in England, one can see the seeds of the revolutionary divide beginning to form. Even though she favors Burke's views of the Revolution, at this point that difference of opinion between her and Williams has no effect on their friendship. Instead, Thrale Piozzi holds Williams in very high esteem, and the following remark from a letter of 3 January 1791 provides some indication of how Williams was viewed by her contemporaries: her "pensive Look and loveliness of Manner engages every one's Affection while her Talents render her extremely respectable."[92] This is an important comment because it gives us some insight into Williams's personality. Thrale Piozzi describes her as a sweet, but serious or pensive person, and, as she notes in another letter, "a better or a more amiable *Woman* can She not be."[93] Williams was regarded as a "respectable" woman of letters, but she also engaged people's affection, and it is this latter quality which especially distinguishes her. Others remarked on it, including Wollstonecraft who wrote in 1792 that what most impressed her about Helen Maria Williams was "the *simple* goodness of her heart."[94]

In spring 1791, having been back in England for several months,

Williams continued to host literary soirées in her home in London. Samuel Rogers counted among the guests at "Miss Williams's" on 21 April 1791, Joanna Baillie, her brother Dr. Matthew Baillie, Mr. Cadell and his daughter, Dr. Cadogan, Edward Jerningham, Andrew Kippis, Henry MacKenzie, Robert Merry, Dr. John Moore, and Mr. William Seward.[95] Meanwhile, Williams was also making plans to return to France for an extended visit. As early as 23 February 1791, Hester Thrale Piozzi told a friend, "Do you know that one of our little darling W's deserts next Summer? Fair Helena is the Person; and She is going to reside in France for two or three years."[96] Williams herself announced her departure in a 15-page poem entitled *A Farewell, for Two Years, to England* (1791).[97] In a letter of 10 May 1791, Piozzi wrote that she found "the farewell Poem . . . mighty pretty,"[98] even though she did not share Williams's revolutionary enthusiasm. Meanwhile, public opinion in England was becoming more divided. While Burke and Fox, both Whig Members of Parliament, had already taken opposite sides on the Revolution, their friendship came to a stormy end in a Commons debate of May 1791, as a result of their disagreement over the French Revolution. Fox was said to have wept at the breach between them, an incident that generated much commentary and several political cartoons.[99] With the dispute between Burke and Fox such a high profile event, perhaps Williams may have wondered whether her support of the Revolution might result in similar breaks with any of her friends, as indeed it did.

In her poem announcing her departure, Williams attempts to strike a position that balances patriotism and revolutionary enthusiasm. As if needing to reassure her readers that she is a loyal Englishwoman, she reflects fondly upon the "native scenes" of England and the "Parental Thames" (*Farewell* 3; 2). Her interest in the Revolution can be defended, she says to any possible detractors, because, as a British woman proud of the nation's historical defence of liberty, she is pleased to see liberty spreading to France (*Farewell* 5–10), and such feelings do not in any way make her less patriotic:

> Scorning those narrow souls, what'er their clime,
> Who meanly think that sympathy a crime;
> Who, if one wish for human good expand
> Beyond the limits of their native land,
> And from the worst of ills would others free,
> Deem that warm wish, my Country! guilt to thee.
> Ah, why those blessings to one spot confine.
>
> (*Farewell* 7)

The poem also includes a long section urging both France and Britain to abolish the slave trade, shifting to a topic which will find her supporters, regardless of their views on the Revolution.

Reviews of the poem offer an important gauge of Williams's literary reputation. In June 1791, the *Analytical Review* gave the poem a short but complimentary notice, noting that liberty was "her favourite topic":

> With her usual happy mixture of energy and tenderness, Miss Williams here pours forth harmonious strains, chiefly on her favourite topic, liberty. The idea of visiting France, now become the first seat of freedom, fires her muse with more than usual ardour. The poem will be read with pleasure by those whose bosoms glow with kindred sentiments.[100]

Others who did not share her political standpoint at this stage still wrote about her favourably. The *London Review*, for instance, approved of her comments on the slave trade, but politely dissented from her on the subject of the Revolution.[101] By now, Williams was regarded as a writer of considerable stature. In the *Farewell* poem she turned to her British audience in her familiar guise as well-loved poetess. Once praised as the "chaster Sappho of our age," she reassures her readers that despite the controversial nature of her writing, she is the same Helen Maria Williams that they loved before.[102] She can combine the delicate work of the muse and her interest in politics. Williams not only regarded herself as having a responsibility to her audience but also depended upon their good opinion of her. In a sense, *A Farewell, for Two Years, to England* asks readers to keep their faith in her, to understand her "love of Liberty" (7), and to wish her well on her second journey to France.

By the time that Williams was preparing to travel in July 1791, the pleasing sentiments of her poem seemed in stark contrast to the tense climate in England that surrounded the second anniversary celebrations for 14 July. That day became a lightening rod for British opponents to the Revolution, with widespread violence by conservative "Church and King" clubs.[103] Chief among these incidents were the Birmingham riots of 14–17 July 1791, when supporters of the Revolution were attacked and buildings burnt, including the home of the prominent Dissenting minister and scientist Dr. Joseph Priestley.[104] While Priestley later emigrated to the United States, he first accepted a move to London as minister for the Hackney congregation, having been invited by John Hurford Stone and others in November 1791 to take over the position vacated by Richard Price, who had died in April of that year.[105] Priestley would certainly have met Williams during his tenure there, since Andrew Kippis had close ties to Hackney, and had, in fact, preached the funeral sermon for Richard Price.[106] Meanwhile, Kippis himself was being pressured to renounce his support of the Revolution. In a letter of 11 July 1791, James Boswell deplored the horrors of the Revolution's "barbarous anarchy" and tried to convince Kippis to dine with him, instead of going to the Crown and Anchor celebration on 14 July 1791.[107] Declining Boswell's invitation, Kippis reiterated his own respect for the Church of England and his loyalty to the King, but insisted that he could not in good conscience miss the Crown and Anchor meeting:

> In drinking the King's Health and in wishing every good Thing to his Majesty and the Royal Family, I should most cordially join; and though I conscientiously dissent from the Church of England, I have always done it with Moderation and Candour, and with the greatest respect for the distinguished ornaments of that Church. But consider, my dear Sir, how I am circumstanced. In my Address at the Funeral of Dr. Price, I have publicly avowed my Exultation in the Emancipation of twenty-five Millions of people from a wretched Tyranny and Despotism; and I feel that this Avowal is perfectly consistent with my firmest attachment to the British Constitution, and the illustrious House of Hanover. But were I to dine with You on Thursday, for the express purpose of avoiding the Crown and Anchor Meeting, I might be charged with renouncing my principles. I must add, that the Alarm and Clamour occasioned by that Meeting appear to me to be altogether ridiculous. You will, therefore, I hope, without depriving me of your Esteem, permit me to decline your friendly Invitation.[108]

Kippis firmly but politely refused the proposal, and even suggested that Boswell's alarm about the revolutionary celebrations was unfounded and "ridiculous." Nonetheless, the incident shows the pressures that were beginning to bear on the most well-respected of Dissenters.

Helen Maria Williams would likely have known about Boswell's letter to Kippis since she was still in England at this time. In fact, Horace Walpole claims that she and Anna Laetitia Barbauld were also invited to the Crown and Anchor celebration, and he uses this as an occasion to cast aspersions on them both. After mentioning that several reformers had been recently arrested, he writes that

> Eleven of these disciples of Paine are in custody; and Mr. Merry, Mrs. Barbauld, and Miss Helen Williams will probably have subjects for elegies. Deborah and Jael, I believe, were invited to the Crown and Anchor, and had let their nails grow accordingly—but somehow or other no poissonnières were there, and the two prophetesses had no opportunity that day of exercising their talents or talons.[109]

Walpole used the names "Deborah" and "Jael" for Barbauld and Williams, perhaps to conjure negative images of the assertiveness of those

Old Testament figures. He also associates them with the "poisson-nières," a term of abuse for French fishwives or marketwomen. Walpole makes Barbauld and Williams out to be malevolent women with long nails or "talons"—rather than "talents." In an earlier letter, he cited Burke's animosity towards British women who supported the Revolution: "Their Amazon allies, headed by Kate Macaulay and the virago Barbauld, whom Mr. Burke calls our *poissardes*."[110]

Whatever Walpole or Burke may have thought of them, Williams and Barbauld remained close during this period, and it is through a letter of Barbauld's that we know that Williams left for France in August. Barbauld wrote to Samuel Rogers on 13 July 1791 that Williams and her family were travelling separately to France that summer: "Perhaps you know that Mrs. Williams and Cecilia are set out for France, and that Helen and the rest of the family are soon to follow. They pay a visit to their old friends at Rouen before they settle at Orleans."[111] Williams probably traveled with her half-sister Persis, while her mother and Cecilia had already left for the du Fossés chateau near Rouen.

Considering only the practical needs of foreign travel, it would have been hard for Williams to visit France in the 1790s without the support, protection, and companionship that her family gave her. Furthermore, the approval of her respectable mother and sisters gave a legitimacy to her writing on the subject. When they arrived in Rouen, Mrs. Williams and Cecilia even had a brief moment of public celebrity, which resulted from their attendance at a meeting of the local branch of the Society of the Friends of the Constitution (Societé des Amis de la Constitution à Rouen), where they presented the Society with a copy of the new French translation of Williams's 1790 *Letters from France*, *Lettres écrites de France à une amie en Angleterre pendant l'été de 1790* (1791) (Woodward 42–46).[112] The Williamses' visit was noted in the *Journal de Rouen*, and recorded prominently in the Society's minutes.

The Society sent a separate letter to Williams, congratulating her on the French translation of her book, and thanking her for demonstrating in it the joy "of a great people at the moment when they became free" (Woodward 43). As Lionel Woodward explains, Williams wrote a reply to the society on 13 September 1791, when she was staying with the du Fossés near Rouen, and the Society copied her reply and printed it with their letter, distributing 3000 copies of both as a double pamphlet, entitled *Lettre de la société des Amis de la Constitution à Rouen à miss Williams et réponse de miss Williams* (Woodward 42). This is a significant recognition in France of Williams's work as a British woman writer. The report in the *Journal de Rouen* praised Williams's talents and used her as an example to Frenchwomen who should, they counseled, develop all the faculties that Heaven has given them. But at the same time, praise of

Williams was overshadowed by the injunction to women to fulfil their proper roles in the family: "That is the best employment of your sex. You are born to persuade and to love. Fill then as mothers of your family the most respectable and the most holy of roles, inspire your children to love liberty and to respect the law" (Woodward 46). Whatever Williams's literary success, the *Journal de Rouen* still confirmed that a woman's primary role was a private not a public one. While some women may have thought the Revolution could change their lives and make them more free, they were often told that they served their country best by raising young patriots. This advice turned into a cult of motherhood that would take hold throughout the decade and beyond.[113]

In 1791, however, there were still hopes for improvements in women's lives, and the Society's recognition of Williams was only one way in which she was establishing a significant reputation for herself in the political and literary circles of France. The appearance of the French translation of her *Letters* and the 3,000 copies of the pamphlet from Rouen brought her increased celebrity, and she reflected on it in a letter to Hester Thrale Piozzi dated 5 September 1791: "I find myself much caressed in this country, but my heart sorrowfully clings to my own, and to those friends from whom I am separated."[114] She added in another letter that these honors " 'play round the head but come not to the heart,' nor do I feel any pleasure from the attentions of the Democrates which at all compensates to my heart for this cruel separation from my friends at home."[115] There is no denying that Williams missed her friends in England, but she also thrived in France, where her circle of friends and acquaintance continued to grow. During her travels in Normandy, recommendations from Madame de Genlis introduced her to the "most considerable families" in Orléans, and when she returned to Paris in December 1791, she built on the friendships she had already established there, becoming the most famous English woman residing in France.[116] One measure of her celebrity status can be taken from William Wordsworth, who had hoped to meet Williams when he visited Orléans in December 1791, bearing letters of introduction from Charlotte Smith: "Mrs. Smith who was so good as to give me Letters for Paris furnished me with one for Miss Williams, an English Lady who resided here lately, but was gone before I arrived. This circumstance was a considerable disappointment to me."[117] At this stage in his life, Wordsworth was a young man of 21, hoping to meet the famous Miss Williams, while his own literary career still lay far ahead of him.

Williams stayed in France till June 1792, when she interrupted her projected two-year stay to return to England for about three months. During her time away, she had written her second book of *Letters from France*, capitalizing on the success of the first one. When she arrived in

London, she was greeted affectionately by friends like Anna Seward, who, though now disapproving of the Revolution, still admired Williams for her commitment to her ideals. In a letter of July 1792 Seward referred to Williams's residence in France as a "heroic emigration," and to Williams herself as "my noble-minded Helen."[118] These high terms of praise are a measure of Williams's continuing public acclaim. She wrote to Hester Thrale Piozzi on 13 June 1792 that "I have come to England to execute some business for my mother" and "I shall remain in England till August, and therefore flatter myself there are many happy days in reserve for me in the dear Library."[119] However, their friendship was under some strain since Thrale Piozzi was now adamantly opposed to revolutionary politics, while Williams's own connections to France were deepening. She was spending more time with John Hurford Stone, a Dissenter and businessman, with close ties to people of influence on both sides of the channel: Sheridan, Fox, Priestley, and Lauderdale in London; and Brissot, Français de Nantes, and Kersaint in Paris.[120] When Williams visited Streatham in summer 1792, Stone accompanied her, and Thrale Piozzi, assuming a romantic connection between them, was shocked when she learned that Stone (1763–1818) was a married man, a topic to be covered in due course.[121]

It is not clear whether it was for political reasons that Williams changed publishers in 1792, but her second volume of *Letters* was published by George Robinson (1737–1801), who remained her publisher for some years. There have been suggestions made that Williams's relationship with Thomas Cadell came to an end because he would not condone her continuing to write about the Revolution, though we recall he had been at Williams's as recently as April 1791, as recorded in Samuel Rogers's diary. Bertrand de Moleville in his *Refutation*, the English edition of which was published by Cadell in 1804, says that Cadell "would on no account undertake to publish the second" volume of Williams's *Letters*.[122] The family-run firm of G. G. and J. Robinson was highly regarded, but it also had a longstanding reputation as the "leading publisher of the English and Scottish Enlightenment,"[123] and was fined in 1793 for "selling copies of Paine's *Rights of Man*."[124]

Williams's new *Letters from France* was published in the summer of 1792.[125] In the opening sentence, she reminds her readers of the story of the du Fossés that they had enjoyed so much in her *Letters* of 1790 (and later recounts the similar class-crossed story of Auguste and Madelaine; 1.2.156–82). Williams boldly asserts that her account of France is more authentic than that of others because she has been in Paris, and she is not reticent about claiming the historical importance of her subject matter: it is "a new era in the history of mankind" (1.2.4–5). When she states that "living in France at present, appears to me somewhat like living in a region of romance" (1.2.4), she, in effect, promises readers that her book will combine an historical account with the excitement that they crave as readers of "romance." The first letter also sets out her ideological position clearly: not only has she retained her initial enthusiasm about the Revolution but she reasserts it in the face of counter-revolutionary discourse. She does not mention Burke's *Reflections*, which she had undoubtedly read by then, but alludes to his famous remark that "the age of chivalry is gone"[126] in her comment that "I sometimes think that the age of chivalry, instead of being past for ever, is just returned" (1.2.5). By stating that she looks forward to the "constitutional reign of Lewis the Sixteenth" she aligns herself with those Whigs who viewed the French government as moving closer to the English model of constitutional monarchy, exhibiting the type of accountability produced in England by the Revolution of 1688 (1.2.6).

Among the many improvements in French society that she thinks might benefit England are those concerning literacy and education. Coffeehouses and lycées are attended by both men and women, as she describes in a letter of 26 February 1792 to Hester Thrale Piozzi:

> Cecilia and I throw aside political discussions at least one hour every day to attend the Lycée, where a number of ladies and gentlemen assemble to hear lectures from the most celebrated professors of Paris on natural philosophy, chemistry, physiology, history, dramatic literature &c and also receive lessons in the greek italian french & english languages—and every Saturday evening by way of recompense for the studies of the week, we have a concert sufficiently good to sooth the mind and give pleasure, tho' not . . . like the sounds I have heard in the Streatham Library.[127]

The instruction at the Lycée represents what, for Williams, was best about the Revolution. As she implies in her *Letters*, this is her vision of an enlightened world where women could develop their minds, where learning was available to men and women alike, and where the sexes could mingle on more of an equal plane:

> I regret we have no such institution in London. What a relief would some people find in being able to escape, for an hour, from those everlasting evenings which are devoted to the dull vacuity of fashionable conversation, or the sad repetitions of card assemblies, and to store the famished mind with a little stock of thought and sentiment, in such a society as the Lycée! (1.2.132–33)

The lycées offered a substitute for the vacuous pastimes relegated to women. Williams's enthusiasm for the public lectures illustrates the deep need that she felt for intellectual stimulation. She described women's minds as "famished," and access to the Lycée provided one forum for learning. Even though only middle-class women are mentioned as being in attendance at the lectures, Williams also remarks on other signs of improved literacy and education:

> I have just been standing with a little circle of country-people, who, after the business of the market was done, ranged themselves round an old woman, who had the advantage over the rest of the groupe, of having attained the accomplishment of reading. She read to them a newspaper, to which the audience listened with such eager attention. (1.2.51–52)

All of these examples can be related to the hopes Williams had for the improvement of women's lives. After all, to use Sylvia Harcstark Myers' categories, she was a second-generation bluestocking, who was building on what the earlier generation of learned women had accomplished.[128] At one point, Williams quotes Hester Thrale Piozzi's comment about the pleasures of learned conversation, which leads her to introduce an anecdote about Samuel Johnson, a man who helped so many women through his encouragement and professional advice:

> One evening at Streatham Park, some person asked Doctor Johnson, how he would choose to distribute the great offices of state which were at that time vacant, amongst the literary ladies of his acquaintance. "Mrs. Carter," said he, "shall be appointed Lord High Chancellor of England." "And what place will you give to the lady of this house [Mrs. Thrale]?" somebody enquired. "We will give *her*," answered Johnson, "a seat in the House of Commons, and she will rise of herself." (1.2.100)

Williams relished the picture of Johnson and a room full of men and women contemplating the possibility of Elizabeth Carter and Hester Thrale (later Piozzi) in Parliament. Even if Johnson had not meant this as a literal possibility, it still conveyed the respect for women that he had so keenly demonstrated in his life and his works, including in the characters of Nekayah and Pekuah in his philosophical romance, *Rasselas*. Williams places this anecdote at the end of one of the letters. She adds no comment of her own, no declaration of the rights of woman, but she lets readers think about the implications of this anecdote. Its inclusion in her *Letters* is important; by aligning herself with Johnson and his reputable bluestocking friends, Williams implied that her own pursuits in France were simply an extension of the work of these earlier "literary ladies" (1.2.100).

Meanwhile, in Paris, she befriended many people renowned for their learning, including women like Madame de Genlis and Madame Roland. Her network of social connections in France was built on her association with men and women whose political views she shared, many of whom held positions of some prominence. The *Letters from France* could have been full of name-dropping, but instead she often preserves her friends' anonymity, referring to them instead as "a Curé of my acquaintance" (1.2.183) or "a friend of mine, who is lately gone to Toulouse" (1.2.156). Her anecdotes derive from dozens of conversations she had with people of all classes, ranging from blacksmiths (1.2.51) to the members of the aristocracy (1.2.73). Although she names very few of her personal acquaintances in this book, one of those mentioned is Monsieur Paul Henri Marron, the pastor of the French Protestant church she attended in Paris; he would become a lifelong friend of her family once they established permanent residence in France. Marron was not a member of the National Assembly, but several of Williams's friends were, and she made several visits to the Assembly (1.2.102), where women attended regularly. John Moore recounted seeing an "abundance of women in the galleries" when he visited later in 1792; and on one occasion he saw Théroigne de Méricourt, whom he found an impressive "amazon" with "a smart martial air."[129] It is possible that Williams may have seen or even met Méricourt, but she leaves no record of it. She was, however, good friends with the more respectable Madame Roland, whom she probably met in Paris during her stay of December 1791 to April 1792.[130] They went together to the Jacobin Club, where Roland's husband had been involved since early 1792 (*Souvenirs* 73),[131] and which was then known as the "cradle and the sanctuary of French liberty" (1.2.110).

Ironically, Williams herself would later denominate it the "den of desolation and carnage" (2.4.128), but in early 1792, the word "Jacobin" had not yet become anathema to Williams. At one large meeting, two thousand people sang songs of liberty and celebrated English and American defenders of liberty. Since Williams regarded liberty as an international cause, her eyes "melted with tears" when it was proposed that the busts of "Price, Franklin, Algernon Sidney, Jean Jacques Rousseau" and others should adorn the Club (1.2.113). She has little patience for aristocratic privileges, preferring the "rejoicing multitudes" in the streets of Paris over the sight of the "splendid equipages" of former days (1.2.74–75). She recalls stories about aristocrats causing accidents with their carriages in the street, including Madame de Pompadour, the mistress of Louis XV, who ran over an old woman and then threw a coin out the window as recompense (1.2.54), an incident later alluded to in Charles Dickens's *A Tale of Two Cities*.[132] Williams even notes with some amusement that democracy has meant a change in dress and manners: "Every man seem at pains to shew that he has wasted as few moments as it was possible at his toilette, and that

his mind is bent on higher cares than the embellishment of his person"
(1.2.81).

This second volume of her *Letters from France* combines an air of
enthusiasm with solemn pronouncements:

> If the blessings of freedom have sometimes been abused, it is because they
> are not yet well understood. Those occasional evils which have happened in
> the infant state of liberty, are but the effects of despotism. Men have been
> long treated with inhumanity, therefore they are ferocious. They have often
> been betrayed, therefore they are suspicious. They have once been slaves,
> and therefore they are tyrants. They have been used to a state of warfare,
> and are not yet accustomed to universal benevolence. They have long been
> ignorant, and have not yet attained sufficient knowledge. They have been
> condemned to darkness, and their eyes are dazzled by light. (1.2.204–5)

Despite Williams's eloquent apologia, her English reading public was
not convinced.

The second volume of the *Letters from France* was received with less
enthusiasm than her first. Now that the almost universal fascination
with the events of 1789 had subsided, most British observers were more
inclined to view the progress of the Revolution with caution. Divisions
were growing between British supporters and opponents of the Revolution, partly due to concerns about the effects that radical ideas could
have in England. Thomas Paine was charged with seditious libel in May
1792, and at the same time a Royal Proclamation against seditious writings was issued. When he was tried and found guilty in absentia in
December 1792, his lawyer, Thomas Erskine, was lauded for his
defence of freedom of speech,[133] and support was briefly galvanized for
groups like the Society for Constitutional Information and the London
Corresponding Society.[134] But, events in France were still regarded
with more scepticism than they had been previously, and this is
reflected in the reviews of the second volume of Williams's *Letters*.

In general, reviewers found themselves unable to agree entirely with
her interpretation of events. The *Critical Review*, for example, conceded
that "the nation in general have gained much," but they added that the
people of France "have paid more dearly for their acquisitions than they
ought to have done."[135] As the gap between the prevailing British view
of France and Williams's widened, critics also called her judgement into
question on the grounds that she was being too emotional in her
response. Reviewers were beginning to sound a disapproving note,
which was often colored by sexist remarks. What the *Critical Review*
applauded as its "Sweet enthusiasm,"[136] the *English Review* dismissed as
uncritical buoyancy, regarding the book as a secondary production
directed at a female audience:

it is not so much addressed to the sagacious politicians of the day, as to the more amiable, though perhaps less sagacious ones; we mean the politicians in petticoats. Its writer is a female democrate, and female democrates should be its readers. . . . In prose we seek for something more than the ebullitions, however elegant, of an enflamed imagination; . . . neglecting to follow the chain of events[.] . . . On the whole, though these letters will not add much to the celebrity of Miss Williams, they will not detract from it. They seem to have been written with great facility; and the writer appears to have known that her name would have some power to sanction a volume, which had otherwise not had those claims to our attention, which this slight work has excited.[137]

Whatever praise Williams is given here, it is deflated by the reviewer's rejection of her efforts to write about the Revolution. Like other "female democrates" and "politicians in petticoats" she lacks the sagacity of male writers and fails to demonstrate historical objectivity because she writes about her own experiences.

Deprecated as the "ebullitions" of an "enflamed imagination," the sensibility previously praised by her reviewers is now a sign of her inferiority; and her ability to move others is even viewed as a form of seduction that her male readers must resist:

We *feel* that we can resist the torrent of Mr. Mackintosh's eloquence, the calm persuasive arguments of Mr. Flower, and the majestic energy of M. Rabaut St. Etienne, more firmly than the seductive insinuations of miss Williams. We formerly endeavoured to convert her, by what we thought the most powerful of arguments, the danger of her leading a life of celibacy, if she continued so furious a democrat. But our arguments, we find, were in vain; and as she is probably now in France, she may have found that democratic principles are not always impediments to the gratification of the social principle, in the most tender connections. We may, perhaps, be allowed to hint that democracy is not equally fashionable in this kingdom; and, if she return without fixing her heart on a French lover, she is still in a little danger. But we must turn to the book, and steel our hearts against the pleasing insinuations of the fair author: we must guard against this enchanted grove, and not be led away captives in fetters of roses.[138]

In an interesting combination of playfulness and censoriousness, the reviewer compliments Williams on being attractive to her male readers, while, at the same time, objecting to her political opinions. Her own work is set in contrast to that of James Mackintosh, Benjamin Flower, and Rabaut St. Etienne, whose opinions are similar to hers,[139] but who lack the "seductive insinuations" or sexual power that she, as a woman, can exert over her readers. This implies a kind of erotic relationship between writer and reader, but the charm of Williams's text constitutes a dubious power. Moreover, the reviewer makes an allusion to her being unmarried, stating that they had warned her before that she would have difficulty finding a husband if she retained her democratic principles. Not only is she depicted as "so furious a democrat," but she has turned out to be just like any other woman, a potential temptress, who could lead men into danger, like Spenser's Acrasia in the Bower of Bliss in the *Faerie Queene*, alluded to in the last line quoted above. The humour couching these comments in a journal normally supportive of Williams's work suggests that the *Critical Review* was indulging in what they probably regarded as a type of gentle teasing of Williams. Nonetheless, their evaluation of her capacity to write on political affairs was demeaning, even though they praised the book overall: "we have been highly pleased with this little book; and, politics apart, can recommend it as truly interesting and entertaining."[140] A backhanded compliment at most, this remark allows that Williams can write an entertaining account of her travels, but it dismisses her as a political commentator. Similarly, the *Analytical Review* praised her book, but regarded her treatment of political subjects as rather superficial, for which they sounded almost grateful: she "does not venture into the depths of politics; but sipping at the brink of the stream, she skims lightly over the subjects alluded to."[141] They imply that this was just the right approach for a woman, to skim "lightly" over the topic of politics. This type of polite but qualified approbation occurred in journals that acknowledged Williams's status as a woman of letters, but also exposed their uncertainty about how to react to her continuing interest in revolutionary politics, now that the general euphoria of 1790 had subsided.

Along with these mixed reviews, this book earned Williams at least one poetic tribute. The poet George Dyer complimented her and other women writers (Mary Wollstonecraft, Ann Jebb, and Anna Laetitia Barbauld) in his poem "On Liberty," also published in 1792. In a note to the poem, Dyer refers directly to Williams's second volume of *Letters*, and, in fact, he quotes from the second stanza of her poem to Dr. John Moore included in that book, with its pastoral image of a new age of prosperity in France: "There, on the Loire's sweet banks, a joyful band / Cull'd the rich produce of the fruitful land" (1.2.10). The women mentioned by Dyer were among the most prominent in late eighteenth-century progressive circles, and they knew each other: Williams and Barbauld were already good friends, as were Wollstonecraft and Jebb; and Wollstonecraft later spent time with Williams in Paris. It was the last two whose lives were most changed by the Revolution. Wollstonecraft's story is well known: she stayed in Paris until 1795, returning to London with a new baby (Fanny Imlay), after publishing a partial history of the French Revolution.[142] Helen Maria Williams's story has a different ending, or perhaps it is better to call it a beginning. As Dyer points out, "Liberty" was the cause that drew Williams to "the Loire's sweet banks."[143] On 5 August 1792, when she left once more for France, she did not know that "liberty" was about to be defiled; nor could she have known that she would never return to England again.

3

"English Historian of the French Revolution"

Having described in the *LETTERS* of 1792, a Paris made congenial by its lycées, and a nation whose example of "enlightened freedom" might soon be emulated "by all the nations of Europe" (1.2.205), Williams was shocked by the events that occurred when she returned to Paris. The second half of 1792 constituted a shift in the development of the Revolution. These were the days of the storming of the Tuileries on the 10th of August; the September massacres; French military victories and decrees; and the trial of Louis XVI and his execution in January 1793. Summarizing the events in France from September to December, a contributor to the *Critical Review* wrote that "every day teems with incident, and a newspaper has become as interesting as a page of Roman history."[1]

Things looked somewhat different to Royalists like Jean Peltier, who commented at the end of 1792, "No period in the history of the world presents us with so crowded a spectacle of atrocious crimes and frightful disasters."[2] While, as a result of this violence, many former supporters in England now opposed the Revolution, in France deputies in the National Assembly fractured into two main camps, the Girondins and the Jacobins, the former accused of elitism, and the latter scorned for their mob appeal. The alliances of Williams and her British friends in Paris were mainly with the Girondins, who blamed the violence of 1792 on the Jacobin leaders, Maximilien Robespierre, Georges Jacques Danton, and Jean-Paul Marat. It was largely because of her network of English and French friends in Paris that Williams did not simply abandon revolutionary politics and return home to London.

The first record we have of Williams's experience of those days is a letter that she wrote to Hester Thrale Piozzi, dated 4 September 1792, in the midst of the massacres of 2–6 September:

September 4th, 1792

My dearest Madam,
    I know your affection & tenderness for me too well not to believe you have some anxiety for me on account of the events which have [been] pass-

ing in Paris since my arrival—if I had written to you half as often as I have thought of you, & the dear elegant retirement of Streatham-Park amidst these scenes of tumult and of death, what a multitude of letters would you have received—but my dearest Madam, many reasons have prevented me from taking up the pen—not only have I felt my mind so much agitated as to make writing a painful task, but I knew there was a great probability that my letters would be stopped—this scrawl may perhaps never reach you, but I cannot delay any longer to send a few lines merely to tell you I am in safety—I leave to some other period the discussion of the scenes which have lately been acting at Paris—they have indeed been such that scarcely even my conviction that this temporary evil will produce permanent good, at all reconcile my mind to that profusion of blood, that dismal waste of life of which I have been the witness—the sword is now drawn, and will be sheathed no more till one party or the other is extirpated—the King's party had made out a most dreadful proscription of many thousand persons & had it triumphed Paris would have been deluged with blood—the popular party have taken their revenge—and the massacre of yesterday has filled my mind with a degree of horror which leaves me scarcely the power of holding my pen—the people of France have indeed been most shamefully betrayed, most cruelly sacrificed to their enemies, but the proscription of yesterday will for ever cast a dark stain on the annals of the revolution—you will hear accounts of it as if it were the mob—but it is a well-known fact that the plan was laid & the list of the proscribed marked by those to whom the people have been the instrument. Adieu my dearest Madam—you will guess from whom this scrawl comes, tho' I shall not sign my name & you will I well know believe me ever & ever with the truest respect & tenderness yours — — —[3]

Circumstances were so dangerous that Williams could "not sign" her name, and she feared that the letter would not even arrive in England: it was a significant change for a writer whose name had "power to sanction a volume."[4] The violence has shaken Williams to the core, making her realize how far away she was from the "elegant retirement of Streatham-Park" and her former life in England. Scarcely able to write, she yet realizes that only more bloodshed will bring an end to the conflict, implying that she knows more than she can safely say.

As David Erdman has noted, "It has been difficult for British historians to imagine that there could have been any honest British citizens whose enthusiasm or even sympathy for the French Revolution had not been dashed irrevocably by the September Massacres."[5] The horror of the massacres did not necessarily mean the end of the Revolution, and many of the British in Paris remained hopeful that things would improve. A group was established called "The Friends of the Rights of Man, associated at Paris," or the British Club, whose members included John Hurford Stone, Joel Barlow, Robert Merry, and John James

Masquerier, all closely associated with Williams.[6] Meanwhile, their Girondin allies Jacques-Pierre Brissot and Pierre Victurnien Vergniaud worked to regain "their political ascendancy" against Robespierre's faction.[7] Erdman points out that the news of General Charles François Dumouriez's victory against the Prussians at Jemappes (6 November 1792) revived hopes for a return to the peaceful progress of the Revolution. On 18 November 1792, the British in Paris celebrated Dumouriez's victory at a party at White's Hotel (presided over by John Hurford Stone), and even toasted Charlotte Smith and Helen Maria Williams as "Women of Great Britain" "who have distinguished themselves by their writings in favour of the French revolution."[8] This toast represents a significant acknowledgement of the contribution that Williams made through her writing. But these accolades would have been viewed differently in England, where support for the Revolution was fast abating.

The celebrations at White's Hotel in Paris also came at a time when Williams was seriously ill, and she would not have attended the festivities, even if women had been allowed to. Williams had been bed-ridden for two months, through October and November 1792, and it was thought that she would not recover. During this period, she worried about the way that her work, though celebrated by the British in Paris, was starting to divide her from some of her friends in England, and she agonized over the personal cost of maintaining her support of the Revolution. It is in her private correspondence, not the published *Letters from France*, that one learns of her determination to hold on to the good opinion of friends in England who were ready to break with her due to her political involvement. The following letter of 12 December 1792 is a reply to one that Thrale Piozzi sent to her, which, although it does not survive, we know from Williams's own remarks contained severe criticism of her continuing residence in France. In this reply, Williams attempts to hold onto their friendship, while also disputing the allegations directed against her:

December 12th, 1792
My dearest Madam,
    At the time your letter arrived I was unable to read it—it reached Paris at the period when I lay almost at the point of death stretched upon a bed to which I have been confined two long months, and from which I had little expectation of ever rising again—never indeed was I before so near journeying to that undiscovered country from whose bourne no traveller returns—I am now recovering slowly, am still confined to my room, and in a state of weakness which scarcely leaves me the power of scrawling a few lines with a trembling hand to congratulate you on sweet Cecilia [Thrale]'s recovery—I feel on my mind a very lively impression of what mothers suffer

when their children are in danger—for my poor mother who watched at my bedside three days and nights without hope of my recovery, has been almost brought to the grave herself from anguish and despair—What a dismal thing is absence from those we love, and how little we know of the feelings of our friends at a distance, while my meditations were fixed on another world you suppose me deeply occupied by the affairs of this world and raging with democratic fury—and on this supposition you write to me (at least I fancied you did) not with your usual kindness, but in somewhat of a harsh tone which cost me some pain—no one my dear Madam, can love you with more sincere tenderness or admire you with more true zeal than myself—I am sure you feel some affection for me, and why should any difference in political opinions cast even a temporary cloud over our friendship it will not be left to us to settle the governments of the earth, do not then I beseech you if you value my peace, let us quarrel about them—as for myself I never took so little interest in politics as I have done lately—I have been too sick and too sorrowful to have the power of considering whether monarchies or republics are best—and at present all my feelings are on the side of Lewis the sixteenth whom whether he be guilty or innocent we know to be unfortunate, which gives him a sufficient claim to pity—indeed even the mob of Paris seemed to feel this sentiment yesterday for they observed the most profound silence as he passed along to the national convention—how imagination is struck by such a fall from greatness—I am happy to find your letter contradicts the reports of commotion in England—be assured I am not indifferent about the tranquillity & welfare of my country—I do not wonder that with your fortune & Streatham-Park, you prefer England to all other countries—people who like ourselves have but a small pittance are glad to go & pitch their tent where that pittance affords more ease and comfort— Say every thing that is kind for me my dear Madam, to Mr. Piozzi, dear Cecilia and our divine Mrs. Siddons, in whose recovery I rejoice most truly so I do in Miss Weston's good fortune—I hope she will be as happy as she deserves—Farewell my dear Madam, believe me sick or well, in all situations ever your most obliged & affectionate friend.[9]

At the end of 1792, Williams struggled against illness and her own despair at the turn the Revolution had taken. Political questions faded in importance as she endured a near fatal illness that made her think of death and the afterlife, or, as she quoted from *Hamlet*, "the bourne from which no traveller returns."[10] Moved by her mother's close attendance at her sick-bed, Williams reflected on the things that are most important in life: her religious faith, her family, and her friends. Her mind was not on monarchies or republics, and she felt offended that Thrale Piozzi would let such subjects—no matter how important—come between them. Thrale Piozzi did not understand the moderate revolutionary politics of the Girondin position, but regarded all supporters of the Revolution as the same. Nonetheless, Williams made an effort to persuade her that their friendship should transcend politics. She made light of the significance of her books on the Revolution by saying that nothing she did would have any effect, so it did not matter if their views differed. Even though Williams had seen the violent consequences of the sharp divisions between Royalists, Jacobins, and Girondins, she still retained the belief that Thrale Piozzi, whom she regarded as a kindred spirit, should not let politics separate them. Williams is poised to discover that she cannot separate her personal world from the political. If she is going to accept being toasted by some, she will have to be prepared to suffer attacks from others—the least of which will turn out to be the "harsh tone" of a friend.

While their relationship was under a strain that would soon lead to Thrale Piozzi breaking off all ties with her, Williams spent Christmas in Paris with her family and her English and French friends. A brief survey of some of the people Williams knew during this period will demonstrate how, since her return in August 1792, her Paris home had become an important gathering place of like-minded writers and politicians (interrupted only by her illness in October and November). For example, soon after her return, at a dinner given by the elderly couple the Bitaubés, she met the writer Sebastian Chamfort, himself a friend of the Comte de Mirabeau and the Marquis de Condorcet.[11] Williams had praised Chamfort in her second volume of *Letters* as a man "of the first literary talents," known for his "brilliant powers of conversation," and his "ardent love of liberty" (1.2.121). It is probably Chamfort who introduced Williams to two men who became important in her later career, his collaborators on the *Decade Philosophique*, Jean-Baptiste Say (the translator of her *Tour in Switzerland* (1798)) and Pierre Louis Ginguené.[12] Chamfort became a regular visitor at Williams's soirées, where he met people like "Vergniaud, Brissot, Bernardin de Saint-Pierre, and Bancal des Issarts."[13] Each visitor to Williams's home could provide similar lists of her noteworthy guests—and, many did. Williams herself mentions many of these friends in her memoirs (*Souvenirs*), including the Venezuelan revolutionary General Francisco Miranda, who had resided with Joel Barlow in London. Miranda's biographer confirms that he was a frequent visitor at Williams's salon, where many gathered for tea on Sunday evenings to discuss literature and politics, including Brissot, Vergniaud, the Chénier brothers, Cambacérès, Chamfort, Bernardin de Saint-Pierre, Manon Roland, Lassource, Barère, Rabaut Saint-Étienne, and Carnot.[14] Such records provide a useful picture of the people who congregated at Williams's home, many of whom earned a place in the world's history books.

We can see from these lists that the social worlds of Madame Roland (1754–93) and Helen Maria Williams were continually overlapping

(*Souvenirs* 97). The only mention of Williams in Roland's surviving papers is in a series of letters from October 1792, concerning Jean-Henri Bancal des Issarts' (1750–1826) romantic interest in Williams.[15] Bancal may have met Williams during his residence in London from November 1790 till July 1791, where he visited Thomas Christie, Thomas Clarkson, and members of the Abolition Society.[16] Though Williams rejected Bancal's proposal in 1792 and again in 1796 when Grégoire acted as his intermediary,[17] she spoke highly of him in her memoirs and *Letters from France*. However, of the many distinguished friends she paid tribute to in her published works, none was more revered than Madame Roland, one of the few women regarded as a major figure in the history of the French Revolution. Roland was an articulate woman who, since the time of her husband's election as a Deputy for Lyons, had been assisting him with the writing of documents and speeches. After their move to Paris, she became an inspirational figure for the men who gathered at their home for political meetings.[18] Her husband was appointed Minister of the Interior in March 1792, and by the fall of that year, after he had broken with the Jacobins, they were both subject to vitriolic attacks in the press, especially in Jean-Paul Marat's *L'Ami du peuple* and Jacques Hébert's *Père Duchesne*.[19] But, for Williams, the like-minded Roland provided a model of intelligent and compassionate womanhood:

> I had been acquainted with her since I first came to France, and had always observed in her conversation the most ardent attachment to liberty, and the most enlarged sentiments of philanthropy; sentiments which she developed with an eloquence peculiar to herself, with a flow and power of expression which gave new graces and new energy to the French language. With these extraordinary endowments of mind she united all the warmth of a feeling heart, and all the charms of the most elegant manners. She was tall and well shaped, her air was dignified, and although more than thirty-five years of age she was still handsome. Her countenance had an expression of uncommon sweetness, and her full dark eyes beamed with the brightest rays of intelligence. (2.1.195–96)

It is clear from this tribute that Williams regarded Roland with the highest esteem and with deep affection. She valued enormously this woman who combined both intelligence and grace, who could converse eloquently, yet maintain her feminine dignity. The homage she pays to Madame Roland recalls the respect Williams felt for other women who valued the life of the mind, those who were a part of her world in London in the 1780s, such as Elizabeth Montagu and Anna Laetitia Barbauld.

In December 1792, Williams began to spend time with another

English woman of letters: Mary Wollstonecraft, who had just arrived in Paris for a six-week visit, which would become a two-and-a-half-year residence.[20] In the following letter of 24 December 1792, Wollstonecraft wrote to her sister Everina about spending time with the renowned Williams, who, recovered from her illness, gave her a warm welcome:

> I have seen very little of Paris the streets are so dirty, and I wait till I can make myself understood before I call upon Madame Laurent &c. Miss Williams has behaved very civilly to me and I shall visit her frequently, because I *rather* like her, and I meet french company at her house. Her manners are affected, yet the *simple* goodness of her heart continually breaks through the varnish, so that one would be more inclined, at least I should, to love than admire her. — Authorship is a heavy weight for female shoulders especially in the sunshine of prosperity.[21]

Wollstonecraft's comment about the "simple goodness" of Williams's heart echoes the remark noted earlier in the *Analytical Review* about Williams's good nature, an important indication that Williams was generally well liked by those who knew her. In addition, it shows that Wollstonecraft felt Williams was managing well despite the pressure that was placed upon a woman of letters. The passage quoted above has, in fact, become well known as an important statement about the predicament of the eighteenth-century woman writer. Wollstonecraft understands that it is not easy for a woman to deal with the attention accompanying her success.

While Wollstonecraft praised Williams for her courage, there were other friends urging Williams to come back to England. Anna Seward went so far as to publish a letter to Williams in *Gentleman's Magazine* in February 1793, which contained this appeal: "Fly, my dear Helen, that land of carnage! . . . Love and respect your country half as well as I love and respect you; and I trust we shall soon cease to view you in a state of cold alienation."[22] France and England had just declared war on each other, and Seward is like the nation's spokesperson, giving Williams one last chance to come home to London with her respectability intact and her rashness forgiven. Williams's decision to stay in Paris at this important historical juncture inevitably alienated her from several friends and affected her public reputation. She was grateful for those who continued to support her, like Penelope Pennington (formerly Weston). Williams wrote several letters to Pennington which survive, and in them she thanked her for her loyalty, calling her the "faithful found among the faithless."[23]

With the publication of the third and fourth volumes of her *Letters from France* in the summer of 1793, Williams demonstrated her determination to find a way to keep writing. From Williams's point of view, after the events of 1792–93, it was not a matter of *not* writing on politics but *how* to write on a political situation she no longer supported unequivocally. She needed new rhetorical strategies in order to write about experiences beyond the scope of the joyful or pathetic scenes recorded in her first two volumes: namely, regicide, political factions, intrigues, and moral failure. This was a transitional period in which she moved towards establishing herself as a serious political commentator, consciously alluding to other "friends of liberty" (1.4.117; 1.4.152; 2.4.1), a term often used in the British reform movement during the eighteenth century.

The third volume of the *Letters from France* opens with a letter dated 25 January 1793, four days after Louis XVI's execution. Williams's tone is at times strikingly different from her earlier books, as tension and frustration replace her former hopefulness in this dirge for "the golden age of the revolution" (1.3.6). In her most extensive criticism yet of the course of the Revolution, Williams views her past hopes as illusions: "the enchanting spell is broken, and the fair scenes of beauty and of order through which imagination wandered, are transformed into the desolation of the wilderness, and clouded by the darkness of the tempest" (1.3.6). In contrast to the many references to harmony and light in the celebratory letters of volume one and two, Williams now has recourse to metaphors of natural turbulence and darkness, which became a conventional part of representations of the Revolution in this period.[24] One of Williams's most significant rhetorical strategies from this point onward was to present herself as a less naive observer, one who would not be easily "enchanted" again. To fashion an ordered literary text out of the political chaos, she chooses a position of rational detachment. Alluding to the King's execution, she writes: "The event which has this week taken place in Paris, will no doubt furnish you with ample matter for speculation" (1.3.1) But there is still a place for the language of sensibility in Williams's prose, as she observes that, "Imagination contemplates with an overwhelming emotion that extraordinary vicissitude of fortune which conducted Louis the Sixteenth from the radiant palace of Versailles, to the gloomy tower of the Temple" (1.3.1). However, in order to maintain her enlightenment hopes for humankind, Williams had to remain stoical, as shown by the following comment:"Upon the whole, the French revolution is still in its progress, and who can decide how its last page will finish?" (1.3.19).

The dangerous times required other sorts of strategies as well. One of them was to publish these volumes anonymously, something she had never done before, and it was certainly not out of a belated sense of feminine reserve that she did so in 1793. The anonymity—such as it was, since reviewers revealed her name—gave her freedom to publish her pro-Girondin account while the Girondins were still fighting for their political and actual lives in summer 1793. Secondly, two other people contributed large sections of the books, as the editor acknowledges in the book's advertisement:

> Though, for particular reasons, the author's name could not be prefixed to these Letters, the reader will, on the perusal of them, be at no loss to determine from what quarter they proceed. It is only fair, however, to premise, that they are not all the production of the same pen. The Letters, Nos. 2, 3, 4, 5, 6, in Vol. III. which contain a history of the campaign of 1792, are by another hand; but the public will easily perceive that they are written by a person who has had the *best* information on the subject that France could afford. The concluding letter is by a third person; but as it contained a very interesting disquisition concerning the popular topics of the times, the publisher conceived he could not render a more acceptable service to the purchasers of these volumes than to insert it. (1.3. n. p.)

It is a testimony to Williams's high public profile that it can confidently be stated that readers will "be at no loss to determine" who wrote most of the letters. But, even though no names are mentioned, a clear distinction is made between what she wrote and what others contributed. One can understand that Williams would not have wanted to be thought to be the author of the last letter in the fourth volume, so acrimonious is its tone. The anonymity of the three writers was preserved, until they were identified in British reviews: "We understand that these letters, except those respecting the campaign of 1792, which are said to have been written by Mr. Stone, and the concluding one, which is attributed to Mr. Christie, are from the elegant pen of miss Williams."[25] Williams's name did appear on the title page of the Dublin edition of the same two volumes in 1794.

As a result of the collaboration, Williams wrote only one-tenth of the material in the third volume (Stone wrote Letters 2, 3, 4, 5, and 6) and two-thirds of the material in the fourth volume (Letter 5, by Christie, dated March 1793, takes up the last 116 pages of the fourth volume). With the contributions of her two colleagues, Williams did not have the burden of doing all the writing herself, but she could get the material into the public's hands fairly speedily. Moreover, it is possible that transferring her central authorial position to men may have given Williams time to decide, both for reasons of personal safety and due to her role as a woman writer, if she could, and just how she *would*, continue to report on events now turned violent. The material on the military campaign, and the excerpts from the letters of Dumouriez and Miranda are pertinent, and even constitute another feat of textual gender-bending since this collaboration with men was not common, but they also disrupt the unity of a multi-volume work in which Williams's narrative voice had been so central and consistent.

The anonymity and the collaboration—both linked to the fact that the times were dangerous for publishing such a book—resulted in the suppression of the authorial persona that readers had grown accustomed to. At one point in the opening letter Williams sounds as if she were ushering in her own detailed account, which then never appears:

> I am a spectator of the representation.—I am placed near enough the scene to discern every look and every gesture of the actors, and every passion excited in the minds of the audience. I shall therefore endeavour to fill up the outline of that picture which France has presented to your contemplation since the memorable epocha of the tenth of August. (1.3.2)

Although she boldly defines herself as an eyewitness who can provide empirical information, she does not give the details one might expect from a person who claims to "be close enough . . . to discern every look and every gesture." In fact, Williams deliberately avoids publishing what she observed, even though she wrote to friends in England about it. She writes under a kind of self-imposed gag order, at odds with the former effusiveness that characterized the two earlier volumes. For example, although she declares that she will report on events from the tenth of August, she does not discuss what she saw. Instead, one can find a vivid account of the 10th of August in the published *Journal* of her friend Dr. John Moore, who saw the dead bodies of the Swiss soldiers at the Tuileries and went to the National Assembly the same day to see Antoine-Joseph Gorsas trying to calm the crowds.[26] Williams was actually an exceptional witness to the storming of the Tuileries, because she could see some of the fighting from her lodgings on the rue de Lille across the river, but one has to read her memoirs to find that out. There she recounts that a Swiss guard approached her hotel, where he was given a glass of water, but died moments later on the doorstep. The next day, friends urged her to walk with them through the Tuileries, insisting that all the signs of the day's bloodshed had been removed, and she was horrified when she came across two corpses and immediately rushed back to her hotel (*Souvenirs* 29–34).

Apparently, Williams wrote to friends about what she saw, and eventually the story got twisted into rumors that damaged her reputation in England, especially after they were circulated in print by people like James Boswell. Although Boswell had been a friend of Andrew Kippis, he was no longer restrained by the politeness shown in his July 1791 letter. A virulent opponent of the Revolution, Boswell used the rumours against Williams in a revised edition of the *Life of Johnson*, published in July 1793. Referring to Johnson's meeting with Williams in 1784, Boswell, having described her as elegant and accomplished, then adds the following footnote:

> In the first edition of my Work, the epithet *amiable* was given. I was sorry to be obliged to strike it out; but I could not in justice suffer it to remain, after this young lady had not only written in favour of the savage Anarchy with which France has been visited, but had (as I have been informed by good authority) walked, without horror, over the ground at the Thuilleries when it was strewed with the naked bodies of the faithful Swiss Guards, who were barbarously massacred for having bravely defended against a crew of ruffians, the Monarch whom they had taken an oath to defend. From Dr.Johnson she could now expect not endearment but repulsion.[27]

It was unfair for Boswell to assume Johnson would have shared his own judgement of Williams. But, in 1793, Williams had more important things to worry about than Boswell's opinion of her, and she waited until the publication of her memoirs to refute this allegation, though she does not mention Boswell by name. As for her decision not to write about this eyewitness account in volume three or four, it seems that she was not prepared to make public this harrowing experience. Since some people criticized her just for being in France, let alone for having political opinions, what would they say about her being literally on the scene? She probably knew her actions would be misinterpreted, and Boswell's slander was the first of many she would suffer at the hands of other British writers.

As for what she did include in these volumes, Williams clearly felt it was important to report on the military campaign, something which she could not observe for herself, even if some women did, as she commented in the fourth volume of the second series of *Letters*: "I am not, like some of the females of this country, skilled in the art of war" (2.4.180). Since the material was published after war was declared between Britain and France, and some of it written in the spring of 1793, by aligning herself with those who celebrated French victories in the Campaign of 1792, she now assumed a more overtly political position. The narrative structure of John Hurford Stone's account of the campaign of 1792 is a confusing combination of present experiences, humorous anecdotes, and retrospective reports on previous military actions. The letters are all dated after the French victory of 20 September, when Dumouriez engineered the Prussian withdrawal from France, an event which gave such confidence to the French revolutionaries. A buoyant mood suffuses most of the report, and the narrator

indulges in a confident feeling of his own safety among the French soldiers (1.3.150). But excitement over French victories subsides when the
narrator observes that villages have no food for travellers; and horse
carcasses and the rotting bodies of dead soldiers block the roadway
(1.3.181). By Letter Six, dated 12 December 1792, when the French
assumed an offensive rather than a defensive role, Stone expresses some
concern that "they seem to be going too fast" (1.3.223).

This mild criticism of the army was not, however, the reason that
these volumes had to be published anonymously. Rather, it was Williams's explicit criticism of the Jacobins that could have led to the arrest
of her and her co-authors, whose names were attached to extracts published in the English newspapers read in France by members of the
Committee of Public Safety. Williams recounts in her *Letters* that it was
because of this danger that she eventually fled to Switzerland in 1794
(2.1.173–74). In her opening letter to this third volume, Williams analyzes the shift in power, as the Mountain gained control of the Convention, and she mentions Robespierre for the first time, demonizing him
in terms that were to become common: with his "countenance of such
dark aspect," he "regulates the most ferocious designs with the most
calm and temperate prudence" motivated by a "deep and extraordinary
malignity" (1.3.7). Similarly, John Moore observed that "Few Men
however can *look* fiercer than Robespierre; in countenance he has a
striking resemblance to a cat-tiger."[28] Such statements draw on the vili-
fication that was already constructing Robespierre's alternate public
image as the most dangerous member of the leading triumvirate that
included Danton and Marat.

Williams accuses these three men of conspiring with people in the
Paris Commune to plan the September massacres, after setting the
stage for anarchy by having "armed every man in Paris, and consequently placed a formidable power in the hands of that swarm of idle
and profligate persons which infest great capitals" (1.3.18). Using a
touch of Burkean rhetoric to attack the followers of the Jacobins, Williams articulates her fear of the anarchy which she sees resulting from
empowering (or at least arming) people whom she views as morally
degenerate. Differences in class surface as she registers her outrage at
the political ascendancy of the uneducated. Since Dissenters, such as
Williams, placed a high value on the capacities of the mind and reason,[29]
the jeering of an uneducated crowd would be regarded as an appalling
reverse:

> a man, in order to gain applause, must harangue in the grossest language of
> the lowest vulgar; and a person of education is hooted for that reason only;

any superiority of mind being considered as an aristocratical deviation from the great principles of equality. (1.3.23)

Class prejudices worked both ways, and sometimes they worked against the literate Girondin. William Hazlitt, a writer who used Williams's *Letters from France* in his *Life of Napoleon*, noted that "the superior accomplishments of the Brissotines were as fatal to them as their moderation and humanity."[30] Williams did not delineate any details of the September massacres, but asked in frustration: "Ah! what is become of the delightful visions which elevated the enthusiastic heart?" (1.3.6).

For other early supporters of the Revolution, like the British reformer Sir Samuel Romilly and Williams's friend Dr. John Moore, the September massacres marked the end of any hopes for the French Revolution. Whereas in 1789 and again in May 1792, Romilly had been proclaiming the Revolution as "the most glorious event, and the happiest for mankind,"[31] on 10 September 1792 he cried out in a letter to his friend Dumont,

> How could we ever be so deceived in the character of the French nation as to think them capable of liberty! wretches, who, after all their professions and boasts about liberty, and patriotism, and courage . . . employ whole days in murdering women, and priests, and prisoners! Others who can deliberately load whole waggons full of victims, and bring them like beasts to be butchered in the metropolis; and then (who are worse even than these) the cold instigators of these murders, who, while blood is streaming round them on every side, permit this carnage to go on.[32]

Contributing to Romilly's moral outrage is his sense of being betrayed by the French after having applauded their Revolution. He also explicitly refers to the bloody facts of the event, while Williams uses metaphors to shift the subject to the level of political interpretation. Even more important because of his friendship with Williams was the reaction of John Moore, who was in Paris at the time of the massacres, and documented his day-to-day experience in his *Journal during a Residence in France*. Although he still attempts on 5 September to salvage his belief in the principles of the Revolution by arguing that liberty itself cannot be blamed for the crimes of despotism, by 14 September the continuing violence has proved insupportable:

> These repeated massacres fill the mind with horror—create a detestation of the people who can suffer such things, and will injure the French revolution more than if the Duke of Brunswick had beaten their armies, and were in possession of Paris itself. I abhor writing any more about them— Wretches![33]

Moore calls the massacres "indelible stains"[34]; Romilly's correspondent Dumont bewails the same "tache indelible"[35]; and Williams too calls the massacres "an indelible stain upon the country" (1.3.17). Indeed, the phrase became the most commonly used to describe those days. In their final rejection of the actions of the French, Moore and Romilly represent a common reaction of former supporters of the Revolution. Williams and Moore, close friends since the early 1780s, had both supported the Revolution in its early period, as she mentioned in her *Letters from France* (1792) — "You, whose warm bosom, whose expanded mind, / Have shared this glorious triumph of mankind"(1.2.13). However, their now differing views on the Revolution may have caused a breach between them, since John Hurford Stone later derided Moore's *Journal* as an "inaccurate" and "stupid performance."[36] Williams is not mentioned in the *Journal*, but Moore may have been thinking of her when he states that if war ensues all British subjects should know where their loyalty lies.[37]

The opening sentence of the first letter of the fourth volume of the *Letters from France* again reveals the tension Williams felt regarding the turn of events in France and, in particular, Robespierre's political influence: "The faction of the anarchists desired that the French king should be put to death without the tedious forms of a trial" (1.4.1). Her sarcasm conveyed her bitterness on watching the Girondins lose an important political battle and the King himself lose his life. When discussing the trial and execution of Louis XVI, her tone is solemn and restrained. She asks that the Royal family be treated compassionately, and referring to the King as "the unfortunate monarch" and the "unhappy monarch" (1.4.9; 22; 31; 33; 38), she argues that the humilation he had already undergone was punishment enough: he did not deserve to die, even though he was, in her opinion, guilty of the crimes with which he was charged. Williams, like other writers, contrasted the humanity and dignity of the King at the time of his execution, with the ferociousness of the onlookers who dipped "their handkerchiefs in the blood" (1.4.38). This last detail was common to most accounts of the execution of Louis XVI, and both republicans and surviving royalists retained superstitions about the potent effects of royal blood, as Daniel Arasse observes in his book *The Guillotine and the Terror*.[38]

Writing from France in the wake of the execution, Williams recognized the danger in the growing power struggle between "the Mountain" and "the Gironde party" (1.4.57), but her criticism was tempered by a philosophical outlook. The insurrection against the Girondins had not yet taken place, so she could still afford a certain degree of hopeful speculation, ending one letter in volume four with a flowery tribute to "uncontaminated, pure, exalted, and sublime liberty" (1.4.73). Despite

Williams's powers of persuasion, her readers might well wonder what faith she can have in "liberty" now, and as if answering such a question, she explains how the genuine "friend of liberty" must praise France when its "cause was just" and condemn France when it becomes "the tyrant" in return (1.4.78). This kind of reasoning enables Williams to detach herself from the reprehensible events occurring after 1789, while maintaining a commitment to "liberty" in the abstract. The downward turn of events forced her to modify the enthusiasm of her first two books on France, and in the third and fourth volumes, she assumes a rational persona, cooly watching events in order to gain a sense of control over the political chaos around her. Thus, she can calmly condemn things that go against her principles of liberty, such as the decrees of 15 December 1792 justifying territorial expansion, but still wax eloquently about what liberty *could* (and may yet) produce. She excuses the crimes of the revolutionaries by saying they had "unhappily strayed" from the original system: "Their minds were yet too young in freedom to appreciate its blessings aright" (1.4.117). She predicts that "Grown wise by experience, they will learn to establish amongst themselves that order and harmony which is the best evidence of the value of liberty" (1.4.118–19). As a way of defusing the situation, Williams uses the biblical parable of seeds falling on stony ground or good ground: "though this may for a time 'fall amongst thorns, and in stony places, and the fowls of the air may devour it,' yet it will certainly at length find every where 'the good ground fitted to receive it' " (1.4.153).

These decorous remarks are followed by Thomas Christie's letter, dated March 1793, in which he reviews the main events of the Revolution, and evaluates the debates in Britain, offering accolades to James Mackintosh (1.4.230) and others, including two women, "Mrs. Macaulay Graham" and "Miss Wollstonecraft" (1.4.220). Although Williams herself is much more gracious to Burke when she mentions him briefly, softening her criticism by praising "Mr. Burke's wit and eloquence (and no one has ever deemed more highly of them than myself)" (1.4.145), the inclusion of Christie's invective against Burke would not have reflected well on her. Christie was a noted Scottish reformer and editor of the *Analytical Review*, but Stone—and, likely Williams—broke with him in late 1793, not long after these books were published.[39] Despite its overall pugilistic tone, Christie's letter concludes the book in the same vein as Williams by predicting that the "vigorous seeds" of liberty will "spring up at the first favourable moment" (1.4.270).

Across the channel, detractors of the Revolution ridiculed such notions about "vigorous seeds" of liberty. The events of late 1792 and the execution of Louis XVI in 1793 seemed to justify conservative reaction and would serve the purposes of Church and King propaganda for years to come. It is telling that the evangelical Hannah More echoed the response "Good Lord, deliver us" from the Litany in the *Book of Common Prayer* when she wrote to Horace Walpole, lamenting the death of Louis XVI: "From liberty, equality, and the rights of man, good Lord deliver *us*!"[40] When France declared war against Britain on 1 February 1793, anti-French commentaries, caricatures, and propaganda, which contrasted British rationality with French barbarity, increased in popularity. The most popular print was *The Contrast*, dating from 1792, which showed a dignified picture of a matron-like woman as the allegorical figure of British Liberty, placed next to a horrific image of a blood-thirsty and muscular hag representing French Liberty. Below each figure were terms applicable to them (words like "religion, "morality," "loyalty" were listed under British Liberty; and "atheism," "perjury" and "rebellion" under French Liberty), followed by the rhetorical question, "Which Is Best." In his book *Shadow of the Guillotine*, David Bindman provides examples of how the print, which was designed by Lord George Murray and engraved by Thomas Rowlandson, was also used on pottery and tea-cloths.[41] Later James Gillray's *French Liberty and British Slavery* (dated December 1792) and Isaac Cruikshank's *French Happiness/English Misery* (dated January 1793) both used a contrast design to discredit supporters of the French Revolution.[42]

The post-1793 period was characterized by this type of patriotic discourse. As might be expected, English radicals were at pains to distance themselves from the judgement against the King, and they bemoaned the way that conservatives used the violent events of 1792–93 to discredit the entire reform movement.[43] But even sensibility was being called into question, attacked for its association with revolutionary politics. This is most vividly demonstrated in a later satirical cartoon by James Gillray, the well-known *New Morality* (1 August 1798), which, in mockery of the French figures of liberty, depicts a triumvirate of blood-thirsty hags, named Justice, Philanthropy, and Sensibility.[44] The demise of sensibility, traced by Janet Todd in her useful study, was untimely for a writer like Williams who continued to argue for its legitimacy.[45]

Another woman writer tried to discredit Williams for using what Stephen Cox has called "sensibility as argument."[46] In late 1793 Laetitia Matilda Hawkins wrote an entire book addressed to Williams, attempting to convince her to give up revolutionary politics and go back to being a poet, which was, in comparison, a much more acceptable role for a woman. Hawkins extensively analyzed Williams's first two books in her anonymous *Letters on the Female Mind, Its Powers and Pursuits. Addressed to Miss H. M. Williams, with Particular Reference to Her Letters from France* (1793), and, although Hawkins's book received little notice

in the press, Steven Blakemore has demonstrated its importance in relation to Williams's public reputation and counter-revolutionary discourse.[47] Williams had written in her *Letters from France* that she
believed that her personal response, her heartfelt support for the ideals
of the Revolution, legitimized her foray into the sphere of political commentary. But Hawkins set out to show Williams "that politics are a
study inapplicable to female powers by nature, and withheld from us
by education."[48] Women were not born for the "deep investigations" of
political study; their duties had a "narrower compass."[49] Hawkins
feared that men may resent the liberties women were taking, and so she
advised conformity and caution, and counselled Williams to return to
her former literary pursuits rather than range beyond them:

> Describe sorrow, paint happiness, plead for frailty, or vindicate the virtues;
> and I will be your reader. But do not, I beseech you, endanger your temper,
> or the delicate texture of your talents, by employing your thoughts on sub-
> jects which, in the eye of genius, must be deemed vulgar.[50]

The problem with this proposal was that it sought to fix women in a
position of passivity. Hawkins granted that women could cry over a
scene of suffering, and even write about it, but they must not investigate
the causes of suffering or proposals for social amelioration. Her analysis
did not account for the radical impulse underlying the culture of sensibility, whereas Williams took the next logical step, which meant putting
into action the principles implicit in her poetry, by working to change
society. Ironically, political realities prevented her from writing poetry,
as she lamented in a private letter of 29 July 1793: "instead of the dear
voice of friendship and the sweet song of the Muses here am I listening
to the dismal sound of the tocsin . . . my poetical enthusiasm is killed in
a country from which the graces have fled, and the muses have emigrated."[51]

As far as Hawkins was concerned, the execution of Louis XVI meant
that those who had before been advocates of the Revolution "must now
abandon the cause."[52] Those words solemnly toll the judgement that
Williams would face from many of her English readers. With language
echoing that of Horace Walpole and Edmund Burke, Hawkins commented that "I have heard you in some circles termed, a *poissarde* and a
firebrand," epithets anticipating the insulting rhetoric that Williams
would be subjected to in years to come.[53] It was during this period that
Hester Thrale Piozzi broke off communication with Williams: "God
keep her in personal safety! Meantime I will not write to her: she has
given me directions, but . . . I will not help those forward who are doing,
or trying to do, mischief."[54] In the autumn of 1793, when volumes three

and four of the *Letters from France* were being reviewed, Williams was in prison in Paris, a circumstance which led a reviewer in the *British Critic* to gloat that "her own fate is the best commentary on the wild doctrines she has vindicated."[55] In reality, Williams's life was endangered because she had not supported the "wild doctrines" of Robespierre and the Mountain. Rather, she had urged a return to order, not foreseeing that the year 1793, which began with the ominous execution of Louis XVI, would end with the Reign of Terror.

For Williams, the most shattering memory of 1793 was not her own relatively brief imprisonment, but the fall from power and the execution of her Girondin friends. She was imprisoned from October to November 1793 (Woodward 91; 96), as a result of a general decree against all the British in France in retaliation for French defeats by the British army, and it was during this time that many of the people she was closest to in Paris were guillotined, including on 31 October 1793 Brissot and Vergniaud in a mass execution of 21 members of the Girondin, and on 7 November her dear friend Madame Roland. Williams might well have said with Talma, whom she quotes, " 'Citizens, citizens, all my friends have perished upon the scaffold!' " (2.4.28). When she was released from prison in late November, the Reign of Terror still persisted, and Williams and her family lived in fear of a second arrest. They had support from their remaining friends, the most resourceful of whom proved to be John Hurford Stone, who seemed galvanized by adversity and helped many friends in Paris, including the Williamses and Marie-Martin-Athanase Coquerel, who married Cecilia Williams in March 1794. But, even Stone's entrepreneurial daring was no match for the Committee of Public Safety, or what Williams called the committee "of public extermination" (2.2.5), which in April 1794 required all nobles and all strangers to leave Paris, forcing the Williamses to move to a village near Marly (2.2.6). Since it was dangerous for former associates of the Girondins to stay in France, she, Stone, and others went into exile in Switzerland around June 1794, an interlude to be discussed in the next chapter.

It was only after the fall of Robespierre that Williams returned to Paris at the end of 1794 to pick up the pieces of her life. She worked for a year on her next major publication, her four-volume second series of *Letters from France*, which recounted the chief events of the Reign of Terror and its immediate aftermath (three volumes were published in 1795 and the fourth in 1796).[56] This second series, together with the first, provided the British reading public with an ongoing history of the Revolution, bringing it to its supposed close at the period of the Directory. Widely reviewed, the *Letters* were either welcomed or denounced, according to the political leanings of individual journals. While the *Gentleman's Magazine* regarded the Revolution as nothing but "a tissue of atrocious crimes," and censured "Helen Maria's" work accordingly,[57] the liberal leaning *Critical Review* praised the *Letters* as forming "a valuable, authentic, and entertaining history of the most astonishing event of modern times."[58]

One cannot hope to understand either the *Letters from France* or Williams's continuing support for the Revolution without knowing the depth of her loyalties to her executed friends and her commitment to the ideals they shared. They formed a type of extended family, since "several members of the Girondin regularly spent their evenings" at her salon (*Souvenirs* 50). As noted earlier, Williams's home had been a popular gathering place for dozens of like-minded politicians, artists, and intellectuals. Although she says little about her salon in her second series of *Letters from France*, what information there is in those volumes, combined with the material from her later memoirs, provides at least a sketch of her close friendships with a number of influential men: Jacques-Pierre Brissot (1754–93), Sebastian Chamfort (1741–94), Jean-Baptiste Fonfrède (1766–93), Jerome Pétion (1756–94), Jean-Paul Rabaut Saint-Etienne (1743–93), and Pierre Victurnien Vergniaud (1753–93), all of whom were executed in 1793 or committed suicide the next year. Her friends from this period who survived the Reign of Terror included Antoine Français de Nantes (1756–1836), Henri Grégoire (1750–1831), Monsieur Marron (1754–1832), General Miranda (1750–1816), Claude Rouget de Lille (1760–1835), Joseph Chénier (1764–1811), Jean-Jacques Cambacérès (1753–1824), Jean-Henri Bancal des Issarts (1751–1826) and Maximin Isnard (1758–1825).

Perhaps what is most notable about Williams's affectionate remembrances of her illustrious friends is her genuine gratitude for the way that they accepted her. This is similar to the way that people like Elizabeth Carter, Catherine Talbot, and Elizabeth Montagu were strengthened by the encouragement of the Bluestocking circles, which included men and women.[59] Williams felt proud to have been thought well of by people she regarded as defenders of liberty. Vergniaud, for instance, rather than ignoring her opinions because she was a woman, actually sought them out: he "spoke freely with me, because he knew my feelings and I dare to say that he respected them" (*Souvenirs* 50). It is a measure of her own courage that Williams was unflinchingly loyal to the members of the Girondin in the summer of 1793, after their proscription, visiting Fonfrède and others when they were under house arrest (*Souvenirs* 59), and giving support to the family of Brissot (*Souvenirs* 22), who themselves became her lifelong friends. At some risk to her own safety, she gave shelter to Jean-Paul Rabaut Saint-Etienne

(2.1.208–11; *Souvenirs* 56), whom she revered as "one of the most enlightened and virtuous men whom the revolution had called forth" (2.1.208). It appears that she thought little about the danger she incurred, but instead deemed "it a privilege to have known the pleasure of their friendship and to have been able to give them support in their last days" (*Souvenirs* 62). Having survived them, she was determined to defend their memory, and felt astonished when they were discredited in the British press:

> when we hear Mr. Sheridan speak in the house of commons of the *faction of the Gironde*, and when we read in Mr. Gilbert Wakefield's answer to Mr. Paine's pamphlet his remark upon the *Brissotine faction*, we are filled with astonishment. They might with as much propriety talk of the faction of Sidney, of Russel, and of Hampden. Such observations are blasphemies indeed from the lovers of liberty; they who ought to pronounce with veneration the names of those illustrious martyrs, who, after the most honourable struggles for their country, shed their blood upon the scaffold in its cause, with heroism worthy of the proudest days of Greece or Rome. (2.2.76–77)

Like the great Whig heroes of the seventeenth century, whom she refers to here—Algernon Sidney (1622–83), Lord William Russell (1639–83), and John Hampden (1594–1643)[60]—the Girondins were martyrs to liberty, a cause that transcended national boundaries. Williams looked to the future for their vindication: "history will judge between Brissot and Robespierre, between the Gironde and the Mountain" (2.2.78). It was a history that she would help to write.

Her loyalty to these men and women defines the ideological position of the second series of *Letters from France*. Part history, part journalism, part melodrama, part documentary, these *Letters* avenge the death of her Girondin friends by combining political analysis and tableaux of sensibility in order to revive in her readers their earlier revolutionary hopes for a better world. Writing as one of the surviving "lovers of liberty," she continued the work that those "illustrious martyrs"(2.2.77)— Brissot, Madame Roland, and Vergniaud, among others—had begun. Although Williams uses the anti-Jacobin rhetoric of a Royalist to attack Robespierre and the Mountain, the language of sensibility dominates her articulation of her political ideals. Having gone to France as a woman of sensibility—effusive, compassionate, and creative—she survived the traumatic Reign of Terror with her ideals intact and even augmented by a caution and scepticism that made her more politically astute. She continued to write in her characteristic manner, seeking to move her readers to accept her own world view. But now her humanitarian purpose related to a specific and urgent political context.

After so many people "whose cultivated minds and enlightened conversation" she enjoyed "were dragged to execution" (2.1.3–4), one
might expect her to be cynical about the prospect for human freedom
and peace; instead, Williams accepts the fall of Robespierre as an incon-
trovertible sign that liberty is still alive. Although some observers were
pessimistic about France's recovery, for others, "it was soon expected
that every trace of the late horrors would be obliterated, and a more
just and lenient system rise on the ruins."[61] Among the English radicals,
Southey trusted that "all will conduce to human happiness,"[62] and
Wordsworth, more famously, that the triumphs of the "young Republic" would "be in the end / Great, universal, irresistible."[63] In the introduction to her new book, Williams's tone is calm and assured:

> Perhaps it will not be uninteresting for you to receive from me a sketch of
> the scenes which have passed in Paris since the second of June, an epocha
> to be forever deplored by the friends of liberty, which seated a vulgar and
> sanguinary despot on the ruins of a throne, till the memorable 28th of July
> 1794, when Liberty, bleeding with a thousand wounds, revived once more.
> (2.1.2)

This passage is typical of Williams's post-Thermidorian rhetoric. Her
image of Liberty is a woman of sensibility, wounded by the ill-usage of
the Jacobins—a representation that parallels the manner in which the
Jacobins replaced the feminine figure of Liberty with the excessively
masculine Hercules.[64] By showing Liberty as a victim of male violence,
Williams provides a chilling reminder of the betrayal felt by her and by
others whose political ideals included improving the status of women.
Having once even played the part of Liberty in a celebration in 1790
her own disappointment is emblematized in this lurid image. Yet, Williams was determined to encourage and document Liberty's revival and
to vindicate the memory of her executed friends. Already she had a reputation as *the* British woman writer in France, and that was something
she could—and, did—build her career on.

Looking back on her arrest and imprisonment in the fall of 1793, Williams explains that she heard news of the decree against all the English
in Paris while she was having tea with J. H. Bernardin de Saint-Pierre,
whose sentimental novella *Paul and Virginia* she would later translate.
This pleasant bourgeois circumstance illustrates the social world Williams inhabited in 1793. Her gender, her nationality, and her class made
it highly unlikely she would ever see the inside of a French prison. But
in the summer of 1793, the imprisonment of her Girondin friends and
Madame Roland, whom she visited, made it clear that no one could
count on being spared. From the first, Williams, her sister Cecilia, and

their mother hoped to avoid arrest because they were "a family of women" (2.1.7); but they soon found that "neither sex nor age gave any claim to compassion" (2.1.7). They were imprisoned for nearly two months, from 9 October to late November 1793, first in the Luxembourg and then in the convent of Les Anglaises (2.1.205; 208).

Williams's account of her prison life demonstrates that English prisoners were, on the whole, well-treated. She and her family initially felt like "defenceless women in a land of strangers" (2.1.11), but when they were transferred to the Luxembourg prison, they found a sociable community, where "strangers meeting in such circumstances fast became friends" (2.1.20). Prisoners read newspapers, received meals from servants, and played cards. Alluding to Dr. Johnson's observation that his tea-kettle was "never allowed time to cool" (2.1.21), Williams remarks that among things shared was her mother's tea-kettle which "was employed from morning till night in furnishing the English with tea" (2.1.21). But prison conditions worsened as hundreds of people were admitted, including some of the Williamses' friends. In Letter Three (2.1.36–56), Williams describes how she and her sister Cecilia held midnight conferences with the Protestant minister La Source and Madame de Genlis's husband, M. Sillery, an anecdote which Hazlitt reprints in the appendix to the first volume of his *Life of Napoleon*, and which Felicia Hemans used in revised form for a poem entitled "Prisoners' Evening Service," noting "The last days of two prisoners in the Luxembourg, Sillery and La Source, so affectingly described by Helen Maria Williams, in her letters from France, gave rise to this little scene."[65] In the same letter that refers to Sillery and La Source, Williams describes her own imprisonment and invokes the psalmist's plea for freedom and "the wings of a dove":

> The walls of that apartment were hung with tapestry which described a landscape of romantic beauty. On that landscape I often gazed till I almost persuaded myself that the scenery was alive around me, so much did I delight in the pleasing illusion. How often, while my eyes were fixed on that canvas which led my wounded spirit from the cruelty of man to the benignity of God—how often did I wish 'for the wings of a dove, that I might flee away and be at rest!' (2.1. 36–37).[66]

In her account of her transfer to the convent of Les Anglaises, she spends little time talking about any physical discomforts and concentrates on the acts of kindness among those imprisoned. The circumstance was made tolerable by the affectionate welcome of the English nuns; nonetheless, it was no idyll. While she was there the new mayor of Paris, Jean Nicolas Pache, decreed that the convent bells and crosses were to be removed and the nuns to discard their habits. The sisters were horrified, but in this instance, the English prisoners helped by organizing a kind of sewing circle to convert the nuns' habits into gowns and their veils into bonnets (2.1.191). One woman named Sister Theresa made by her unfailing devotion to God a lasting impression on Williams, and her companionship became Williams's "chief consolation" (2.1.192). Further comfort was provided by the friends who came to visit at the prison gate, especially Thomas and Monique du Fossé, who assisted the Williamses financially, and Marie-Martin-Athanase Coquerel, Monique's nephew, who arranged for their release in late November and three months later in March 1794 married Williams's sister, Cecilia.[67] Meanwhile, Williams feared being arrested again: "many were deprived of liberty, because they were rich; others, because they were learned; and most who were arrested enquired the reason in vain" (2.1.207).

In between the stories of her imprisonment, Williams sandwiches a lengthy outline of the events leading up to "the fatal 31st of May" (2.1.170), when the Jacobins led an insurrection against the Girondin members of the Convention. For Williams, this was the event that caused her the greatest shock: in her narrative history of the French Revolution, the cataclysmic event was neither the September massacres nor the execution of Louis XVI, but the proscription of the 29 deputies on June 2, 1793: "From that fatal decree may be dated all the horrors which have cast their sanguinary cloud over the glories of the revolution" (2.1.81). The fall of the Girondins led her to view the events of the Revolution from an overtly partisan position which made political martyrs out of the Girondins and defined the Jacobins as the enemy. Brian Rigby shows that this was not an uncommon view among British middle-class radicals, and the editors of the *Analytical Review* held that there was "only one 'real' Revolution—the rationalist, humanist, constitutionalist Revolution of the Girondins."[68] But, the Girondins were accused of being too indecisive, too self-interested, and too bourgeois. It is this last which surfaces most clearly in Williams's own writing, for her interpretation of the rise in power of the Jacobins is built upon her sense of class difference. She sets the middle-class and educated Girondins apart from the unruly Jacobin-duped mob. Developing her class analysis, she explains that the Jacobins used propaganda to manipulate the uneducated masses: the evidence was "so ill-fabricated that they only deceived those who could not read" (2.1.138).

As part of her own anti-Jacobin rhetoric she describes the Committee of Public Safety (2.2. 156) and leaders such as Henriot (2.1.29), Collot d'Herbois (2.2.157–67), and Hebert (2.2.14–15) as cannibals. Robespierre himself and all that he did was "polluted," including the

Festival of the Supreme Being; his supporters, like David, acted uncon-
scionably, and, as far as Williams was concerned, "David's shame will
be as durable as his celebrity" (2.2.76). On a number of occasions Williams used the term "sanguinary monsters" (2.4.178) to describe Robespierre's Jacobins. While it was Mallet du Pan who said that "the
Revolution devours its children,"[69] Williams also noted that the atmosphere of suspicion turned to paranoia: "It is the punishment of tyrants
and villains to live in continual terror of each other" (2.3.70). The difference between the Revolution of 1789 and 1793 even left her agreeing, if only partially, with her ideological opponent Edmund Burke: "I
thought of that passage in Mr. Burke's book, 'In the groves of *their*
academy, at the end of every vista I see the gallows!' " Ah Liberty! best
friend of mankind, why have sanguinary monsters profaned thy name,
and fulfilled this gloomy prediction" (2.2.89–90). The persistent evoca-
tion of the monstrous to describe Robespierre's supporters and their
work is common to accounts of the Reign of Terror, though Elizabeth
Bohls has also observed that Williams's diction resembles the "discourse of Gothic horror" in its references to the "savage, subhuman
quality" of the men of the Terror.[70]

In her coverage of the trial and execution of the Girondins, Williams
promotes their own self-representation as Republican martyrs following in the footsteps of their political predecessors who struggled against
the Fall of the Roman Republic in the first century B. C. As Harold T.
Parker has noted "this identification of one's self or one's friends with
the persecuted of antiquity became popular [because] to illustrious victims of the guillotine it gave a wanted assurance of posterity's esteem,
while it required of them . . . a conviction that history (in this case,
posterity's praise) repeated itself."[71] While some individuals, like
Roland's husband, imitated Brutus in their choice of suicide, others
faced execution with a stoical deportment to show concern not for their
own personal suffering, but for the demise of the republic. For instance,
Williams writes that her friend Girey Dupré, on his way to the guillotine "sung in a triumphant tone a very popular patriotic song" with the
chorus, "Rather death than slavery!" (2.1.222). Such anecdotes produce legends, and in *The Body and the French Revolution*, Dorinda Outram, following Harold T. Parker, argues that "the heroic self-control
and joyful acceptance of death prevented a sense of death's finality and
deflected energy into the future onto the survivors" so that these men
became mythical public figures.[72]

As for the representation of the behavior of women who were executed, Outram argues that "no female in the canon was portrayed as
acting from devotion to an ideal or as an autonomous individual" but
only out of concern for those near and dear to her.[73] However, the most

memorable women whose behaviour refutes this are Charlotte Corday and Madame Roland, who, as Chantal Thomas has shown, adhered to masculine models of heroism: "they took up positions squarely on the terrain of men's thought and action, and there they proved to be daunting rivals in full command of virtues assumed to be exclusively masculine."[74] Following Thomas, I would add that Williams too acknowledged not only a familial bond, but a political will in the women whom she describes as bravely going to their deaths.[75] As Chris Jones argues, Williams's "female victims are not the heroines of sentimental novels, languishing in imagined terrors or prey to mental distraction, but strong women facing the guillotine with the heroic firmness of those dying in a great cause."[76]

Outram only discusses Corday briefly and focuses on the myth of Corday's blushing severed head, rather than the more significant and authentically documented aspects of her behaviour during the trial and at the time of execution. Williams and others describe Corday using terms that explicitly emphasize her Roman stoicism: She "was probably excited by the examples of antiquity to the commission of a deed, which she believed with fond enthusiasm would deliver and save her country" (2.1.129). In her own defence after being tried for Marat's murder, Corday explained that she "trusted that her example would inspire the people with that energy which had been at all times the distinguished characteristic of republicans" (2.1.131). Even for those who did not approve of Corday's having murdered Marat, she still had the aura of a heroine with her dignified deportment, eloquent speech, and composure. A young man named Adam Lux wanted to erect a statue in her honor, inscribing it "Greater than Brutus" (2.1.134), while an opposite sentiment was felt by the supporters of Marat who used the epithet "a New Corday" as a term of suspicion.[77]

Madame Roland is also canonized among the Revolution's female martyrs. Unlike Corday, Roland was a well-known public figure before her arrest, having taken an active interest in her husband's work and gaining a reputation herself as an eloquent writer and speaker—for which she was vilified by the Jacobin press. When Williams visited her in the Saint Pelagie prison she found Roland reading Plutarch, the same text, significantly, that Corday brought to Paris. An excerpt from the memoirs is included in an Appendix to this volume of the *Letters from France*, but other papers which Roland entrusted to Williams had to be burned on the night of the latter's own arrest (2.1.198). Williams describes her friend as "one of the most accomplished women that France has produced" and a cultivated and ardent supporter of liberty, who showed "heroical firmness" before the tribunal (2.1.195–97). Roland's posthumous popularity burgeoned after the publication in

1795 of her memoirs in French and then English. When Anna Laetitia Barbauld read the *Appeal to Impartial Posterity, by Madame Roland*, she rated the book higher than Rousseau's *Confessions*.[78] Others on the political left in England joined in this kind of eulogy, including Sir Samuel Romilly, who wrote: "Her enthusiasm, her party zeal, her masculine courage, and unalterable serenity under the most imminent dangers, are exactly calculated, in the present state of France, to excite the most enthusiastic veneration for her memory."[79] Not all commentators were as favourably disposed. In the *Female Revolutionary Plutarch*, for instance, Lewis Goldsmith uses Roland as an example of improper female behaviour: "Madame Roland received a severe lesson of the dangers in which ambitious women involve themselves, by undutifully aspiring to notoriety in troublesome times, and by interfering with what does not regard their sex."[80] For Williams, on the other hand, Roland would always remain "a celebrated woman" and "glorious" martyr (2.1.197; 199).

These concerns about proper female conduct are related to the more general issue of women's political activism in the Revolution. By 1793, Williams's association with the members of the Girondin meant not only that she valorized those associated with her cause, like Corday and Roland, but that she resented the actions of the radical women in Paris whose fight for bread and the constitution led them to side with the Jacobins and contribute to the defeat of the Girondins on 31 May 1793. Although she herself would be disparagingly labeled a "female politician" she in turn used the word as a term of abuse to belittle those who worked against the Girondins. In the following passage, Williams summarizes the events that led to the Convention's October 1793 ban on women's political organizations:

A certain class of the women of Paris, who gave themselves the title of revolutionary women, had been serviceable auxiliaries to the conspirators, and had taken place of the poissards, who not having all the energy which the present exigencies required, had yielded the palm to their revolutionary successors. These female politicians held deliberative assemblies, and afterwards presented their views to the convention, while they influenced its debates by their vociferations in the tribunes, which they now exclusively occupied. On the days of tumult which preceded the 31st of May they had mounted guard in person at the convention, and prevented the execution of certain orders which they disliked. They now presented themselves at the bar of the assembly, and demanded the exclusion of the former nobles from every function civil or military, the renewal of all the administrations throughout the republic, the examination of the conduct of the ministers, the arrest of every suspected person, the raising of the whole nation in mass, and obliging the women to wear red caps. The convention having shewn some disinclination to comply with these modest requisitions, these female politicians insulted some of the members, and the society was dissolved by a decree. (2.1.139–40)

In an essay entitled "The 'Citoyennes' Against the Girondins," Shirley Elson Roessler provides an analysis that allows us to understand why Williams, as a Girondin supporter, would have been outraged by the actions of the Republican Revolutionary Women.[81] As Elson Roessler recounts, the proceedings of the Convention in spring 1793 were frequently disrupted by vociferous members of the women's clubs. At one point in March 1793, women were briefly removed from the Convention (1.4.56), and Girondins like Maximin Isnard spoke against the women who were obstructing entrances to the Convention. A band of women attacked Isnard as he left the Convention, and Gorsas reported that others were assaulted by a "troop of women calling themselves revolutionaries, a troop of furies, avid of carnage."[82]

As Elisabeth Roudinesco observes, "The massive presence of these women in the galleries of the Convention, their anti-parliamentary fury, and their excesses of every kind, may perhaps explain why it was that the few representatives still in favor of political equality for women came very soon to abandon this position."[83] In October 1793, while Williams's friends awaited execution, she felt at least some vindication when the women's political clubs were banned. She saw no parallel between their militant actions and her own form of political activism, and so did not view this clamping down on women's freedom of expression as having any effect on her as a writer. Yet, the arguments used to ban women's clubs also kept women's deputations out of the Convention, on the basis that women should not interfere with politics but stay at home. There would be little chance that women could interfere with politics any more since during this period, not only were women's clubs banned (30 October 1793), but Théroigne de Méricourt was institutionalized (1794); several prominent women were executed—Marie Antoinette (16 October 1793), Olympe de Gouges (6 November 1793), Madame Roland (7 November 1793); and nothing is known of what happened to the founders of the Revolutionary Republican Women (Claire Lacombe from August 1795, and Pauline Léon from August 1794).[84]

As a Girondin history, the second series of the *Letters from France* may not contain sympathetic portraits of Jacobin women, but it does pay tribute to the women (and men and entire families) who were victims of the guillotine. Roland and Corday were among the most famous, but they were only two of the 16,000 people executed during the Reign of Terror.[85] Studies of official reports and unofficial accounts of executions reveal an interesting history of the narrative construction of what Daniel Arasse calls "scaffold scenes."[86] Williams emphasizes those victims whose behavior at the scaffold showed a stoicism that seemed a kind of political or moral statement. She compares them favourably to heroes like Socrates or Seneca, who

> have perhaps less claim to admiration than those blooming beauties, who in all the first freshness of youth, in the very spring of life, submitted to the stroke of the executioner with placid smiles on their countenances, and looked like angels in their flight to heaven. (2.1.213)

In the construction of these quasi-religious tableaux, Williams emphasizes youthfulness and physical attractiveness. The women will be remembered as "blooming beauties," like 19-year old Mademoiselle St. Amaranthe, described by Williams as "one of the most beautiful women in France," who on the day of her execution walked "towards the vehicles of death with that firmness which belongs to innocence" (2.2.70;72).

As individual after individual assumes the same calm demeanor, they achieve a collective identity, which, in its aura of purity and innocence contrasts with the violent aggression associated with the vociferous mobs of lower-class women rioting for bread. The former, then, is a respectable form of feminized heroism, a stoicism displayed by large numbers of women, though headed by the illustrious examples of Corday and Roland. These anecdotes also exemplify "filial piety" (2.2.108). Williams makes no reference to the patriarchal tyranny which she exposed in her famous story about the Baron Du Fossé in volume one of the first series of *Letters*. Endowing these nameless female heroes with perfect family relationships, Williams, with anecdote after anecdote, follows young girls, daughters, nursing mothers, fathers, and brothers to the guillotine, where her version of the family romance effaces the ghoulish reality of the execution. Later Wordsworth would describe this procession in *The Prelude*:

> the old man from the chimney-nook,
> The maiden from the bosom of her love,
> The mother from the cradle of her babe,
> The warrior from the field—all perished all—[87]

The idealization of the victims brings into question any claims to historical accuracy, and it is best to use caution when interpreting any reports of scaffold scenes. Sociologist John Lofland, commenting on public executions,[88] notes that the hour-long procession from the prison gave victims some opportunity to establish "a public character,"[89] but once at the scaffold, the guillotine worked quickly, and the crowd could see or hear little. Daniel Arasse argues that actual instances of heroic behaviour at the time of execution were probably rare, and whether or not a victim appeared heroic was based on how reporters interpreted both the victim's behaviour *and* the reaction of the crowd—and the effect reporters wanted to have on their readers.[90] For Williams, these anecdotes suit her pro-Girondin account. She is engaged in the kind of myth-making that Ann Rigney discusses in *The Rhetoric of Historical Representation*, a study of Michelet's, Blanc's, and Lamartine's reconstruction of the Revolution. Rigney analyzes the "discursive and narrative strategies actually deployed by the different writers in representing and giving meaning to events;" for example, Michelet insists "on the heroic deaths of the Girondins," while Blanc belittles the Girondins.[91] Inevitably, writers' politics shape their texts, and the *Letters from France* are no exception.

Williams did not attend any executions, but she had passed the squares where the executions took place and saw the carts transporting people to the guillotine. When she was forced to live outside of Paris in early 1794, during the months following her imprisonment, she was taken past "the square of the revolution, where we saw the guillotine erected, the crowd assembled for the bloody tragedy, and the gens d'armes on horseback, followed by victims who were to be sacrificed" (2.2.7). From the stories she heard or read, she deliberately chose to concentrate on images of the prisoners before the moment of execution, in postures that might be called "virtue in distress." For one thing, it would be unseemly for a woman to linger on the act of execution, and for another, her rhetorical strategy was to emphasize the innocence of the victims, in order to show them as martyrs to the cause of liberty. Conversely, counter-revolutionaries emphasized the bloodshed in order to make the French out to be animals and demons, and therefore to discredit the entire Revolution.[92]

By concentrating on the victims' purported "noble contempt of death" (2.1.220), Williams can evade the gruesome facts of execution. But this was not always the case. She stated with horror that "The scaffold was every day bathed with the blood of women" (2.1.214–15), and she noted cases where even pregnant women were executed despite a law that protected them till after they gave birth: "two days before the fall of Robespierre, eight women who had been respited having declared themselves pregnant, were dragged to the scaffold" (2.2.107). Departing from her usual decorum, Williams relates one especially disturbing anecdote about the execution of a nursing mother—a peasant from a village in the north of France:

> When she received the fatal stroke, the streams of maternal nourishment issued rapidly from her bosom, and, mingled with her blood, bathed her executioner. (2.3.122)

This shocking scene enacts the Jacobin defilement of the Republic through the defilement of the mother-figure, key to Republican iconography. It recalls the image in the engraving by Clement after Boizot, entitled "Republican France Offering Her Breast to All the French" (1794), which portrays the Republic as a bare-breasted nursing mother ready to feed her children.[93] Williams's anecdote demonstrates that under the Terror that image was desecrated as woman after woman, pregnant, nursing, or virgin, were decapitated. Splashed by milk and blood, the executioner is marked as a traitor to the Republican ideals of feminine virtue. Through Williams's telling, the contrasting white and red liquids, symbolizing life and death, produce one of the most unforgettable images of the Reign of Terror.

The second volume in this series of *Letters from France* continues with stories of more victims, yet the collection of anecdotes often lacks a clear chronology. Williams includes a letter by the Protestant Minister Paul Henri Marron (1754–1832) about his two-month imprisonment in the Talaru maison d'arret, before she discusses the revolt at Lyons and the battles between the Vendean troops and the army of the Republic, for which she provides virtually no dates. In this series of *Letters* she also uses a number of appendices collecting works by people like Brissot and Roland, which though cumbersome, do lend weight to her own arguments. Reviewers had mixed reactions to these *Letters*. The *English Review* stated that even though she displays "good sense and observation, philanthropy, and sentiments not altogether extravagant on the grand subject of political liberty," nonetheless, "she should have given explanations, and used definitions": her "sketches are not well arranged, clear and satisfactory," and "what they lack is judgement, taste, and skill in historical composition."[94] In her defence, Williams must have found it difficult to write a chronological narrative including information about debates and military exploits, using the form of the travel letter. She did not attempt to write proper history, and she pushed the epistolary mode beyond its capacity.

In 1795, anyone writing about the Revolution found herself in what Rigney describes as an anachronistic position,[95] which in this case meant knowing how the Terror ended. The third volume of this second series of *Letters from France* opens with a reference to this double perspective: on the one hand Williams has to recount the events of the Terror, and on the other hand she faces the now bright future of the "young Republic": "My pen, wearied of tracing successive pictures of human crimes and human calamity, pursues its task with reluctance; while my heart springs forward to that fairer epocha which now beams upon the friends of liberty" (2.3.1). Williams must suppress her characteristic optimism, glancing quickly at the transformed capital—"Paris, so lately besmeared with blood — Paris, the refuge of barbarism, and the den of carnage, once more excites the ideas of taste, elegance, refinement, and happiness" (2.3.10) — before turning to narrate the course of events in the Departments. Still refusing to exploit and sensationalize the bloodshed, she does not linger on the crimes of Carrier (such as the mass drownings or "noyades" in Nantes) but leaves the full account to traditional historians in order to spare herself and her readers from the numbing effect of hearing too much about the *"noyades, fusillades, mitraillades, and guillinades"* (2.3.51).

Nonetheless, she forges ahead, like a wartime journalist, turning from the Vendée to other regions, outlining the massacres overseen by Maignet at places like Bedouin and Orange in the South; and "the atrocities of Lebon" (2.3.112) in the North. Again she emphasizes affecting stories of young French soldiers returning to find their homes destroyed, and of families who, after being accused by an "inebriated jury" (2.3.115), "died with the serenity of virtue, and with the hope of immortality" (2.3.128). And from the sublime to the ridiculous, she also recounts the story of the family of Monsieur Viefville, who were put to death because their parrot said "Vive le roi" (2.3.119). Williams also devotes about 20 pages to affecting scenes of the release of prisoners, about which Thomas Carlyle stated, "The Prisons give up their Suspect; emit them faster and faster."[96] Williams's own inflated rhetoric evokes the spirit of the times, presenting, in a manner worthy of a final scene in a Walt Disney movie, the release of the first people from the Luxembourg, her friends Monsieur and Madame Bitaubé who embrace the nine hundred prisoners lined up to say goodbye (2.3.185). These stories produced the desired effect: the *Analytical Review*, praised the "benevolent historian" for winning "a tear of sympathy" from her readers.[97] The fourth and last volume of the *Letters from France* does provide a coherent outline of events up to the introduction of the new constitution in August 1795. Apart from anti-Jacobin rhetoric and the military reports, much space (2.4.52–116) is devoted again to scenes of post-Robespierrian "domestic felicity" (2.4.53). Hedva Ben-Israel identifies this as what became the traditional outlook on the Revolution for nineteenth-century commentators: it "insists on separate treatment for the various aspects of the Revolution; it allows praise for reforms and moral indignation at crimes."[98]

Among the events of the post-Thermidor period recorded in the *Letters from France* was the Jacobin uprising of Prairial (20 May 1795), which was especially notable for the prominent role played by women, whom Williams castigates here, along with their male counterparts:

> the insurgents made their appearance, headed as usual by women, who filled the tribunes, and passages leading into the assembly, with vociferations for

bread and a constitution; but whose furious looks and menacing gestures indicated more strongly a thirst for blood. (2.4.132)

Williams was not the only one to criticize these "female politicians," though some historians have looked upon Prairial as "the apogee of women's political involvement in the revolutionary struggle."[99] So concerned were the governing leaders about the violent militancy of the women of Prairial that they imposed severe sanctions on women's activities and again temporarily banned them from the Convention.[100] Times had changed since Williams exulted in the freedom of attending the National Assembly with her sister Cecilia. But from her perspective, the present restrictions were necessary, because no mob could be trusted. Georges Lefebvre explains that "almost all the bourgeoisie, from republicans to partisans of the Old Regime, were solidly against the popular movement. The experience of the Year II had taught them class discipline, and now they held power."[101] Williams regarded the establishment of the Directory as the end of the Revolution and a restoration of peace:

To finish the revolution was an idea of all others the most soothing to the public mind, which, agitated for six years past by the most convulsive political tempests, felt perhaps less the love of order, than the irresistible desire of repose. (2.4.172)

In her later books, she will explore what those "six years past"—"the most eventful in the history of mankind" (2.4.174)—and the ensuing period would mean for the rights of man—and woman.

4

A Tour in Switzerland:
The Sublime and the Political

By THE MIDDLE OF THE 1790S, WILLIAMS HAD ATTAINED AN UNPRECE-
dented position for a woman writer of her day by becoming a well-
known authority on an international event of immeasurable historical
importance. She had the perseverance to complete her eyewitness
accounts of the Reign of Terror, and her very endurance became a noteworthy subject, though the Tory *British Critic* registered its disapproval
that she "still continues to fall prostrate before the holy [revolutionary]
fire, whose flames have scorched and nearly consumed her."[1] But Whig
journals, such as the *Critical Review*, were pleased that she was "able to
resume her pen," and the *New Annual Register* respected her for being as
ardently attached "to the cause of liberty" as ever.[2] What would she do
after completing the *Letters from France*? No one would blame her for
retiring her pen at this point, but the story was not over; Robespierre
was gone, but Europe was still adapting itself to the changes produced
by the Revolution. Williams had the background, the access to information, and the self-confidence to continue writing about the events taking
place around her. By the end of the 1790s, she would publish a popular
English translation of J. H. Bernardin de Saint-Pierre's French classic
of 1788, *Paul and Virginia*; and complete a two-volume book on Switzerland. Her *Tour in Switzerland* contains a great deal of commentary on the
governments in the Swiss cantons, but it also records a unique interlude
in Williams's life when she exchanged the noisy streets of Paris for the
beauty of snow-capped mountains.

Before leaving for Switzerland, Williams began work on her translation of *Paul and Virginia*, which was later published by Vernor and Hood
in London in 1795. She sold the rights to them in June 1797 for twenty
pounds,[3] and although other translations appeared, hers became the
standard English edition well into the nineteenth century.[4] In her Preface, dated June 1795, Williams tells her readers about the circumstances in which she completed the translation. She was subject to
frequent house searches, and on several occasions had parts of the

translation and other papers seized and taken to "the Municipality of Paris, in order to be examined as English papers; where they still remain, mingled with revolutionary placards, motions, and harangues; and are not likely to be restored to my possession."[5] In the position of a persecuted writer, Williams asks that her readers

> receive with indulgence a work written under such peculiar circumstances; not composed in the calm of literary leisure, or in pursuit of literary fame; but amidst the turbulence of the most cruel sensations, and in order to escape awhile from overwhelming misery. (Preface, *PV* viii–ix)

For Williams, working on the translation, entering the world of Paul and Virginia, was an "escape" from the "misery" of Robespierre's France, when she could not enjoy "the calm of literary leisure," such as a writer is usually thought to enjoy. These circumstances give the translation additional interest for having been somehow stamped by the struggles of the Revolution, a not inappropriate association for a work that has at its core a rejection of the corruption of the Ancien Régime.

Bernardin's novel was democratizing in its effect since it honored the dignity of the humble Paul and Virginia, who were raised by their mothers in a remote area on the island of Mauritius. They lived simply, working the land and taking pleasure in the beauties of nature. It was only when Virginia was sent to France to be educated by her wealthy great-aunt that their pastoral idyll was destroyed. Virginia was returning to the island to be reunited with her family and Paul, when she died in a shipwreck. Her mother, Paul's mother, and Paul himself were all so close that they died from heartache soon after, as if they were one body that had been corrupted by the disease of aristocratic culture.

William Wordsworth purchased a copy of this translation in 1795, and his poem *The Ruined Cottage*, composed in 1797, uses a similar narrative structure, with a story being told by an old man about a family that used to live in a now abandoned spot.[6] The narrator in *Paul and Virginia* is surprised that the passerby wants to hear the tale of the humble family:

> But what European, pursuing his way to the Indies, will pause one moment to interest himself in the fate of a few obscure individuals? What European can picture happiness to his imagination amidst poverty and neglect? The curiosity of mankind is only attracted by the history of the great. (*PV* 4–5)

Such sentiments abound in Wordsworth's Preface to the *Lyrical Ballads*, which defended his choice of rustic subjects for his poetry. The story of Paul and Virginia would have appealed to a poet like Wordsworth who himself became known for bringing a human face to poverty, as Gary

Harrison has put it.[7] The eighteenth century saw a renewed interest in pastoral themes and representations of country life. One finds an echo of Thomas Gray's *Elegy* in Bernardin's remarks about the absence of a formal grave marker for Paul and Virginia: "no marble covers the turf, no inscription records their virtues, but their memory is engraven upon our hearts" (*PV* 213). The pathos of this image enables one to see why Williams was so suited to translating Bernardin's novel. It is reminiscent of lines from one of her early poems of sensibility, in which she shows the importance of virtue over material possessions:

> No riches from his scanty store
> My lover could impart;
> He gave a boon I valued more —
> He gave me all his heart!
>
> .   .   .   .
>
> The frugal meal, the lowly cot
> If blest my love with thee!
> That simple fare, that humble lot,
> Were more than wealth to me.
>
> ("A Song," *Poems* 1:29–30)

This is one of Williams's most perfect lyrics from the 1780s, and, as mentioned in the first chapter, it had a second life as an actual song, set to music by the British composer Robert Cooke in 1800. Its simplicity and its theme of the dignity of the poor have much in common with Wordsworth's poetry of rural life.

Helen Maria Williams had something of a revival as a poet because of her translation of *Paul and Virginia*. Although Bernardin had no poems in his original version, she added eight sonnets of her own making: "Sonnet To Love," "To Disappointment," "To Simplicity," "To the Strawberry," "To the Curlew," "To the Torrid Zone," "To the Calabria-Tree," and "To the White Bird of the Tropic." These became well known in their own right, and were reprinted in a collection of verse entitled *Poems. Moral, Elegant and Pathetic* (1796), which included works by Gray and Pope, but which featured Williams's name most prominently on the title page.[8] In her translation of *Paul and Virginia*, Williams attributed the sonnets to Madame de la Tour, Virginia's mother, and this was perhaps the most significant alteration she made to Bernardin's book, though she also omitted certain passages "of general observations" (*PV* vii). English readers were accustomed to poetry-writing heroines, and Williams refashioned Bernardin's Madame de La Tour into a woman who sometimes "poured forth the effusions of melancholy in the language of verse" (*PV* 19).

The best of the sonnets in *Paul and Virginia* is "To the Curlew."

Ostensibly a description of a bird seen by the seashore, it can also be read as a reflection of Williams's own emotions, writing as she did in a state of instability, and in exile from her own home, like Madame de la Tour:

Sonnet to the Curlew

Sooth'd by the murmurs on the sea-beat shore,
His dun grey plumage floating to the gale,
The Curlew blends his melancholy wail,
With those hoarse sounds the rushing waters pour.
Like thee, congenial bird! my steps explore
The bleak lone sea-beach, or the rocky dale,
And shun the orange bower, the myrtle vale,
Whose gay luxuriance suits my soul no more.
I love the ocean's broad expanse, when drest
In limpid clearness, or when tempests blow,
When the smooth currents on its placid breast
Flow calm as my past moments used to flow;
Or, when its troubled waves refuse to rest,
And seem the symbol of my present woe.

(*PV* 79)

The fictional Madame de la Tour's recollection of a calmer past that contrasts with the "troubled waves" of her "present woe," is not unlike Williams's experience in Robespierre's France. The passage also recalls the classical picture of the plight of exile from Ovid's *Tristia*, in which "verses" are written "amid the wild roar of the sea."[9] In her Preface Williams asked her readers to "receive with indulgence a work written" "amidst turbulence" and not "in the calm of literary leisure," and Ovid long ago wrote the following in a similar vein:

And so, kindly reader, you should grant me the more indulgence if these verses are—as they are—poorer than your hopes. They were not written, as of old, in my garden . . . I am tossing of a winter's day on the stormy deep, and my paper is sprayed by the dark waters.[10]

Williams was also a writer in exile when she went to Switzerland in 1794, and in her *Tour*, after meeting someone reading the *Tristia*, she quotes from her friend Anna Laetitia Barbauld's poem "Ovid to his Wife: Imitated from different parts of his Tristia."[11] Ovid's speaker laments his forced departure from his home, but for Williams, after living in France, "a country where arts have given place to arms" (Preface, *PV* viii), and where her literary papers were confiscated, she was relieved to leave for Switzerland. She completed her translation of *Paul and Virginia* in 1795 after her return to Paris.

When Williams travelled to Switzerland, some concern was raised about her being accompanied by the recently divorced John Hurford Stone. As mentioned earlier, Williams and Stone probably met in the 1780s, since he is listed as a subscriber to her *Poems* (1786), and he was an active member of the Dissenting congregation at Hackney, where Kippis's good friend Dr. Richard Price was minister. The Stones were prosperous coal merchants, based in London, and John Hurford Stone went to France both as a supporter of the Revolution and as a business-man, who sought to take advantage of the commercial opportunities opened up by the Revolution. In Paris he became a close friend of the Williams family, and when his wife divorced him there in 1794, there was speculation that he and Williams married, though there is no evidence of this.[12] Still, her trip to Switzerland with Stone was taken as proof of their liaison, even though they did not travel alone. Williams tried to explain to friends that she had little choice about making the trip: it was that or risk execution as an enemy of Robespierre. She later learned that Andrew Kippis had to defend her against the "relentless Slander"[13] of rumours that were circulating about her in England. The situation was compounded when Stone became a permanent member of the Williams household in Paris, when they returned from Switzerland, an arrangement that Williams claimed was wholly honorable. In her own defence Williams wrote to Penelope Pennington in 1803, "to assert in the language of scripture 'my witness is in heaven, and my record on high.' "[14] Returning to the subject years later, she explained that Stone was, in a way, adopted into the family: "we gave Mr. Stone an asylum in his misfortunes, a thing common amidst the storms of revolution, he was 25 years a member of our family."[15] Still, her critics continued to deprecate her for her association with Stone, not only for their purported personal liaison but also for political reasons, since Stone himself had been branded a traitor in the English press.

Letters that John Hurford Stone wrote from Paris to his brother William Stone were seized in 1794 as possible evidence of a treasonous conspiracy.[16] John Hurford Stone had asked his brother to gather up testimony from a number of influential men in London in order to convince France not to attempt an invasion of England. One of their friends Benjamin Vaughan, a Member of Parliament, left England in 1794 when he too was implicated in the matter.[17] William Stone was finally tried and acquitted in January 1796, having as his counsel the Whig lawyer Thomas Erskine, who had represented Thomas Paine earlier, and had successfully defended Thomas Hardy, Thomas Holcroft and John Horne Tooke in the famous treason trials of December 1794.

Despite the acquittal, the trial cast a cloud of suspicion over the Stone family, and William Stone eventually joined his brother in France. John Hurford Stone had also been "charged as a conspirator," but was never tried because he did not return to England.[18] Excerpts from the letters published in the press coverage of the William Stone trial highlighted John Hurford Stone's political connections and his commercial dealings up until 1794 when he left for Switzerland. The letters reveal Stone's entrepreneurial spirit. Rather than being paralysed by the horror of the Reign of Terror, Stone kept working, often helping others financially, as he told his brother in a letter of February 1794:

> I am respected, tho' I keep aloof from all political acquaintance. I am indeed the chief support of my unfortunate countrymen; and my time is employed in relieving and alleviating their wants.—I am also happy to inform you, that my own affairs go on very prosperously.[19]

Among the many ventures that John Hurford Stone pursued was a factory which he operated with Marie-Martin-Athanase Coquerel, who married Helen Maria Williams's sister Cecilia in March 1794,[20] another sign of the intimacy between Stone and the Williams family. The security given to the Williams family at this point in time due to Cecilia's marriage would prove to be very important, especially when Helen Maria Williams's English mentor Andrew Kippis passed away the next year in London. Her memorial poem to Kippis appeared in the *Gentleman's Magazine* in January 1796. Coquerel's father was Laurent Louis Martin Coquerel, the brother of Monique Coquerel, who married Thomas du Fossé, as recounted in Williams's first volume of *Letters from France*. In summer 1794, Stone used his business acumen and his contacts to procure French passports for Switzerland, where he, Helen Maria Williams, and others stayed for six months.[21] Williams's mother had urged Helen Maria to go with Stone to escape a possible second arrest during the Reign of Terror.[22] Once in Switzerland, Basel was her home base, where she was the guest of Colonel Johann-Rudolf Frey, whose son Jean Rodolphe Frey had married Monique and Thomas du Fossé's daughter, Madeleine Sophie du Fossé in 1792.[23] This enabled Williams to travel with propriety since her new brother-in-law, Marie-Martin-Athanase Coquerel, was now related to the Frey family. In her words, she was placed under the Freys' "particular protection, and introduced in consequence to the best society in that country."[24]

The trip to Switzerland was an escape from Robespierre, but it was not an escape from the Revolution. Williams and her friends associated with those "whose political and literary interests paralleled" their own.[25] Her "venerable friend, Colonel Frey" was known as a "distinguished liberal," and another man she met J. L. LeGrand would work on the Swiss constitution of 1798: "Mr. Le Grand, member of the great council, an ardent and enlightened friend of the French Republic, had taught his infants to lisp the cherished sound of liberty, and chaunt its favourite airs with such fond enthusiasm, that his house seemed to me a chapel worthy of William Tell" (*Tour* 1:118–19).[26] A person like LeGrand must have reminded her of her Girondin friends, as did one of her compatriots in exile the aforementioned Benjamin Vaughan, whom she describes as "one of the most correct, the most pure and exalted characters with which I ever held communion."[27]

Traveling in Switzerland for six months, Williams kept a journal of her visit, and whether or not she had planned to write a book about her trip, she had a reason to do so by 1797. While the Swiss confederation had long been admired for the ability of its diverse cantons to live harmoniously together,[28] the eighteenth century was a period regarded as a time of renaissance in Switzerland, promoted by the Helvetic Society, established in 1761 to rejuvenate the confederation.[29] But, it was also a time of political unrest in various regions. Although a canton like Berne was a model of administrative efficiency, there, and in many parts of Switzerland, "citizenship was a privileged hereditary position granted to a minority."[30] Some areas already had a history of liberal activism, and the example of the French Revolution drew renewed attention to certain political inequalities in different parts of Switzerland.[31] Swiss exiles from various regions worked for reforms through the Swiss Club in Paris, including activists from the Pays de Vaud, led by Frédéric César de La Harpe (1754–1838). Williams's book combined an interesting travel narrative (based on the journal she kept in 1794) with a report on the state of politics in the Swiss cantons in 1797. *A Tour in Switzerland; Or, A View of the Present State of the Governments and Manners of those Cantons: with Comparative Sketches of the Present State of Paris* appeared in early 1798, only weeks before French intervention in Switzerland, timing which automatically and deliberately involved the book in the politics of the moment.

What ensured Williams an audience for the *Tour* was the fact that, even without the revolutionary drama of 1798, Switzerland itself was a subject of great interest in the eighteenth century. Although in earlier times it had been generally thought of as a nightmarish, rocky landscape to be endured on the way to Italy, by the middle of the eighteenth century, as Ernest Giddey explains, the country had gained a romantic allure and became a favoured destination on the Grand Tour.[32] Interest in the region was fuelled by important literary works such as Albrecht von Haller's poem on *The Alps* (1732), and Jean Jacques Rousseau's best-selling epistolary novel *Julie, ou La Nouvelle Heloise* (1761). In the

1770s, learned and scientific books were very popular, such as Johann Kaspar Lavater's study of *Physiognomy* (1775) and the geologist H. B. de Saussure's *Voyages dans les Alps* (1779). A popular travel book by the British clergyman William Coxe, *Sketches of the Natural, Civil, and Political State of Swisserland* (1779), or as it was later called *Travels in Switzerland*, was translated into a famous French edition by Ramond de Carbonnière (1781).[33] British travellers, including William Wordsworth on his Alpine tour of 1790, and Helen Maria Williams in 1794 (*Tour* 2:223), often relied on both Coxe and Ramond, enjoying the more poetic additions of the French version.[34] Nonetheless, it was common for books on Switzerland to deal with that country's political structure, since it was a subject of longstanding interest to foreign observers. As Peter Barber explains, seventeenth-century accounts such as Gilbert Burnet's *Letters containing an account of what seem'd most remarkable in travelling thru' Switzerland* "focused as much on the history, constitution, legal system, economy and politics of the cantons and on the customs of the people as on the noteworthy sights."[35]

In the Preface to her *Tour in Switzerland* (1798), Williams offers the political content as the justification for the book, explaining that while others have already described the alpine scenery, and she will do that too, the main function of her book is to "trace the important effects which the French Revolution has produced" in Switzerland (Preface, *Tour* n. p.). Her goal, as Chris Jones has aptly summarized it,[36] is to deconstruct the myth of Swiss liberty in order to convince her readers that the Swiss should follow France's lead in political revolution.[37] Previously, Swiss society had been held up as a model of human liberty. The British Whig writer Thomas Hollis, who visited Switzerland in 1748, remarked that from all of his travels he "nowhere saw so general an ease through all the ranks, and so much seeming content and happiness as in Switzerland"[38]; and William Coxe opens his *Travels in Switzerland* with his famous observation that "I feel great delight in breathing the air of liberty."[39] Joseph Addison wrote that "It is very wonderful to see such a knot of governments, which are so divided among themselves in matters of religion, maintain so uninterrupted an union and correspondence, that no one of them is for invading the rights of another."[40] Based on praise such as this, Switzerland was looked upon as an ideal society for others to emulate. But its flaws had not gone unnoticed, and in order to advocate change, Williams concentrates on these, reminding her readers of what John Trotter, the secretary of Charles James Fox, described as the "oppression and cruelty" of the "aristocracies of Switzerland."[41]

In her first chapter, Williams explains that she had gone to Switzerland expecting to enjoy wonderful scenery and enlightened society, but only the glorious scenery lived up to expectation. Although these words seem an affront to her host nation, they indicate the uncompromising stance Williams would take *vis-à-vis* Swiss politics. In a country touted for its simplicity and social virtues, she was surprised to find that Basel had the same vices as anywhere else, and this leads to a long critique of urban life with extensive remarks on Parisian society under the Directory. It is only in Chapter Four that she finally turns her attention to Switzerland's "scenes of solemn grandeur" (*Tour* 1:47).

It is possible to reconstruct Williams's 1794 itinerary, though the chronology is uncertain since she provides few dates; in fact, one has to agree with the reviewer who, in an otherwise quite favourable review of the book, complained that "Throughout the authoress is too inattentive to perspicuity, particularly in regard to chronology and geography."[42] Nonetheless, her tour can be divided into three separate journeys: the northern, the southern, and the western. Williams's travels in Switzerland were constrained because she was travelling with a French passport, which meant that she was not allowed to cross the Swiss border into any Austrian or Italian territory (*Tour* 1:47). The first trip was in the northern area, from her temporary home base at Basel, on to Baden, Zürich, the falls at Schaffhausen and then to Solothurn, before returning to Basel. The second trip was to the South, through Lucerne and Altdorf, past the Devil's Bridge and St. Gotthard's Pass, to Bellinzona, and as far south as Lugano, where she stayed in August 1794, a date ascertained by a surviving letter that she wrote to Hester Thrale Piozzi.[43] Her journey back to Basel was through St. Bernardin—where she composed her "Hymn Written Among the Alps"—then past Coire and Wallenstadt. After spending two or three weeks in Basel (*Tour* 2:137), her third journey, in the autumn, was to the west, again to Solothurn, then, Bienne, Neuchatel, Lausanne and as far south as St. Maurice, then to Sion, Freiburg, and Berne. Her travels covered most of the popular tourist destinations, except for the Lauterbrunnen and Grindelwald area, and Mont Blanc and the Chamonix, which Coxe had visited. The latter areas would later gain literary importance in works such as Mary Shelley's *Frankenstein* (1818), Percy Shelley's "Mont Blanc" (1817), and Wordsworth's *Prelude* (1850). Williams did not travel as far south as Mont Blanc, but she recounts meeting a group of young men from the region, which was now French territory, France having annexed the Duchy of Savoy in 1792: " 'Bon jour, citoyens; Bon jour, citoyennes.' We answered these republican compliments in the same style in which they were made, and concluded that this was a group of the new French citizens of Mont Blanc" (*Tour* 2:177).

Neither Williams nor Archdeacon Coxe wrote a systematic guide for travellers, such as one finds in John Murray's Victorian classic *Hand-*

book for Travellers in Switzerland, with its separate entries on modes of travel, Swiss inns, and alpine passes.[44] But one can garner information about travelling in Switzerland from Coxe's various stories of using sail boats, mules, and crampons to make his way across the country, and from Williams's own personal anecdotes. While politics and geographical highlights dominate her *Tour*, one finds instances of a more traditional pastoral scene which would appeal to the conventional traveller, such as the time when she stops "to botanize" among "a rich variety of herbs and delicate mountain-flowers" (*Tour* 2:3) and then enjoys a picnic of dried fruits and coffee (*Tour* 2:4). Travelling conditions were often dangerous, with unpredictable storms, and roads threatened by avalanches, though Williams seems to have relished the adventure. She found that drinking water straight from an icy waterfall was even better than drinking coffee (*Tour* 2:5), and on a difficult road to Glarus, she remarked that "the dangers of the way were often forgotten in admiration of the scene through which it led" (*Tour* 2:63).

Occasionally, some special arrangements were made for Williams in order to ease the hardships of the journey. She never used crampons to travel across the ice;[45] instead, she rode a mule or was assisted by guides. At times the climbing was difficult for everyone:

> the latter part of our journey was extreme toil; at some distance from the top, the mule which had hitherto carried me was left tied to a rock, and our guides supported me up the rugged steep; my fellow travellers, who were furnished with crampons, little machines buckled to the feet, with points to enable the wearer to keep his hold, purchased their security by excessive fatigue from wearing them. (*Tour* 2:5)

In this particular case, on their descent from St. Bernardin, her mule ran away, and the guides carried her on a makeshift "chair," using shrubs, leather straps, and walking sticks (*Tour* 2:14). It was common for guides to carry travelers: Thomas Gray reports that on his journey near Mount Cenis, eight men carried him and Walpole and their party for several miles, with the English gentlemen each "wrapped up in our furs, and seated upon a sort of matted chair."[46]

In an incident in the warmer climate of the Italian-speaking cantons, Williams's group was in a boat returning to Bellinzona when they were nearly capsized by a sudden storm. She recounts the story with humor, explaining that her companions made the journey despite the warnings of their boatmen because they wanted to get back to Bellinzona to read the newspaper: "storms, when weighed against newspapers, were found light in the balance" (*Tour* 1:256). They reached their destination "after much terror on my part, and much labor on that of my fellow travellers"

(*Tour* 1:257). Near St. Gotthard, she watched from the sidelines while her "fellow travellers amused themselves with a diversion not very common in the middle of July, that of throwing snowballs at each other" (*Tour* 1:180).

In Bellinzona, Williams met the French emigrants Monsieur and Madame de C., whose own history she recounts as a type of moral tale. One would not normally expect Williams to strike up a friendship with émigrés, but Madame de C. was an accomplished woman who was sympathetic to the Revolution. After explaining that she had used the rules of physiognomy designed by Lavater (whom she met soon after arriving in Switzerland [*Tour* 1:66]) for reading "the charming countenance of Madame de C." (*Tour* 1:279), Williams then adds that "there was something like enchantment in finding in a rude hamlet, at the foot of savage rocks, and untrodden Glaciers, the most polished graces of intellectual culture" (*Tour* 1:282). Madame de C. "had often wept over the miseries of the oppressed people" in Paris (*Tour* 1:288), but she followed her husband into exile in 1792. Her trials really began when she arrived in Bellinzona and learned that he had run off with his mistress. Having to support herself for the first time in her life, Madame de C. did embroidery work and drawing, and like a heroine of a novel, found comfort in nature, where "alone amidst those scenes of solemn grandeur, [she] indulged that mournful musing, when the mind wanders over its vanished pleasures" (*Tour* 1:314). She forgave Monsieur de C. when he returned, and they lived happily together in a cottage, an example to other emigrants that "rank and splendour" could be relinquished without regret (*Tour* 1:322). To appreciate a humbler life is a sign of an enlightened mind, and Madame de C.'s maid, Victoire, errs in not being sympathetic to the Revolution and not being able to adjust to life in the Swiss countryside, after the glittering halls of Paris. Victoire prided herself on having lived at Versailles, waiting on court ladies, and she had no sympathy for the democratizing changes of the Revolution. She felt it an insult to be addressed as "tu" or "citoyenne," and she imagined the "monsters" in Paris had by now "sown all the Tuilleries with potatoes . . . and made all the women wear red caps" (*Tour* 1:283–84). As revolted by the vulgar habits of the Jacobins as she was by their acts of violence, Victoire also disdained living in rural Switzerland, asking how she could be "happy among the savages here, who can't speak one word of French! — Oh, what I would sometimes give for a walk upon the boulevards! I am so tired of rocks and snows!" (*Tour* 1:284).

Unlike Victoire, Williams had been longing to see Switzerland since she read about it in Dr. John Moore's travel book of 1783, and she regarded the Swiss landscape with the eyes of a poet: "It was not without the most powerful emotion that, for the first time, I cast my eyes on that solemn, that majestic vision, the Alps!—how often had the idea of those stupendous mountains filled my heart with enthusiastic awe!" (*Tour* 1:57).[47] The *Analytical Review*, rather like Victoire, remained unconvinced, having read one too many descriptions of the Alps:

> Torrents, alps, lakes, have roared, towered, spread; forests have waved, and landscapes frowned or smiled in sudden alternatives of spring and winter, in many a page, before those of H. W., to little better purpose than to weary the reader, and leave him in a chaos of undiscriminated imagery.[48]

But the *European Magazine*, while agreeing that the *Tour* had little claim to novelty since "every spot has been so often trodden and so minutely described," yet added that no one was more sensitive to the beauties of nature than Williams:

> As, however, those who have a true taste for the sublime and beautiful of nature, no country, perhaps, affords more objects of gratification than Switzerland; so we know of no pen by which such scenes are more agreeably portrayed than by that of Helen Maria Williams.[49]

This is an important tribute, in which the reviewer credits Williams with a skill superior to that of every other writer who has attempted to describe the Swiss landscape.

It could easily be argued that the descriptions of nature in the *Tour* are among its most memorable sections. Excerpts from the book have been used to exemplify the eighteenth-century sublime.[50] One of these was taken from her description of the Rhinefall of Schaffhausen, in which she evokes a sense of terror and awe before the sublime landscape. In the early part of the trip, Williams visited the famous waterfall, which she would have read about in Coxe's travel book.[51] It was left to Williams, though, to supply the following poetic rendering of the scene:

> . . . although I had been assured that the cataract of the Rhine was "but a fall of water," it had excited so tormenting a curiosity, that I found I should be incapable of seeing anything else with pleasure or advantage, till I had once gazed upon that object. When we reached the summit of the hill which leads to the fall of the Rhine, we alighted from the carriage, and walked down the steep bank, whence I saw the river rolling turbulently over its bed of rocks, and heard the noise of the torrent, towards which we were descending, increasing as we drew near. My heart swelled with expectation—our path, as if formed to give the scene its full effect, concealed for some time the river from our view; till we reached a wooden balcony, projecting on the edge of the water, and whence, just sheltered from the torrent, it bursts in all its overwhelming wonders on the astonished sight. That stu-

pendous cataract, rushing with wild impetuosity over those broken, unequal rocks, which, lifting up their sharp points amidst its sea of foam, disturb its headlong course, multiply its falls, and make the afflicted waters roar—the cadence of tumultuous sound, which had never till now struck upon my ear—those long feathery surges, giving the element a new aspect—that spray rising into clouds of vapour, and reflecting the prismatic colours, while it disperses itself over the hills—never, never can I forget the sensations of that moment! when with a sort of annihilation of self, with every past impression erased from my memory, I felt as if my heart were bursting with emotions too strong to be sustained.—Oh, majestic torrent! which hast conveyed a new image of nature to my soul, the moments I have passed in contemplating thy sublimity will form an epocha in my short span! —thy course is coeval with time, and thou wilt rush down thy rocky walls when this bosom, which throbs with admiration of thy greatness, shall beat no longer! (*Tour* 1:59–61)

While Williams explains how the scene is set up ready for tourists, with a "wooden balcony" ushering them to the sight of the "wild" waterfall, her own response bursts out of the bounds of the predictable. Friends may have told her not to expect much—it was "but a fall of water"—but what she sees surpasses expectations, and the effect upon her of the sound, the spray, and "the feathery surges" is turned into evocative prose. She describes how the sight affects her physiologically, emotionally, and spiritually, When one reviewer observed that she concentrated less on "the objects themselves, than their effects on the beholder," he was noting what might now be called her mystical approach to nature.[52] This is "nature" in the Wordsworthian sense of the writer's subjective experience: to record not only what one sees, but what one feels. Her response to the Rhinefall culminates in what she called a sense of "annihilation of self." She attributed this to her awe before the great power of nature, which revealed simultaneously her own earthly mortality:

> such objects appear to belong to immortality; they call the musing mind from all its little cares and vanities, to higher destinies and regions; more congenial than this world to the feelings they excite. I had been often summoned by my fellow-travellers to depart, had often repeated 'but one moment more,' and many 'moments more' had elapsed before I could resolve to tear myself from the balcony. (*Tour* 1:61)

This scene also privileges Williams's powers of perception because she—not her companions—is the central figure whose perceptions define the moment. With her keen sensibilities, she finds it difficult to tear herself away from the falls, wanting "but one moment more."

Williams's response to the waterfall may also owe something to the romantic depictions of the Swiss landscape in Rousseau's *La Nouvelle Heloise*, especially the famous scenes when St. Preux travels in the mountains of the Vallais region and remarks on a spiritual experience that occurs in the alpine heights. Williams later quotes directly from Rousseau when giving an account of her travels through the Alps of St. Bernardin during the second part of her trip (*Tour* 2:7). Mountains have long served as archetypal settings associated with revelation and religious experience, and for Helen Maria Williams seeing the Alps prompted feelings of devotion. Where else, she asks, might one feel so much in awe of "the author of nature": "no spot can surely be more congenial to devotional feelings, than that theatre where the divinity has displayed the most stupendous of his earthly works" (*Tour* 2:10). Her thoughts are very much like those of Thomas Gray who wrote of the Alps: "Not a precipice, not a torrent, not a cliff, but is pregnant with religion and poetry."[53]

After climbing St. Bernardin, Williams wrote her hymn to the Alps, offering it to her readers in place of any attempt to describe the Alps in a scientific manner. She deprecates her own "imperfect observations" (*Tour* 2:15), but her knowledge of geology must have been fairly good since the Appendix includes her own translation of Ramond's essay on the glaciers. She also wrote a whimsical poem on the scientific theories in Erasmus Darwin's *The Botanic Garden* (1791), which she entitled "The Complaint of the Goddess of the Glaciers to Doctor Darwin" (*Tour* 2:293–95). This piece was reprinted in her *Poems* of 1823, but it was the "Hymn Written Among the Alps" which was given the most prominent place in that volume as the concluding poem in the collection. The first of its twenty quatrains is in keeping with the sense of devotion in Williams's earlier religious verse:

> Creation's God! with thought elate,
>   Thy hand divine I see;
> Impressed on scenes, where all is great,
>   Where all is full of thee!
>
> (*Tour* 2:16)

Williams attempts to show how the alpine scenery reflects God's power, and even within the constraints of the stanzaic pattern she manages to create a sense of the sublime. The poem is filled with descriptions of the native wildlife, avalanches, waterfalls, "lucid" lakes, chalets, shepherds, and the "liquid light" of glistening minerals on the mountainside (*Tour* 2:18; 2:19). This building up of rich imagery concludes in the same manner as the poem began, with her tribute to the Creator: "In nature's vast, overwhelming power, / THEE, THEE, my GOD, I trace!" (*Tour* 2:19).

When William Wordsworth reflected on his own visit to the Alps in the summer of 1790, he observed that, "Among the more awful scenes of the Alps, I had not a thought of man, or a single created being; my whole soul was turned to him who produced the terrible majesty before me."[54] While so many scenes among the Alps filled observers with feelings of devotion, others were known for arousing sensations of horror and terror, as Wordsworth found when he felt a bewildering sense of dislocation near Gravedona, across from the Swiss border.[55] Helen Maria Williams similarly takes note of the terrifying landscapes that she passes, declaring, for instance, that the Valley of Schellinen, leading to St. Gotthard mountain, could have supplied Milton with images of hell for *Paradise Lost* (*Tour* 1:158). She felt that one could find in the Swiss landscape, which has inspired many artists, "all those combinations of imagery which croud the dreams of the poet" (*Tour* 2:153). In 1987, John Wraight noted the "very large number of British writers who have been inspired to write poems or essays about Switzerland itself," and he included Helen Maria Williams alongside Goldsmith, Collins, Wordsworth, Shelley, Byron, and many others.[56] Few of these other writers, however, treated contemporary Swiss politics at any length. Even Byron's hauntingly beautiful poem "The Prisoner of Chillon" (1816) is set in the sixteenth century. It is perhaps a testimony to Williams's sense of her own political involvement that she willingly interrupted her raptures over the landscape to present, without apology, her critique of the state of Swiss politics.

In a sense, Williams's tour of Switzerland was shaped by the perspective she gained from her Swiss friends, who would have been reliable sources of information about revolutionary activity in the cantons, providing her with the facts and figures that are used throughout the book and contribute to its air of authority.[57] But she also appeals to her readers' emotions by asking them to visualize in their minds the situation of the inhabitants of Basel who are without any rights. Imagine, she asks, how those people living near the French border feel when they observe the improvements in the lives of their French neighbours, or, to use her metaphor, they can hear "the shouts of equality, fraternity and the rights of man" (*Tour* 1:99) from across the border. As a Dissenter, Williams sympathized with those who were systematically excluded from the liberties others enjoyed. Historian Wilhelm Oechsli, discussing the "economic subordination of the subject rural district," explains that "The countryman of Basel, like the countryman of Zurich, was remorselessly excluded from ecclesiastical benefices, from higher educational positions, and from commissions as officers; he was forbidden to sell silk or to weave ribbons upon his own account, or to enter a business as partner."[58] In *Political Justice* (1793), William Godwin dealt in general with this subject, offering the following tableau in "On Property":

> the peasant and the labourer work till their understandings are benumbed with toil, their sinews contracted and made callous by being forever on the stretch, and their bodies invaded with infirmities and surrendered to an untimely grave! What is the fruit of this disproportioned and unceasing toil? In the evening they return to a family, famished with hunger, exposed half-naked to the inclemencies of the sky, hardly sheltered, and denied the slenderest instruction . . . all this while their rich neighbour—but we visited him before.[59]

Helen Maria Williams draws on her expertise as a writer of sensibility to construct a moving tableau—reminiscent of this scene from *Political Justice*—in order to illustrate the effects of Swiss disenfranchisement. A poor but hard-working family toils away, but never profits from their labor, because they must take the goods they produce to the burgher who sets the price and keeps them in poverty:

> in vain the father of a family may cultivate his field of flax, and prepare it for use; in vain his wife may spin, his infants turn the wheel which winds the thread, and he himself weave the woof; the web when woven is not at his disposition—he has no right over the produce of his labour, no power to dispose of what he has acquired by the sweat of his brow and the toil of his hands. (*Tour* 1:104)

This is just the type of social injustice that provoked Williams into a passionate cry of indignation: "a more vexatious law than this is, I believe, scarcely to be found in the whole code of despotism" (*Tour* 1:104).

Her objections to the state of affairs in Zürich were similar. In all of her work, she stresses the way that political and moral progress and the development of arts and science go hand in hand. For that reason she was disappointed that Zürich, known as the "Athens of Switzerland" (*Tour* 2:85), should labor under what she regarded as a "despotic government" (*Tour* 2:86): the "taste for letters, whatever tendency it may have had to purify their manners, has been ineffectual to correct the vices of the [oligarchic] government" (*Tour* 2:85). Even though Zürich could boast "men highly enlightened and ardent in the cause of liberty" (*Tour* 2:88), Williams found them silent about injustices in the rural areas of their own canton. Without naming the village of Stäfa, Williams alludes to what would become known as the Stäfa affair, when in 1794 its residents unsuccessfully petitioned for further rights. Having been impressed with the charitable and educational institutions in

Zürich in 1794, Williams was disappointed that the grievances of the canton's own oppressed classes had not been addressed.

Taking every opportunity to promote political liberty and social progress, Williams describes the new state of France under the Directory as an oasis of education and culture, with its libraries, its museums, and its plans for a national system of schooling (*Tour* 2:125–28). There is no mention of the great Swiss educator Heinrich Pestalozzi, a protegé of her friend Phillipe-Albert Stapfer.[60] Williams does applaud the Reading Society in Lucerne, which exemplified her ideal of a place where progressive cultural and political interests met. The Society's members discussed the Revolution in France to the extent that it worried the ruling oligarchy, which in 1791 ordered that "all publications referring to the French Revolution, and especially the Procès Verbal and the French journal, should henceforth not be read at the library and should be removed from it."[61] Peter Kamber confirms that several members of the Reading Society later became leaders in the Helvetic Republic.[62] Williams would also have welcomed the Society's liberal attitude towards women because, although no women were listed as members of the Reading Society, in 1796 the Reading Library had a special catalog for ladies (271 items), and women of the higher classes were known for being educated, or as Williams noted, "The ladies of Lucerne are remarked for their beauty, and give an higher interest to their personal charms, by cultivating the graces of the mind" (*Tour* 2:122).[63] At some point, Williams's portrait was painted by the Zürich artist Johann Heinrich Lips (1758–1817).

Whatever the shortcomings of Swiss society, which included problems of censorship, Williams celebrated signs of progress, especially those that emphasized that conditions were ripe for enlightened change. The presence of progressive coteries such as the Reading Society (Williams does not mention political societies) should assure her readers of Switzerland's readiness for change: "There is no inconsiderable number of enlightened men in every Canton of Switzerland, who are anxious to see the abuses of their government reformed, by restoring to the community those privileges which are now the property of a few individuals" (*Tour* 2:119).

However, there is little room for praise in a book whose function is to argue for the necessity of revolutionary change. Williams has to work hard to counteract the positive image of the cantons, lauded in books such as Coxe's popular *Travels in Switzerland*. William Coxe was the leading interpreter of the Swiss for British readers, and Gavin Rylands de Beer explains that "Of all accounts of travels through Switzerland in the eighteenth century, none enjoyed such a high reputation for accuracy and completeness as that of Archdeacon William Coxe."[64] It would especially be an uphill battle convincing her readers that there was any-thing wrong with the governments in the democratic cantons. Glarus, for instance, was reputed to be the epitome of Swiss pastoral democ-racy. Once again it was Coxe who had lavished praise on its cattle, cheese, and butter; and its voting for every man over age 16.[65] Coxe's comment that "Nothing delights me so much as the inside of a Swiss cottage" helped to shape the British view of Switzerland.[66] Williams focuses instead on what she regards as a lack of progress in the "Democracies of Switzerland" (*Tour* 2:78). The southeast Catholic regions of Uri, Schwyz, Unterwalden, Zug, and Glarus were "hostile to the French Revolution" (*Tour* 1:215), and in her view, "No other part of Switzerland is so unenlightened" (*Tour* 1:213). Chris Jones points out that Williams's adversarial stance put her at a disadvantage, since readers could respond more favourably to the pleasing pictures in Coxe than they could to her dissection of governmental practices.[67]

On the third and last part of her tour, Williams travelled through western Switzerland. She did not go to Geneva, likely because of the political turmoil there, but she gave her readers a sketch of its recent history. Even a disinterested tourist would have had difficulty avoiding the subject, since anyone arriving in the picturesque Lausanne when Williams did would have seen that it was "filled with emigrants from France, and also from Geneva" (*Tour* 2:156). The Genevans were escaping the very recent Jacobin revolution which had occurred just a few weeks before in July 1794. Williams praises the Genevans for throwing "off the chains" of despotism in the general insurrection of 1789 (*Tour* 2:156). However, she had little sympathy for this Jacobin insurrection of 1794, and, writing after the fact, she can report that they were soon replaced by moderate republicans (*Tour* 2:171–72).

The *Tour in Switzerland* concludes with five chapters on Berne, the canton about which Williams probably knew the most, due to her friendship with Frédéric César de La Harpe. In German-speaking Berne a small number of wealthy families controlled the governing sen-ate (the Great Council of Two Hundred), which had refused to give into demands that a sixteenth-century treaty gave sovereignty to the French-speaking inhabitants of the subject region of the Pays de Vaud. Presenting a history of the dispute, Williams argues for the justice of the claims of the Vaudois and anticipates the settlement of its grievances, imagining that La Harpe will earn "the glory of giving independence to his country, if that event takes place" (*Tour* 2:253). Williams also eulo-gises his cousin, the Baron Amédée de La Harpe, who left Switzerland after he and others were issued severe sentences for their political activ-ism and for participating in festivities celebrating the Fall of the Bastille

(*Tour* 2:237–48). Some of these men had already been sentenced to long terms in "the dungeons of Chillon" (*Tour* 2:237).

The Bernese oligarchy took rigorous steps to control republican activities, which were often aided by the French and by members of the Swiss Club in Paris. The circulation of revolutionary pamphlets was answered by Berne's use of censorship, spies, and the "police supervision of foreigners,"[68] the last of which involved Williams in an incident in 1794:

> On our arrival at the gates of Berne, we were questioned with stern severity respecting our country, our names, our professions, whence we came, whither we were going, and above all, what were the motives of our visit. Nothing can be more calculated to destroy all impressions of Swiss freedom than this absurd kind of police, which has so completely the air of despotism, and which is particularly disagreeable to the English traveller, who recollects that in his own country, strangers from every quarter of the globe are received without inquiry or distrust. (*Tour* 2:197)

The police presence was unsettling, and the author of the *Letters from France* (the first four volumes had appeared by 1794) had reason to be alarmed by their questions.

Williams found an apt symbol for the Bernese oligarchy in the famous prison Chillon Castle, which she disparagingly named the "Swiss bastille" (*Tour* 2:180). Located in the Pays de Vaud, the Castle was used as a prison until 1798, and at the time of Williams's visit in 1794, it held some prisoners from the Pays de Vaud who had spoken out against the government of Berne in 1791. The Castle had been made famous in Rousseau's *La Nouvelle Heloise* as the place where his heroine, Julie, was nearly drowned attempting to save her son. In honor of Rousseau's fictional heroine, travelers visited the spot, in Williams's words, like "sentimental pilgrims, who, with Heloise in hand, run over the rocks and mountains to catch the lover's inspiration" (*Tour* 2:179). Even Archdeacon Coxe romanticized his visit, as would Percy Shelley, on his trip to Clarens and Chillon, years later in 1816.[69] Williams asks her readers to resist this "reading" of the landscape and to let the facts about the Castle take precedence over fiction:

> The tear of sensibility which has so often been shed over this spot for the woes of fiction, may now fall for sorrows that have the dull reality of existence. It is not the imaginary maternal shriek [of Julie] that pierces the ear, it is the groan of the patriot rising from the floor of his damp dungeon. (*Tour* 2:180)

Making her readers feel guilty for ignoring the real human suffering taking place within the walls of the romanticized Castle, Williams tries to redirect their sensibility to the actual experiences of the imprisoned patriots of the Pays de Vaud.

In order to influence public opinion in favor of the rights of the Vaudois, Williams must also counteract positive reports about Berne. On his first journey to Switzerland, Coxe had been disappointed with Berne, but 10 years later he found it much improved and the aristocratic senate a model of moderation. She compares Coxe's views to those of Edmund Burke, who described Berne as "one of the happiest, most prosperous, and best governed countries on earth" (*Tour* 2:205). Burke delivered his praise in the *Reflections* in 1790, warning that France was out to destroy Switzerland by sowing the seeds of discontent there.[70] Williams agreed with Burke that one can find "cultivation, ease and prosperity" in Switzerland, but it served as a model of liberty only because there was so little before to compare it to, or to quote her metaphor "as the glow-worm becomes a luminary when all around is darkness" (*Tour* 2:206). As Williams sees it, the French Revolution has changed everything, and its example will improve Switzerland, by giving it laws to protect individual rights and positively assert the principles of liberty (*Tour* 2:274).

Along with repudiating other English observers, Williams attacks the Swiss counter-revolutionary movement, focusing on the work of Jacques Mallet du Pan, whose *Considérations sur la nature de la Révolution de France* (1793) was read and translated throughout Europe.[71] In the spring of 1792, pressure from French emigrés in Freiburg and Soleure had forced the French ambassador, Barthelemy, whom Williams visited in 1794, to move from Soleure to Baden and then Basel (*Tour* 2:189; 2:261). With an emigrant army formed in Berne, Soleure, and Freiburg, French travellers in Switzerland had to "hide every symbol of liberty" (*Tour* 2:256–57). One of Williams's travelling companions got himself into trouble with royalist refugees near Lucerne because of the engraving on his snuff box (*Souvenirs* 85–86): "[he] was careful to slide hastily into his pocket the lid of his box, on which was painted the emblems of liberty, and the rights of man" (*Tour* 2:105–6). On another occasion when Williams and her companions visited the region of the Vallais, they read placards listing the "various degrees of corporal punishment" which would be inflicted on anyone found discussing "French principles" or reading French newspapers, and they actually cut short a trip, out of fear of an innkeeper's royalist sympathies, when he began boasting of the many aristocrats, Lords, and Dukes whom he had met as a mountain-guide (*Tour* 2:182; 2:191).[72] These incidents give readers concrete examples of the restrictions and dangers that characterized the unsettled days of 1794.

When she came to finish her book three years later, the political landscape had changed considerably. She had friends in power in the French Directory, like Antoine Français de Nantes (1756–1836), and she had put the horrors of the Reign of Terror behind her. The Campo Formio peace agreement between Austria and France had been reached on 17 October 1797 (*Tour* 2:22–23), largely due to the military victories of Napoleon Bonaparte, whom she called a hero for all of the world (*Tour* 2:57). Now she looked for France's influence on other governments, beginning with those in the closest vicinity, like Switzerland (*Tour* 2:275–76). With the prospect of a just political landscape before her, Williams concludes her book with the following panegyric:

> With sincere reluctance I bade Switzerland farewell. Who can leave such a country without regret? If we find its governments defective, or its societies dull, there is always a resource against every feeling of dislike, or of weariness, in the meditation of that glorious scenery, the view of which renders the mind insensible to human evils, by lifting it beyond their reach. Switzerland has opened to me a new world of ideas; its landscapes are indelibly impressed upon my memory; whenever the delightful images of nature present themselves to my imagination, I find that I have been thinking only of Switzerland. (*Tour* 2:276–77)

Recalling the beauty of the Swiss landscape in these last remarks softened the political edge of Williams's book. Williams admitted that whatever the defects of its governments—whatever its political landscape—Switzerland's geographical landscape seized the imagination and it was what she would remember most from her own tour. Ironically, it is these gracious words, not her political arguments, that have been recalled in our own century: this last paragraph was quoted as recently as 1952 by the Swiss National Tourist Office, on the concluding page of a compendium of literary comments on Switzerland.[73]

Published in March 1798, Helen Maria Williams's *Tour in Switzerland* received long reviews in the British press, showing that despite not having lived in England for the past six years, she was still regarded as an important writer. The *Monthly Magazine* announced the publication of her book with a good deal of excitement: "A Tour in Switzerland, from the brilliant pen of Miss Williams, will be published in early March."[74] By the time her book appeared, however, French actions in Switzerland had led to a great deal of bloodshed, which she deplored and had not anticipated. Still, reviewers found much to recommend in the *Tour*: the *Analytical Review* and the *European Magazine* were especially fascinated by Williams's picture of Parisian and Swiss society and by her meeting with Lavater, but like other reviewers they were less comfortable with the politics of the book.

While liberal journals downplayed the political elements of the *Tour*, because they believed Williams had misjudged the situation in Switzerland, conservative reviewers denounced the book and engaged in ad hominem attacks on Williams, maligning her as "Mrs. Stone."[75] The *Anti-Jacobin*, with its usual excess, vilified her as a "poissarde," and lamented "the hard fate of the brave, the free, and once happy SWISS, now disunited by the perfidious, and plundered, massacred, and enslaved by the rapacious and bloody Satellites of the French Directory."[76] Other reviewers tried to reclaim Williams as a writer of sensibility. The *Monthly Review*, disliked the political parts of her book and admonished "the female reformer" while praising her poem about the Glacier Goddess.[77] The *European Magazine* reprinted her "Hymn Written Among the Alps" and declared that "As a Poetess Miss Williams attracts us much more than as a politician."[78] Concerned that she would be criticized for seeming to support the French invasion, they reminded readers that the "fair Tourist" had written her book before "the subjugation of Switzerland by France."[79] Even the *Monthly Magazine*, which expressly recommended the political information in the *Tour*, took pains to distance Williams from the events that occurred after her book was written.[80] Once again she was in the uncomfortable position of making idealistic predictions that did not correspond to resulting political realities.

But the same immediacy that made the book a hazardous undertaking for her was its chief selling point. In the Preface to his French translation, published in early 1798, Jean-Baptiste Say describes Williams as one of the preeminent English supporters of the French Republic and asserts that her account of her travels in 1794 will explain and justify the revolution taking place *currently*, as the French armies, in his words, break the fetters that still enchain most of the Swiss population.[81] The French edition, *Nouveau Voyage en Suisse*, was widely promoted[82] and in a letter to Joseph Priestley dated 12 February 1798, John Hurford Stone recommended Williams's new book as a guide to the state of Swiss politics, explaining that French troops were helping the Swiss Cantons to destroy their

> tyrannic oligarchies, and [melt] the whole into an Helvetic Republic, founded on the basis of the Rights of Man. Of the nature of their past governments, and the abuses which they contain, you will have a pretty just idea, [in] . . . a View of Switzerland, written by Miss H. M. Williams.[83]

Ironically, this letter never reached Priestley, because it and a letter to Benjamin Vaughan (both of whom were now living in the United States) were intercepted and published a few months later in London in May 1798 as examples of treasonous correspondence.[84] Although the publication of these private letters—linking Williams with Stone—cast a shadow on the respectable reviews of her Swiss *Tour*, they revealed nothing about her politics that readers did not already know; they were, in fact, used primarily in an American campaign to discredit Joseph Priestley.[85] What the confiscated letters do reveal is the hopeful mood in the Williams household. Stone, who chatted about his friends LeGrand and Talleyrand, told Benjamin Vaughan, "the political world rolls so rapidly, that we scarce have time to look around us, and admire the revolution of one spot, before we are called off to look after another."[86] Even Williams's sister Cecilia added a cheerful note to the same letter ("I snatch a little scrap of M's paper to recall myself to your remembrance"), and Williams told Vaughan about her *Tour* and ended her postscript on a personal note: "My mother and sister are well, and I have two charming little nephews—the eldest is already an excellent republican."[87] In the early months of 1798, Williams was optimistic about the future. If her own life was like a happy family in a tableau of sensibility, it was one in which the genre had expanded to include not only the unconventional presence of the divorced John Hurford Stone, but also a place for the active and independent woman who wanted to make a contribution to the world. Her friends were once again in power in France, and the British press still looked with expectation to books that came "from the brilliant pen of Miss Williams."[88]

Helen Maria Williams
by Ozias Humphry; engraved by Joseph Singleton, 1792
Copyright The British Museum.

Rev. Andrew Kippis
by William Artaud; engraved by F. Bartolozzi, 1792
By courtesy of the National Portrait Gallery, London.

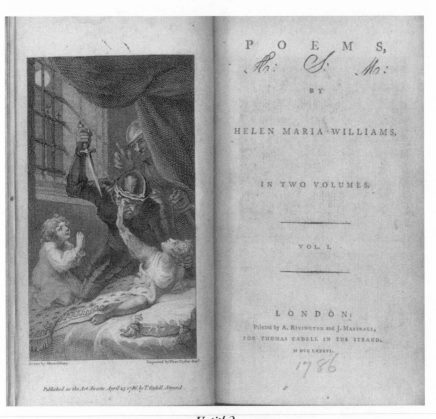

Untitled
Maria Cosway, frontispiece for Williams's *Poems*, 1786
Private Collection

Don Dismallo Running the Literary Gantlet
Anon. 1790
Copyright The British Museum.

Hélène Maria Williams
n.d.
engraved by H. Lips
Cliché Bibliothèque nationale de France, Paris.

Helen Maria Williams
1816
The Bodleian Library, University of Oxford, Ms. Montagu d. 5 fol. 296v.

Athanase Coquerel
1849
Cliché Bibliothèque nationale de France, Paris.

Héléna Maria Williams
n.d.
Cliché Bibliothèque nationale de France, Paris.

5

The Napoleonic Era

IN HER NOTE TO BENJAMIN VAUGHAN, ENCLOSED WITH STONE'S LETters of February 1798, Williams expressed a happiness that was soon replaced by sorrow due to an unexpected death in her family. Her sister Cecilia died suddenly in September 1798, possibly from complications arising from her third pregnancy. Cecilia Coquerel was survived by her husband Marie-Martin-Athanase Coquerel, and her two children, Athanase Laurent Charles Coquerel, born 27 August 1795 (with John Hurford Stone and Williams as his godparents) and Charles Augustin Coquerel, born 17 April 1797 (with Jean-Scipion Sabonadière and Persis Williams as his godparents).[1] The boys had been baptized by Paul Henri Marron, and he would also conduct Cecilia's funeral (Woodward 137). While Helen Maria Williams, her mother, and Persis took over the care of the young boys, it was very difficult for the family to deal with the loss of Cecilia, as Williams later wrote:

> can you wonder that my heart is almost broken, when you recollect, what I have lost? the grave, the relentless grave for ever covers from my sight my sister!—my eye meets no more the dear companion of my childhood—the beloved friend of my life! she, who shared in all its destiny, all its emotions—all its interests—all that has left the traces of existence on the memory, or the affections!—she, on whom I ever leant for consolation!—whose placid sweetness soothed my too acute feelings, and whose uniform chearfulness of disposition corrected the melancholy habitual to mine—No!—the world has nothing to offer me that can compensate for the loss of my sister—nothing, nothing can fill the void she has left in my desolate heart![2]

Williams movingly expresses how much her bond with her beloved sister meant to her. This time of personal grief coincided with a complex period in European history, when Napoleon Bonaparte took to the world stage.

Just as Williams's career as a poet of sensibility had been irrevocably altered by the French Revolution, so did the rise to power of Napoleon Bonaparte in 1799 alter the course of her career once again. When the nineteenth century critic John Alger wrote that Helen Maria Williams "admired the Bonaparte of Brumaire, but loathed Bonaparte the Despot," he might well have been describing the reaction of many of Williams's contemporaries.[3] But unlike her friends in Britain, Williams lived in Paris, and her own career as a writer was endangered by Bonaparte who knew and disapproved of her work. Having praised Bonaparte in rapturous terms in her *Tour in Switzerland* (1798) and *Sketches of the French Republic* (1801), Williams became disillusioned when his image of greatness became tainted by his acts of self-aggrandizement, his militaristic imperialist quest, and his systematic program of censorship, which eventually forced her to stop writing. Williams and Bonaparte met around 1801, when he praised her *Sketches*; but later that year his dissatisfaction with the political content of her poem on the Peace of Amiens began 20 years of animosity between them. This chapter chronicles the development of her career during the Napoleonic era, from the days when the world seemed full of possibility, in what she hopefully called the "age of rights" (*Sketches* 2:216), to the period of censorship under Napoleon which lasted until 1815.

In 1801, Williams published the two-volume *Sketches of the State of Manners and Opinions in the French Republic*, which covers events from 1799 to 1800, a period that marked the end of a decade of revolutionary activity and the beginning of a new century. France had an optimistic future, entrusted to the leadership of its national hero, Napoleon Bonaparte. Williams reports on the successes and failures of an intense period of political change, in diffusive coverage of a wide range of material, such as events in Switzerland and Naples, the achievements of Bonaparte, and the establishment of a new Constitution. By noting in this work, alongside her support of the achievements of the Revolution her own critique of public affairs, concerning topics such as French military actions and the status of women, Williams reinforces her role as a political commentator who seeks to correct and shape policies. The *Critical Review* was impressed by the range of topics in *Sketches* and thought highly of her literary achievements: "The name of Helen Maria Williams has already acquired no small degree of celebrity in the republic of literature: her admirers are not confined to this island, nor indeed to this quarter of the globe."[4] It was generally acknowledged that Williams had become a writer of international repute.

The Preface to *Sketches* is an important document in itself since it reveals how Williams has changed since she wrote her first *Letters from France*. It has a formality and seriousness of tone, a maturity, that shows how Williams had gained confidence in her own abilities and her influence as a writer. It is a confidence she had earned, after writing about revolutionary politics for more than a decade. Having heard that she had been vilified in British journals like *The Anti-Jacobin*, Williams presents a dignified defence of herself. She deflects these attacks on her character by an appeal to ethos and pathos, implicitly creating an image of her own courage by reminding her readers that since she survived the Reign of Terror, she was quite fit to survive attacks in the press.

> I am aware of the censure which has been thrown on writers of the female sex who have sometimes employed their pens on political subjects; nor am I ignorant that my name has been mentioned with abuse by journalists, calling themselves Anti-Jacobins. But however malignant may be the aim, these Anti-Jacobin darts fly harmless; those who have lived amidst the scenes of a French Revolution, have learnt to parry or despise more formidable weapons. (*Sketches* Preface n. p.)

With her controlled tone, Williams implies that it would be beneath her to take seriously the attacks of the prejudicial *Anti-Jacobin*. She has more important work at hand in observing and recording the progress of liberty at this period in "human history" (*Sketches* Preface n. p.). The *Monthly Review* commended her for this stance, and, although its praise for the book was not unqualified, it credited her authority on the subject of revolutionary politics: "Few English women, or even English men, have enjoyed a more ample opportunity of observing . . . the revolutions in France."[5]

Appearing only three years after her *Tour in Switzerland*, which looked forward to French intervention in the Swiss cantons, her new book opens with a sharp critique of French military action. Williams explains that when she wrote the *Tour of Switzerland* she thought that "the necessity of a general reform [in the Swiss cantons] had been universally proclaimed," so conditions seemed ripe for change (*Sketches* 1:11). However, within months of completing the *Tour in Switzerland*, she learned that the French army's manner of "moulding" the Swiss government resulted in bloodshed that went far beyond the "friendly" guidance she had envisioned, and in this next book she records her disappointment that the blaze of French liberty had once again burned out of control (*Tour* 2:275). Although she had harshly criticized the government of Berne in the *Tour*, she now rebukes France for overthrowing the Bernese government "by the bayonet" (*Sketches* 1:10), especially since she believed that the governments of Switzerland would have changed on their own. This violence simply made things worse, and Williams scorns the "revolutionary Optimists" who excuse bloodshed as "transient blemishes in the grand drama of the Revolution" (*Sketches* 1:12). Both she and Jacques Mallet du Pan, though writing from opposite ideological positions, condemned the plundering of Swiss treasuries

(*Sketches* 2:20–21).[6] France's actions in Switzerland exasperate Williams because they made a mockery of her own glowing hopes for the future of republican government. Her friend La Harpe, who had been a member of the Swiss Directory shortly after its founding in April 1798, became critical of French relations with Switzerland and was forced off the Directory in January 1800.[7]

In England, there was a great outcry against the invasion of Switzerland. Anna Laetitia Barbauld published a poem in March 1800 lamenting the war, and "her distress at the French invasion of Switzerland was widely shared among English liberals," as William McCarthy and Elizabeth Kraft have noted.[8] Other poems followed, including William Lisle Bowles's *The Sorrows of Switzerland* (1801), and Wordsworth's "Thought of a Briton on the Subjugation of Switzerland" (1807). Williams did not write a poem on the topic, but she did address the situation in her Preface to the second French edition of her *Tour* (1802), and her prose account in *Sketches* harkens back to sentiments expressed in her early anti-war poetry, as she laments "the mourning widow," the "desolate children," "the ruined cottage" (*Sketches* 1:12). She recalls walking with a friend in Switzerland in 1794, both of them pleased that they were sheltered from the fury of war, unaware that "the blue mountains" would soon, too, be "the seat of the wild uproar of savage passions" (*Sketches* 1:14). Another British writer, William James MacNevin, visiting Switzerland in 1802, mentioned "Miss Williams's elegant letters from Swisserland" in his own travel book.[9] But he also noted that the sublime landscape of the Schaffhausen falls, so memorably described by Williams, was now terribly altered by the ravages of the French invasion: "my reveries was interrupted too soon by the sight of some destructive traces of the late war. They were ruins of another fine bridge, which the French army broke down for its security."[10] Williams herself received reports in letters from her friends that the beautiful scenes of Switzerland have now had "their august solitudes invaded, and disturbed by the clang of arms, the shouts of the victor, the cry of the vanquished, and all the dissonant uproar of war—war!" (*Sketches* 1:24). Seeking the ideal of a bloodless revolution, she was destined to be disappointed.

Nowhere was this more true than in Naples. When she recounts the history of the short-lived Neapolitan Republic (actually called the Parthenopean Republic), which was founded on 26 January 1799 and overturned just six months later on 8 July 1799, her sympathy is for the ousted revolutionaries, and she views Naples in the context of a series of European revolutions, following the ur-model of the French Revolution: "Its rise and fall are so nearly connected that the interval will occupy but a short page in the history of the Revolutions which

usher out this eventful century" (*Sketches* 1:167). Her account, which
includes copies of treaties in lengthy appendices, was influential in
shaping British opinion about the events in Naples, and it was widely,
though not always favourably, cited, especially because of her comments about the controversial actions of Admiral Nelson and the Hamiltons.

Much of Williams's information she owed to her acquaintance with
some of the surviving revolutionary leaders who had taken refuge in
Paris. Viewing the events in Naples from their perspective, she asserts
that the formation of the republic was unanimously welcomed by the
people.[11] But the accepted view among historians is that supporters of
the Neapolitan revolution were a minority group made up of the educated and artistic class. Many members of the peasant and working
classes, known as the lazzaroni, fought against the revolutionaries and
the French armies.[12] Before commenting on their defeat, Williams
describes a scene of jubilation among her friends, a mirror image of the
golden days of the French Revolution of 1789:

> Newly awakened to liberty, the hearts of the Neapolitans began to dilate at
> the prospect of the progressive happiness which lay before them. Joy was
> painted on every countenance, and fairer suns seemed to embellish their
> charming horizon. The grateful names of Liberty, of Country, of Equality,
> electrifying the natural enthusiasm of a people of warm imaginations,
> impelled them forward with rapid steps in their republican career. . . .
> Almost every where the tree of liberty was planted by the intervention of
> the clergy, who, clothed in their sacred robes, implored the blessing of
> Heaven on their regenerated country. (*Sketches* 1:156–57)

Despite this picture of a people rejoicing in their new republic, it took
only a short time for the counter-revolutionary forces to overthrow the
republican government.

Cardinal Ruffo began what Williams calls the royalist reign of terror
in Calabria in February 1799, arriving in Naples on 13 June 1799.
Naples was one of the few Republican strongholds, and it was attacked
with "Robespierrian ferocity" (*Sketches* 1:168): "Calabrians, galley-
slaves, ruffians, and Lazzaroni," were thirsting "for blood, and pillage"
(*Sketches* 1:172). Williams's description of the "slaughter" in Naples
equals the very few graphic scenes from her books on the Reign of Terror: "Heads of patriots bathed in gore were carried on pikes in triumph
through the streets; their palpitating flesh was gnawed by these monsters of fanaticism" (*Sketches* 1:172). In this case, however, the "monsters" are not Jacobins but royalists, in a conflict that was especially
class-oriented. Williams was outraged that the prisons were "thronged

with persons who formed the pride and ornament of the Neapolitan nation" (*Sketches* 1:172–73). Her remarks resemble those of socialist historian Benedetto Croce who wrote that "The reaction of those days has no parallel in history; nowhere else has a monarch ever sentenced to prison, death, and exile, prelates, gentleman, generals, admirals, writers, scientists, poets, philosophers, jurists, and nobles—the intellectual and spiritual flower of the country."[13]

What also troubled Williams was that the counter-revolutionaries were helped by the British, most notably Admiral Nelson, whose actions at Naples stand as the most controversial of his career. English troops in the Isle of Procida aided the royalist "insurgents in the interior," "directed their operations," and "excited revolt in the places near the coasts" (*Sketches* 1:161–62). Recounting these events placed Williams in an awkward situation as an Englishwoman, because she supported the actions of France in endeavouring to establish a republic, not the actions of England which aimed at returning the monarchy. It is when she can comment approvingly on British behaviour, without relinquishing her political allegiances, that she can proudly claim her British identity, as she does when praising two British Commodores: Trowbridge, who saved the lives of many patriots by not forcing their ship to return to Naples where they would be executed (*Sketches* 1:201–2), and Foote, who treated kindly those who surrendered. However, among the British, few regarded Foote as the hero that Williams found him to be.

Sir William Hamilton, the British Ambassador to Naples, along with Admiral Nelson, refused to honor the treaties Foote had negotiated for the Castles of Nuovo and Ovo. Acting on the direct orders of the King and Queen of Naples, Nelson overruled the treaties, and hundreds of Neapolitan republicans were imprisoned. In recounting this event, Williams preserves her own image as a loyal Englishwoman by heaping praise upon her country's reputation for honorable conduct, and viewing the actions of Nelson and Sir Hamilton as an aberration, a shameful betrayal of British principles of honor and liberty. She quotes a letter from a Neapolitan patriot who was shocked that

> "the sons of the English nation, the first-born of liberty in Europe; the heirs of so many philosophers, who were the founders of public morality, and of the rights of nations, thus the acknowledged defenders of the principles of freedom throughout the world, found themselves humbled to the condition of becoming satellites of the cruelty of the king of Naples." (quoted in *Sketches* 1:199)

Among those executed under Nelson's orders was 70-year old Prince Caraccioli, the enlightened envoy of Sicily who had joined the republican cause in its last months. He was tried and executed in a space of less than 24 hours. In the words of Nelson's nineteenth-century biographer Sir Nicholas Harris Nicolas, this would become "the affair which, more than any other, has been used to load Nelson's memory with obloquy."[14] Nicolas, who attempted to discredit Williams, disparaged her as "the very writer whose statements were the original source of most of the injustice that has been done to Lord Nelson. Miss Helen Maria Williams, a lady deeply imbued with Republican principles."[15] Still, even Nicolas cannot explain Nelson's "motive for ordering the immediate execution of Caraccioli."[16] However, focusing on the Caraccioli episode detracts from the larger issue at hand which was Nelson's annulment of the treaties and involvement in ordering the execution of prisoners. Williams herself gives only cursory attention to Caraccioli's execution and concentrates on the many other victims who were denied the terms agreed to for their surrender. Robert Southey, who used Williams's book to write his *Life of Nelson* (1813), also criticized Nelson for delivering the prisoners "over to the vengeance of the Sicilian court," calling it a "deplorable action! a stain upon the memory of Nelson, and the honor of England!"[17] As accounts of these events arrived in England, the controversy surrounding Nelson's actions began to ferment. In February 1800, Charles James Fox reminded the House of Commons of "the horrors" that accompanied the successful campaign in Naples.[18] When Williams's book appeared, it raised the ire of Nelson supporters and of Nelson himself, who wrote disparaging comments about her in his own copy of the *Sketches*, which is preserved in the British Library (Woodward 214).

Some commentators attempted to excuse Nelson's actions in Naples by blaming his mistress Lady Emma Hamilton, the young wife of the British Ambassador, for leading him to act dishonorably in the first place. Nicolas cites one biography of Nelson which states that "The judgment of Lord Nelson, in this cruel transaction, was influenced and warped by the artful influence of Lady Hamilton . . . The trial and execution of Caraccioli were indecently and unjustly accelerated by this wicked siren."[19] Although Williams never blames Emma Hamilton for Nelson's actions, nor refers to their relationship, she does criticize her for exhibiting a hardness of heart when the Hamiltons saw Caraccioli and other prisoners in chains on the deck of the ship:[20]

[what] could lead Lady Hamilton to ascend the deck, and witness so sad a spectacle. These honourable victims, bound hand and foot like the vilest criminals, could present no attitudes as a study for an amateur . . . whether the deck-scene in the bay of Naples be calculated to cherish the favourable sentiments entertained of my country women, I leave you to judge. I have,

however, heard from the only individual who escaped the butchery which afterwards took place, that this sad spectacle was not beheld by Lady Hamilton with complete indifference. She, it seems, gracefully lifted her handkerchief to her eyes during part of the tragedy. (*Sketches* 1:182–84)

Emma Hamilton reminds her of Elizabeth Montagu's description of Lady Macbeth, who "would have been a monster out of nature, had not one trait reminded us of the woman" (*Sketches* 1:184). Williams scorns the "British Ambassadress, [who was] gallantly attended like another Cleopatra, and rowed along the bay in nautical magnificence, before the floating prisons of these unfortunate patriots" (*Sketches* 1:195).

It is another woman who is more deserving of admiration: the Neapolitan revolutionary, Eleanora de Fonseca Pimentel, whom Williams names in a list of dozens of patriots executed by the Supreme Junta established by the King of Naples. Williams writes at some length about "Eleonora Fonseca, a woman highly esteemed for her literary acquirements" (*Sketches* 1:215). Usually referred to by the name Pimentel, she was the talented daughter of expatriate noble Portuguese parents. As Emiliana P. Noether explains, Pimentel pursued literary and scientific studies, producing publications that earned her "a commendation and pension" from the King of Naples in 1790.[21] However, she was suspected of Jacobin sympathies as early as 1794, and from February to June 1799 she edited a republican journal called *Monitore napoletano*, which reported on the progress of the new government. While Pimentel was critical of some of the actions taken by the French in Naples, she was, much like Williams herself, committed to "the underlying principles of the French Revolution."[22] Williams lamented the loss of a woman who, in her words, "was guilty of having loved the cause of liberty, and of having written in its favour" (*Sketches* 1:220). Like so many of the intellectuals, writers, journalists, and artists executed five years earlier during Robespierre's Reign of Terror, Pimentel became one in a long line of "illustrious martyrs of liberty" (*Sketches* 1:222).

After concluding her report on events in Naples, Williams turns abruptly from political matters to recount a fictional tale, the story of Perourou, the bellows-mender, preparing her reader for the unexpected transition by stating that for a moment, she will set aside the political events and vicissitudes of the day:

Every thing that could tear the mind from the late change of things was welcome; and I felt pleasure in turning from the change of Empires, the rise and fall of Kingdoms and Republics, to copy the humble revolutions of domestic life; forgetting for a moment the stratagems of Suwarrow (sic), and the terrors of the [Jacobin] *Manege*, in the malicious vengeance of the Lyons-engravers, and the fourberies of *Perourou*. (*Sketches* 1:248)

Williams never indicated who actually wrote the original tale of the bellows-mender; we can assume that it was not her own story since she refers above to copying it, and when it was published separately as a best-selling chapbook, she was cited as the translator.[23] Her description of it as a story about "revolutions of domestic life" is apropos because it is a Pygmalion-like story, that shows a lower-class man rising to a higher class when he is given the chance to educate and improve himself. The change in Perourou's status is not initiated for his own benefit, however, and that is what Williams means by the "fourberies" or trickery in the story.

Perourou, an uneducated bellows-mender, is hired by the rejected suitor of a beautiful woman named Aurora to exact his revenge against her. He teaches Perourou to talk and act like a wealthy gentleman, hoping the latter will win the hand of the rich Aurora. After months of training, Perourou is successful in his suit, and the rejected lover—a wealthy engraver—shames Aurora with the knowledge that Perourou was really only a bellows-mender. She takes refuge in a convent, but Perourou uses the education he has received to become a successful businessman, and he wins Aurora back. They live together happily, even forgiving the vindictive engraver. E. W. Pitcher classifies the story as a "philosophic tale" that demonstrates "the power of the common man,"[24] and it is the type of story that would appeal to Williams because of its emphasis on the democratic value of education. As Pitcher explains: "if a member of the lowest order in society be educated and given sufficient money and the right connections, that person will develop into as competent a businessman and as polished a socialite as another person born to the class which takes those abilities for granted."[25] An amusing story with a happy ending, it relieves Williams and her readers from the political news of the day, but it is still consistent with her own ideals.

It is no wonder Williams sought relief in a literary tale, for 1799 was a tumultuous year, and after the neo-Jacobin coup d'état of 30 Prairial (June 18, 1799) in France, Williams's friends in Basel (probably the Frey family) urged her "to take speedy refuge" (*Sketches* 1:245); but she stayed in Paris, where a few months later she cheered the coup d'état of 18 Brumaire (November 10, 1799), that resulted in Bonaparte being made First Consul, and his choosing Jean-Jacques Cambacérès and Charles François Lebrun as his Second and Third Consuls. Williams actually went to St. Cloud the day after 18 Brumaire, since she normally went there on horseback for daily exercise.

For some time past I have considered the Park of St. Cloud as my domain, since, in my daily rides on horseback in search of health, I often prefer those solitudes to the Bois de Boulogne, for ever haunted by the Parisian beau monde. To the Park of St. Cloud, then, my horse, on the immortal nineteenth of Brumaire, turned his steps mechanically; and traversing the village and the court of the Chateau, filled with troops, conveyed me in perfect safety to my accustomed hills and woods. . . . we beheld, through the trees, Deputies of the Five Hundred sauntering in the walks; and as it was the first time I had beheld them in their costume, though they had worn it two years, I was the more struck with their picturesque appearance, moving along in flowing robes, like tragedy-heroes. (*Sketches* 2:2–3)

She and her friend observed part of the swearing-in ceremony for the 500 members, noting that some members pronounced "with an emphatic gesture, the words 'hatred to *all tyranny*'" (*Sketches* 1:6). Williams seemed very comfortable, and not at all intimidated by the proceedings, as she mingled with some of the deputies on the terrace, "gazing on the autumnal tints and variegated forms of the lofty elms" and later "met with Deputies of our acquaintance, who gave us some intimation of what was going forwards" (*Sketches* 2:6; 2:10). It is not clear whether she was present for the moment of crisis when Bonaparte's power was threatened, but she recounts it vividly, either from her own observation or, more likely, that of the deputies whom she knew.

The formation of Bonaparte's government would enable France to become stronger and more stable which was, she argued, essential for the health of Europe itself because "the existence of liberty in Europe is fixed on the fate of the French Republic" (*Sketches* 2:21). Bonaparte and Sieyès oversaw the preparation of a new constitution for France, which won overwhelming support of the French electorate in a plebiscite held during Nivôse (December 1799 to January 1800).[26] Defending the new constitution, Williams also defends her right to have an opinion on it—since she mingles "with the political throng"—but for an expert analysis she includes in the appendix a paper by Cabanis:

> Do not be alarmed—I am not going to play the part of an analyser of constitutions, and act the lofty politician. My flights are always very near the surface; but though in seats of learning are sometimes found the most unapt of scholars, it is impossible to live in Paris, and mingle with the political throng, without catching some ideas on the important subjects in agitation. I shall, however, spare you my own reflections, and send you the opinion of the person [Cabanis] I have already cited. (*Sketches* 2:39)

As we saw in her *Letters from France*, Williams is acutely aware of how her readers might react to her discussing matters that may be out of her depth. However, when a friend asked her if she got to cast a vote in the plebiscite on the constitution, her negative answer prompts her to consider this great blind-spot in revolutionary politics, and she devotes an entire letter to the subject, entitled "On the State of Women in the French Republic," reprinted in the *New Annual Register* for 1801.

Women in France were not allowed to vote, and that fact was a glaring reminder of how little the Revolution had benefited women. Williams approaches the issue of women's suffrage by way of an analysis of the status of women in French society, in particular their lack of educational opportunities. She argues that by denying women a formal education, the government shows a complete disregard for women's rights of citizenship. It is because of her commitment to the ameliorative potential of education that Williams insists that politics must be approached from an informed position. She is quick to denigrate women of any class who get their opinions from "the mob, either high or low" (*Sketches* 2:50), and who, therefore, lack the education and the self-restraint necessary to work for change in a rational manner. There are a small number of women of "ardent or enlightened minds" (*Sketches* 2:50), who can discuss these subjects seriously because they have been self-educated, and presumably Williams herself would be included in such a category. But, in general, she finds that French women at the turn of the century are apolitical, most having "preserved a strict neutrality" on political subjects (*Sketches* 2:49), a position which she reminds her readers was recommended to British women in *The Spectator* (*Sketches* 2:48).[27] Though obviously not apolitical herself, Williams is still sympathetic to women who choose not to involve themselves in politics: if women "have shrunk from the fraternal embrace," it is because the Revolution has often "been terrifying, or repulsive" (*Sketches* 2:50), in its Jacobin madness. Moreover, the Revolution has provided very few "positive benefits" for women (*Sketches* 2:51), perhaps because its leaders had not troubled themselves to take an interest in women's rights, with the exception, she adds, of Condorcet, Sieyès, and Sieyès's associate Charles Théremin.

In her analysis of the status of women, Williams goes right to the heart of the matter by addressing the question of whether women have their sights on the bastions of male power, to be "Leaders of armies, or Rulers of states" (*Sketches* 2:52). She immediately allays men's fears by saying that women do not aspire to such important positions, but then she unsettles their complacency by adding that women might actually be good at these jobs if given a chance. Boldly presuming to speak for "every woman" (*Sketches* 2:53), Williams praises the work of Charles Théremin, the author of *De la Condition des Femmes dans les Républiques* (Paris, 1799), who condemned the inequality of laws that grant education for males but not for females (*Sketches* 2:53). Williams then begins an extended discussion of the rights of women, which would become the lengthiest she would ever publish on the subject:

> What claim has the Republic to the attachment of that part of the human race from whom it withholds the first privilege of our nature, the first gift of Heaven—instruction and knowledge? How should the heart of woman glow with the love of liberty, or her understanding assent to the force of truth?—She receives no lesson in the schools of wisdom or philosophy—she is considered as a being unworthy to participate in the higher acquisitions of the mind, and unfitted for those intellectual attainments which ennoble our nature—while inscriptions on every portal where instruction is dispensed throughout the Republic, invite man to enter, while, in every region of learning which he seeks to explore, his path is carefully traced, his footsteps firmly guided, and the accumulated wisdom of ages unfolded to his research, she, whose bosom glows with the sacred rays of genius, or the proud desire of pre-eminence, finds the gates of learning rudely barred against her entrance. She has no professor but her music-master—no academy but that of dancing—She may fill the hours which domestic duties leave vacant by dress, dissipation, cards, or public amusements; but, although destined to be the companion of man through life, let her not aspire to the lofty privilege of comprehending his studies, or becoming the associate of his labours—She to whose forming care the first years of the Republican youth are confided, is expected to instil principles which she has never imbibed, and teach lessons which she has never learned— . . . No!—When Republican Lawgivers shall have established public institutions where women may receive the blessings of a liberal education, when they shall have allotted for her whose mind is enlightened by study, and refined by nature, some honourable and dignified employments, which, if she is destitute of fortune, may shield her from the cruel alternative of penury, with all its train of ills, or of uniting herself to a man whom her heart despises or rejects— . . . when she is supplied with the means of knowledge, and of honourable independence, then will she kneel, with that glowing enthusiasm . . . and bless the tutelary sway of the Republic. (*Sketches* 53–57)

Williams argues her case clearly: the Republic will only earn the allegiance of women when it treats them like intelligent human beings, deserving of "instruction and knowledge." Williams movingly describes the way that women have been excluded from any form of education and made to feel inferior, deemed "unfit" for those "intellectual attainments" which, she argues, "ennoble our nature." Most earlier treatises on the education of women centred on this same argument of intellectual equality. We can compare, for instance, Mary Astell's *A Serious Proposal to the Ladies* (1694), a proposal to establish an Anglican women's college that would "stock the kingdom with pious and prudent ladies."[28] Astell's Tory politics are far removed from Williams's, and she was not interested in women gaining political rights, but she argued vehemently for their right to an education:

> The ladies, I'm sure, have no reason to dislike this proposal, but I know not how the men will resent it to have their enclosure broke down, and women invited to taste of that tree of knowledge they have so long unjustly *monopolized*. But they must excuse me if I be as partial to my own sex as they are to theirs, and think women as capable of learning as men are, and that it becomes them well.[29]

One notices immediately a difference in tone: Astell's somewhat bitter reproach is a striking contrast to the more eloquent plea that Williams uses, as she aims for an air of oratorical dignity.

How just is it, Williams asks, that the very inscriptions set in stone over school entrances invite men alone to pursue a life of the mind. Their footsteps are "firmly guided" all along the way, while a woman "finds the gates of learning rudely barred against her entrance." Williams's remarks anticipate the unforgettable anecdotes from the first chapter of Virginia Woolf's *A Room of One's Own*, when Woolf's protagonist is forced off the grass of the men's college by a Beadle and then forced out of the library by a gentleman "barring the way with a flutter of black gown."[30] However, Williams goes one better than Woolf's later chapter on Judith Shakespeare, by sketching her own brief portrait of a woman of genius, who could produce the highest intellectual or artistic achievements. While other writers in favour of women's education, like Hannah More (*Strictures on the Modern System of Female Education*, 1799), argued for its moral and intellectual benefits, they usually set limits on the nature and extent of women's achievements by confining their role to the home or to charitable works.[31] Williams offers a rare sight, that of the gifted woman fulfilling her potential, wherever it would take her: "she, whose bosom glows with the sacred rays of genius." It is for this gifted woman, too, that Williams wants the Republic to establish "public institutions where women may receive the blessings of a liberal education." Furthermore, the Republic must allow women to pursue not simply menial work but respectable jobs and careers that have been closed to them in the past, a point Mary Wollstonecraft also made in the *Vindication of the Rights of Woman*:

> is not that government then very defective, and very unmindful of the happiness of one half of its members, that does not provide for honest, independent women, by encouraging them to fill respectable stations? . . . How many women thus waste life away the prey of discontent, who might have practised as physicians, regulated a farm, managed a shop, and stood erect, supported by their own industry.[32]

These comments by Wollstonecraft are among the more revolutionary in her treatise, but they tend to be almost hidden away, in the second half of her long *Vindication*, and are subordinated to her main argument that educated women make better wives and mothers—an argument more palatable to her readers—and one to which Hannah More returns. Considering the length of Williams's chapter, her arguments for women's employment have a prominent place, and it is quite important, in tracing the tradition of feminist arguments, to recognize that the subjects of education and employment are inextricably linked in her view of the status of women.

While she speaks out on the need for education and employment, Williams deals with political rights per se in a less direct manner, by conjuring an Amazon from classical literature to do it for her, a "political Thalestris, warring for the rights of women" (*Sketches* 2:58). Thalestris, an Amazon Queen described in the works of Strabo and Plutarch, was a figure of some interest to eighteenth-century readers, appearing in various literary works, including Alexander Pope's *The Rape of the Lock*, where she helped Belinda in the battle of the sexes.[33] Through the character of Thalestris, Williams points out some of the inconsistencies in Charles Théremin's treatise, *De la Condition des Femmes dans les Républiques*. On the positive side, Théremin advocates women's education and women's right to positions in state education and family tribunals. But, as Candice Proctor has shown, he does not believe women should have any political rights, because their husbands can speak for them.[34] To this, Williams's Thalestris counters that, if women are given civil rights and privileges, they must also have political rights, and their independence of mind must be acknowledged because no one can assume that their opinions on all matters would coincide with those of their husbands.

Having had her say through Thalestris, Williams then turns to other issues. Her tone becomes serious again when she takes a moment to honor women's bravery during the Revolution:

It was women, who, in those days of horror, proved that sensibility has its heroism—and that the affections of the heart can brace the nerves with energy, that mocks the calculations of danger. It was women who penetrated into the depths of dungeons, who flew to the abodes of despair—who were the ministering angels that whispered hope and comfort to the prisoner—who wiped the cold damps from the brow of the extenuated sufferer— . . . And if the women of France knew how to sympathize in the sorrows of others, who knew so well as themselves how to suffer and how to die?—Have we not seen the daughter, led in the bloom of beauty to the scaffold with her parents, seeming to forget that she had herself the sacrifice of life to make, and only occupied in sustaining their sinking spirits?—Have we not seen the wife refusing to survive her husband, provoke also the fatal sentence, which it was her choice to share, and mingle her blood with his under the axe of the executioner? — What Roman virtue was displayed by Charlotte Corday! — what more than Roman fortitude dignified the last moments of Madame Roland! (*Sketches* 2:63–64)

The vignettes of feminine bravery here are similar to scenes in the second series of *Letters from France*, analyzed in Chapter Three. The women she honors are "ministering angels" who maintain their femininity, while displaying strength and courage.

Following her essay on the condition of women, Williams gives proof of her argument that women have the intelligence to consider important subjects, by herself treating several matters concerning law and religion in France, all of which demonstrate her progressive political position. She analyzes at length a new book by Francois d'Ivernois *On the Causes of the Usurpation which are to bring about the Fall of Bonaparte* (1800), belittling his gloomy theories about the French Republic (*Sketches* 2:226–74). On other subjects, she criticizes the practice of bribing judges and makes an eloquent defence of "trial by jury," as essential to civic liberty (*Sketches* 2:79). Making the same appeal to liberal principles, she defends her censure of the Catholic church (*Sketches* 2:90), while also criticizing the Directory for persecuting it (*Sketches* 2:202–3). She goes further, arguing that Christianity provides the foundation upon which human society should be structured because it promotes such "revolutionary" ideals as equality, virtue, and love:

> Although Christianity institutes no exclusive form of government, they have discerned that it promotes the spirit of equality, which suffers us to call no man master on earth; not that levelling system, which, under pretence of destroying distinctions, degrades genius and debases virtue; but that equality which, while it teaches man his rights, instructs him better in his duties, and becomes the firmest guarantee of the new commandment left by the Saviour of the world, and which has hitherto unhappily retained its novelty, that we should love one another. (*Sketches* 2:122)

On many occasions Williams has argued for political change to be shaped by moral and humanistic ideals, and here she makes explicit that such changes must reflect the teaching of Christ. She does not by any means associate political progress with a movement towards atheism. In her *Letters from France*, her *Tour of Switzerland*, and again in this book, she laments the increase in atheism that accompanied the Revolution, and to combat it, she later adds her own gentle "homily against Atheism" (*Sketches* 2:208).

As Williams admits, the letters in the second-half of the second volume of *Sketches* wander from one topic to another: "But where are we wandering? How came the controversies between the conformists and non-conformists of France to lead us to Saltzburg and the treaty of Campo Formio?" (*Sketches* 2:113) and, later, "But where am I wandering with the poets of Italy! I began my letter with . . . the departure of Bonaparte" (*Sketches* 2:140). In passing, she mentions, disparagingly, Burke's essay on the regicide peace (*Sketches* 2:132) and then outlines recent French military victories, pausing to applaud Bonaparte's incomparable courage traversing the Alps in the spring of 1800 (*Sketches* 2:137). Williams does not acknowledge any conflict in, on the one hand, praising Bonaparte's military prowess while, on the other hand, condemning the war itself. She appropriates Bonaparte for the cause of pacifism, claiming that he wanted peace, but the coalition governments refused his terms (*Sketches* 2:155). Bonaparte's victory at Marengo against the Austrians enabled him to return to a more-than-hero's welcome in Paris in July 1800. The burgeoning industry of myth-making surrounding Bonaparte was something to which she could happily devote her own pen.

In keeping with her stories of sensibility, and reminiscent of a scene in her poem *Edwin and Eltruda* which showed Eltruda nursing an injured linnet, she tells a story about Bonaparte being moved by a "piteous spectacle" of a barbet-dog or spaniel, loyally standing by the corpse of its master, an Austrian soldier (*Sketches* 2:189) at the Battle of Castiglione. This scene "put to flight every harsh and hostile feeling: Bonaparte gave orders to stop instantly the pursuit and carnage" (*Sketches* 2:190). The following passage demonstrates how sensibility and politics remained entwined for Williams, for she says that if *she* were "the negotiator for peace" she would "send with my dispatches to every cabinet, the portrait of the little dog at the battle of Castiglione" (*Sketches* 2:190). Williams once again imagines herself as a politician, but one who would use pathos to generate feelings of compassion, as we see in her plan to send out pictures of the dog as a symbol of the senselessness of war. One could argue that the spaniel triggered a moment of awareness in Bonaparte, shocking him out of the soldier's habitual gaze on victims of war, leading him to extend his pity to the human victims. The proportion of sympathy may appear skewed, but Williams clearly values the anecdote as a means to paint her hero as a Man of Feeling. It was reprinted in the *Critical Review*, which found it a "curious" anecdote, and which dubbed Williams, not disrespectfully, "our political sentimentalist."[35]

It is easy to see how Williams would have been attracted to the pathetic story of the barbet-dog, since it can be grouped with other incidents such as those she describes in her poetry, that demonstrate a sympathy for animals. This is a subject she treats at length in this book, defending her late friend Madame Helvétius, who spoke out against cruelty to animals and was ridiculed for it. Williams explains that it would be hypocritical if the Revolution did not encompass the humane treatment of animals, and again she proposes what she would do if she had a position of political power:

> Had I any influence in the proposal or fabrication of laws, I should be tempted to leave the human race a while to its own good government, and form a code for the protection of animals. In this age of rights, can no one be found fantastically humane enough to make their wrongs a theme of public attention? In other countries laws are instituted for their protection . . . In England, an ill-treated horse, or over-driven bullock, has the law for its avenger. The rights of animals there form a part of the social compact. (*Sketches* 2:216)

In a fine piece of persuasive writing, Williams attempts to convince her readers to admit that the frequent displays of "brutal inhumanity" against animals in the very streets of Paris put the nation to shame:

> Can no law succour that wretched horse, worn to the bone from famine and fatigue, lashed by his cruel tyrant into exertion beyond his strength, while he drags, in some vile vehicle, six persons, besides his merciless owner? For myself, I confess, that at the view of such spectacles, the charm of nature seems suddenly dissolved—to me the fields lose their verdure, and the woods their pleasantness—nor is my indignation confined to the unrelenting driver of these loaded machines; I consider the passengers who tacitly assent to the pain he inflicts, perhaps bribe his avarice to hasten on, as more than his accomplices in barbarity. Is it beneath the attention of legislators to lessen the sufferings of those tender animals which we see heaped on each other in carts, their heads hanging down on each side of the machine, in every position of torture? . . . France may be a great, and civilized, and free nation, but till such evils are redressed, let it not boast of its humanity. (*Sketches* 2:218–19)

Clearly, Williams will not turn a blind eye to the faults of the French. Her arguments for animal rights show her own refusal to indulge in complacency or to compromise her ideals by accepting anything less than a fully humane society, which would live up to the promise of the "age of rights" (*Sketches* 2:216).Her ideals were to be frustrated by the human frailty and the imperial ambitions of Napoleon Bonaparte.

By spring 1797, Bonaparte's name was "a household word through-out Europe"[36] because of his successful military exploits in the Italian campaign of 1796 to 1797. Although Britain and France had been at war since 1793, Bonaparte was a subject of admiration among many

British observers, and was featured in the May 1797 issue of *Monthly Magazine*, in an article on "Eminent Persons" which praised him for everything from his achievements in the battlefield to his wife's beauty.[37] Bonaparte was a hero in the making, even in the British press, so it was not unusual for Williams to eulogize him in her *Tour of Switzerland*, published in early 1798. In his recent study on Napoleon and the Romantics, Simon Bainbridge explains that commentators routinely compared Napoleon to great figures in history, which Williams also does when, for example, she claims that Bonaparte "belongs not exclusively to France, or her revolution; like Homer, or Newton, Bonaparte belongs to the world" (*Tour* 2:55–57).[38] This hyperbolic praise continued in *Sketches*, where she explains that the French people viewed Bonaparte as "invulnerable as Achilles, and invincible and fortunate as Caesar" (*Sketches* 2:158). Her occasional references to Bonaparte in this book seem aimed at pressuring the British government to accept his terms for peace, and she refers directly to a famous speech given by Richard Sheridan in the British House of Commons in June 1800, in which he argues for ending the war with France (*Sketches* 2:184). Rather than disparaging Bonaparte as the enemy, Sheridan respects his genius, exclaiming that: "Unfortunately for us . . . Never since the days of Hannibal have such splendid events opened on the world."[39] The terms of Sheridan's praise for Bonaparte exemplify the burgeoning industry of myth-making surrounding the French general (and First Consul), about whom Coleridge, for one, remarked breathlessly in a letter of October 1799 to Southey: "Buonaparte—! Buonaparte! dear dear DEAR Buonaparte."[40]

Williams would have been envied by her British countrymen had they known that she actually conversed with Buonaparte on one occasion. Not long after Brumaire, Williams met him by chance when she was out horseback riding in Boulogne with her friend Nicholas Thiessé, a member of the Tribunate. She regarded it as a great compliment when Napoleon said he had just finished reading her report on Naples in the French edition of *Sketches*, which had been translated by Sophie Grandchamp.[41] In her memoirs, Williams admitted to having been awe-struck:

> My enthusiasm was totally fervent. He was very polite because he had not yet attained that point of power in which, afterwards, only one of his glances would nearly make M. le Comte Volney disappear. He said to me that he had just read my description of the counter-revolution in Naples, and that he would answer for the truth of that which I reported. He said several things which were in reality quite ordinary; but my admiration accentuated the value of his words. (*Souvenirs* 132–33)

Since this is a retrospective account of her conversation with Bonaparte, written in her memoirs of 1827, her description of her own enthusiasm is qualified by her later opposition to him. Her admiration for the First Consul began to fade as the people she knew started to find themselves in conflict with him. At different points from 1801 to 1802, her friends La Harpe, Kosciuszko,[42] and Lafayette,[43] who supported Bonaparte previously, began distancing themselves from him because of his foreign policies. Thiessé was rebuked for objecting to some of the proposals for Bonaparte's Code Civil, and it soon became clear that the First Consul had little tolerance for opposition. The incident led to Thiessé's withdrawal from public life, and Williams remarked in her memoirs, "The error of my admiration for Buonaparte was not to last much longer" (*Souvenirs* 133). Bonaparte's restructuring of the governing bodies of the Tribunate and the Senate in April 1802 was telling, as Louis Bergeron points out: "The decay of representative institutions was only a part, in fact, of a general encroachment on public liberties, and in particular on freedom of expression."[44] As part of the "general encroachment," the system of press censorship directly affected Williams and her liberal circles, as will be discussed shortly.

On another level, the events of this period did, however, bring a measure of relief to a war-weary continent. After France had been at war for nearly 10 years, the peace accords of 1801–02 meant that people could travel again. Tourists streamed into Paris, and Williams's salon, noted for its "republicanism,"[45] was one of the most popular.[46] The diaries and letters of her visitors provide a valuable record of what some referred to as her "conversations"[47] or "conversazione,"[48] where the rooms were full to capacity. One person commented on the "crowd of politically remarkable persons" at Williams's;[49] and another was impressed by the "assemblage altogether of 60 or 70 people, almost all celebrated for something or other."[50] Her salon was known for bringing together people from around the world, or as a German guest put it: "you may meet all the important faces of several countries."[51]

For information about Williams's salon, one can turn to Gary Kelly's analysis and also to contemporary sources such as the diary of one of Williams's visitors in 1802, a young Irish woman named Catherine Wilmot.[52] Wilmot travelled throughout Europe with Lord and Lady Mount Cashell, the latter of whom (née Margaret King) is best known for having had Mary Wollstonecraft as her governess.[53] This early entry of January 1802 lists Williams's entire family (Persis, Mrs. Williams, the children Athanase and Charles Coquerel, their widowed father (Marie-Martin-Athanase Coquerel), and John Hurford Stone). As mentioned earlier, her sister Cecilia had died unexpectedly in 1798, and Williams, who loved her deeply, regarded this as a tragedy from which she never recovered (Woodward 136–37).[54] Wilmot's description of Williams herself is uncannily similar to the undated portrait of her in black mourning clothes:

> Miss Williams is in perpetual mourning for her sister; she wears, added to her Black dress, a long black gauze scarf thrown over her head, and hanging down to her feet. I never saw manners so desirous to please, as hers, nor a countenance more corresponding to this idea. She speaks in a tone of voice that sounds like an invalid and tho' large in her Person, a general air of languor reigns throughout her exterior. We were invited to her [Miss Williams's] house the day after our introduction. Her family consists of an old Scotch, high-blooded lady, her Mother, two little nephews, their Father, a young Frenchmen. Mr. Stone is also their intimate; it was he who befriended Charlotte Corday on her tryal. He is an Englishman and one of the most sensible ones I ever saw. Their Hotel is in the midst of a delightful garden and we spend the evening in her Library, which was particulary corresponding with her style of society, the latter being compos'd of Senators, Members of the National Institute (in their blue embroider'd coats) and every one in the literary line.[55]

Although it seems surprising that Wilmot thought her hostess appeared languid amid the excitement of the crowded library and the beauty of the garden, it is possible that she was perceiving the strain that Williams was under during this period, as the latter explained in a letter to Penelope Pennington:

> the continual pressure of a mortal malady on my lungs, from which you may perhaps remember I suffered much even in the early days of our acquaintance, but which, increased and irritated by all I have suffered, and above all by the last and the most evil of my sorrows, the loss of my beloved sister, my poor Cecilia!, is leading me irrevocably to the tomb.[56]

The mourning clothes that so intrigued Wilmot, which Williams wore out of respect for Cecilia, were in keeping with the "extreme simplicity"[57] of dress that Williams chose for herself. Not only her private sorrows, and her Protestant upbringing, but also her disillusionment with Napoleon made her sober appearance seem like a statement of resistance to the vanities of the world—and of the Consular (and subsequently the Imperial) period.

Despite the strain she was under, Williams hosted a successful salon. The regular presence of Members of the National Institute and the Tribunate was a sign of Williams's secure place in French liberal and intellectual circles. Moreover, as Catherine Wilmot was quick to observe, it also showed how her soirées differed from those of others. A party given by General Berthier with "the most brilliant displays of light, luxury, and attire that human vanity could contrive," contrasted the intellectual "brilliancy" of Williams's salon.[58] Among the people that Williams's guests were most eager to meet were the renowned liberal politicians Henri Grégoire, Lazare Carnot, and Thaddeus Kosciuszko. Wilmot was thrilled to see the "famous Polish General, Kosciuszko," and her comments are typical of many of Williams's guests: "We have been introduced to the Abbé Grégoire and have met him two or three times at Miss Williams' " and "The other night at Miss Williams' we were introduced to Carnot. I was very much pleased at seeing a man of such celebrity."[59] The most famous woman in Paris was Madame de Staël, and it is not known if she ever visited Williams's home, but Catherine Wilmot did see them both at a party in January 1802, given by William Loughton Smith, an American diplomat.[60] This is important because, although Staël and Williams had many mutual friends, this is the only record that actually places them together in the same room. We can assume that they met that night at Smith's, if on no other occasions before Staël's exile in 1802, or after her return to Paris in 1817.

One might well wonder how Williams could afford to host such a large salon. In June 1802 her financial state was so comfortable that she could move from the apartments that Catherine Wilmot had described in January, to a home on the elegant Quai Malaquai in the faubourg Saint-Germain. Her friend Joel Barlow reported to his wife Ruth that he returned from a visit to London to find that "Helen is moved onto the Quay Malaquai."[61] One visitor Bertie Greatheed asked in his diary: "where are the resources to have so good a house?"[62] For those who knew them well, their prosperity was no mystery. John Hurford Stone, now a permanent member of Williams's family, was an adventurous entrepreneur, and in a letter written many years later, Williams told her friend Penelope Pennington that, around 1801, a high-ranking friend advised her and Stone on a business investment that secured them a fortune:

> our oldest *french* friend, having obtained one of the highest stations in the government, offered us an easy and honourable means of acquiring a considerable fortune, which he gave in common to Mr. Stone, and myself—an ample fortune was soon obtained, and as we believed, secure beyond the powers of chance—it became necessary and for many reasons, even obligatory, to change in some respects our mode of living—I had always seen the best society of Paris, and no stranger of distinction from any country came without being introduced to me—but my increased fortune enabled me, (as it usually does) to render my house still more agreeable—we had a fine Hotel at Paris, a delicious country house in the english taste, carriages, and all the elegancies of life.[63]

The friend whom she refers to was probably Antoine Français de Nantes (1756–1836), a brilliant financier and public administrator who served in many important government posts throughout his long career.[64]

One of her visitors from England in 1802, was William Shepherd, a Presbyterian minister and former student of Andrew Kippis. He remarked not only on the number of famous people he met, but also on Williams's gift as a hostess to make all of her guests feel welcome:

> Here we found a numerous assemblage of natives of various parts of Europe, some French gentlemen, members of the legislative body—the ex-director Carnot—a Neapolitan Principessa—a Bishop of the same country—a Polish countess—the ci-devant viceroy of Sardinia—several English gentlemen—and though last, not least, General Kosciusko. This party was soon divided into various groups, each of which was engaged in its peculiar subject of conversation. I could not but admire the judicious politeness with which our hostess equally distributed her attentions among her numerous guests.[65]

Shepherd, who published this account in a travel book after a second visit to France in 1814, was quite moved by the fact that Williams treated him so kindly, when she could have devoted her attention to her more renowned friends. Another of her guests who was more accustomed to cosmopolitan literary society was Caroline von Wolzogen (1763–1847), herself a published author and German salonnière. In the 1780s, Wolzogen had contributed to Sophie von La Roche's pioneering journal, *Pomona for the Daughters of Germany*, the first of its kind in that country. Wolzogen published a novel in 1798 and later wrote a biography of her famous brother-in-law, Friedrich von Schiller.[66] She described her 1802 visit to Williams in a letter to her sister Charlotte von Schiller:

> A pleasant society is here, in which you may meet all the important faces of several countries, viz. at the house of a political and literary lady, Miss Williams. She is very pleasant (*artig*) and polite, and receives every second night.[67]

It is a useful gauge of Williams's international reputation to see that she won the approval of another woman of letters. Finding her hostess "pleasant and polite," Wolzogen respected her as a "political and literary lady."

Williams's close friends the American couple Joel and Ruth Barlow also left a record of Williams's salon since Joel wrote regularly to his wife while she was convalescing in Vosges in the summer of 1802. After a party on 7 July, Barlow informed Ruth, "I was at Helen's last night; I believe she has a party almost every night—30, or 40, or 50, chiefly

English. There have been a good many lords and sirs among them."[68] Barlow joked with his wife about being exasperated by the crowds at Williams's "great parties": "It is quite stifling. English lords & ladies, Italian princes & duchesses brought together to inhale each other's exhalations & judge of the state of each other's lungs by a free exchange of gasses, compliments & politics."[69] Despite the off-putting crowds, Williams's home was on the "must-see" list for many travellers.[70] Thomas Poole left this record of his visit in August 1802:

> I have been three times to Helen Marie Williams's *conversations*. You meet here a very interesting society. Many of the *literati*. A poet and a poetess recited some verses about to be published. I met here Lord Holland, the American and Swiss Ambassadors, Carnot, etc. etc.[71]

When Caroline von Wolzogen went to see Williams again in September she wrote, "At Miss Williams', I saw the other day a crowd of politically remarkable persons, Fox, Kosciusko, La Harpe, Carnot, a very pleasant English lady (a pupil of Mrs. Wolstoncraft), and Lord Holland."[72] One writer who did not attend her *conversazione* was Maria Edgeworth, known for her conservatism: "Miss Williams we did not chuse to go to see though many English do. She is not in any of the societies we are in but sees a vast deal of company. My father I believe will pay her a visit just before we go and he will do the same by Mme de Genlis for similar reasons."[73] Whether for her politics or her association with Stone, Edgeworth did not think it was proper to visit Williams. Even Charles James Fox had been advised not to attend Williams's soirées, but he did go, and was given a place of honor.[74] On 6 October 1802, Joseph Farington noted that her decidedly liberal guest list included the great Whig lawyer Thomas Erskine, who had defended Stone's brother in 1796, and the Irish radicals Arthur O'Connor and Edward Blaquiere: "went to Miss Williams Conversazione. There we saw Erskine, — La Harpe, — Mackintosh & his wife, — Greathead, — Arthur O'Connor, — Joel Barlow, — Stone, — Coll. Blaquiere, Son of Lord Blaquiere, — Mrs. Cosway &c."[75] The British writer Amelia Opie and her husband and their friend Maria Cosway (who drew the frontispiece for Williams's *Poems*, 1786) were frequent guests. Opie's biographer described Williams as the "republican hostess" whose "salon was noted in Paris, especially among the French liberals."[76] When she had to return to London in October 1802, Opie said that " 'Paris has not disappointed me. The society I leave with regret; but chiefly I regret General Kosciuszko and Miss Williams.' "[77]

At this point in time, expressing admiration for Kosciuszko, whom so many visitors were keen to meet, could sometimes be construed as a political statement in itself since he was out of favour with Bonaparte.[78] Williams's friendship with the Polish hero was a sign of her own political allegiances. She often served as an intermediary for those who wished to meet Kosciuszko. In the following letter, she extends such an invitation to Lord Holland:

> Helen Maria Williams presents her Compliments to Lord Holland — General Kosciusko [sic], who now inhabits a little retreat near Paris, regrets extremely having been prevented coming on the evening when Lord Holland did her that honour — may she venture under the auspices of Kosciusko, to request his Lordship will confer on her the favor of repeating his visit on Wednesday evening next, when Kosciusko will come to Paris on purpose to meet him, between eight and nine — Lord Holland will easily believe that H. M. Williams considers the visits of so distinguished a friend of liberty as himself, as some compensation for what she has sacrificed, and suffered in its defence. — [79]

Lord Holland accepted Williams's invitation and visited her salon several times, where he did, in fact, meet Kosciuszko. The last part of the invitation is especially interesting because Williams not only describes Holland as a "distinguished" "friend of liberty," but, using the third-person, she also presents herself as someone who has undergone sacrifices and suffering in its defence. She is asking Lord Holland to recognize her as a friend of liberty, just as Kosciuszko obviously has. Nonetheless, whatever interests they may have had in common, Holland was not persuaded by Kosciuszko or anyone else to change his mind about Bonaparte; instead, he and his circle became the chief British apologists for Napoleon.[80]

The exciting social life of Paris in 1802 was inevitably affected by the political tensions and difficulties that marked this period of short-lived peace. In September 1802, the British painter Joseph Farington recorded in his voluminous diary important information about Williams's family and the political nature of her salon. He is the only visitor to have recorded a conversation he had with Williams's half-sister Persis, who, though not the "star" of the family, still had stories to tell about life in Paris during the Revolution:

> Garvey & Opie came to us. At 9 o'clock I went with the latter, Fuseli and Moore to Miss Helen Maria Williams, where we found about 50 people. Among them Lady Mount-Cashell, — The Abbe Gregoire, West & his Son, — Joel Barlow, — Stone, Boddington, — Gerard the Historical painter, Mrs. Opie &c&c. Mrs. [Persis] Williams, sister to Miss H. M. Williams by a former wife, told me the French dress had been changed since the days of terror: *then* every one studied to appear as mean and careless as possible, the

men dirty and unshaved. When that wore of a plain dress was continued and was now the fashion after the manner of the English. — She said that the state of apprehension they were constantly in during the days of terror could scarcely be described. The most guarded expressions only were uttered even before near friends and before servants, an indiscreet word having often proved fatal.[81]

The atmosphere of suspicion during the Reign of Terror that Persis Williams describes was not unlike that which developed as relations between France and England continued to deteriorate, and as Bonaparte's actions became increasingly troubling to liberal observers.

In April 1802, Bonaparte dissolved the Tribunate, a move which most historians have interpreted as an attempt to do away with the intellectuals and republicans "who stood in his way,"[82] replacing them with new and more "docile" members.[83] Williams's friends Thiessé (as mentioned earlier), Pierre Louis Ginguené and Jean-Baptiste Say were among the ideologues whom Napoleon forced out of the Tribunate. A month after this political purge, Bonaparte reintroduced slavery in the colonies on 20 May 1802, an act which Joel Barlow regarded with disbelief: "No legislative body till the tenth year of the French Republic has outraged human nature so far as to make a law to establish it [slavery]."[84] Bonaparte's assumption of the title of First Consul for life on 2 August 1802 further alienated former supporters. Thomas Poole had remarked on meeting Carnot at Williams's: "Carnot was one of the two who lately had courage to oppose in the Senate Buonaparte's being consul for life."[85] Simon Bainbridge points out that by the time Bonaparte was made First Consul for life in August 1802, many of his British enthusiasts, including Coleridge, Southey, Wordsworth, and Landor had given him up, and their response is perhaps best expressed by Coleridge who described his experience as "the having hoped proudly of an individual and the having been miserably disappointed."[86]

By late 1802, neither Stone nor Williams were favourites of Bonaparte. As early as 17 January 1800 he had shut down "sixty of the seventy-three political journals in Paris" ostensibly to counter royalist opposition to the coup of Brumaire.[87] He soon developed a system of police supervision of the press and censorship of the theatres.[88] Bonaparte was once quoted as saying, "if the press is not bridled, I shall not remain three days in power."[89] He even wanted to extend his control over British papers, objecting to unflattering references to himself and offering bribes to British editors.[90] Not only did Bonaparte have English papers translated for him, but he actually wrote numerous articles for the official French paper, *Le Moniteur*.[91] It was sometime during 1801 that Williams began, in her words, to see Bonaparte for what he

really was (*Souvenirs* 137), and when she indirectly struck out at Napoleon in print, his response showed her the dangers of tangoing with
such a man. The incident was a decisive moment in her relationship to
Napoleon, and she recounts it in three different books, her *Narrative*
(1815; 193–95), her *Poems* (1823; xii–xii) and her memoirs (*Souvenirs*
1827; 137–51), from which we can gather the following outline. When
she wrote her "Ode to Peace," published in the *Morning Chronicle* on 17
November 1801, to celebrate the preliminary treaty between France
and Britain (signed in October), Williams deliberately omitted any reference to Bonaparte, in order to test his vanity. This resulted in a public
dispute between Williams and Napoleon because the Ode infuriated
him, and several months later he had her house searched and Williams
and her mother imprisoned for 24 hours.[92]

The incident reminds one of Madame de Staël's account of how
Bonaparte reacted when she refused to pay tribute to him in her books:

> Bonaparte wanted me to praise him in my writings. It is not that one more
> eulogy would have been noticed in the fumes of incense surrounding him.
> But he was annoyed that I was the only well-known French writer to pub-
> lish during his reign without making the least mention of his stupendous
> existence.[93]

Staël was later expelled from France, a fate that Williams was spared,
perhaps because she was less of a threat to Bonaparte.[94] When one
examines Williams's "Ode to Peace," it seems likely that Bonaparte was
looking for a personal compliment in the poem because he could hardly
have been dissatisfied with it otherwise, since it presents France in a
favourable light, viewing the peace as a symbol of the world's acceptance of the rightful existence of the French Republic. While Williams
pays tribute to Britain her "parental Isle," she also criticizes its "mis-
guided efforts" in having tried to deny France its liberty (*Poems* 1823,
142). This is in contrast to the poet laureate Henry James Pye's "Ode
for the New Year, 1802," also printed in the *Morning Chronicle*. Pye's
poem, with the "Olive Bough" entwined around Britannia's "Monarch's brow," is a model of patriotic rhetoric, depicting England as the
avenger of worldly wrongs against "the Gallic Conqueror's pride" and
"fierce ambition."[95] On the other hand, Williams's ode ultimately oper-
ates outside the conventions of patriotic verse, since her position is
defined neither by French nor British interests; rather—in accordance
with her earlier statements at the commencement of the French Revolution—she situates herself as a citizen of the world, concluding her poem
with three stanzas urging all nations to advance towards a "New Age"
of "Liberty and Light" (*Poems* 1823, 144).

Williams felt that the controversy surrounding the "Ode" proved her point about Napoleon's character by revealing the extent of his vanity and by exhibiting his control over the press:

> The only memorable circumstance in the history of this Ode, is its having incurred the displeasure of Buonaparte: he found it in a corner of the Morning Chronicle, and it was translated into French by his order. He pretended to be highly irritated at the expression "encircled by thy subject-waves," applied to England, and which he said was treasonable towards France; but what he really resented was, that his name was not once pronounced in the Ode. However singular it may seem that he should have paid the slightest attention to such a circumstance, it is nevertheless true. The ambitious find time for every thing, and while they appear to be wholly absorbed by great objects, never lose sight of the most minute if connected with their own egotism. (*Poems* 1823, xii–xiii)

In her multiple accounts of the event, she uses the word "triumph" more than once, representing herself as a type of military victor who "came out triumphant" from the ordeal (*Souvenirs* 149; *Narrative* 195). At one point, the police visited her "apartment several times" and "forgot nothing. They examined all my papers, and even the toys of my nephews, and took me and my mother, who was old and ill, to the Prefecture" (*Souvenirs* 149). Williams found the police unduly suspicious, and their actions were a reflection of Bonaparte's excessive concern for his public persona:

> Bonaparte had a great anxiety not only to spread his name throughout the world, but to learn what the world said of him, particularly the English. He did not understand English, but he had a board of translation, and was regularly served each morning with the daily London papers done into French. . . . In one of these surveys my name fell under his notice, prefixed to a few verses I had written on the peace at Amiens. He inquired why they were not translated? The translator, with whom I was acquainted, answered that this had been omitted in conformity to his orders to translate nothing of literature or poetry in which his name was not mentioned. But could this be possible? An Ode on Peace, without any mention of the Great Pacificator, — Le Grand Pacificateur! — words which now resounded throughout all France; words that were engraved on marble in palaces and stuck up below his bust, placed as a sign-post at the door of every hedge-alehouse on the highway.[96]

While Williams was severely critical of Bonaparte's newfound ostentation, he was still a hero in the eyes of the world at large and praised by many in the same rapturous terms that Williams had used in her *Sketches* of 1801.

The summer of 1802 brought thousands of visitors to Paris, many of whom hoped to catch a glimpse of Bonaparte. But as the year came to an end, France was increasingly becoming a police state, with a rise in police surveillance, the suspension of the jury system in some places, and the increase of Napoleon's personal legislative powers. The diary of the British artist, Bertie Greatheed, senior, a friend of Williams who resided in Paris in 1803, provides invaluable information about the general atmosphere of tension in Paris during this period.[97] Greatheed regularly spent time at Williams's home, which Bonaparte had placed under surveillance by late 1802: "The house it seems is hated and every thing done there known to the first Consul."[98] In his diary entry for 1 February, he writes: "we all went to Helen Maria Williams, where there generally are interesting characters, but the house is almost taboo, in consequence of its republicanism, and we are told the government keep an exact watch over all who frequent it."[99] Greatheed also reported that he and his wife were afraid of being spied upon by Bonaparte's men: "As for Nancy I never saw her alarmed at government before, she is afraid of every word she says being reported, but I myself scarcely think it safe to write down these observations."[100]

Soon Greatheed had come to loathe Bonaparte's despotic policies: "this war will be for liberty, or rather against the universal despotism of one man, and the consequent slavery of Europe."[101] Upon the resumption of war between France and England on 18 May 1803, Greatheed went to get a passport to leave the country and was shocked to be told he was a "Prisoner of War."[102] He went to Williams for help, but it was not until five months later on 5 October 1803 that the Greatheeds received their passports.[103] The family was lucky to leave; other British visitors in Paris were conveyed to prison towns, as a result of a general order to detain British men between the ages of 18 and 60.[104] Bonaparte had told Cambacérès in July 1803 that there were too many English in Paris and they should be removed.[105] Williams's friend James Forbes was briefly a "detenu" at Verdun, though conditions were quite comfortable for "travelling gentlemen" of means.[106] For some reason, John Hurford Stone was not subject to this rule, probably because of his significant property and business interests in Paris, as well as his connections to many officials still in high-ranking positions. However, around the time that war between Britain and France was renewed, Williams found herself again in trouble with Napoleon.

In April 1803, her newest work, an edition of *The Political and Confidential Correspondence of Lewis the Sixteenth*, brought her to Napoleon's notice when one of his police officers reported that the correspondence might promote royalist interests, since it portrayed Louis XVI in a favourable light. As it turned out, the edition proved to be nothing but trouble for Williams, pleasing neither Bonapartists nor Royalists. It was confiscated by the authorities for two months in 1803 and then pirated in 1804 (Woodward 167). Worse still, it became the occasion for a book-length attack on Williams, by the royalist A. F. Bertrand de Moleville. His *Refutation of the Libel on the Memory of the Late King of France, published by Helen Maria Williams* complains of her "revolutionary delirium" and describes her as "a woman whose wretched pen has been long accumulating on itself disgrace after disgrace by writings of a similar nature."[107] Worst of all, several years later it was discovered that Williams had been duped by the people who sold her the letters. The *Correspondence* was found to have been forged by the people who sold it to her, even though she had been assured that it was authentic.[108]

The initial confiscation of the work in 1803 came at a time when Bonaparte had already begun to establish various forms of censorship, which would become entrenched by the end of the decade.[109] In a letter to Regnier, the Minister of Justice, dated 7 July 1803, Bonaparte cited Williams's edition as an example of the type of "dangerous work" that demonstrated the need for state censorship.[110] In July 1803 the entire edition was seized, which represented a considerable amount of money to Williams. She immediately wrote letters to the judge in charge of the case, and her influential friend Antoine Français de Nantes did the same on her behalf. Lionel Woodward has reprinted some of these documents, including several of Williams's letters to the judge, in which she actually flatters Napoleon, calling him a great man and a genius, which, considering her antipathy towards him, illustrates how desperate she must have been to get the books back (Woodward 153–68). At this point, too, she would have known about the difficulties of Madame de Staël, an even more famous woman of letters than herself, who by the fall of 1803 had been forced into exile. Known for his antipathy to intellectual women, Napoleon once remarked that women "may dance and amuse themselves, but they shall not thrust their noses into politics."[111] Although Williams's ingratiating appeal for the release of her book was successful (the books were released on 29 August—Woodward 163), she now realized Napoleon was too formidable an antagonist, and for the next ten years, she virtually stopped publishing—until after the Battle of Waterloo.[112]

Having to relinquish her career when she was an established writer in her forties, was a very heavy price for her to pay for residence in France. Bonaparte's control over the press and restrictions on freedom of speech were widely denounced in England. Few have disputed Herbert Richardson's statement that "under the regime of Napoleon the liberty of the press was practically extinct."[113] Napoleon attempted to "suppress hostile criticism"[114] of his government and to "use the press as an arm of foreign policy."[115] Nonetheless, Napoleon did have considerable support in France itself. Martyn Lyons points out that the influence of the ideologues was limited, and there had been little opposition to the restructuring of the Tribunate and Senate.[116] Many people in France were content with the "domestic stability and international prestige" that Bonaparte brought them.[117] Albert Leon Guérard, analyzing Napoleon's popular appeal, describes a French population who were flattered by his victories and "cared little whether Benjamin Constant were free to deliver speeches that they would never hear, or Madame de Staël free to write books that they (o fortunas nimium) would never read."[118] The title of Pieter Geyl's *Napoleon: For and Against* illustrates how opinion continues to be divided.[119] Even during the Napoleonic wars, Bonaparte had his defenders in England, though they were in the minority. In 1810, Anne Plumptre openly defended Bonaparte against a myriad of charges that had been laid against him in the British press. Her book, *A Narrative of A Three Year's Residence in France*, was based on her travels in France from 1802 to 1805, mostly in the southern region. Though she spent eight months in Paris and may have visited Williams, their points of view were antithetical, since Plumptre disputed the claim that Bonaparte had suppressed freedom of speech.[120]

What censorship meant for Helen Maria Williams was that she could not write about the changes in European politics and society as they occurred; instead her remarks published after 1815 reflect perceptions shaped by Napoleon's entire reign. When she was finally free to publish again in 1815, she explained the reasons for her silence and described the psychological effects of the repression she endured:

> I have been often asked by my countrymen of late, why I have so long discontinued to describe the scenes which are passing around me? . . . But the iron hand of despotism has weighed upon my soul, and subdued all intellectual energy. The Chevalier de Boufflers used to call Bonaparte 'le cochemare de l'univers,' the night-mare of the world; and indeed the idea of the consequences with which those were menaced who ventured to collect forbidden materials for history, was sufficient to chill this sort of courage. (*Narrative* 3)

The "iron hand" was a common metaphor to describe Bonaparte's reign. It was so often used that Anne Plumptre mocked those who complained of Bonaparte's *"iron* sceptre."[121] But Williams shows how the policies of censorship affected her and others, subduing "all intellectual energy" and chilling their courage. Rather than indulging in self-pity over this forced interruption of her literary career, however, she sees herself as part of a larger oppressed community.

Her position as an established observer of the political scene is evident in her post-Napoleonic writing, which, attentive to the practical effects of Napoleon's policies, is distinguished by its tone of composure, for unlike other commentators, she neither lionizes Napoleon nor demonizes him, despite her anti-Bonapartism. In her political *Letters* of 1819, where she expresses hope for the administration of the moderate Louis XVIII, she deals at some length with the Napoleonic legacy, granting the importance of some of the achievements of the Napoleonic Code and the Concordat, but otherwise portraying Napoleon as a military despot, beloved only by his army. Nonetheless, she may have been remembering some of her own earlier attraction to him when she admits that his appearance as a general on the battlefield cast a spell over all those who saw him (*Restoration* 128).

Ironically, her relationship with Napoleon did not end even after his death in 1821, because he lashed out at her from the pages of the popular memoirs of Barry O'Meara, entitled *Napoleon in Exile; or a Voice from St. Helena* (1822). According to O'Meara, Napoleon had read Williams's *Narrative of the Events Which Have Taken Place in France*, which was translated into French in 1816,[122] and he was furious that she accused him of wearing a steel-plated vest and helmet to protect himself.[123] Williams defended the veracity of her statements in the Preface to her book of *Poems* in 1823, where she also informed readers of her concerns about the growth of a posthumous cult of Napoleon, warning that pity for his misfortunes on St. Helena should not make one forget his abuse of power (*Poems* 1823, xiii). She looked back to the glory days of the Brumarian Bonaparte and admitted again that she too was once a devotee, that there was a time "when I offered incense at his shrine, when I never pronounced his name without emotion . . . [but] he was not then an Emperor" and "his imperial purple at length cured my enthusiasm" (*Poems* 1823, xli–xlii). Williams cautions her readers that an emotional response to Napoleon must be tempered by a rational understanding of the political implications and practical effects of his government. This was something that she understood only too well, as one of many writers forced into silence during his reign.

6

Venerable Woman of Letters

DESPITE THE DIFFICULTIES SHE ENCOUNTERED UNDER THE NAPOLE-
onic regime, Williams maintained a distinguished place in the literary
circles of Paris. The French dramatist Jean-François Ducis (1733–
1816), who met her in 1805, said "She is a person of infinite grace,
spirit, and talent" (Woodward 170). Charles Pougens, who recalled her
with affection in his memoirs, arranged for the publication of a French
edition of her poems in 1808, translated by "two celebrated" poets,
Marquis Stanislas-Jean Boufflers (1738–1815), a longtime friend of
Williams's, and Joseph-Alphonse Esménard (1767–1811).[1] The selection did not include any overtly political poems, but consisted mainly of
works in the more Romantic style, such as her sonnets from *Paul and
Virginia* and her two poems on the Alps. The one original English work
that Williams published during this period was a short poem in 1809 to
her two nephews—a topic that government censors could not object to.[2]
It was only after the Restoration that Williams built what was, in effect,
a second literary career, publishing after 1814 several books on politics,
a volume of poetry, and a number of important works of translations.
By the time English visitors were allowed back to France, her home
was once again a meeting place for an international group of writers,
artists, politicians, and intellectuals. The Wordsworths were delighted
to meet her; Southey thanked her for writing "such interesting memoirs
of the most interesting times";[3] and, if one reviewer tried to discredit
her by calling her a "warm old female Whig," another wrote in praise
of "those liberal and patriotic feelings, for which the muse of Miss W.
has long been celebrated."[4] Although her family suffered financial
losses due to the commercial instability following the change in government, visitors still congregated at her home, where they met people like
the eminent scientist Alexander von Humboldt or the well-known Protestant Minister Paul Henri Marron. Williams's lifelong friendship with
Humboldt symbolizes the way that her public stature was still structured by political alliances, for Humboldt came to be regarded as the
most famous man in Europe after Napoleon, with whom he, like Williams, was out favor.

In 1810, Helen Maria Williams was asked to translate into English Alexander von Humboldt's important works on his expeditions to South America.[5] In a letter to Williams dated 10 May 1810, Humboldt conveyed his pleasure at being told by a mutual friend that she had begun her work on the translation. He stated that he knew enough of "the charm of the style of Miss Helena Williams to sense how her elo-quent pen" would add the right words in the translation to move the imagination of readers.[6] Humboldt's confidence in Williams's abilities was an auspicious beginning to their working relationship; they were well-matched, sharing similar political ideals and a wide-ranging intel-lectual curiosity. Williams had already demonstrated an interest in South America—with her early poem *Peru* (1784)—and an interest in scientific exploration, contributing her poem "The Morai" to Andrew Kippis's *Life of Captain Cook*. This last point is mentioned in her Preface to Humboldt's *Personal Narrative* as an explanation for her undertaking this work:

> The narratives of travellers, and, above all, the description of those remote countries of the globe, which have immortalized the name of Cook, have always had a particular attraction for my mind; and led me in my early youth, to weave an humble chaplet for the brow of that great navigator, which my venerable friend, Doctor Kippis, inserted in the history of his life.[7]

One of Humboldt's favourite novels was the work Williams had trans-lated into English, J. H. Bernardin de Saint-Pierre's *Paul and Virginia*, which Humboldt is said to have read out loud to Aimé Bonpland when they travelled in South America.[8] Although they did not know each other during the period of the French Revolution, both Williams and Humboldt were in Paris to celebrate the Festival of the Federation in July 1790.[9] A progressive liberal, Humboldt, who believed in "slow reform under a monarchy," had been grateful to the King of Spain for giving him permission to travel to Spanish America and conduct scien-tific research, but that did not prevent him from denouncing the Span-ish slave trade and from later supporting the independence movement of Simon Bolívar.[10] Humboldt's political views meant that he was regarded with suspicion by Napoleon, who tried to force him to leave Paris in 1810. Fortunately, Humboldt had friends in high places who helped him, just as Williams's friends did when she came into conflict with Napoleon in 1802–03.[11]

Williams translated into English two of Humboldt's major works, the shorter *Researches* (1814) and the seven-volume *Personal Narrative* (1814–29), both of which were based on Humboldt's and Aimé Bon-pland's five-year trip to South America from 1799 to 1804. Humboldt had returned to Paris in 1807, where he worked on writing and publishing his scientific findings, a process that continued over a period of 27 years (until 1834), and which resulted in some 30 volumes of scientific and travel writing published in French.[12] The one-volume *Researches* was published simultaneously in French and German, and consisted of miscellaneous essays on Mexico and Peru.[13] With its "essays on pre-Spanish antiquities and American Indian cultures," Helmut de Terra explains, it "acquainted Europe with the cultural achievements of ancient America."[14] While *Researches* was historical in focus, the *Personal Narrative* described contemporary culture, introducing readers to the customs, geography, and botany of Mexico and South America, while also providing an interesting travel narrative. Comprised of several volumes, the *Personal Narrative* was published in French as *Relation Historique* in three instalments in 1814, 1819, and 1825; Williams's English translation appeared from 1814 to 1829. Both *Researches* and *Personal Narrative* were important books that established Humboldt's scientific reputation. As Malcolm Nicolson explains, by the 1820s, Humboldt "had become arguably the most famous natural scientist in the world," inspiring his contemporaries and the next generation of scientists, the most important of whom was Charles Darwin.[15] Reading the *Personal Narrative* was a pivotal moment in Darwin's life, for it inspired his desire to travel and to become a scientist like Humboldt, as he explained in this letter: "All the while I am writing now my head is running abut the Tropics: in the morning I go and gaze at Palm trees in the hot-house and come home and read Humboldt: my enthusiasm is so great that I cannot hardly sit still on my chair."[16] It was Helen Maria Williams's translation that Charles Darwin read.

Humboldt had been very pleased with her translation, remarking in one letter that "I cannot find the words that could express strongly enough the admiration with which I read these new sheets."[17] Still, because of the length of the work, the task of writing and translating it was arduous for both Humboldt and Williams. In 1812, at a relatively early stage in the process, Humboldt expressed his own weariness about the task: "I am still working on that interminable journey and it bores me terribly."[18] Williams, equally weary of it by 1817, wrote to her friend Penelope Pennington:

at present I have only one moment in which to tell you that I am half dead with a colossal literary and scientific task—the translation of a part of M. de Humboldt's great Work—of which also I shall talk to you in detail—I am from that spirit of procrastination which prevails in our nature, already too late—I must labour without ceasing a month longer, and shall then repose myself.[19]

The "labour" was also done out of financial necessity since Williams now needed the source of income, having lost most of her fortune in financial reverses after the Restoration of 1815.

She was not wholly satisfied with the remunerative terms given by Longman, Humboldt's British publisher. Apparently, Humboldt himself had made the arrangements with Longman during a trip to London to visit his brother, Wilhelm von Humboldt. Williams wrote to Robinson on 25 March 1819 that "the only thing in heaven or earth that M. Humboldt does *not* understand, is business."[20] But she couldn't blame Humboldt because "he had given me a great proof of his devotedness in 'binding his loins to such a feat', he had done his best, and therefore I acquiesced in conditions with which I was little satisfied."[21] Williams's affection for Humboldt is clearly evident here in her willingness to agree to his less than efficient business decisions. It was out of friendship for him that she had agreed in 1817 to translate into English the short sentimental tale *The Leper of the City of Aoste*, written by Xavier de Maistre, the brother of Joseph de Maistre.[22] Her last volume of poetry *Poems on Various Occasions* (1823) contains a poem in honor of Humboldt, "To the Baron de Humboldt, on His Bringing Me Some Flowers in March" (255). Their friendship and working relationship continued to the end of Williams's life: he left Paris to reside in Berlin in early 1827, and Williams died in December of that year. Humboldt, who lived till 1859, continued to write to Williams's nephews, Athanase and Charles Coquerel.[23]

Along with the ongoing "noble task" of translating Humboldt, Williams produced several original works during this later period—*A Narrative of the Events Which Have Taken Place in France from the Landing of Napoleon Bonaparte on the 1st of March, 1815, till the Restoration of Louis XVIII* (1815); *On the Late Persecution of the Protestants in the South of France* (1816); *Letters on the Events Which Have Passed in France Since the Restoration in 1815* (1819); *Poems on Various Subjects* (1823); and *Souvenirs de la révolution française* (1827)—all of which deal with contemporary European politics, either at length or in part, as in the case of *Poems* (1823). Since the *Letters from France* had been widely read in England as a guide to the French Revolution, there was a good deal of expectation regarding Williams's book on Napoleon. Even though it had been 14 years since she last published an original work in England, she had not been forgotten. Once again respected as an "eye-witness of all that passed,"[24] she garnered favourable reviews that matched those of the 1780s and 1790s:

> our expectations had been highly raised by the promise of a work on a subject of such universal interest, from the pen of a writer so eminently quali-

fied by every circumstance of talent, experience, and local information, to do justice to the theme, and they have been amply realised.[25]

Even the Tory *Quarterly Review* was generous, preferring her book from among several reviewed together: "Of these, decidedly, the best is that of Miss Helen Maria Williams, which, though its style is occasionally affected, is written with accuracy, with a free and, we had almost said, an impartial spirit."[26] The *Narrative* was a success, and a new portrait of Williams was published in London in February 1816.

In the heady days of the victory of Waterloo, it would not have been difficult to find readers for an anti-Bonapartist account of the Hundred Days, the period from March to June 1815, when Napoleon briefly returned to power. With connections to people at all levels of military, governmental, and artistic circles, Williams was, as one reviewer noted above, "eminently qualified" to narrate these events and the subsequent triumph of the Allied powers. The book did not cover the Battle of Waterloo since accounts of it were already plentiful in the British press, but it did touch on the controversial subject of the removal of art works from French museums. Above all, readers had a voracious appetite for information about Bonaparte, and the pages of Williams's book were full of anecdotes that demonstrated his character. Though she at first regarded him as a hero, she explained that the "rapid successive grada-tions to the consulate for life [1802], and thence to the imperial purple [1804], dispelled all illusion" (*Narrative* 8). She compares his female supporters to the "tricoteuses de la guillotine" of former days, and insists that women's popular infatuation with Bonaparte was no more (*Narrative* 35–36; 44).

It was conscription, Williams argued, that turned the women of France against him. In terms reminiscent of the tableaux of sensibility from her earlier work, she shows how domesticity and motherhood united all women, from high to low, even the lower class Dames des Halles: "the women of this class also were wives and mothers" (*Narra-tive* 48), and they too were tired of endless wars. Williams included her-self among these women since she worried about the possible conscription of her two nephews. In fact, she presents herself not only as an observer of the political scene, but also as a mother, the adopted mother of the two children of her deceased sister Cecilia:

> You know that I have adopted since their infancy my two nephews, the chil-
> dren of my only sister: you have not forgotten Cecilia, who in dying left
> them to my care. I have educated and loved them, —not with what is called
> instinctive fondness, which perhaps is an illusion, but with the steadfast
> affection of long habit, which binds us by such endearing ties to the objects

we have reared and cherished. If there is something more tender in nature than the sentiment I feel for them, they know it not; for they can recollect no mother but myself, and therefore they reward my cares with all the feelings of filial attachment. My nephews then are unto me as children. (*Narrative* 45–46)

Her assumption of the conventionally feminine role of devoted sister and aunt forced her readers to see her in a new light, and this contributed to the ethical appeal of the book.

The ease with which Williams could tolerate if not welcome the royalist fervor, demonstrated by women singing Royalist songs, or the sight of "fresh-blown lilies twined round every hat" (*Narrative* 47; 163), surprised some of her readers who thought she had become an apostate to the revolutionary cause. But this was not the case. Her account is anti-Bonapartist and favorable to Louis XVIII, not because she had become a royalist, but because he seemed the best alternative after Napoleon. In fact, she insists that "The spirit of constitutional representation is abroad, and will walk the world" (*Narrative* 207). She explicitly rejects "the ultra-royalists" who are "more royalist than the king, and who wish to bring back France to its state previous to the revolution" (*Narrative* 250). The *Narrative* ends with an eloquent plea for a changed political scene where liberty can flourish in peace:

> Upon the whole, let us hope that the political convulsions which have devastated Europe will be succeeded by the blessedness of tranquillity; and that moderation, magnanimity, and, above all, the long profaned but ever-sacred name of liberty will become the order of the day of the nineteenth century. (*Narrative* 254–55)

Weary herself of the "political convulsions," Williams dreamed of a change, not only in France, but in her personal circumstances. Her own mother had died in 1812 and was buried in Père Lachaise cemetery: "that spot where my mother is buried is encircled with Scotch firs, that seem to blend the associations of country with the sorrows of affection" (*Restoration* 24). In 1816, she wrote to Penelope Pennington about her mother's death: "I lost my poor mother four years ago—she died like an angel, fully prepared for a better existence, and enjoying all her faculties to the last moment."[27] When Williams visited the camp of English soldiers in 1815, she felt nostalgic for her own country, pleased to hear her native language and moved by a funeral service for a Scottish soldier: "After a long lapse of time passed in a foreign country, who can hear unmoved a religious ceremony performed in that language in which the first prayer of childhood had been uttered" (*Narrative* 219). In these later years, she did consider visiting England with her nephews, and wrote in 1816 to Penelope Pennington that, "I should like to shew them one day the country of their mother—my poor Cecilia."[28] Though she later abandoned the idea, such a journey seemed possible with so many English visitors in Paris.

The transition in government was not all good, however: many businesses were adversely affected, including the china factory and the publishing company run by John Hurford Stone and Marie-Martin-Athanase Coquerel (Woodward 171–72). Coquerel retired in Normandy, and Williams even contemplated migrating to America. In a letter to her friend Ruth Barlow dated 16 June 1815, she spoke wistfully about retiring to a cottage in America with her nephews:

> We more than most others have been the victims of the great political convulsions which have shaken Europe—the splendid enterprize of Humboldt's works, and the elegant manufactory of painted ware, have alike suffered a temporary, but cruel suspension, amidst those mighty dispersions so hostile to all commercial speculations. Peace alone can renew our affairs, and restore our prosperity—how often have I wished for the wings of a bird, to have taken flight towards your favoured shores, at such a happy distance from European commotions—if the American Government would endow me, & my nephews with a cottage on the bank of one of your majestic rivers, thither would I hasten, and pass my days in composing orisons in praise of liberty—but such happiness belongs to the dreams of fancy![29]

Williams shows a longing in this letter for a pastoral life, living in a cottage on a river, composing poetry. Even as she articulated her dream, she knew it was unlikely. She remained in Paris, where she continued to be involved in the causes and the controversies of her day.

Williams's political writing during this period focused on the safeguarding and entrenchment of human rights, especially in the areas of religious freedom and government representation. In the wake of the White Terror of 1815, she wrote a short polemical book (62 pages) entitled *On the Late Persecution of the Protestants in the South of France* (1816). Like the *Narrative* published the previous year, this book continued the type of up-to-date reporting that Williams became famous for years earlier with her *Letters from France*, *Tour in Switzerland*, and *Sketches*. Yet, because of the importance of her work on the French Revolution, critics have minimized if not altogether ignored her contribution to the writing of Protestant history.

On the Late Persecution, written in the form of a long letter dated 10 February 1816, is a report on the violent uprisings against Protestants that occurred in the south of France in 1815. A long-standing member of the Protestant community in Paris, Williams was committed to protecting the newly-won rights of Protestants which were under threat during the period of instability following the transition of power after Waterloo. This book includes a brief historical account of the process by which French Protestants gained their rights under the law, and an analysis of the uprisings of 1815. Although the intervention of the English government and the restored French monarchy suppressed the White Terror, Williams warns of the dangers of a return to what she calls Catholic "fanaticism."[30] and makes it clear that she will be there to record vigilantly any further outrages against the Protestant community, acting as its able and vocal defender. Her own involvement in that community meant that Williams had access to its oral history: "How often have I heard my friends relate the trials and dangers of their fathers! They had often heard the story of the hair-breathed escapes of their parents from Catholic fury, when they assembled in caves, and desarts, to celebrate divine worship" (*Persecution* 19). As her history approaches more recent events, Williams acknowledges the importance of Napoleon's Concordat of 1804 for solidifying the rights of French Protestants, and Bonaparte's fall meant the loss of certain legal protections.[31]

Williams's account of the White Terror provides the emotional center of her short history, and recalls the impassioned tones of her second series of *Letters from France*: "A fanatical multitude, breathing traditionary hatred, was let loose: the cry of 'Down with the Hugonists!' resounded through the streets. Massacre and pillage prevailed" (*Persecution* 46). A selection of vivid details demonstrates to readers how much this persecution seemed at odds with the orderly practice of religion that people had come to expect in the "modern" world of 1815: "the temples of the Protestants were broken open, and every thing contained in them—the registers, psalm-books, the gowns of the ministers, were torn into shreds—and burnt"(*Persecution* 51). These violent images recall not only the plight of the French Huguenots but also instances of religious persecution in British history. The days of shredding and burning "registers, psalm-books, the gowns of the ministers" were supposed to have been over.

Williams highlights one particularly notorious episode when a mob attacked a congregation during a church service. Here again she uses first-hand information, because she knows the minister involved, Monsieur Juillera and his wife,[32] who gave her a minute-by-minute account:

"I held my little girl in my hand," writes Madame Juillera, the wife of the minister, a woman of a superior mind, and with whom I am personally acquainted: "I held my little girl in my hand, and approached the foot of the pulpit,—my husband rejoined us,—I thought of my nursing boy, whom I had left at home, and should embrace no more! I recollected that this day was the anniversary of my marriage—I believed that I was going to die, with my husband and my daughter." (*Persecution* 49)

This heart-rending and suspenseful testimony creates some of the same persuasive content as Williams's stories of families perishing on the scaffold in her *Letters from France*.

Williams's concentration on an emotional narrative over a more objective history was a necessary part of her rhetorical strategy in order to gain the sympathy of her British readers. In her conclusion, she uses both ethical and emotional appeals in a tribute to Britain, which she celebrates as the greatest nation in the world:

> The period was now arrived, when England fixed her stedfast eye on the Protestants of the South of France. The story of their persecution has reached her ear. The feeling of their wrongs had penetrated her heart. Indignation beat high in every British bosom. . . . Favoured and glorious England! How poor are the trophies of other nations compared with those which encircle her brows! She has ever the pre-eminence in all the counsels of philanthropy; the arbitress of moral action—the guardian of the wronged, whatever region they inhabit, with whatever colour they may be tinged. While England exists, justice will never want a sanctuary, nor the oppressed a refuge. (*Persecution* 55–56)

While this passage has the rhetorical function of showing good will to her British readers, some of whom may have accused her of disloyalty for moving to France, one also senses Williams's love for her former homeland. This panegyric perhaps contains something of her unspoken loss, even though she never expressed regret for coming to France. In fact, in 1817 she and John Hurford Stone applied for and were granted French citizenship.[33] This was a practical step, considering that they were unlikely to leave the country now that Stone's health was failing and Williams's nephews were completing their education.

Despite her reduced circumstances, visitors to Paris continued to seek Williams out.[34] In 1816, the Irish author Lady Morgan (1776–1859), who had read the *Letters from France* in her youth, enjoyed meeting one of her "great bluestocking idols."[35] She was struck by how serious Williams's salon was, finding it composed of "a sober and learned" gathering, where, even the servant "looked as wise and literary as the rest of the party."[36] When Morgan mentioned she had made the ball gown they were complimenting her on (she was on her way to another party), "all the serious ladies in their black bonnets exclaimed their amazement that a 'femme savant' could sew!"[37] Morgan wrote a bestselling book on her visit to France and remarked upon the "many ladies of distinguished literary merit" whom she met: "The celebrated

Helen Marie Williams has long been a resident in Paris, surrounded by a large circle of distinguished friends, who meet every Sunday evening at her hotel."[38] Williams's other guests during this period included Robert Southey (now British Poet Laureate), the Swiss politician Philippe-Albert Stapfer, and the American George Ticknor, who left the following account:

> [1817] May 2—This evening I have passed, as I do most of my Sunday evenings, very pleasantly, at Helen Maria Williams's. The company generally consists of literary Englishmen, with several Frenchmen, well known in the world—such as Marron the preacher, whom Bonaparte liked so much, Stapfer the Swiss minister, who concluded the treaty of 1802, several professors of the College de France, etc.[39]

Ticknor also mentions seeing Mary Jane Godwin at Williams's soirées in 1817. Though she is usually known only as William Godwin's second wife—the successor to Mary Wollstonecraft—Mary Jane Godwin was also a woman of letters. She and Godwin published children's books and ran a bookstore called M. J. Godwin and Company.[40] Although she was not liked by her famous step-daughter, Mary Shelley, Williams's nephews (the Coquerel boys) adored her and looked forward to her visits.[41] When she was in London, Mary Jane Godwin attended to some publishing matters for Williams, who appreciated being able to talk to her about the practical details of the literary life. Williams remarked in a letter that they were "both women of business without alas, much of the happy leisure we deserve."[42]

By the end of 1817, Williams had a "sad chapter" of her "domestic history" to relate to Mary Jane Godwin: John Hurford Stone's health was in serious decline, and he had been confined to his room since September.[43] Williams and her older half-sister Persis spent all of their time tending to him and saw very little company, as she told Mrs. Godwin, "I now only receive two or three friends who take a quiet dish of tea with me as you used to do so kindly."[44] Stone's health continued to deteriorate, and he died on 22 May 1818. He was buried in Père Lachaise, as Williams's mother had been, and as Williams herself would be, all three next to each other. Engraved on his tombstone were the words (in French) an "enlightened champion of Religion and Liberty."[45] Especially interesting is the way the inscription concludes with a personal comment identifying Williams, in a public acknowledgement of their close relationship: "Last Tribute to a Long Friendship. H. M. W."[46] In the following letter, Williams conveyed the news of Stone's death to an old friend, the Reverend William Shepherd, a Presbyterian minister:

> I am suffering a deep affliction—Mr. Stone, whom you no doubt remember, expired a month ago, after a long and lingering decay—altho' prepared for

this cruel event, I find it difficult indeed to console myself for the loss of a
friend of twenty five years, who had passed thro' all the storms of the revolution with me and my family, and to whom I was attached by a sacred sentiment, a tie which death only could dissolve—since this event took place, my
door has been shut to all the world—but I shall try to find courage next
week to see not what is called company, but one or two friends.[47]

Williams describes John Hurford Stone as a "friend of twenty-five
years." She stresses his bond to her entire family, but also speaks of
being attached to him by "a sacred sentiment, a tie which death only
could dissolve." Whatever the nature of their relationship, this last
phrase tell us unequivocally of her love for him.

After Stone passed away, Williams was left to manage on her own,
though her nephews continued to help her. In a letter dated 26 June
1819, she said that she lived in a small apartment with her half-sister
Persis and her nephew Charles Coquerel, while her eldest nephew
Athanase worked as a Protestant minister in Amsterdam.[48] That same
year she had a case before the courts to try to recover some of the
investments she had lost.[49] In the meantime, she attempted to make
some money with the publication of another book on French politics,
but British publishers initially showed no interest. On 25 March 1819,
Williams wrote to Henry Crabb Robinson to ask for his help in secur-
ing a publisher, and it was through his kind offices that the book finally
appeared in print. One of the problems that Williams faced was that
"everyone in England was tired of works on France" (Woodward 185).
However, in the wake of the White Terror, there was an interest in the
situation of French Protestants, though not all of it sympathetic. Robinson had informed Williams of a book by Reverend Thomas Raffles, *Letters During a Tour Through Some Parts of France* published in 1818, in
which Raffles claimed that not a single pious family could be found
among the members of the Oratoire in Paris (Woodward 187), and that
the Protestant clergy spent their evenings playing cards.[50] Williams not
only felt a responsibility to counter Raffles's scathing portraits, but
Robinson had already advised her to lengthen her book. She recognized
that a supplemental letter on the Protestant situation would provide
added interest and "it will be more *piquant* in England than further
political observations"[51]: "some english gentlemen have since told me
that not only Mr Raffles, but other persons, had attacked the French
Protestants, so I thought I could do nothing better than write a little
defence of them, supported by a variety of facts."[52]

Williams still derived confidence from the fact that her residence in
Paris gave her work an authenticity that other commentators could not
claim:

I replied perhaps a little haughtily that the English reader might be permitted to be tired of books published by travellers who, after having spent a fortnight in Paris, hastened to write their adventures, but that the public in England had accustomed me to a favourable hearing, because they knew that my long residence in this country, my situation, and connections, qualified me to give them real information.[53]

Robinson had to edit the manuscript quite heavily due to gallicisms in the style of Williams and her nephew Charles Coquerel who assisted her.[54] After unsuccessfully making the rounds of several publishing houses, and consulting William Godwin and others, he became very concerned on Williams's behalf: "I called on [John James] Masquerier; he too has been troubled by Miss Williams's affairs; he has had to speak with booksellers and he fears her necessities are great. She has sold all her property, he says. If so, and she be now in want, what must her future state be?"[55] It was a relief for all concerned when Baldwin accepted the book, but, unfortunately, it made no profits, even though it came out in a second edition.[56] Williams was surprised by this, as she told Robinson, because "accustomed from the age of seventeen when I began to scribble, to receive some pecuniary contribution, it seems strange to me to receive nothing for this autumn composition."[57]

Though it may not have been a best-seller, her full-length book on the Bourbon Restoration, entitled *Letters on the Events Which Have Passed in France Since the Restoration in 1815* (1819), was important enough to warrant translation into French.[58] Although continuing to support Louis XVIII, whom she describes as a philosopher-King and defender of liberty (*Restoration* 181), Williams admits to being very discouraged by the prominence of the ultra-royalists, whom she views as aiming to crush "the revolutionary principles of equal rights, independence, [and] tolerance" (*Restoration* 5). One can feel her weariness when she remarks: "I have been silent only because I have been discouraged, for the interval has been crowded with events" (*Restoration* 3). With an experienced eye, she reflected back on what the French legislature used to be like some 30 years ago, having occasionally observed its sessions and having had many friends who were members of the various legislative bodies over the years (*Restoration* 64). After Bonaparte's "imperial despotism" she welcomed a return to representative government, while cautioning that "National representation is making rapid progress in France, but has not yet reached maturity" (*Restoration* 64). Her awareness of party politics recalls her accounts of the differences between the Girondin and the Mountain in her *Letters from France*: "The Chamber of Deputies is composed of parties professing the most opposite opinions; it may be divided into four classes, under the denomination of the

Ultras, the *Centre*, the *Doctrinaires*, and "though last, not least," the *Liber-aux*, or *Independans*" (*Restoration* 67). With her own political affiliations still left of centre, she noted that the "*coté gauche*, composed of the *Liber-aux* or *Independans*, forms the van-guard of French liberty," and she was concerned about attempts to weaken their influence (*Restoration* 69; 179).

In most cases, Williams's analysis of Restoration France was based on how it compared positively or negatively to life under the previous governments. Censorship policies, for instance, were slightly improved from what they were under Bonaparte, but the loss of the Concordat represented a step backward, and she regarded its removal as "perhaps the greatest blunder that has been committed by the French govern-ment since the restoration" (*Restoration* 100). This change allowed for the promotion of the interest of the ultras because, as Adrien Dansette explains, although the Charter of 1814 permitted freedom of worship, it also proclaimed Catholicism as the state religion.[59] Continuing the vigilance she showed in her 1816 book on the White Terror, Williams's concern about how the rights of Protestants will be affected by this change and by a rise in Catholic activism is reflected in Letter Two on the "Persecution of the Protestants," Letter Eleven on the "Bible Soci-ety," and Letter Thirteen on "Catholic Processions." As a Dissenter, Williams viewed the Catholic revivalist missions as attempts to control people through the spread of superstition and fanaticism (*Restoration* 116). It was a period when "zealots" burned copies of Voltaire, and Catholic processions became occasions for "anti-Protestant riots."[60] Concerned about the return of religious intolerance, Williams con-cludes her book with a supplementary letter entitled "Defense of the French Protestants," which attempts to construct a positive public image of Protestants as pious and disciplined Christians.

The writing of this supplementary letter and the book itself when she was nearly 60 years old indicates Williams's commitment to making what contribution she could to the support of social and political change. Perhaps in 1790 she may have envisioned herself enjoying her old age in leisure rather than continuing to fight for the liberty the French Revolution had promised. But 1819 was a period still "crowded with events" that required her vigilant observation (*Restoration* 3). It was not to be expected that a woman so involved with the politics of the Revolution would retire from the public scene when political mat-ters were once again the main topic of conversation:

Such is the present avidity for political intelligence, that Paris is filled with reading-rooms, which are crowded from morning till night, with old and young, all alike eager to seize upon some new pamphlet, and obtain information of what is passing. At the *Athenée*, a long established literary institution, nothing attracts so brilliant a crowd of both sexes as the discussion of some political question by M. Benjamin Constant. (*Restoration* 108)

Despite the unsettling early years of the Bourbon Restoration, Williams hoped that people like Benjamin Constant would carry forward the ideals of the revolutionary years.

This was a time when leftists sided with the King and "the government of the Duke de Richelieu," in opposition to the powerful Ultras, organized by the King's brother, the Count d'Artois,[61] and so Williams's support of Louis XVIII marked a continuation of her leftist politics. As mentioned earlier, others misunderstood her vocal support of the King as a renunciation of her political ideals. One reviewer wrote "This warm old female Whig, however, transformed into a sort of nondescript between a Revolutionist and a Bourbonist, reprobates Bonaparte, and rejoices in the return of Louis XVIII."[62] As she explained in 1819, "I disavow your ill-founded conjectures respecting my prolonged silence: the interest I once took in the French Revolution is not chilled" (*Restoration* 1). Williams was not repudiating her support of the Revolution; rather, she was looking for the continuation of the story that had begun in 1789. When Williams wrote that "Every eye is fixed on the Charter" (*Restoration* 181), she was articulating a cherished view among those on the left that the Charter held the key to their rights. Benjamin Constant, in the election years of 1828–29, was quoted as saying in a speech in Strasbourg, "La Charte, rien que la Charte, et toute la Charte."[63]

Williams set her hopes on the legal entrenchment of rights and freedoms. She regarded the achievement in France of a nationally representative government—even as a constitutional monarchy rather than a Republic—as one of the proudest legacies of the French Revolution. As might be expected, however, she was ridiculed for her optimism by her longtime adversary the *British Critic*. While some critics attempted to find evidence of changes in her views, the *British Critic* mocked her for the persistence of her liberal politics:

And indeed it is truly edifying to observe the undiminished interest which this profound lady still takes in the welfare of all the nations of the earth; how she detests cruelty and injustice (the case of the *ex-nobles* always excepted)—how she adores the sacred cause of 'civil and religious liberty all over the world'—how she warms up at the very mention of virtue. On any of these subjects, she obviously can hardly write without the tears streaming down her cheeks; notes of admiration conclude every sentence; Oh!'s, and Ah!'s choke her utterance before she can begin them.[64]

Conservative reviews like the *British Critic* and *Anti-Jacobin* had long been attacking sensibility as synonymous with the anarchy of Jacobinism.[65] Janet Todd notes that in the long period of war between France and England from the 1790s to 1815, sensibility was viewed with alarm. The climate of national insularity also produced a retreat from the international outlook that Williams represented.[66] By 1819, the popularity of sensibility had long since subsided, and because of Williams's reputation as a writer of sensibility, the reviewer in the *British Critic* used it as the basis for his ridicule. Her emotions, the "tears streaming down her face," were equated with "womanly weakness," or an emblem of liberalism that emasculates male liberals as well. If anything, the *British Critic* treated Williams more viciously in 1819 than it had before, comparing "her" "Jacobinism" to "a leprosy in the understanding, for which there is no cure."[67] In contrast, one finds a more measured comment in the *Monthly Magazine*, which, although disagreeing with her on several points, begins its review with the statement that "Miss Williams is one of the most eloquent writers of her time."[68]

Williams's next original publication after the *Letters* of 1819 was not another prose work on politics, but a book of poetry. With *Poems on Various Subjects* (1823), Williams reclaimed her identity as poet, 41 years after the appearance of her first poem *Edwin and Eltruda* (1782). She included in the book many pieces from the 1780s so that it functioned as a collected poetic works, preserving for posterity the earlier poems that were out of print. While the collection recalls Williams's initial popularity as a poet in the 1780s and 1790s, its inclusion of poems addressed to friends and members of her family written during the Napoleonic and post-Napoleonic decades offers a valuable context for understanding her later years, a period of her life about which little is known.

In many ways, this book illustrates the different phases in Williams's literary career, a subject she reflects upon in her prefatory essay, where she explains that she gave up her poetry to write about the French Revolution: "I have long renounced any attempts in verse, confining my pen almost entirely to sketches of the events of the Revolution" (*Poems* 1823, ix). Once she began publishing her prose works on the French Revolution, she published little poetry except for the sonnets in her translation of *Paul and Virginia* and a few poems in her *Letters from France* and her *Tour in Switzerland*. In a letter of 1820, she acknowledged how much she missed spending time on her poetry:

> with how much pleasure I left politics, the laws of election, and the charter—to take care of themselves, while I was led by Mr. Wordsworth's soci-

ety to that world of poetical illusion, so full of charms, and from which I have been so long an exile.[69]

This is a significant comment because it reveals Williams's own awareness of what she had lost in giving up poetry for her political work. She expresses a wistful longing for the world of poetry but, at the same time, implies that it functions as an escape from reality—a "world of poetical illusion, so full of charms." Rather than enjoying that illusory world, she has been engaged with the real world of "politics, the laws of election, and the charter." Such a privileging of politics over art is perhaps indicative of just how much Williams was formed by the spirit of the age of enlightenment; for her, the praxis of government and the state took precedence over the pleasures of the imagination.

Equally significant is the fact that this comment was made in response to her meeting William Wordsworth. They had both been poets in the 1780s: she (his elder by nine years) was at the centre of London's literary circles, and he was an unknown schoolboy whose first published poem was in her honor. Wordsworth had tried to meet Williams on another trip to France in 1791 and was disappointed to have missed her. He was an avid reader of her poetry and her prose works, including *Letters from France*, which he borrowed from the Pinney family in 1795.[70] While Wordsworth also tried his hand at prose with his unpublished *Letter to the Bishop of Llandaff* (1793), and the short-lived journal *The Philanthropist*, he gave up any serious pursuits in that line and devoted himself to his poetic vocation; Williams, on the other hand, concentrated on political writing.

Because both were drawn into the worlds of poetry and politics in the 1790s, the shape of their careers illustrates the choices that each made about what direction their lives would take. Although their paths had intersected many times in the past, they only met for the first time in October 1820.[71] A letter by Dorothy Wordsworth reveals that they were delighted with each other's company: Williams "is a very sweet woman, and we were much pleased with our visit."[72] Since Wordsworth had been an ardent fan of Williams's work in his youth, his continuing admiration for her work—and now his enjoyment of her company— would have been a comfort to Williams, especially since she realized that her long absence from England meant that she could not expect to be well known there. Their conversation would have drifted back to the 1780s and 1790s, reminding her of those years when she was at the centre of London's literary circles. Moreover, the Wordsworths were still interested in her political writing, since Dorothy requested a copy of her *Letters on the Events Which Have Passed in France Since the Restoration in 1815* (1819).[73]

This late meeting with Wordsworth reveals other important facts about Williams's life during this period. Once she took up permanent residence in France, Williams found it difficult to keep up with the British literary world, particularly in the long years of Napoleon's reign. Lady Morgan explained that this was a problem for writers in both countries: "the little intercourse which necessarily subsisted between England and France, prior to the year 1814, has left the two countries reciprocally strangers to some of the most popular writers, in their respective languages."[74] In 1814, when visitors flooded to Paris, Williams was once again in contact with British writers. By this time Wordsworth was a poet of some repute, but when Henry Crabb Robinson first mentioned Wordsworth to her in 1814, she had never heard of him. All of this had changed by 1820; by then Crabb Robinson had sent her some of Wordsworth's poems and probably told her about Wordsworth's longtime respect for her own work.[75] Perhaps when they met Wordsworth even encouraged her to reissue the early works. He is mentioned in the *Poems* 1823, which seems a fitting culmination of the literary relationship that began when 36 years earlier he had published his first poem, "Sonnet on Seeing Miss Helen Maria Williams Weep at a Tale of Distress." In a note to her sonnet "To Hope," which was originally published in her novel *Julia* in 1790, Williams pays tribute to Wordsworth in a comment that also reveals the ways that their careers had intersected so many years ago, when she was the popular poet and he the unknown young man reading her work:

> I commence the Sonnets with that to Hope, from a predilection in its favour, for which I have a proud reason: it is that of Mr. Wordsworth, who lately honoured me with his visits while at Paris, having repeated it to me from memory, after a lapse of many years. (*Poems* 1823, 203, note)[76]

Wordsworth became for Williams a link to her past, which was especially important to her in these later years, as she reflected on the course of her own life and literary career.

Throughout the long years of the Napoleonic Wars (when Williams stopped publishing and lost touch with the literary scene in England), her own influence there obviously waned. She told Penelope Pennington in a letter dated 28 October 1822 that she had abandoned the idea of visiting England:

> tho' I am very earnestly solicited by some kind english to revisit my country, I feel that the visit would have more in it of sadness than joy—what a mutation in society across the long lapse of years—what a void should I feel in finding myself in England only amidst strangers.[77]

In the Preface to *Poems* (1823) she acknowledges that her "literary patrons belonged to 'the days of other years'" (xiv). Yet, she also told John Bowring, who along with Edward Blaquiere had arranged for the book of *Poems* to published by Whittaker, that people were continually asking her for copies of her poems, and so she hoped the collected edition might sell well.[78] For those readers in 1823 who did not remember her as "the lovely female bard" of the 1780s (as Anna Seward had called her then), they might at least have heard of her as a controversial political writer. Most of the reviews of her *Poems* treated her with the respect due to an elder writer. For instance, the *European Magazine* remarked on the beauty of her later prose compositions and "the dignity and consistency of her sentiments."[79] The *Monthly Review* commended "those liberal and patriotic feelings, for which the muse of Miss W. has long been celebrated,"[80] and paid tribute to her writings on the Revolution, even while acknowledging her work had caused controversy in the past:

> The name of Miss Williams has been so long and so frequently before the public, and her literary character, from its outset, has been so connected with some of the deepest and most pathetic feelings of human nature during revolutionary periods, that it cannot have been easily dismissed from general recollection. Her labours in the vast field of modern literature and research have, indeed, been equally various and persevering, occupying the whole of the present together with the latter part of the past century: her opinions have given rise to some discussion; and her political as well as literary views have subjected her to much periodical animadversion.[81]

The reviews of the *Poems* followed Williams's lead in using the occasion to look back upon her earlier career: "It is pleasurable to see the name of this lady again in print, as it recalls to our imagination the older times, when her talents were a passport for her into the society of Johnson."[82] Such a statement shows how Williams belonged to two different worlds: first, the world of Samuel Johnson's London; and, later, the very different world of post-Napoleonic Europe.

Since the *Poems* of 1823 act as a type of collected works, that nostalgia was both inevitable and desirable. In fact, Williams seeks to reassure her readers that they will discover the Williams of old—the poet—not the political writer. She explains to her readers that they will find only four poems that "have any reference to public events" (*Poems* 1823, x): the epic *Peru*, the poems on the slave trade and on the Bastille, and the "Ode" on the Peace of Amiens. Her brief remarks imply that readers might be wary of her book if it was too political. This book seeks to bring readers into the "world of poetical illusion" rather than the world of "politics, elections and the laws of the charter."[83] However, even many of the non-political poems demonstrate Williams's very political life because they include those written in honor of friends like Thomas Clarkson and Joel Barlow, who were associated with her favourite political causes.

Like the tributes to Andrew Kippis and John Moore published in her earlier years, these later poems to friends are constructed for public viewing, and, therefore, they reveal little private information, but they are affectionate in tone, often written for a particular reason, in thanks for a gift, to acknowledge a visit, or for a formal occasion.[84] As a group, the poems promote the causes championed by her friends by concentrating on how each contributed to the public good. By implication, they demonstrate Williams's own interest in the world of politics, arts, and sciences, and her ongoing status in distinguished circles. This is also true of one of Williams's last poems, an unpublished elegy written in 1824, a year after *Poems* appeared. It was in honor of her friend Abraham-Louis Bréguet (1747–1823), a Swiss inventor and watchmaker of Huguenot descent, who was a member of the Institute: "Lines written by Helen Maria Williams, on the funeral of M. Bréguet, member of the Institute of France, and the Bureau de longitude, in the Cimetiere de l'Est."[85]

The poem to Thomas Clarkson, "The Travellers in Haste," which also mentions Bréguet, was written in 1814. In it, Williams shows that Clarkson was so busy with his work against slavery that he had no time or inclination to visit the theatres and art galleries in Paris: "His embassy is from the slave, / His diplomatic skill to save" (*Poems* 1823, 260). Clarkson visited Williams regularly during his missions to Paris, and she knew his wife Catherine, herself an early supporter of the French Revolution, about whom she wrote, "it is impossible to know [her] a little, without wishing to know her more."[86] In 1814, conservative abolitionists like Wilberforce and the émigré Comte de St. Morys advised Clarkson not to mingle with any members of the former Amis des Noirs who were disparaged as revolutionaries, but Clarkson replied that he knew "but two classes of persons—the friends and the enemies of Africa. All the friends of Africa are my friends, whatever they may be besides."[87] Clarkson continued to work with the venerable Henri Grégoire.[88] A friend of Williams's for many years, Grégoire had been active in the Amis des Noirs in 1799, when it took the radical step of giving membership to women, and Williams herself was singled out for special recognition: "The society invited the wives of all of its members to join as well as the English poetess, Helene Williams."[89] In 1797, her Swedish abolitionist friend Charles Wadstrom (1746–99) had written to Grégoire about a soirée at Williams's, and in 1799 Williams wrote an obituary for Wadstrom, which was published in the *Decade*

Philosophique (the journal edited by her friends Jean-Baptist Say and Pierre-Louis Ginguené) and reprinted in England in the *Monthly Magazine* in 1799.[90]

In 1814, Williams helped Clarkson distribute his abolitionist pamphlet by sending copies to Frédéric César de La Harpe and to the Duke of Pampo Chiaro at Vienna (Woodward 180). In a letter dated 20 September 1815, Clarkson mentions having dinner with his 19-year old son at Williams's home, where his wife Catherine had forwarded a letter to him.[91] Later around 1820, Williams prepared notes for Clarkson on the notorious case of the French slave ship the Rodeur, which he used for his speech at the Congress of Verona in the fall of 1822, published as *Cries of Africa, to the Inhabitants of Europe; or a Survey of that Bloody Commerce called the Slave-Trade*.[92] The Rodeur, whose conditions were so poor that ophthalmia spread through the ship, blinding nearly all the slaves and crew, was also mentioned in a speech by Benjamin Constant who founded the new French abolitionist committee, Société de la Morale Chrétienne (1822).[93] Williams's nephew Charles Coquerel, who published a pamphlet on the slave trade in 1820, was an active member of the Société, which was dominated by Protestants.[94]

This collection of poetry also contains several family poems, revealing how Williams had taken on increasing domestic responsibilities after the death of her sister Cecilia in 1798. Then she had to juggle the demands of the literary world and child-rearing: as she explained in a letter to Penelope Pennington, she was busy with "the labours . . . of a literary occupation, the regulation of a large family, the care of my mother now feeble and infirm, [and] of my two infant nephews."[95] Mrs. Williams (who died in 1812) and Williams's half-sister Persis both assisted with the childcare, but Williams took on the role of second mother to Cecilia's children.

Because her private life is rarely mentioned in her work, these late poems addressed to her nephews and marking occasions in their lives, enable us to picture Williams in a different context from that of the salonnière. Even a poem on the death in 1815 of the family dog, Bibi, creates an image of Williams and her loved ones at home, "Lines on the Tomb of a Favourite Dog" (*Poems* 1823, 264).[96] In *Verses Addressed to My Two Nephews, on Saint Helen's Day, 1809*, written when Athanase would have been 14 and Charles 12, she marks the occasion of their school vacation with an earnest address: "Listen, dear Boys! nor take amiss / A lesson, with a parting kiss" (*Poems* 1823, 248). For a time, the boys were educated in Geneva, and then transferred in 1811 to the new Protestant academy in Montauban in the south of France.[97] In preparing the boys for the future, Williams asks them to use this one day a year—

Saint Helen's Day—to remember her, and to reflect seriously on their lives, putting aside "Pleasure" for "Reason" (249):

> When come the years—for come they must—
> When her ye love is laid in dust;
> Her who for you has learn'd to prove
> A mother's care—a mother's love!
> From you all ill has sought to chase,
> And fill a mother's vacant place:
> Still on this day, to duty true,
> Remember that she liv'd for you!
>
> (*Poems* 1823, 249)

Since there is little surviving material about Williams's domestic life, especially during the period under Napoleon, this poem is an important record of the nature and extent of her involvement with her nephews' upbringing. It is also significant that Williams published this poem in Paris in 1809. As the only work that she published for a 10-year period, it presents to the public a view of Helen Maria Williams not as the political writer that they were used to, but as a more conventional woman, spending her time raising two children, fulfilling the duty she owed to them, her deceased sister, and her family. In a letter to Charles Coquerel she wrote, "that you may become every year *wiser* and *better* is the most ardent prayer of your ever affectionate aunt" (1813; Woodward 176).

Williams was very proud of Athanase and Charles as they grew into manhood; and she would have been gratified to see that they remained loyal to her memory after her death. Charles, who helped her on her later publishing projects, became a journalist and Protestant historian and mentioned Williams with pride in his essay on "the school of women authors," in his book on the history of English literature (1828).[98] Athanase wrote the following tribute to her in a Preface to an English edition of his book *Christianity* (1847):

> I was brought up half an Englishman, the nephew and adopted son of one of the most remarkable female writers of modern times, who justly bears the title of *English Historian of the French Revolution*, whose works have been translated into all modern languages, and are even now often had recourse to by many authors of the present day. Her poems have been translated by the celebrated Chevalier de Boufders; she herself translated the Travels of the celebrated Humboldt, and remained to the last the friend of Clarkson and Wilberforce, of Southey, Wordsworth, and Rogers, of Mrs. Barbauld and Mrs. Opie—Helen Maria Williams. This eminent woman, whose pen was constantly devoted to the defence of liberty, and who was very near

losing her life in the cause, when imprisoned during the reign of Terror in the palace of the Luxembourg, with several deputies of the illustrious party of the Gironde, filled a mother's vacant place for my brother and myself, and brought us up.[99]

Describing himself as her "nephew and adopted son," Athanase regarded his aunt as "one of the most remarkable female writers of modern times." Writing in 1847, he seems to have had in mind the poem of 1809, since a phrase from the last sentence in this passage ("filled a mother's vacant place for my brother and myself") is nearly a direct quotation from the *Verses*: "And fill a mother's vacant place" (*Poems* 1823, 249). His own words stand as an affectionate response to her poem, some 40 years later.

The only other poem Williams is known to have published before her 1823 collection appeared was a present to Athanase to commemorate his wedding in 1819 to Nancy Rattier, a Swiss woman from Montauban: *The Charter; Addressed to My Nephew Athanase C. L. Coquerel, on his Wedding Day, 1819*.[100] Its first words describe Athanase as the "Child of my heart!" (266), who reminds her of his mother—her beloved sister Cecilia:

> My heart for thee has learn'd to prove
> The throbbings of a mother's love,
> Since on thy cradle fell the tear
> That mourn'd a sister's early bier;
> And sure that angel's sainted prayer
> Has shed sweet influence o'er my care.
>
> (*Poems* 1823, 267)

Williams suggests that the young couple look upon their marriage vows as a form of agreement like the French Charter. Since she was preoccupied with the subject of the Charter at this period, Athanase and others would have been amused to see her use this political analogy. Her advice seems especially aimed at ensuring a type of equality in the marriage, with Athanase not becoming a domineering husband (or "ultra") and with his bride not being a passive partner:

> Ah! may no *ultra* thirst of power
> Embitter life's domestic hour;
> No principles of feudal sway
> Teach without loving, to obey;
> The heart such joyless homage slights,
> And wedlock claims its Bill of Rights.
>
> (*Poems* 1823, 268)

The gently humorous references to ultras and the "Bill of Rights," result in a treatment of the subject of marriage in terms that seem appropriate for a political writer. Composing the poem when she was nearly 60, Williams concludes by reminding the young couple to value each other even in old age when beauty is gone, because the "compact" they have signed

> Includes wan age, with wrinkled brow,
> With tresses grey, with visage pale,
> And eyes whose liquid lustre fail;
> For then the hand, that shrivell'd thing,
> Shall still display the nuptial ring.
>
> (*Poems* 1823, 271)

Unfortunately, Nancy Coquerel died in 1825, but Williams wrote poems about two of Nancy's children, "Lines addressed to A. C." and "Lines to Helen, a new-born infant, 1821."[101] The latter piece on her namesake's fragile health (276) is especially poignant due to the baby's early death. Another girl born after the *Poems* appeared was her sister's namesake Cécile. She followed in her great-aunt's footsteps, by becoming an author, publishing poetry and children's stories, under her married name Cécile Gay and the pen-name Saygé.[102]

In her "Lines addressed to A. C." dated New Year's Day 1821, Williams refers to Athanase's first-born and namesake as the "heir of my maternal love" (*Poems* 1823, 273). Imagining the baby growing up to experience the adult world of cares, she hopes that he will have inner strength to sustain him, during the "weary wing" of time (274). Little did Williams know that her great-nephew would need these words of encouragement years later when he was a controversial Protestant minister in Paris. In the 1860s French Protestants became polarized between the evangelical majority and the liberal minority. Athanase Coquerel, Jr., was thought of as an extremist liberal, and the Council of Churches forbade him from preaching.[103] After his dismissal, he published several books in the 1860s, had a break-away congregation in Paris, and preached in England and the United States. He was known for his humanitarian work, organizing "societies for the relief of the poor, catechetical classes, libraries, lectures."[104]

Helen Maria Williams would have understood something of the life that her great-nephew had chosen, having herself paid a price for a very public career. The introductory essay included in *Poems* (1823) demonstrates that, the familial poems notwithstanding, Williams still remained an outspoken and ardent defender of liberty. The essay involved her in a contemporary controversy raised by a series of articles in the *Edin-*

burgh Review about the state of French science and literature—articles that were widely discussed because of their reactionary nature. In her essay, Williams, who had already written privately about these articles in a letter to Mary Jane Godwin dated 10 June 1821, takes issue with the derogatory comments about France made in a review of works by her friend Joseph Chenier, including *Tableau Historique de l'Etat et des Progrès de la Littérature Française* (1816).[105] Although she does not mention the reviewer's name, she may have eventually learned from Thomas Moore that the reviewer was Richard Chevenix (1774–1830), whom Moore knew. Insisting on the dearth of French achievements in arts and science since the Revolution, Chevenix contrasts this intellectual poverty with British achievements by listing hundreds of eminent British artists, scientists, and poets; charitable and religious societies for social reform; and scientific discoveries. Chevenix even lists forty British women writers—though Williams herself is not among them. In her letter to Mary Jane Godwin, Williams remarks that others "will perhaps think I am angry at being omitted on the list of *forty* female writers—but this would be an error—I am not surprized at the silent disdain of the E. Review. Those countrymen of mine [have] never spoilt me by the slightest mention either of my prose, or verse."[106] Williams adds that her compensation for such slights is that she has been praised in the past by men whom she respects like Sir James Mackintosh and William Godwin (Mary Jane's husband).

Constructing her own self-image as an experienced woman of letters who is above such matters, she concerns herself in the Preface with a more pressing issue, namely the anti-revolutionary point of view promoted by the articles. She interprets Chevenix's attack on the current state of science and literature in France as an attack on the French Revolution itself, and answers in kind by defending the Revolution. She refers to "the admirable philosophical discourses of M. Daunou on history, the brilliant memoirs of M. Le Montey, the transcendent genius of Madame de Stael" and the talents of several politicians, which are at least equal to those of their Ancien Régime counterparts who defended "a less noble cause" (*Poems* 1823, xvi). Williams looks towards the future and the new actors on the public stage, the men and the women carrying forward the legacy of the Revolution who—"belong to the new order of things" (xvi). Although a Centre-Left coalition had dominated France since the Restoration,[107] the Ultras had gained strength steadily, and liberals like Williams were increasingly concerned about the influence of the reactionary Count d'Artois (who would become King Charles X in 1824), especially after decisive electoral victories for the Ultras from 1820 to 1822.[108] Her nephew Charles Coquerel worked for Benjamin Constant's campaign against Charles X, *Aide-toi, le ciel d'aid-*

era.[109] Williams was upset that the *Edinburgh Review* would publish what Thomas Moore called "Chevenix's *ultra-ism*"[110] at a time when the right-wing parties were dominating in the French government: "and all this rancour is poured forth at the very moment when the civilized world should write against the league of barbarians — really those articles belonged of right to the Quarterly Review, and the E. Review has encroached on its property."[111]

If Chevenix's reviews were a boost for "the league of barbarians," Williams hoped that her own essay would speak out for the other side, both in defence of the Revolution and in support of its heirs, especially the liberal minority in the Chamber of Deputies (*Poems* 1823, xvii). Prior to publishing the book, in a letter to John Bowring dated 24 June 1822, she expressed her sense of urgency that the book appear soon, so the preface would still be current.[112] In responding to Chevenix's charges that the Revolution had a negative effect on the intellectual climate of France, Williams conceded that during decades of political upheaval, people living through the Revolution, Napoleon, and now the Restoration had "little leisure for letters and arts" unlike those living in countries with an "old settled" government (*Poems* 1823, xviii). Yet, many still sought consolation and comfort in books, "turning for a moment to Literature, from the turbulence of a world in commotion" (*Poems* 1823, xviii).

In an attempt to illustrate that French poetry has not suffered because of the Revolution, Williams cites several male and female poets from this period. A friend of P. D. E. Lebrun (1729–1807), she recounts his recitals in her salon, claiming that he "was a greater poet for having witnessed the Revolution" (*Poems* 1823, xxii). Even Jacques De Lille, an opponent of the Revolution, earned her respect for refusing, just as Jean-François Ducis had, Bonaparte's persistent offers of patronage. Williams also mentions three women in her list of nine talented French poets (Vigée, Tissot, Merville, Millvoye, Viennet, Madame de Salm, Madame Dufrénoy, Madame Babois, and Esmenard). Not only is their inclusion an important sign of Williams's knowledge of other literary women, but she draws further attention to their work, in a brief footnote: "Madame de Salm has written several didactic poems of great merit; she is eminently the poet of reason; Madame Dufrénoy has acquired great celebrity by some beautiful love elegies, and some philosophical essays in prose" (*Poems* 1823, xxxiii). Despite recent efforts in feminist literary history to rediscover early women writers, little attention has been paid to the writing of female poets in the early nineteenth century, with scholars concentrating instead on French women writers and activists in the period after the July Monarchy and the Revolution of 1848.[113] It will be useful, then, to review briefly some information about these three writers mentioned by Williams. Madame Marguerite-Victoire Babois (1760–1839) (the niece of Ducis) was a poet best known for her *Elégies et poésies diverses* (1810) on the death of her daughter and her *Elégies nationales* (1815) on the Restoration.[114] Adelaide Dufrénoy (1765–1825) was a poet and essayist, who had some friends in common with Williams in the early days of the Revolution, such as Chamfort, but later Dufrénoy became a member of Bonaparte's imperial court, accompanying Marie Louise to Cherbourg in 1813. Dufrénoy was one of the few women officially honored for her literary talent, receiving awards from the Institute in 1815 and the Academy of Cambrai in 1824.[115]

Williams's praise of Madame de Salm is especially important because Salm (1767–1845) was one of the most renowned female writers of the early nineteenth century. It is possible that Salm and Williams may have known each other since they were both associated with the journal *Decade Philosophique* in the 1790s and early 1800s, and Salm had republican sympathies, though according to Elizabeth Colwill, she only declared them publically later in life, after the July Revolution of 1830.[116] Salm took part in debates printed in the *Decade Philosphique* on the subject of women writers, defending "woman's right to education, intellectual autonomy, and a public voice."[117] In 1799, in a paper delivered at the Lyceum of Arts and published later as *Rapport sur un ouvrage intitulé "De la condition des femmes dans les républiques"*, Salm replied to Charles Théremin's book *De la condition des femmes dans les républiques*.[118] Williams, who became a friend of Théremin's, also took issue with some of his points in her book *Sketches* (1801), as we have seen.[119] Salm's poem in defence of women entitled *Epitre aux femmes* was much talked about when it appeared in 1797, and when reissued in 1811, it reignited debates about women writers.[120] During the period of the Napoleonic empire, Salm lived outside of Paris, but she continued to publish, and Colwill notes that "In an era and a milieu notoriously inhospitable to women of genius, her work, read in her absence, was applauded by thousands at the Parisian Athénées."[121] Despite personal tragedies, Salm regained her "beautiful literary crown,"[122] and in 1841 she published a work tracing her own life as a female author, her autobiographical poem *Mes Soixantes Ans*.

After Williams's *Poems* appeared in 1823, she began working on her own memoirs—her last book *Souvenirs de la révolution française* (1827). A fourth author portrait may have appeared around this time, and she told Samuel Rogers in 1825 that she would keep on writing as long as she could draw breath: "I am among the number of past things, but I can still hold my pen, and am scribbling a little sketch which will perhaps have some interest."[123] The book was primarily written in Amsterdam, where she and Persis went to stay with their nephew Athanase and his wife and children. Soon after their arrival, Persis Williams died on 23 December 1823, and in the letter to Samuel Rogers, Williams describes how much her older half-sister had meant to her:

> I lost not long since the last surviving member of my own family, Mrs. Persis Williams, the most virtuous character I ever met with, if virtue consists as I believe it does, in living only for others—she had always been to me a second mother—she was old, but I see no reason in that circumstance for regretting the objects of our affection less—we had passed life together, and had remembrances that were our own—I should now be quite alone in the world if my nephews did not still give interest to my life.[124]

Having lost Persis, John Hurford Stone, Mrs. Williams, and (much earlier) Cecilia, Williams was now the only member of her generation left in her family. She stayed with her nephew Athanase for more than two years. James Mackintosh visited her in Amsterdam in 1824, and she added to her literary associates the Dutch poet and translator of Homer, Jan van's Gravenweert (1790–1870).

Williams's last book on the French Revolution, though written by her in English, was only published in the French edition translated by her nephew Charles Coquerel. It appears that she had made plans to publish an English edition, since, in his introduction, Coquerel mentions that the book has not yet appeared in London (*Souvenirs* viii), but no English version has been discovered. *Souvenirs* was published in early 1827, and Williams sent a copy of it to Benjamin Constant with a letter dated 10 May 1827, in which she mentions that she has recently moved back to Paris from Amsterdam.[125] The book covers events in France from the beginning of the Revolution through the Napoleonic Empire, with a small section on the Restoration. Writing this book when she was in her 60s, Williams clearly saw it as her last opportunity to offer concluding comments on the Revolution and its aftermath. As we saw in the *Letters from France*, although Williams prided herself on being a "witness" to the Revolution and regarded her work as implicitly valuable because she described what "passed before [her] very eyes," she does not recount anecdotes that are especially personal in nature (*Souvenirs* 2; 1). Any references to herself concern her public role as a writer and salonnière; for instance, she wrote about what happened to her on 10 August 1792 only to counter misleading rumours about those incidents.

The period following the Bourbon Restoration saw the publication of a number of memoirs of the Revolution, but they were primarily written from the royalist point of view. In total over a thousand memoirs of the

French Revolution would be published from 1815 to 1914, of which about 80 were written by women.[126] Women's memoirs contained "pages of testimonial fixed determinedly on famous events and personages, and other pages devoted to aspects of their personal lives that have nothing to do with public history."[127] Marilyn Yalom notes that although women's memoirs described "famous events," they "were not given to political analysis," "with the notable exceptions of Mme de Staël and Mme Roland."[128] Staël's *Considerations of the Principal Events of the French Revolution* (1818), published the year after her death, has even been analyzed for its selective omission of the personal element,[129] while Roland's posthumous first-person political memoirs, *An Appeal to Impartial Posterity* (1795, 4 vols.), made her "the most celebrated memoirist of the French Revolution."[130]

Seeking to differentiate her book from the typical memoir, Williams explained to her readers that *Souvenirs* was more like a serious report than a memoir, and that, unlike others, she was not using it as an excuse to write about herself—"People might perhaps believe that I am only publishing this report of my opinions on the diverse events of the French Revolution as a pretext for giving my Memoirs, because of the current fashion for this type of work; but they would be sadly surprised" (*Souvenirs* 4). Sensationalist memoirs had little historical value: "The vulgar intrigues, the ordinary anecdotes of private life, can furnish only material for racy books, and France possesses more than one masterpiece in this genre" (*Souvenirs* 4–5). Williams disdained most memoirs for being too personal and amateurish, but she does refer favorably to the *Memoirs* of Madame de Larochejaquelein (1817; *Souvenirs* 89), prized for what Yalom calls its "exceptional literary and historical merit."[131]

Williams implies that the publication of a book promoting the cause of liberty was necessary to ensure that Royalist memoirs would not become the standard interpretations of the Revolution. While *Souvenirs* does cover some of the same ground as her earlier books, it also enables her to take a retrospective position, writing at a greater distance from the events, so that she can now analyze her own earlier reactions and try to explain the failures and the successes of the past. She admits to having been young and naive (*Souvenirs* 8), but that did not lessen her pride in her political commitment and particulary her attachment to the Girondins, whom Gary Kates has called "not only a political faction, but a circle of friends."[132] Their proscription was, for Williams, the decisive moment in the history of the Revolution for it precipitated the execution of so many of the people she knew. Now in her final book, she recalls them once again, and her anecdotes illustrate the climate of fear that shrouded the period of the Reign of Terror, when house searches and arbitrary seizures of papers were common (*Souvenirs* 55–60). Williams's family had to destroy many private papers in order to protect themselves from possible arrest, including manuscripts "of Madame Roland, letters of Lasource, and other *conspiratorial* correspondence" (*Souvenirs* 81). Papers belonging to Madame de Genlis also had to be burned, though Genlis, who had become a type of unofficial paid advisor to Bonaparte in 1800,[133] accused John Hurford Stone of deliberately failing to return materials that she had given him for safekeeping. Williams wrote a long defence of Stone in the *Souvenirs* (66–72), explaining that Mrs. Williams, fearing a house search in 1794, was forced to burn the manuscripts that Genlis's daughter had given Stone (*Souvenirs* 70). It was a complicated series of events that took place over 30 years before, but Williams was determined to counter what she regarded as Genlis's misrepresentation of Stone.

Williams knew this was her last time to correct any erroneous statements made about her friends or about the events that occurred during the revolutionary and Napoleonic periods. She was pleased with some of the histories that were being written, like that of Thiers (*Souvenirs* 50), but was concerned that historians like Mignet, who were too young to have seen the Revolution, were somewhat cold in their account of its events (*Souvenirs* 104). Williams took issue with Madame de Staël for her severe treatment of Pétion and Brissot in the *Considerations of the Principal Events of the French Revolution* (1818). Staël's friend Count Narbonne suffered a political defeat at the hands of the Girondins, and, according to Christopher Herold, "no love was lost," between Staël and Madame Roland.[134] Williams was a close friend of both Roland and Brissot, and she wrote of the latter, "I cannot stop myself from adding still one word in defence of another patriot, of whom Madame de Staël has said that his principles were no less dissolute than his style" (*Souvenirs* 21–22). Staël's portrait of Brissot would have especially bothered her since Williams had undertaken some responsibility for his posthumous reputation, having been asked by his widow to prepare an English edition of his memoirs, in order to raise money for their children (*Souvenirs* 22). Although she never completed the project, her nephews gave John Bowring the papers for it. The manuscript was a curious artifact, partly written on discarded pages from old editions "of Joseph Andrews, and upon the backs of certain decrees of the Revolutionary Government."[135] The odd union of a novel by Fielding and revolutionary papers seems symbolic of the way that Williams bridged the literary and political worlds of eighteenth-century England and France. Even though she identified with and admired Staël as a woman of letters, her personal and political loyalties were more important than any bond she might have felt with her on that account. With friends like Brissot, Pétion, and Roland, she had shared the most important years of her life.

Williams thrived among the Girondins because they encouraged the interest that she, as a woman—and a writer—took in the Revolution. In the following passage from *Souvenirs*, she preserves for her readers a moment from her own personal history, describing what she felt was an atmosphere of equality between men and women at the dinners which she regularly attended at the home of Pétion and his wife:

> The women appeared to forget the need to please, and the men thought little of admiring them. In their salon there were things better than gallantry. A mutual esteem, a common interest in the great questions of the day, was what appeared more important. We spoke of liberty in a tone profound and sincere, which even approached eloquence. (*Souvenirs* 19–20)

At these soirées, women were not expected to be pleasing little Sophies, à la Rousseau, but were free to discuss important issues. This expansion of gender roles is a subject she addresses elsewhere in *Souvenirs*, in the context of praising Madame Roland, "one of the first people she knew in France" (*Souvenirs* 73). Williams begins by describing the traditional roles of women:

> In general the duties and activities of women are enclosed in the walls of the home. We are allowed in effect permission to soften the cares and inquietude of human life . . . But women are not allowed to leave the restricted circle where men have confined them and intervene in the important questions or interests of human concern that they debate and decide upon. Women can without a doubt be moved by the sacred name of their country; but men have decided that they must not occupy themselves with its affairs. (*Souvenirs* 72)

This is a concise picture of women's subordination: traditionally, woman's place was in the home, where she was valued as a care-giver and nurturer; she was "allowed" to "soften" others' cares, but not to intervene in "important questions." Women lived in a state of passivity since their lives were shaped by the decisions made by the men who governed them. This patriarchal authority is illustrated in the choice of verbs used in this description, since it is men who "allow," "confine," and "decide." There could not be a clearer demarcation between male and female roles. According to Williams, Madame Roland proved things could be different:

> All of a sudden, breaking these chains, a woman with a male genius appeared in the world, declaring herself capable of patriotism, and capable of discussing the most important political questions. (*Souvenirs* 72)

The image of someone breaking out of the chains of custom—a forceful image in both revolutionary and abolitionist discourse—is used to show how a woman can challenge the limitations her society has imposed. Of all the women she would ever know, it was Madame Roland who epitomized for Williams the ability to take an active interest in the "important questions" of the day, without the loss of femininity. By describing her as having "a male genius," Williams probably meant that Roland was as intelligent as any of the eminent men in her circle. In the many years that followed her execution in 1793, the memory of Roland remained an inspiration and a source of strength for Williams.

Williams uses the final pages of this book to draw to a close the work that she began some 37 years earlier in 1790, with her first *Letters from France*. At the beginning of the *Souvenirs*, she repudiated those who accused her of vacillating in her political opinions, and she returns to this subject once again: "Before concluding these pages, may I be permitted to offer some personal comments and to repeat that I hope to have fully justified my opinions during the course of the revolution and to have shown that if the events themselves have changed, my feelings have not" (*Souvenirs* 198). Her commitment to the principles of liberty, she argues, was not subject to the winds of change but was a lifelong passion:

> Accustomed from my youth to place all of my hopes on the noble causes that embrace the broad interest of humanity, and having learned early that the word "tyranny" is synonymous with misery, I have always loved liberty with a sincere love. I hope that I have proven that my principles (and the political principles of a woman always derive from her feelings) have always been on the side of the oppressed. I could not rest an indifferent spectator of the events happening in front of me. It is not true that I have preached, turn by turn, as others say, the symbols of the terror, the imperial eagle and the white flag. I believe I have lived through the revolution with more constancy. Far from humbly acknowledging myself guilty of such a fault, I dare, on the contrary, to reclaim a part of the merit belonging to the friends of liberty, for having so long defended the cause. I have at least the good remembrance of having placed at their feet the small portion of talent and all the zeal that I could offer them; and maybe sometimes the voice of my heart is heard by the heart of those who read me, because a sincere conviction is not without some power. (*Souvenirs* 198–99)

Though referring modestly to her own talents as "small," Williams feels proud of having earned a place among the "friends of liberty," for "having so long defended the cause." Unlike the many Royalist accounts appearing after 1815, her *Souvenirs* revisit the tragedy and the sublimity of the Revolution from the point of view of one who still has a personal investment in its ideals.

In the concluding pages of her last book, Williams looks back on what, by any account, was a remarkable life and literary career. She reflects on her loyalties to France, where she has spent much of her adult life and where she hopes to find "a final resting place" (*Souvenirs* 201), and her loyalties to the country of her birth: "England, my native isle which will always be dear to me, and to which I am proud to belong" (*Souvenirs* 201). Williams had taken to heart Richard Price's injunction to be a citizen of the world, and her international outlook is exemplified in the conclusion of her book, where she looks for leadership among the statesmen of Europe and beyond, citing the courage of men as diverse as George Canning and Simon Bolívar (*Souvenirs* 195–96). Williams also comments briefly on the Greek struggle for independence from Turkish rule, having herself corresponded with several members of the London Greek Committee, including Edward Blaquiere. It is in keeping with her forward-looking perspective and her interest in the "important political questions" of the day (*Souvenirs* 72), that she should append to her memoirs a long poem on the recent fall of Missolonghi and the death of Lord Byron in 1824 (*Souvenirs* 208–12). Even in her elderly years, Williams responded vigilantly to "the cry of the people" (*Souvenirs* 197), and once again she assumed the role of the poet of sensibility, who observed with compassion that "Europe, Europe weeps" over "fetter'd Greece opprest!" (*Souvenirs* 203; 207). The Williams of 1827 is not very different from the Williams of the 1780s. Having lived under the threat of Robespierre, Bonaparte, and the Ultras, she still preserves her hopes for a better and more caring world. In this her denouement, Williams exhibits the grace and maturity that complete her portrait as an eighteenth-century woman of letters, "whose pen was constantly devoted to the defence of liberty."[136]

Notes

INTRODUCTION

1. Helen Maria Williams, *Souvenirs de la révolution française*, trans. Charles Coquerel (Paris: Dondey-Dupré, 1827), p. 198. Subsequent quotations from this work are cited parenthetically in the text. All translations from the French are my own.

2. Helen Maria Williams, letter to Samuel Rogers, 24 April 1825, in the Sharpe Papers, University College London. This material is published with the permission of the Library, University College London.

3. Helen Maria Williams, *Poems on Various Subjects* (London: Whittaker, 1823), p. x. Subsequent quotations from this work are cited parenthetically in the text.

4. Williams's works are included in anthologies such as *British Women Poets 1660–1800: An Anthology*, ed. Joyce Fullard (Troy: Whitson, 1990); *The Sublime: A Reader in British Eighteenth-Century Aesthetic Theory*, ed. Andrew Ashfield and Peter de Bolla (Cambridge: Cambridge University Press, 1996); *Romantic Women Poets: An Anthology*, ed. Duncan Wu (Oxford: Blackwell, 1997); and *Eighteenth-Century Poetry: An Annotated Anthology*, ed. David Fairer and Christine Gerrard (Oxford: Blackwell, 1999). Recent editions of Williams's work include: *Julia*, intro. Gina Luria (New York: Garland, 1974); *Letters from France*, eight volumes in two, intro. Janet Todd (Delmar: Scholars' Facsimiles & Reprints, 1975); *Letters written in France in the summer of 1790*, intro. Jonathan Wordsworth (Spelsbury: Woodstock, 1990); trans. *Paul and Virginia* by J. H. Bernardin de St-Pierre, intro. Jonathan Wordsworth (Spelsbury: Woodstock, 1990); *Poems* (Spelsbury: Woodstock, 1994); *Julia, A Novel*, ed. Peter Garside (London: Routledge/Thoemmes Press, 1995); *Helen Williams and the French Revolution*, ed. Jane Shuter, History Eyewitness Series (Austin: Raintree Steck-Vaughn, 1996); *An Eyewitness Account of the French Revolution*, ed. Jack Fruchtman, Jr. (New York: Peter Lang, 1997); *Letters Written in France in the Summer, 1790*, eds. Neil Fraistat and Susan Lanser (Peterborough: Broadview Press, 2001).

5. The *Letters from France* were published in individual volumes in 1790, 1792, 1793 (2), 1795 (3), and 1796, and later arranged into two series of *Letters from France*, each with four volumes. All references will be to the modern reprint *Letters from France*, eight volumes in two, intro. Janet Todd (Delmar: Scholars' Facsimiles & Reprints, 1975). The series number, volume number, and page number will be cited in the manner used for this first quotation (1.1.14). Subsequent quotations from this work are cited parenthetically in the text.

6. Helen Maria Williams, letter to Colonel Barry, 25 June 1790, quoted in Lionel Woodward, *Une anglaise amie de la révolution française: Hélène-Maria Williams et ses amis* (Paris: Librarie Ancienne Honoré Champion, 1930. Geneva: Slatkine Reprints, 1977), p. 32. Subsequent quotations from Woodward are cited parenthetically in the text. All translations from the French are my own.

7. Rev. of Williams's *Letters from France*, in *Critical Review* 14 (August 1795):361.

CHAPTER 1. THE POETRY OF SENSIBILITY

1. A number of sources enable one to determine that Helen Maria Williams was born on 17 June 1761 and died on 15 December 1827. Her naturalization papers from 1817 in the Archives Nationales in Paris (BB 11/ 125/1) give her date of birth as 17 June 1769. The year should read 1761, since that date corresponds to the notice of her death below.

> Mr. Charles Coquerel et Mr A.-L.-C. Coquerel, Pasteur de l'Église Réformée d'Amsterdam, ont l'honneur de vous faire part de la perte très douloureuse qu'ils ont éprouvée en la personne de Madame Héléna-Maria Williams, leur Tante, décédée en sa maison, rue Neuve-Ste-Eustache, No. 47, le 15 décembre 1827, âgée de 66 ans.
>
> Paris, le 16 décembre 1827

A copy of this announcement, sent out by her nephews the day after her death, is held in the Bodleian Library (ms. Montagu d. 19, ff. 185; Woodward, p. 196). Helen Maria Williams was buried at Père Lachaise cemetery in Paris at the following location: "la concession No. 965 P de 1827, située dans la 39ème division, 11ème ligne face à la 38ème division et 1ère tombe à partir de la 40ème division" (The Conservator, private correspondence, 28 May 1998). See also Woodward, p. 11. Her will is in the Archives de Paris, Cote D Q7 3549.

2. Persis Williams was born in Cork, Ireland, the daughter of Charles and Persis Williams. In her elderly years, she and Helen Maria Williams went to live with their nephew Athanase Coquerel in Amsterdam, where she died on 23 December 1823, around 80 years of age (record of the Municipal Archives, Amsterdam).

3. The record of the marriage of Charles Williams and Helen Hay can be found in the extracted records for St. Martin-in-the-Fields, Westminster, 1757–70, microfilm number 0561156, batch M001452, in the International Genealogical Index (I. G. I.), consulted at the Family History Centre, The Church of Jesus Christ of Latter-Day Saints, Dartmouth, Nova Scotia.

4. The christening record for Helen Hay, daughter of George Hay and Mary Balfour, 27 December 1730, Kilmany, Fife, Scotland, can be found in the extracted records from Kilmany, Fife, 1706–1821, microfilm number 1040165, batch C114372, in the International Genealogical Index, as cited above.

5. George Hay and Mary Balfour had their marriage registered in two parishes: 15 August 1713 in Errol, Perth, and 28 September, 1713, Kingsbarns, Fife. The record of their marriage can be found in the CD-Rom Records for the International Genealogical Index, as cited above.

6. For information about David Hay, see Woodward, p. 12. David Hay is listed as a Captain in the Royal Regiment of Artillery, in *List of the General and Field-Officers to September 1758* (London: Millan, n. d.), p. 137. For information on the governors of Minorca, see Desmond Gregory, *Minorca, The Illusory Prize: A History of the British Occupation of Minorca between 1708 and 1802* (Rutherford: Fairleigh Dickinson University Press, 1990), Appendix A, n. p.

7. See the account by Athanase Coquerel, Jr., in Ernest Stroehlin, *Athanase Coquerel fils* (Paris: Librairie Fischbacher, 1886), p. 9.

8. The burial of Charles Williams on 23 December 1762 in St. John the Evangelist Church, Westminster (London) is recorded in volume 51 of the burial fee book.

9. Charles Williams's will and burial record were located for me by the genealogist John Dagger, of Tonbridge, Kent. The will is held at PROB 11/882 q. 535 fo. 354v–5r. It was dated 25 February 1761 and proved on 29 December 1762. It reads as follows:

I Charles Williams of West Clandon, in the County of Surry formerly the Secretary of the Island of Minorca considering the uncertainty of this Mortal Life and being now of perfect mind and memory do make, ordain, constitute, and Appoint this my last Will and Testament first revoking and annulling all and every former Will or Wills heretofore by me of any time made first. I give and bequeath to my Daughter Persis Williams an Annuity of fifty pounds payable to me at the Exchequer for and during the term of her natural life And after payment of my just debts and funeral Expenses I give and bequeath unto my dearly beloved Wife Helen Williams the remainder and residue of all my Real and Personal Estate of what nature and kind it may consist not doubting her favour care and Affection to my Children. And in case of Necessity contributing to the support of my Mother. And I do hereby Nominate and Appoint my said Beloved Wife Helen Williams whole and Sole Executrix to this my last Will and Testament In Witness whereof I have hereunto set my hand and seal in West Clandon aforesaid this 25th Day of February in the year of our Lord 1761.

10. Joseph Farington, *The Diary of Joseph Farington*, ed. Kenneth Garlick and Angus MacIntyre, vol. 5 (New Haven: Yale University Press, 1979), p. 1835.

11. In the same passage from *Poems* 1823, she wrote of her melancholic disposition.

12. Athanase Coquerel, Preface, *Christianity*, trans. Rev. D. Davison (London: Longman, 1847), p. ix.

13. See Marie Bartoszewski, "La Famille Coquerel," in the Société de l'Histoire du Protestantisme Français, 54 rue des Saints-Pères, Paris. See also Jules Dèveze, *Athanase Coquerel fils sa vie et ses oeuvres* (Paris: Librairie Fischbacher, 1884), p. 58. At the time of his death, Helen Maria Williams's nephew donated thousands of books to the library of the Société, including many books that had belonged to Williams, which had been passed down to him. His own son, Athanase, Jr., asked for the Minorca Bible to be returned to the family since it "was very dear to my grandmother and to her sister." Stroehlin, *Athanase Coquerel fils*, p. 9.

14. Athanase Coquerel fils, "Charles Coquerel," *Le Lien, Journal des églises réformées de France*, Second Series, volume 7, number 4 (15 février 1851):243.

15. Stroehlin, *Athanase Coquerel fils*, p. 8–9. Helen Maria Williams, *Letters on the Events Which Have Passed in France Since the Restoration in 1815* (London: Baldwin, 1819), p. 194. Subsequent quotations from *Restoration* are cited parenthetically in the text.

16. For information on the Princes Street Presbyterian Church in Westminster, see Anon., "Historical Retrospect of Presbyterian Churches and their Ministers," *Weekly Review* (1872), n. p.

17. Williams's poem "On the Death of the Rev. Dr. Kippis" was published in *Gentleman's Magazine* 66 (1796):66. It has been reprinted in *Eighteenth-Century Women Poets*, ed. Roger Lonsdale (Oxford: Oxford University Press, 1989), p. 418–20.

18. Andrew Kippis, Advertisement, *Edwin and Eltruda. A Legendary Tale*, by A Young Lady (London: Cadell, 1782), p. i.

19. Percival Stockdale, *The Memoirs of the Life, and Writings of Percival Stockdale; containing many interesting anecdotes of the illustrious men with whom he was connected*, 2 vols. (London: Longman, Hurst, Rees, and Orme, 1809), 2:218–19.

20. Seward, "Sonnet to Miss Williams, On her Epic Poem PERU," *London Magazine* (February 1785):113–14.

21. Kippis, Advertisement, *Edwin and Eltruda*, p. ii.

22. "On the Death of the Rev. Dr. Kippis," p. 66.

23. On the "Honest Whigs" see Craig C. Murray, *Benjamin Vaughan (1751–1835): The Life of an Anglo-American Intellectual* (New York: Arno Press, 1982), p. 22; and Albert Goodwin, *The Friends of Liberty: The English Democratic Movement in the Age of the French Revolution* (Cambridge: Harvard University Press, 1979), p. 54.

24. *The New Annual Register for the year 1782* (London: Robinson, 1783), p. 202–4; and p. 242–43.

25. Helen Maria Williams, *Poems*, 2 vols. (London: Cadell, 1786), 1:69–70. Subsequent quotations from this work are cited parenthetically in the text.

26. Charlotte Burney, *The Early Diary of Frances Burney 1768–1778 with a Selection from . . . the Journals of Her Sisters Susan and Charlotte Burney*, ed. Annie Raine Ellis, 2 vols. (London: George Bell and Sons, 1889), 2:301–2.

27. Burney, *The Early Diary* 2:305.

28. John A. Vance, *Joseph and Thomas Warton* (Boston: Twayne Publishers, 1983), p. 5.

29. See William Hayley, *Memoirs of the Life and Writings of William Hayley, Esq*, ed. John Johnson, 2 vols. (London: Colburn, 1823), 1:349; 1:410–11; 2:418–19; 1:425; 1:467; 1:479.

30. Ibid. 1:294.

31. William Wordsworth asked Charlotte Smith for a letter of introduction to Helen Maria Williams, since he hoped to meet Williams during his visit to France in 1791. See *The Letters of William and Dorothy Wordsworth: The Early Years 1787–1805*, ed. Ernest de Selincourt, 2nd ed. rev. Chester L. Shaver (Oxford: Clarendon Press, 1967), 1:69. See Hayley, *Memoirs of William Hayley* 1:322; 1:330.

32. Stuart Curran, "Romantic Poetry: The I Altered," in *Romanticism and Feminism*, ed. Anne K. Mellor (Bloomington: Indiana University Press, 1988), p. 187. See also Margaret Anne Doody, "Women Poets of the Eighteenth Century," in *Women and Literature in Britain 1700–1800*, ed. Vivien Jones (Cambridge: Cambridge University Press, 2000), p. 217–37.

33. Hayley, *Memoirs of William Hayley* 1:289.

34. Ibid. 1:292–93.

35. Richard Polwhele, *The Unsex'd Females* (New York: Garland, 1974), p. 32, note.

36. Goodwin, *The Friends of Liberty*, p. 52–56.

37. *The New Annual Register . . . for the Year 1783* (London: Robinson, 1784), p. 275.

38. The *Ode on the Peace* was also favourably noticed in a short article in the *Monthly Review* 69 (August 1783):167.

39. See Kathleen Nulton Kemmerer, *"A Neutral being between the sexes": Samuel Johnson's Sexual Politics* (Lewisburg: Bucknell University Press, 1998), p. 13–22; James G. Basker, "Dancing Dogs, Women Preachers and the Myth of Johnson's Misogyny," *The Age of Johnson* 3 (1990):63–90; Isobel Grundy, "Samuel Johnson as a Patron of Women," *The Age of Johnson* 1 (1987):59–77.

40. Burney, *The Early Diary* 2:317; my italics.

41. James Boswell, *The Life of Samuel Johnson*, 3 vols. (Dublin: R. Cross, et al., 1792), 3:428–29. Although Boswell would later add a derisive note about Williams because of his own abhorrence of the French Revolution, at this time no such shadow was cast over her reputation.

42. Mary Hamilton, *Mary Hamilton Afterwards Mrs. John Dickenson at Court and at Home. From Letters and Diaries 1756–1816*, ed. Elizabeth and Florence Anson (London: John Murray, 1925), p. 187.

43. For a brief discussion of Thomas Seward's poem, see Sylvia Harcstark Myers, *The Bluestocking Circle: Women, Friendship, and the Life of the Mind in Eighteenth-Century England* (Oxford: Oxford University Press, 1990), p. 126–28

44. Anna Seward, letter to Helen Maria Williams, 25 August 1785, in *Letters of Anna Seward*, 6 vols. (Edinburgh: Constable, 1811), 1:76.

45. Margaret Ashmun, *The Singing Swan* (New Haven: Yale University Press, 1931), p. 144.

46. Anna Seward, letter to Mrs. Martin, 5 June 1786, in *Letters of Anna Seward* 1:151–52.

47. James Averill notes that "The short poem of recognition to a fellow poet was a minor genre popular in the late eighteenth century." See *Wordsworth and the Poetry of Human Suffering* (Ithaca: Cornell University Press, 1980), p. 33. The very active presence of women poets is demonstrated in this particular issue of *London Magazine*, since Seward's poem is next to Williams's own "Sonnet to Twilight," sonnets by Charlotte Smith, and a poem addressed to "Miss Smith of Bignor Hall." See *London Magazine* (February 1785): 113–14. Another poet who signed her name as "ELIZA" (perhaps Eliza Knipe Cobbald) had earlier published "To Miss Helen Maria Williams: On her Poem of Peru," in *Gentleman's Magazine* 54 (July 1784):532.

48. Anna Seward, "Sonnet to Miss Williams, on her Epic Poem PERU," *London Magazine* (February 1785):113–14.

49. Averill, *Wordsworth and the Poetry of Human Suffering*, p. 30.

50. William McCarthy, *Hester Thrale Piozzi: Portrait of a Literary Woman* (Chapel Hill: University of North Carolina Press, 1985), p. 93–95.

51. Horace Walpole, letter to Lady Ossory, 4 November 1786, in *Horace Walpole's Correspondence with the Countess of Ossory*, ed. W. S. Lewis and A. Doyle Wallace, vol. 33 of *The Yale Edition of Horace Walpole's Correspondence* (New Haven: Yale University Press, 1965), 33:533.

52. For information on Dr. John Moore, see W. L. Renwick, "Introduction," *Mordaunt* (1800; London: Oxford University Press, 1965), p. ix–xviii. See also Henry L. Fulton, "Disillusionment with the French Revolution: The Case of the Scottish Physician John Moore," *Studies in Scottish Literature* 23 (1988):46–63.

53. Williams's mother (a Hay of Naughton) may have been related to Moore's maternal grandmother, who was a Hay of the family of the Earls of Kinnoull. Much information about Moore can be gained from the biography of his son and namesake by Carola Oman, *Sir John Moore* (London: Hodder and Stoughton, 1953).

54. John Moore sent this poem to Robert Burns on 8 November 1787. It is reprinted as follows in William Wallace, *Robert Burns and Mrs. Dunlop* (London: Hodder and Stoughton, 1898), p. 35.

At Miss Williams's desire I send you a copy of some lines I wrote to her lately when she was at Southampton. She said she wished to send you her picture drawn by me. The truth, however, is they are all exaggeration, for she is remarkably pretty; but on her being a little out of humour at my laughing at her nose, and chin, and stooping, which she expressed in a letter, I wrote in answer the enclosed.

> I confess I have said—but pray do not pout—
> That your chin is too fond of your aquiline snout,
> Like the world disposed from inferiors to fly,
> It always looks up to the features on high.
> That I said of your back, and I still must say so,
> It resembles the back of an Indian canoe:
> What was strait as an arrow, you've bent like a bow.
> I must own too I hinted your waddling walk
> Was much like a parrot's—and sometimes yr talk.
> Yet these observations as plainly you'll view,
> Tho' they glance at your person, don't touch upon *you*;
> For *you* never can think—you're too much refined—
> That your body is *you*—you's entirely your mind.
> And when yr sweet genius so gracefully flows,
> In melodious verse or poetical prose,
> Who thinks of your chin or the turn of yr toes?
> For you, my dear Helen, have proved by your works
> That women have souls, in the teeth of the Turks.

Your person and face in the hands of those
Who think upon ought but the care of their bodies
It is true would be ranked for beauty and air
In a pretty high class of the graceful and fair,
And would doubtless attract from the thoughtless and gay
A more pointed regard to yr fabrick of clay,
But all those you will treat with scorn eternal
Who sigh for the shell and taste not the kernel.

55. Helen Maria Williams, *Poems* (London: Cadell, 1791).
Only a few new poems were added. The second edition opened with her 1788 poem on Captain Cook, "The Morai," and the first volume also introduced her previously unpublished "Sonnet to Robert Burns, the Scotch Poet" and a piece from her novel *Julia* called "An Address to Poetry." The second volume included a new piece "Duncan, an Ode."
56. A letter of Hardinge's from 20 March 1786 indicates that Dr. John Moore paid him two pounds for subscriptions for himself and Mrs. Moore. See John Nichols, *Illustrations of the Literary History of the Eighteenth Century*, vol. 3 (London: Nichols, Son, and Bentley, 1818), p. 148. In the Preface, Williams thanked Hardinge (without naming him): "I owe to one Gentleman in particular, whose exertions in my behalf, though I was a stranger to him, have been so marked, so generous, and indeed so unexampled, that it is a very painful task which his delicacy has imposed upon me, in not permitting me to mention his name" (*Poems* n. p.).
57. Anna Seward's letter is quoted in *The Autobiography and Correspondence of Mary Granville, Mrs. Delaney*, ed. Lady Llanover, 3 vols. (London: Richard Bentley, 1862), 3:394.
58. For a more detailed discussion, see my " 'Storms of Sorrow': The Poetry of Helen Maria Williams," *Man and Nature* 10 (1991): 77–91.
59. William H. Cummings, "No Riches from his Little Store," *Notes and Queries* 28 July 1906:75.
60. See John Walker, "Maria Cosway: An Undervalued Artist," *Apollo* (May 1986):318–24.
61. James Thomson, "Winter," *The Seasons*, ed. J. Logie Robertson (London: Oxford University Press, 1965), p. 354–56.
62. Janet Todd, *Sensibility: An Introduction* (London: Methuen, 1986), p. 11.
63. M. Ray Adams, "Helen Maria Williams and the French Revolution," *Wordsworth and Coleridge: Studies in Honour of George McLean Harper*, ed. Earl Leslie Griggs (New York: Russell, 1967), p. 93.
64. See Cecil Price, *The Dramatic Works of Richard Brinsley Sheridan*, vol. 2 (Oxford: Clarendon Press, 1973), p. 624–46.
65. Hannah More, *The Works of Hannah More. A New Edition in Eighteen Volumes* (London: T. Cadell and W. Davies, 1816), 1:181.
66. Frances Greville, "A Prayer for Indifference," in *Eighteenth-Century Women Poets*, ed. Roger Lonsdale (Oxford: Oxford University Press, 1989), p. 193.
67. Rev. of Williams's *Poems*, in *European Magazine* 10 (August 1786):91.
68. Wordsworth published this sonnet in the *European Magazine* in March 1787. See Wordsworth, *Poetical Works*, ed. Thomas Hutchinson, rev. ed. Ernest de Selincourt (Oxford: Oxford University Press, 1969), p. 484.
69. For Esther Schor's discussion of this sonnet, see *Bearing the Dead: The British Culture of Mourning: from the Enlightenment to Victoria* (Princeton: Princeton University Press, 1994), p. 69–72.
70. Oman, *Sir John Moore*, p. 63.

71. *The Letters of Robert Burns*, ed. J. De Lancey Ferguson, vol. 1 (Oxford: Clarendon), p. 77.

72. Thomas Gray, *Elegy Written in a Country Church-Yard*, in *Thomas Gray and William Collins: Poetical Works*, ed. Roger Lonsdale (Oxford: Oxford University Press, 1977), p. 36, line 51.

73. Helen Maria Williams, letter to Robert Burns, 20 June 1787, in *The Edinburgh Magazine, and Literary Miscellany; a New Series of the Scots Magazine* 1 (September 1817):109.

74. On Colonel Barry, Edward Bloom and Lillian D. Bloom note the following: "Ultimately a colonel in the army (1793), Henry Barry (1750–1822) served during the American Revolution as aide-de-camp and private secretary to Baron Rawdon (*later* Rawdon-Hastings). For a short time thereafter he was posted to India. Although he remained in the army until 1794, he was well known in English literary and scientific circles by 1789." Rev. Thomas Sedgwick Whalley (1746–1828) was the "nonresident pastor of Hagsworthingham, near Spilsby, Lincs, prebendary of Wells, poet, traveler, and friend of . . . Hannah More." See Edward Bloom and Lillian D. Bloom, eds., *The Piozzi Letters: Correspondence of Hester Lynch Piozzi, 1784–1821*, 3 vols. (Newark: University of Delaware Press, 1989–93), 1:297, n. 2; 1:115, n. 11.

75. Kippis is quoted in P. W. Clayden, *The Early Life of Samuel Rogers* (London: Smith, Elder, 1887), p. 76.

76. All citations from "The Morai" will be from *The Life of Captain James Cook*, by Andrew Kippis (London: Robinson, 1788; Chiswick: Whittingham, 1822), p. 213–18. Subsequent quotations from this work are cited parenthetically in the text.

77. See Clare Midgley, *Women against Slavery: The British Campaigns, 1780–1870* (London: Routledge, 1992).

78. Judith Jennings explains that not all abolitionists thought women should be involved in petitions to Parliament, though they could show their benevolent support by other means. Judith Jennings, *The Business of Abolishing the Slave Trade 1783–1807* (London: Frank Cass, 1997), p. 43. Boycotting sugar was sometimes ridiculed; Moira Ferguson cites the example of Maria Edgeworth, who, although friendly with abolitionists, did not abstain from sugar and made fun of the Barbaulds for bringing their own East Indian sugar when they visited her for tea. See Moira Ferguson, *Subject to Others: British Women Writers and Colonial Slavery, 1670–1834* (New York: Routledge, 1992), p. 179–80. Political cartoonists parodied the boycott in prints like Gillray's *Anti-Saccharrites, —or— John Bull and his Family leaving off the use of Sugar* (March 27 1792), and Isaac Cruikshank's *The Gradual Abolition of the Slave Trade, or Leaving off Sugar by Degrees* (15 April 1792).

79. See Ferguson, *Subject to Others*, p. 150.

80. On Kippis's election to the London Committee, see J. R. Oldfield, *Popular Politics and British Anti-Slavery: The Mobilisation of Public Opinion against the Slave Trade 1787–1807* (Manchester: Manchester University Press, 1995), p. 43.

81. See Ellen Gibson Wilson, *Thomas Clarkson: A Biography* (New York: St. Martin's Press, 1990), p. 41.

82. See Ellen Gibson Wilson, *Thomas Clarkson*, p. 28. For a discussion of the Committee's membership and formation see Judith Jennings, *The Business of Abolishing the Slave Trade*, p. 34–37.

83. See J. R. Oldfield, *Popular Politics and British Anti-Slavery*, p. 50–51 and note 47, p. 67.

84. See Dale H. Porter, *The Abolition of the Slave Trade in England, 1784–1807* (New York: Archon Books, 1970), p. 49.

85. Judith Jennings quotes Seymour Drescher as saying that with the Wedgwood

design "Abolitionists 'used commercial techniques . . . to rivet public attention' " (*The Business of Abolishing the Slave Trade*, p. 40). Jennings cites Drescher, *Capitalism and Anti-Slavery* (Oxford: Oxford University Press, 1987), p. 73.

86. Oldfield explains the history of the print in *Popular Politics and British Anti-Slavery*, p. 163–66. For more information see Hugh Honour, *The Image of the Black in Western Art*, vol. 4, *From the American Revolution to World War I* (Cambridge: Harvard University Press, 1989), p. 315, note 136; and p. 64–65.

87. Oldfield, *Popular Politics and British Anti-Slavery*, p. 165.

88. Ellen Gibson Wilson, *Thomas Clarkson*, p. 57; Lady Morgan, *France*, 2nd. ed., 2 vols. (London: Henry Colburn, 1817), 2:331.

89. These memoirs are only known to exist in the French translation made by Williams's nephew.

90. See the list of subscribers in Appendix C of Vincent Carretta's edition of Olaudah Equiano's *The Interesting Narrative* (Harmondsworth: Penguin, 1995), p. 317–21.

91. See the discussion and colour reprint of the painting in Honour, *The Image of the Black in Western Art* 4:91–93.

92. Burns's comments on her Slave Trade poem are dated December 1787 in James Currie, *The Life of Robert Burns* (Edinburgh: Chambers, 1838), p. 31–32; but they appear to have been sent with the letter of July-August 1789 in *The Letters of Robert Burns*, 2nd. ed., ed. J. de Lancey Ferguson and G. Ross Roy (Oxford: Clarendon, 1985) 1:428–31.

Williams's reply is reprinted here:

Dear Sir—I do not lose a moment in returning you my sincere acknowledgements for your letter, and your criticism on my poem, which is a very flattering proof that you have read it with attention. I think your objections are perfectly just, except in one instance. You have indeed been very profuse of panegyric on my little performance. A much less portion of applause from *you* would have been gratifying to me; since I think its value depends entirely upon the source from whence it proceeds—the incense of praise, like other incense, is more grateful from the quality than the quantity of the odour.

I hope you still cultivate the pleasures of poetry, which are precious even independent of the rewards of fame. Perhaps the most valuable property of poetry is its power of disengaging the mind from worldly cares, and leading the imagination to the richest springs of intellectual enjoyment; since, however frequently life may be chequered with gloomy scenes, those who truly love the muse can always find one little path adorned with flowers and cheered by sunshine.

Helen Maria Williams, letter to Robert Burns, 7 August 1789, in Currie, *The Life of Robert Burns*, p. 55.

93. Seward had recently been ridiculed in the press and been unfavourably compared to Ann Yearsley, so she did not want to risk the comparison again. See Anna Seward, letter to Josiah Wedgwood, 18 February 1788, in *Letters of Anna Seward* 2:28–33; and in *Women Romantics 1785–1832: Writing in Prose*, ed. Jennifer Breen (London: Everyman, 1996), p. 46–48.

94. Anna Seward, letter to Mrs. Taylor (Mary Scott), 13 January 1790, in *Letters of Anna Seward* 2:345–46. For many years Anna Seward had corresponded with the poet Mary Scott, author of *The Female Advocate* (1774), a survey of British women poets. Their correspondence continued after Scott's marriage to a Unitarian minister in May 1788, and from time to time they wrote about Williams's poetry and her books on the French Revolution. Scott died on 5 June 1793. See Roger Lonsdale, ed., *Eighteenth-Century Women Poets*, p. 320–21. See also Anna Seward, letter to Theophilus Swift, 9 July 1789, and letter to Helen Maria Williams, 3 March 1789, in *Letters of Anna Seward* 2:286–87; 2:247. For general background, see Amanda Vickery, *The Gentleman's Daugh-*

ter: Women's Lives in Georgian England (New Haven: Yale University Press, 1998), p. 258–60.

95. Rev. of Williams's *A Poem on the Bill Lately Passed for Regulating the Slave Trade*, in *Monthly Review* 80 (March 1789):237.

96. Ferguson, *Subject to Others*, p. 3.

97. Helen Maria Williams, *A Poem on the Bill Lately Passed for Regulating the Slave Trade* (London: Cadell, 1788), lines 37–38. Subsequent quotations from this work are cited parenthetically in the text.

98. Dale H. Porter reports that "Eventually a limit was set at five slaves for every three tons up to 200 tons, and one per ton thereafter" (*The Abolition*, p. 40).

99. Ibid., p. 38.

100. The text is quoted from *Description of A Slave Ship* reprinted in Honour, *The Image of the Black in Western Art* 4:65.

101. Ferguson, *Subject to Others*, p. 158.

102. She pays special tribute to Prime Minister William Pitt and Lord Richmond (though this section was omitted when she revised the work for her *Poems* 1823; 51–80).

103. Oldfield, *Popular Politics and British Anti-Slavery*, p. 117.

104. Hannah More, letter to Horace Walpole, September 1791, in *Horace Walpole's Correspondence with Hannah More*, ed. W. S. Lewis, Robert Smith and Charles H. Bennet, vol. 31 of *The Yale Edition of Horace Walpole's Correspondence* (New Haven: Yale University Press, 1961), 31:358.

105. Horace Walpole, letter to Hannah More, 29 September 1791,in *Horace Walpole's Correspondence with Hannah More* 31:361–362.

106. Nancy Armstrong, *Desire and Domestic Fiction: A Political History of the Novel* (Oxford: Oxford University Press, 1987), p. 97.

107. Helen Maria Williams, *Julia, A Novel; Interspersed with Poetical Pieces*, 2 vols., intro. Gina Luria (New York: Garland, 1974), 1:105; 1:89. Subsequent quotations from this work are cited parenthetically in the text.

108. See Janet Todd, *Sensibility*, p. 55–57.

109. William Cowper, *The Task*, in *The Task and Selected Other Poems*, ed. James Sambrook (London: Longman, 1994), Book 1:749.

110. G. J. Barker-Benfield, *The Culture of Sensibility: Sex and Society in Eighteenth-Century Britain* (Chicago: University of Chicago Press, 1992), p. 201.

111. See Eleanor Ty, *Unsex'd Revolutionaries: Five Women Novelists of the 1790s* (Toronto: University of Toronto Press, 1993), p. 73–84.

CHAPTER 2. CITIZEN OF THE WORLD, 1789–1792

1. William Smith traveled with Benjamin Vaughan to Paris in 1790. See Richard W. Davis, *Dissent in Politics 1780–1850: The Political Life of William Smith, MP* (London: Epworth, 1971), p. 69–74.

2. Andrew Kippis taught at Hoxton from 1763–84 and began teaching at the new Dissenting academy at Hackney in 1786. See the *Dictionary of National Biography* entry for Kippis. On Godwin, see Charles Kegan Paul, *William Godwin: His Friends and Contemporaries*, 2 vols. (New York: AMS, 1970), 1:63.

3. The Corporate Act (1661) required that those holding a civic or municipal office had to have taken the sacrament of the Church of England during the past year. The Test Act (1673) required that those holding civic or military offices had to take additional oaths regarding the practices of the Church and allegiance to the Crown. See Goodwin, *The Friends of Liberty*, p. 77.

4. Ibid., p. 85.

5. Andrew Kippis, *A Sermon Preached at the Old Jewry* (London: Cadell, 1788).

6. Goodwin, *The Friends of Liberty*, p. 86.

7. Ibid., p. 63–64; p. 101–2.

8. On Lord Lansdowne's Bowood circle, see Goodwin, *The Friends of Liberty*, p. 99–107.

9. Samuel Romilly, letter to E. Dumont, 28 July 1789, *Memoirs of The Life of Sir Samuel Romilly*, 3 vols. (London: John Murray, 1840), 1:356.

10. William Doyle, *The Oxford History of the French Revolution* (Oxford: Oxford University Press, 1989), p. 161.

11. For information on Godwin's relationship to Kippis and his involvement in the Revolution Society, see William St. Clair, *The Godwins and the Shelleys: The Biography of a Family* (London: Faber, 1989), p. 44–45; p. 31–33.

12. Kegan Paul, *William Godwin* 1:64.

13. On the vote count results, see Goodwin, *The Friends of Liberty*, p. 97; p. 89.

14. See H. T. Dickinson, *British Radicalism and the French Revolution* (Oxford: Basil Blackwell, 1985), p. 7. William St. Clair explains that "when the third bill to repeal the Test and Corporation Acts was presented in 1790, it was resoundingly defeated by a majority of 189, compared with only 20 the year before. Church bells were rung in many Anglican steeples and exultant graffiti chalked on meeting house walls reminded dissenters that 102 years after the Glorious Revolution they were still officially rebels and traitors" (*The Godwins and the Shelleys*, p. 47).

15. Anna Laetitia Barbauld, *Address to the Opposers of the Repeal of the Corporation and Test Acts*, in *The Meridian Anthology of Early Women Writers*, ed. Katharine M. Rogers and William McCarthy (New York: New American Library, 1987), p. 263–76.

16. Godwin's diary lists the following people at the Anti-Tests supper: "Fox, Beaufoy, Hoghton, Sawbridge, Adair, Watson, Heywood, B. Hollis, Shore, Geddes, Vaughan, Fell, Stone, Woodfall, Listers" (Kegan Paul, *William Godwin* 1:65).

17. Helen Maria Williams, letter to Hester Thrale Piozzi, 27 February 1790, John Rylands University Library of Manchester. Material from this collection is reproduced by permission.

18. Officially, the Declaration of the Rights of Man allowed non-Catholics freedom of conscience but not freedom to worship. This came gradually, due to the efforts of several influential Protestants, especially one who was a member of the National Assembly, Jean-Paul Rabaut St. Etienne, who would become a friend of Williams, once she joined the Protestant community in Paris: "a decision of the directory of Paris (11 April 1791) made it possible for non-Catholics to rent former Catholic buildings for the celebration of their religious services." See Burdette C. Poland. *French Protestantism and the French Revolution: A Study in Church and State, Thought and Religion, 1685–1815* (Princeton: Princeton University Press, 1957), p. 156, 158, note 27.

19. Charles Stanhope, *A Letter from Earl Stanhope, to the Right Honourable Edmund Burke; Containing a Short Answer to His Late Speech on the French Revolution* [February 24] 1790, reprinted in *Political Writings of the 1790s*, ed. Gregory Claeys, 8 vols. (London: Pickering, 1995), 1:10.

20. Hereafter *Letters written in France, in the Summer 1790* will be referred to as the first volume of the *Letters from France*.

21. Cynthia Lowenthal, "The Veil of Romance: Lady Mary's Embassy Letters," *Eighteenth-Century Life* 14 (1990):68.

22. William Wordsworth, *The Prelude: 1799, 1805, 1850*, eds. Jonathan Wordsworth, M. H. Abrams, and Stephen Gill (New York: Norton, 1979), 1805: Book 10:692–93.

23. Richard Price, *A Discourse on the Love of Our Country*, in *Richard Price: Political Writings*, ed. D. O. Thomas (Cambridge: Cambridge University Press, 1991),p. 182.

24. Ibid., p. 181; italics mine.

25. See Darline Gay Levy and Harriet B. Applewhite, "Women and Militant Citizenship in Revolutionary Paris," in *Rebel Daughters: Women and the French Revolution*, ed. Sara E. Melzer and Leslie W. Rabine (New York: Oxford University Press, 1992), p. 79–101.

26. Mary A. Favret, *Romantic Correspondences: Women, Politics, and the Fiction of Letters* (Cambridge: Cambridge University Press, 1993), p. 63.

27. Mona Ozouf, *Festivals and the French Revolution*, trans. Alan Sheridan (Cambridge: Harvard University Press, 1988), p. 45.

28. Edmund Burke, *Reflections on the Revolution in France*, ed. Conor Cruise O'Brien (Harmondsworth: Penguin, 1987), p. 175.

29. Stephen Cox, "Sensibility as Argument," in *Sensibility in Transformation: Creative Resistance of Sentiment from the Augustans to the Romantics: Essays in Honor of Jean H. Hagstrum*, ed. Syndy McMillen Conger (Rutherford: Fairleigh Dickinson University Press, 1990), pp. 63–82; p. 64–65.

30. Anna Seward's comments about Williams and Burke are, respectively, from letters dated 10 January 1791 and 19 December 1790, in *Letters of Anna Seward* 3:52; 3:48–49.

31. Price, Preface to the Fourth Edition, *A Discourse on the Love of Our Country*, *Richard Price: Political Writings*, p. 177.

32. Burke, *Reflections*, p.159.

33. Ibid., p. 175.

34. Mary Wollstonecraft, *A Vindication of the Rights of Men*, in *Mary Wollstonecraft: Political Writings*, ed. Janet Todd (Toronto: University of Toronto Press, 1993), p. 27.

35. Burke, *Reflections*, p. 164–65.

36. Catharine Macaulay, *Observations on the Reflections of the Right Hon. Edmund Burke, on the Revolution in France, In a Letter to the Right Hon. Earl of Stanhope.* (London: C. Dilly in the Poultry, 1790), p. 26.

37. Burke, *Reflections*, p. 176.

38. David Bindman, *The Shadow of the Guillotine: Britain and the French Revolution* (London: British Museum, 1989), p. 36–37.

39. Cowper, *The Task*, Book 5:385; 389–90.

40. Doyle, *The Oxford History of the French Revolution*, p. 160–61.

41. Bindman, *The Shadow of the Guillotine*, p. 90–91.

42. Price, *A Discourse on the Love of Our Country*, p. 182.

43. Isaac Kramnick, "Introduction," *The Portable Enlightenment Reader* (Harmondsworth: Penguin, 1995), p. xiv.

44. Burke, *Reflections*, p. 117.

45. Ibid., p. 184.

46. Barbauld, *Address to the Opposers of the Repeal of the Corporation and Test Acts*, p. 274.

47. Rev. of *LF* 1.1., in *Gentleman's Magazine* 61 (1791):63. All references to reviews of the *Letters from France* will use the abbreviation *LF*, and indicate the series and volume number.

48. *Gentleman's Magazine* 61 (1791):63.

49. Henry Fielding, *Tom Jones*, ed. John Bender and Simon Stern (Oxford: Oxford University Press, 1996), p. 238.

50. Quoted in Bridget Hill, *The Republican Virago: The Life and Times of Catharine Macaulay, Historian* (Oxford: Clarendon, 1992), p. 131; p. 132.

51. Burke, *Reflections*, p. 281.

52. Ibid., p. 281.

53. Cox, "Sensibility as Argument," p. 64.

54. See Geoffrey Tillotson, Paul Fussell, Jr., Marshall Waingrow, and Brewster Rogerson, *Eighteenth-Century English Literature* (San Diego: Harcourt, Brace, Jovanovich, 1969), p. 1261; and Linda Kelly, *Richard Brinsley Sheridan* (London: Sinclair-Stevenson, 1997), p. 144–51.

55. Roland Quinault, "Westminster and the Victorian Constitution," *Transactions of the Royal Historical Society* 6.2 (London: Butler and Tanner, 1992), p. 87. I am grateful to Sandra Holton for this reference.

56. For information on female spectators in the British House of Commons, see P. D. G. Thomas, *The House of Commons in the Eighteenth Century* (Oxford: Clarendon, 1971), pp. 148–49; and R. G. Thorne, *The History of Parliament: The House of Commons 1790–1820* (London: Secker and Warburg, 1986), p. 334.

57. Darline Gay Levy and Harriet B. Applewhite, "Women and Militant Citizenship in Revolutionary Paris," p. 80; p. 81.

58. See Candice E. Proctor, *Women, Equality, and the French Revolution* (New York: Greenwood, 1990), p. 112.

59. Elisabeth Roudinesco, *Madness and Revolution: The Lives and Legends of Théroigne de Méricourt*, trans. Martin Thom (London: Verso, 1991), p. 33–49; 40.

60. Joan B. Landes, *Women and the Public Sphere in the Age of the French Revolution* (Ithaca: Cornell University Press, 1988), p. 118.

61. "By the summer of 1791, women were participating avidly in clubs and popular societies, joining fraternal societies for both sexes, and attending as spectators the galleries of section assemblies, the national legislature, and radical clubs professing republican ideas." See Joan B. Landes, *Women and the Public Sphere*, p. 117.

62. Most accounts of the Fall of the Bastille record the presence of women, though few were actual combatants. In June 1790, nearly a thousand people who took part in the siege were awarded the title *Vainquere de la Bastille*; this included "one woman, a laundress." See Christopher Hibbert, *The French Revolution* (Harmondsworth: Penguin, 1980), p. 82–83; and Catherine Marand-Fouquet, *La Femme au temps de La Révolution* (Paris: Stock/Laurence Pernoud, 1989), p. 54–55.

63. Catherine Marand-Fouquet, *La Femme au temps de La Révolution*, p. 92.

64. Ruth Graham explains that "prosperous women also considered themselves patriots and supported the Revolution. Since September [1789], when the King's minister, Jacques Necker, asked for personal sacrifices to avert national bankruptcy, these women appeared at the National Assembly to offer their jewels and valuables." Ruth Graham, "Loaves and Liberty: Women in the French Revolution," in *Becoming Visible: Women in European History*, ed. Renate Bridenthal and Claudia Koonz (Boston: Houghton Mifflin, 1977), p. 241–42. Two illustrations on this subject are reprinted in *Les Femmes et la Révolution française*, volume 2, ed. Marie-France Brive (Toulouse: Presses universitaires du Mirail, 1990), n.p. One is a drawing entitled *Citoyennes de Paris faisant hommage de leurs bijoux*, and the other is a picture done in 1791 by Louis Gauffier, entitled *La Générosité des femmes romaines*. On this subject in general, see Madelyn Gutwirth, *The Twilight of the Goddesses: Women and Representation in the French Revolutionary Era* (New Brunswick: Rutgers University Press, 1992).

65. See Jacqueline LeBlanc, "Politics and Commercial Sensibility in Helen Maria Williams's *Letters from France*," *Eighteenth-Century Life* 21 (February 1997):32.

66. See Burke, *Reflections*, p. 159–79.

67. Julie Ellison, "Redoubled Feeling: Politics, Sentiment, and the Sublime in Williams and Wollstonecraft," *Studies in Eighteenth-Century Culture* 20 (1990):202.

68. See "History of Monsieur Du F— —" *Universal Magazine* 18 (December 1790):455 and 19 (January 1791):41; and Robert D. Mayo, *The English Novel in the Magazines* (Evanston, Illinois: Northwestern University Press, 1962), p. 260.

69. See Deborah Kennedy, "Revolutionary Tales: Helen Maria Williams's *Letters from France* and Wordsworth's 'Vaudracour and Julia,'" *The Wordsworth Circle* 21 (1990):110–15; and F. M. Todd, "Wordsworth, Helen Maria Williams and France," *Modern Language Review* 43 (1948):456–64.

70. Edmund Burke, *The Correspondence of Edmund Burke, July 1789-December 1791*, ed. Alfred Cobban and Robert A. Smith, vol. 6 of *The Correspondence of Edmund Burke* (Cambridge: Cambridge University Press, 1967), p. 91.

71. Lynn Hunt, *The Family Romance of the French Revolution* (Berkeley: University of California Press, 1992), p. 21.

72. Ibid., p. 20.

73. Janet Todd, *Sensibility*, p. 16.

74. Ibid., p. 16.

75. Rev. of *LF* 1.1, in *Analytical Review* 8 (1790):431–32.

76. Letter to the editor, *Gentleman's Magazine* 61 (April 1791): 299–300.

77. The satirical print *Don Dismallo Running the Literary Gantlet* was published in London on 1 December 1790, by Wm. Holland, No. 50 Oxford Street. See Dorothy George, *Catalogue of Political and Personal Satires Preserved in the Department of Prints and Drawings in the British Museum*, vol. 6 (London: British Museum, 1978), p. 703–5.

78. Nicholas K. Robinson, *Edmund Burke: A Life in Caricature* (New Haven: Yale University Press, 1996).

79. See Diana Donald, *The Age of Caricature: Satirical Prints in the Reign of George III* (New Haven: Yale University Press, 1996).

80. See Linda Colley's discussion of Georgiana Cavendish, the Duchess of Devonshire, in *Britons: Forging the Nation 1707–1837* (New Haven: Yale University Press, 1992), p. 242–50.

81. Helen Maria Williams, letters to Edward Jerningham, c. 1790, Huntington Library.

82. Jerningham's poem was published in the *Universal Magazine* 18(December 1790):472.

83. Williams sent Colonel Barry a copy of her *Letters* (1790). See Williams, letter to Colonel Barry, 17 November 1790, British Library.

84. Rev. of Wollstonecraft's *A Vindication of the Rights of Men*, 2nd. ed., in *Analytical Review* 8 (December 1790):416–19; 416.

85. Barbara Brandon Schnorrenberg, "An Opportunity Missed: Catharine Macaulay on the Revolution of 1688," *Studies in Eighteenth-Century Culture* 20 (1990):232.

86. See Claire Tomalin, *The Life and Death of Mary Wollstonecraft* (New York: Meridian, 1974), p. 94.

87. Rev. of Wollstonecraft's *Vindication of the Rights of Men*, in *Critical Review* 70 (December 1790):694. See Gary Kelly, *Revolutionary Feminism: The Mind and Career of Mary Wollstonecraft* (London: Macmillan, 1992), p. 90. Janet Todd notes that Wollstonecraft "displayed herself as the provoked and impartial rationalist exasperated by . . . a vain, trivial, and effeminate man." See Janet Todd, Introduction, *Mary Wollstonecraft: Political Writings* (Toronto: University of Toronto Press, 1993), p. xii.

88. See William Roscoe, *The Life, Death, and Wonderful Atchievements of Edmund Burke: A New Ballad* (1791), reprinted in George Chandler, *William Roscoe of Liverpool* (London: Batsford, 1953), p. 386–90; p. 389–90.

89. These lines are from a New Year's Day poem written by Williams for Thrale Piozzi on 1 January 1791. See *Thraliana: The Diary of Hester Lynch Piozzi*, ed. Katharine C. Balderstone, 2 vols. (Oxford: Clarendon), 2:794.

90. Burke, *Reflections*, p. 170. Helen Maria Williams, letter to Colonel Barry, 17 November 1790, the British Library. This material is published with the permission of the British Library Board.

91. Hester Thrale Piozzi, letter to Charlotte Lewis, 8 December 1790, in *The Piozzi Letters* 1:342.

92. Hester Thrale Piozzi, 3 January 1791, *Thraliana* 2:794.

93. Hester Thrale Piozzi, letter to Rev. Leonard Chappelow, 23 February 1791, in *The Piozzi Letters* 1:348.

94. Mary Wollstonecraft, letter to Everina Wollstonecraft, 24 December 1792, in *Collected Letters of Mary Wollstonecraft*, ed. Ralph M. Wardle (Ithaca: Cornell University Press, 1979), p. 225–26.

95. P. W. Clayden, *The Early Life of Samuel Rogers*, p. 165–76.

96. Hester Thrale Piozzi, letter to Rev. Leonard Chappelow, 23 February 1791, in *The Piozzi Letters* 1:348.

97. Helen Maria Williams, *A Farewell, for Two Years, to England. A Poem* (London: Cadell, 1791). Subsequent quotations from this work are cited parenthetically in the text.

98. Hester Thrale Piozzi, letter to Charlotte Lewis, 30 May 1791, in *The Piozzi Letters* 1:353.

99. *The Battle of the Whigs* and *The Volcano of Opposition* are both reproduced in colour in Nicholas Robinson's *Edmund Burke: A Life in Caricature*, p. 149; p. 155.

100. Rev. of *Farewell to England*, in *Analytical Review* 10 (June 1791):188.

101. Rev. of *Farewell to England*, in *European Magazine* 20 (August 1791):114.

102. "To Miss Helen Maria Williams, on Reading Her Novel of Julia." *Gentleman's Magazine* (April 1790):355.

103. Albert Goodwin discusses the history of the "Church and King" clubs in *The Friends of Liberty*, p. 67–68.

104. Ibid., p. 180–82.

105. See *The Theological and Miscellaneous Works of Joseph Priestley*, ed. John Towill Rutt, 25 vols. (n. d.; New York: Kraus Reprint, 1972), 1:170–71.

106. Andrew Kippis, *An Address Delivered at the Internment of Richard Price, D. D., F. R. S.* (1791), cited in the entry for Kippis in the *Dictionary of National Biography*.

107. See Thomas Crawford, *Boswell, Burns and the French Revolution* (Edinburgh: Saltire Society, 1990), p. 39–40.

108. Andrew Kippis, letter to James Boswell, 12 July 1791, Beinecke Rare Book and Manuscript Library, Yale University.

109. Horace Walpole, letter to Mary Berry, 26 July 1791, in *Horace Walpole's Correspondence with Mary and Agnes Berry and Barbara Cecilia Seton*, ed. W. S. Lewis and A. Dayle Wallace, vol. 11 of *The Yale Edition of Horace Walpole's Correspondence* (New Haven: Yale University Press, 1944), 11:320. See Fielding, p. 155.

110. Horace Walpole, letter to Mary Berry, 20 December 1790, in *Horace Walpole's Correspondence with Mary and Agnes Berry and Barbara Cecilia Seton* 11:169–70.

111. This letter from Anna Laetitia Barbauld to Samuel Rogers, 13 July 1791, is quoted in P. W. Clayden, *The Early Life of Samuel Rogers*, p. 204. See *The Piozzi Letters* 1:353.

112. *Lettres écrites de France à une amie en Angleterre pendant l'été 1790*, traduit de l'Anglais par M. de la Montagné (Paris, 1791).

113. By 1794, as Ruth Graham states, "Everywhere the Rousseauean ideal of pregnant and nursing women personified the regeneration of France. . . . Gone were the Amazons, the activists, the petitioners for women's rights, the clubs of revolutionary women." See Ruth Graham, "Loaves and Liberty," p.250.

114. Helen Maria Williams, letter to Hester Thrale Piozzi, 5 September 1791, John Rylands University Library of Manchester.

115. "La societé des amis de la constitution at Rouen sent me a very flattering letter

of thanks for my french journal, and ordered three Thousand copies of an answer I sent them, to be printed." Helen Maria Williams, letter to Hester Thrale Piozzi, 12 October 1791, John Rylands University Library of Manchester.

116. Helen Maria Williams, letter to Hester Thrale Piozzi, 12 October 1791; Helen Maria Williams, letter to Hester Thrale Piozzi, 26 February 1792, John Rylands University Library of Manchester.

117. William Wordsworth, letter to Richard Wordsworth, 19 December 1791, *The Letters of William and Dorothy Wordsworth: The Early Years 1787–1805* 1:69.

118. Anna Seward, letter to Helen Maria Williams, 26 July 1792, in *Letters of Anna Seward* 3:148.

119. Helen Maria Williams, letter to Hester Thrale Piozzi, 13 June 1792, John Rylands University Library of Manchester.

120. Information about John Hurford Stone can be gathered from *A Complete Collection of State Trials*, edited by T. B. Howell and Thomas Jones Howell, vol. 25 (London: Longman, Hunt, Rees, Orme, and Brown, 1818), which contains letters from him to his brother William Stone, who was arrested for treason in 1794 and tried and acquitted in 1796. There is an entry for Stone in the *Dictionary of National Biography*, and he is mentioned in numerous books on the British Club in Paris.

121. Thrale Piozzi wrote: "Helena Williams should mind who she keeps Company with — so indeed should Hester Piozzi: that fine Man She brought to our house lives in *no* Emigrant's Hotel at Paris but a common Lodging, in a Place where Numbers Lodge: he carried *no* Wife over with him, nor *no* Children, they are left at Hackney I am told — her Mother and Sister are at Montreuil." Hester Thrale Piozzi, letter to Penelope Weston, 15 September [1792], *The Piozzi Letters* 2:68.

122. A. F. Bertrand de Moleville, *Refutation of the Libel of the Memory of the Late King of France, published by Helen Maria Williams, under the title of Political and Confidential Correspondence of Louis the Sixteenth*, trans. R. C. Dallas (London: Cadell & Davies, 1804), p. 21.

123. Gary Kelly, *Women, Writing, and Revolution: 1790–1827* (Oxford: Clarendon, 1993), p. 44, note.

124. For information on George Robinson, see the *Dictionary of National Biography*.

125. This volume was entitled *Letters from France: Containing Many New Anecdotes Relative to the French Revolution and the Present State of French Manners* (London: Robinson, 1792).

126. Burke, *Reflections*, p. 170.

127. Helen Maria Williams, letter to Thrale Piozzi, 26 February 1792, John Rylands University Library of Manchester.

128. Sylvia Harcstark Myers, *The Bluestocking Circle*, p. x.

129. John Moore, *A Journal during a Residence in France, from the Beginning of August, to the Middle of December, 1792. To Which is Added, An Account of the Most Remarkable Events that Happened at Paris from that Time to the Death of the Late King of France*, 2 vols. (London: Robinson, 1793), 1:116–17.

130. *Memoirs of Madame Roland: A Heroine of the French Revolution*, trans. and ed. Evelyn Shuckburgh (London: Barrie and Jenkins, 1989), p. 55.

131. Mary Seidman Trouille, *Sexual Politics in the Enlightenment: Women Writers Read Rousseau* (New York: State University of New York Press, 1997), p. 172.

132. See Charles Dickens, *A Tale of Two Cities*, ed. George Woodcock (Harmondsworth: Penguin, 1986), ch. 8, p. 140–43.

133. On the trial of Thomas Paine see Carl B. Cone, *The English Jacobins: Reformers in Late 18th Century England* (New York: Charles Scribner's Sons, 1968), p.131; p.137–39; and Jack Fruchtman, Jr., *Thomas Paine: Apostle of Freedom* (New York: Four Walls Eight Windows, 1994), p. 288–91.

134. The London Corresponding Society was a radical group established in January 1792. See Cone, *The English Jacobins*, p.131; and Goodwin, *The Friends of Liberty*, p. 215. On English radicalism in the 1790s, see Michael T. Davis, ed., *Radicalism and Revolution in Britain 1775–1848* (London: Macmillan, 2000).

135. Rev. of *LF* 1.2, in *Critical Review* 6 (September 1792):65–72; 66.

136. Rev. of *LF* 1.2, in *Critical Review* 6 (September 1792):68.

137. Rev. of *LF* 1.2, in *English Review* 20 (July 1792):57–60.

138. Rev. of *LF* 1.2, in *Critical Review* 6 (September 1792):65–66.

139. James Mackintosh, *Vindicae Gallicae: A Defence of the French revolution and its English Admirers against the Accusations of the Rt. Hon. Edmund Burke* (1791); Benjamin Flower, *The French Constitution, with Remarks on Some of Its Principal Articles* (1792); and Jean-Paul Rabaut Saint-Étienne, *Considerations on the Rights and the Duties of the Third Estate* (1788) and *The History of the Revolution in France* (1793).

140. Rev. of *LF* 1.2, in *Critical Review* 6 (September 1792):72.

141. Rev. of *LF* 1.2, in *Analytical Review* 13 (August 1792):386–88; 386.

142. The book was *An Historical and Moral View of the Origin and Progress of the French Revolution; and the Effect if Has Produced on Europe*, vol. 1 (London: Johnson, 1794). Claire Tomalin entitles her chapter for this period "A Book and A Child." See Tomalin, *The Life and Death of Mary Wollstonecraft*, p. 162; and Janet Todd, *Mary Wollstonecraft: A Revolutionary Life* (London: Weidenfeld & Nicolson, 2000), p. 217.

143. George Dyer, "On Liberty," *Poems* (London: J. Johnson, 1792), p. 36.

CHAPTER 3. "ENGLISH HISTORIAN OF THE FRENCH REVOLUTION"

Portions of this chapter appeared in "Spectacle of the Guillotine," *Philological Quarterly* 73 (1994): 95–113. The chapter title, "English Historian of the French Revolution," is a phrase used by Athanase Coquerel to describe Williams, in "Reply to Dr. Strauss's Book 'The Life of Jesus,'" in *Voices of the Church*, ed. Rev. J. R. Beard (London: Simpkin, Marshall, 1845), p. 27.

1. "Review of Public Affairs: France," in *Critical Review* 6 (December 1792):571.

2. Jean Peltier, *The Late Picture of Paris, or Narrative of the Revolution of the Tenth of August*, vol. 1 (London, 1792), p. iii.

3. Helen Maria Williams, letter to Hester Thrale Piozzi, 4 September 1792, John Rylands University Library of Manchester.

4. Rev. of *LF* 1.2, in *English Review* 20 (July 1792):60.

5. David Erdman, *Commerce des Lumières: John Oswald and the British in Paris, 1790–1793* (Columbia: University of Missouri Press, 1986), p. 228.

6. Erdman, *Commerce des Lumières*, p. 226; p. 305.

7. Linda Kelly, *Women of the French Revolution* (London: Hamish Hamilton, 1987), p. 72.

8. Quoted in Erdman, *Commerce des Lumières*, p. 230.

9. Helen Maria Williams, letter to Hester Thrale Piozzi, 12 December 1792, John Rylands University Library of Manchester.

10. Williams is here quoting from Hamlet's soliloquy: "The undiscovered country from whose bourn / No traveller returns." William Shakespeare, *Hamlet* 3.1. 76.

11. Another guest at the supper, Baron Thiébault, recalled that the Bitaubés had arranged the supper because Chamfort wanted to be introduced to Williams (*Memoires du Général Baron Thiébault*, ed. Fernand Calmettes [Paris:Plon, 1894], p. 312).

12. On Chamfort, Ginguené, and Say, see Claude Arnaud, *Chamfort: A Biography*, trans. Deke Dusinberre (Chicago: University of Chicago Press, 1992), p. 254.

13. See Arnaud, *Chamfort*, p. 226.

14. C. Parra-Pérez, *Miranda et la Révolution Française* (Paris: Librairie Pierre Roger, 1925), p. 11.

15. *Lettres autographes de Madame Roland, addressées a Bancal-des-Issarts*, ed. Henriette Bancal-des-Issarts (Paris: Eugène Renduel, 1835), p. 350–55.

16. Francisque Mège, *Le Conventionnel Bancal des Issarts* (Paris: H. Champion, 1887), p. 30.

17. Later, after his imprisonment during the revolutionary wars, when Bancal returned to Paris in 1796, he had Grégoire write a letter on his behalf to Williams, proposing marriage. Williams did not accept him, but he married another woman, Marie Girard in January 1803, with whom he raised a large family. See Mège, *Le Conventionnel Bancal des Issarts*, p. 166.

18. Arnaud, *Chamfort*, p. 222.

19. Trouille, *Sexual Politics in the Enlightenment*, p. 163–92.

20. Claire Tomalin, *The Life and Death of Mary Wollstonecraft*, p. 119.

21. Mary Wollstonecraft, letter to Everina Wollstonecraft, 24 December 1792, in *Collected Letters of Mary Wollstonecraft*, p. 225–26.

22. See *Letters of Anna Seward* 3:208–9.

23. Helen Maria Williams, letters to Penelope Pennington, 1803 and 26 June 1819, in Piozzi-Pennington letters, Princeton University Library. Material from the Piozzi-Pennington letters is to be found in the Manuscripts Division of the Department of Rare Books and Special Collections of the Princeton University Library.

24. See Ronald Paulson, *Representations of Revolution 1789–1820* (New Haven: Yale University Press, 1983), p. 56.

25. Rev. of *LF* 1.3 and 1.4, in *Analytical Review* 17 (October 1793):127.

26. On the tenth of August 1792, see John Moore, *A Journal during a Residence in France* 1:41–70.

27. James Boswell, *The Life of Samuel Johnson*, 2 vols. (London: J. M. Dent, 1906), 2:515.

28. John Moore, *A Journal during a Residence in France* 1:338.

29. See Brian Rigby, "Radical Spectators of the Revolution: the Case of the *Analytical Review*," in *The French Revolution and British Culture*, ed. Ceri Crossley and Ian Small (Oxford: Oxford University Press, 1989), p. 67–73.

30. William Hazlitt, *The Life of Napoleon Bonaparte* 6 vols. (Paris: Napoleon Society, 1895), 1:203.

31. Romilly, *Memoirs* 2:2.

32. Romilly, *Memoirs* 2:4–5.

33. John Moore, *A Journal during a Residence in France* 1:391–92.

34. Ibid. 1:323.

35. Romilly, *Memoirs* 2:16.

36. John Hurford Stone, letter to William Stone, *A Complete Collection of State Trials* 25:1216.

37. John Moore, *A Journal during a Residence in France* 1:348.

38. Daniel Arasse, *The Guillotine and the Terror*, trans. Christopher Miller (Harmondsworth: Penguin, 1991), p. 61–65.

39. Stone wrote in a letter to his brother dated 16 February 1794: "I shall say no more of this man [Christie], as you say he is sunk into oblivion, but just to mention that amongst other extravagances, and claims, made in consequence, is that of a young girl who has obtained judgement against him for seduction, to the amount of 1200L." See *A Complete Collection of State Trials* 25:1222.

40. Hannah More, letter to Horace Walpole, 7 February 1793, in *Horace Walpole's Correspondence with Hannah More* 31:375.

41. Bindman, *The Shadow of the Guillotine*, p. 119. For a coloured copy of this print, see Donald, *The Age of Caricature*, p. 153. For an analysis of the print as representing the shifts in Williams's public reputation from chaste poet (British liberty) to raging democrat (French liberty), see my " 'Benevolent Historian': Helen Maria Williams and Her British Readers,"in *Rebellious Hearts: British Women Writers and the French Revolution*, eds. Adriana Craciun and Kari E. Lokke (New York: State University of New York Press, 2001), p. 317–336.

42. For the Gillray print, see Bindman, *The Shadow of the Guillotine*, p. 127; and for the Cruikshank print, see Donald, *The Age of Caricature*, p. 151.

43. H. T. Dickinson, *British Radicalism in the French Revolution*, p. 26–31.

44. Gillray's *New Morality* is widely reprinted, but a rare colour reprint can be found in *Hyenas in Petticoats: Mary Wollstonecraft and Mary Shelley*, by Robert Woof, Stephen Hebron, and Claire Tomalin (Kendal: Wordsworth Trust, 1997), p. 126–27.

45. Janet Todd, *Sensibility*, p. 129–49.

46. Cox, "Sensibility as Argument," p. 64–65.

47. Steven Blakemore, "Revolution and the French Disease: Laetitia Matilda Hawkins's *Letters* to Helen Maria Williams," *Studies in English Literature* 36 (1996):673–91.

48. Laetitia Matilda Hawkins, *Letters on the Female Mind, Its Powers and Pursuits. Addressed to Miss H. M. Williams, with Particular Reference to Her Letters from France*, 2 vols. (London: Hookham and Carpenter, 1793), 1:25. Vivien Jones describes how, especially after 1792, "the spectacle of women writing republican history was a triple violation — of sexual morality and generic decorum as well as national political loyalty." See "Women Writing Revolution: Narratives of History and Sexuality in Wollstonecraft and Williams," in *Beyond Romanticism*, ed. Stephen Copley and John Whale (London: Routledge, 1992), p. 179.

49. Hawkins, *Letters on the Female Mind* 1:7 and 1:104.

50. Ibid. 1:33; 2:25.

51. Helen Maria Williams, letter to Hester Thrale Piozzi, 29 July 1793, John Rylands University Library of Manchester.

52. Hawkins, *Letters on the Female Mind* 1:209.

53. Ibid. 2:106.

54. Hester Thrale Piozzi, letter to Penelope Pennington, 10 August 1793, in *The Piozzi Letters* 2:135–36.

55. Rev. of *LF* 1.3 and 1.4, in *British Critic* 2 (November 1793):252.

56. Williams began to write the first volume of the Second Series of *Letters* when she was in exile in Switzerland in 1794 and completed subsequent volumes upon her return to Paris. According to Williams, six letters were written in Switzerland: Letter One is dated "Switzerland, September 1794" (2.1.1); and, then, in Letter Seven (undated) but marked as "Paris," she explains that "since my last letter was written, I have left Switzerland, and returned to Paris" (2.1.169). An abridged version of these letters has been published for young readers: Jane Shuter, ed., *Helen Williams and the French Revolution*, (Austin: Raintree Steck-Vaughn, 1996).

57. Rev. of *LF* 2.1 and 2.2, in *Gentleman's Magazine* (August 1795):673.

58. Rev. of *LF* 2.3, in *Critical Review* 16 (January 1796):1.

59. Sylvia Harcstark Myers discusses this throughout *The Bluestocking Circle*.

60. The Whig politicians Algernon Sidney (1622–83) and Lord William Russell (1639–83) were executed in 1683 after being implicated in the Rye House plot to execute Charles II and his brother, the Duke of York. John Hampden (1594–1643), an opponent of Charles I and a member of the Long Parliament, died in battle during the English Civil War. See Jack Fruchtman, Jr., ed., *An Eye-Witness Account of the French Revolution by Helen Maria Williams* (New York: Peter Lang, 1997), p. 164; p. 245 note.

61. John Adolphus, *History of France from the Year 1790 to the Peace Concluded at Amiens in 1802*, 3 vols. (London: George Kearsley, 1803), 2:6.

62. Robert Southey, letter to Horace Walpole Bedford, 22 August 1794, in *New Letters of Robert Southey*, ed. Kenneth Curry, vol. 1 (New York: Columbia University Press, 1965), p. 73

63. William Wordsworth, *The Prelude*, 1805: Book 10:577–85.

64. See Lynn Hunt, *Politics, Culture, and Class in the French Revolution* (Berkeley: University of California Press, 1986), p. 94–98.

65. Felicia Hemans, *Poetical Works* (Philadelphia: Lippincott, 1855), p. 364.

66. See Richard C. Sha's discussion of this episode in his "Expanding the Limits of Feminine Writing: The Prose Sketches of Sydney Owenson (Lady Morgan) and Helen Maria Williams," in *Romantic Women Writers: Voices and Countervoices*, ed. Paula R. Feldman and Theresa M. Kelley (Hanover: University Press of New England, 1995), p. 204.

67. See Bartoszewski, "La Famille Coquerel."

68. Rigby, "Radical Spectators of the Revolution," p. 79.

69. Jacques Mallet du Pan, *Considerations on the Nature of the French Revolution and on the Causes Which Prolong Its Duration*, introduction by Paul H. Beik (New York: Howard Fertig, 1974), p. 90.

70. Elizabeth Bohls, *Women Travel Writers and the Language of Aesthetics, 1716–1818* (Cambridge: Cambridge University Press, 1995), p. 130.

71. Harold T. Parker, *The Cult of Antiquity and the French Revolutionaries: A Study in the Development of the Revolutionary Spirit* (New York: Octagon, 1965), p. 173.

72. Dorinda Outram, *The Body and the French Revolution: Sex, Class, and Political Culture* (New Haven: Yale University Press, 1989), p. 101.

73. Outram, *The Body and the French Revolution*, p. 85.

74. Chantal Thomas, "Heroism in the Feminine: The Examples of Charlotte Corday and Madame Roland," in *The French Revolution 1789–1989: Two Hundred Years of Rethinking*, ed. Sandy Petrey (Lubbock, Texas: Texas Tech University Press, 1989), p. 80.

75. Judith Scheffler contends that Williams presents the female victims as apolitical. See "Romantic Women Writing on Imprisonment and Prison Reform," *The Wordsworth Circle* 19 (1988):99–103.

76. Chris Jones, "Helen Maria Williams and Radical Sensibility," *Prose Studies* 12 (1989):12.

77. See *Women in Revolutionary Paris, 1789–95: Selected Documents Translated with Notes and Commentary*, eds. Darline Gay Levy, Harriet Bronson Applewhite, and Mary Durham Johnson (Chicago: University of Illinois Press, 1979), p. 180.

78. Anna Laetitia Barbauld, *Memoirs, Letters, and A Selection from the Poems and Prose Writings of Anna Laetitia Barbauld*, ed. Grace A. Oliver (Boston: J. R. Osgood, 1874), p. 207–8.

79. Romilly, *Memoirs* 2:48.

80. Lewis Goldsmith, *Female Revolutionary Plutarch*, vol. 3. (London: John Murray, 1806), p. 404.

81. See Shirley Elson Roessler, "The 'Citoyennes' against the Girondins,"in *Out of the Shadows: Women and Politics in the French Revolution, 1789–95* (New York: Peter Lang, 1996), p. 113–24; and Dominique Godineau, *The Women of Paris and Their French Revolution*, trans. Katherine Streip (Berkeley: University of California Press, 1998),p. 128.

82. Antoine-Joseph Gorsas is quoted in Shirley Elson Roessler, *Out of the Shadows*, p. 122–23.

83. Roudinesco, *Madness and Revolution*, p. 129.

84. See Roudinesco, *Madness and Revolution*, p. 271; p. 272; and Godineau, *The Women of Paris*, p. 391; p. 394.

85. Statistics on the Reign of Terror are taken from Donald Greer, *The Incidence of the Terror during the French Revolution: A Statistical Interpretation* (Cambridge: Harvard University Press, 1935).

86. Arasse, *The Guillotine and the Terror*, p. 58; p. 68.

87. Wordsworth, *The Prelude*, 1805: Book 10:330–33.

88. John Lofland, "The Dramaturgy of State Executions," *State Executions Viewed Historically and Sociologically* (Montclair, N.J.: Patterson Smith, 1977), p. 292.

89. Lofland, "The Dramaturgy of State Executions," p. 308.

90. Arasse, *The Guillotine and the Terror*, p. 93–104.

91. Ann Rigney, *The Rhetoric of Historical Representation: Three Narratives of the French Revolution* (Cambridge: Cambridge University Press, 1990), p. ix, 60, 50–51.

92. See Regina Janes, "Beheadings," *Representations* 35 (1991):23.

93. The engraving is reprinted in an article by Mary Jacobus, "Incorruptible Milk: Breast-feeding and the French Revolution," in *Rebel Daughters*, ed. Sara E. Melzer and Leslie W. Rabine (Oxford: Oxford University Press, 1992), p. 62.

94. Rev. of *LF* 2.1 and 2.2, in *English Review* 26 (October 1795):247–48.

95. Rigney, *The Rhetoric of Historical Representation*, p. 41.

96. Thomas Carlyle, *The French Revolution*, ed. K. J. Fielding and David Sorensen, 2 vols. (Oxford: Oxford University Press, 1989), 2:419.

97. Rev. of *LF* 2.3, in *Analytical Review* 23 (January 1796):23.

98. Hedva Ben-Israel, *English Historians on the French Revolution* (Cambridge: Cambridge University Press, 1969), p. 13.

99. Elson Roessler, *Out of the Shadows*, p. 194. See also Godineau, *The Women of Paris*, p. 343.

100. For Elson Roessler's comment and her quotation of the decree (from the *Moniteur* 24:515), see *Out of the Shadows*, p. 193.

101. Georges Lefebvre, *The French Revolution from 1793 to 1799*, trans. John Hall Stewart and James Friguglietti (London: Routledge & Kegan Paul, 1967), p. 144.

CHAPTER 4. A TOUR OF SWITZERLAND:
THE SUBLIME AND THE POLITICAL

Portions of this chapter are reprinted with permission from "Revolutionizing Switzerland: Helen Maria Williams and 1798." In *Republikanische Tugend*, ed. Michael Böhler, et al. (Geneva: Slatkine, 2000), p. 547–55.

1. Rev. of *LF* 2.1;2.2, in *British Critic* 6 (October 1795):493.

2. Rev. of *LF* 2.1;2.1, in *Critical Review* 14 (August 1795):361; and Rev. of *LF* 2.3;2.4, in *New Annual Register* (1795):244.

3. Her letter to Vernor and Hood is located in the Evelyn Collection in the British Library.

4. See Philip Robinson, "Traduction ou Trahison de *Paul et Virginie*? L'exemple de Helen Maria Williams," *Revue d'Histoire Littéraire de la France* 89 (September–October 1989):846.

5. Helen Maria Williams, Preface, *Paul and Virginia*, by J. H. Bernardin de St.-Pierre (Oxford: Woodstock, 1989), p. vi. Subsequent quotations from this work are cited parenthetically in the text.

6. See Jonathan Wordsworth, Introduction, *Paul and Virginia* (Oxford: Woodstock, 1989), n. p.

7. Gary Harrison, *Wordsworth's Vagrant Muse: Poetry, Poverty, and Power* (Detroit: Wayne State University Press, 1994), p. 60

8. *Poems. Moral, Elegant and Pathetic, viz. Essay on Man, by Pope; The Monk of La Trappe, by Jerningham; The Grave, by Blair; An Elegy in a Country Churchyard, by Gray; The Hermit of Warkworth, by Percy; and Original Sonnets by Helen Maria Williams* (London: Vernor and Hood, 1796).

9. Ovid, *Tristia*, trans. Arthur Leslie Wheeler, Loeb Classical Library (Cambridge: Harvard University Press, 1975), 1.11.7.

10. Ibid., 1.11.35–40.

11. See Anna Letitia Barbauld, "Ovid to his Wife, in *The Poems of Anna Letitia Barbauld*, ed. William McCarthy and Elizabeth Kraft (Athens: University of Georgia Press, 1994), p. 74.

12. The following statement in *The Times* in September 1794 added grist to the gossip mill and alarmed Williams's friends back in England: "Private letters from Paris, mention the marriage there of Mr. Stone, a person well known in this country, with Miss Helen Williams, the Poetess. Stone had previously got divorced from his wife." *The Times* 18 September 1794, p. 2. Hester Thrale Piozzi wrote to her friends about it; and Penelope Pennington asked her: " 'Is what all the Papers have announced *true*, that Helen Williams *is married* to that *Stone*? — Oh what a falling off from all true Sentiment is there!!!.' " See Hester Thrale Piozzi, *The Piozzi Letters* 2:239–40, note 5.

13. Helen Maria Williams, "On the Death of Rev. Dr. Kippis," p.66.

14. Helen Maria Williams, letter to Penelope Pennington, 1803, Piozzi-Pennington letters, Princeton University Library. She is quoting Job 16:19.

15. Ibid., 26 June 1819, Piozzi-Pennington letters, Princeton University Library.

16. The account of the trial of William Stone is taken from *A Complete Collection of State Trials*.

17. Benjamin Vaughan, M. P., was known to have written a paper for Stone, arguing against the invasion. Thinking that he might be arrested, he left for France and then travelled in Switzerland with Stone and Williams. See Craig C. Murray, *Benjamin Vaughan*, p. 338–44.

18. *A Complete Collection of State Trials* 25:1394.

19. Ibid. 25:1226.

20. John Hurford Stone, letter to William Stone, 26 December 1793: "Cecy. Williams is about to be married to a young citizen of Normandy, the nephew of the nobleman whose history her sister writes in the first volumes; and as he is acquainted with the cotton manuf. and we have here English workmen, who are otherwise starving, we have engaged in a manufactory of English fashion cotton hose, of which he has the superintendence" (*A Complete Collection of State Trials* 25:1214).

21. Woodward devotes nearly all of his chapter on the Swiss *Tour* to the mystery of Stone's alleged "mission" in that country (Woodward 113–27). He quotes from several conflicting documents; some accuse Stone of spying for Pitt, others of collecting information for France. Without further research, the matter remains inconclusive.

22. Helen Maria Williams, letter to Penelope Pennington, 1803, in Piozzi-Pennington letters, Princeton University Library.

23. See Bartoszewski, "La Famille Coquerel."

24. Helen Maria Williams, letter to Penelope Pennington, 1803, in Piozzi-Pennington letters, Princeton University Library.

25. Craig C. Murray, *Benjamin Vaughan*, p. 347.

26. Williams describes Colonel Frey in *A Tour in Switzerland; Or, A View of the Present*

State of the Governments and Manners of those Cantons: with Comparative Sketches of the Present State of Paris, 2 vols. (London: G. G. and J. Robinson, 1798) 1:117. Subsequent quotations from this work are cited parenthetically in the text. See Craig C. Murray, *Benjamin Vaughan*, p. 348. On LeGrand, see R. R. Palmer, *The Age of the Democratic Revolution*, vol. 2 (Princeton: Princeton University Press, 1964), p. 405.

27. Helen Maria Williams, letter to Penelope Pennington, 1803, in Piozzi-Pennington letters, Princeton University Library.

28. Switzerland was a confederation founded in 1291 by the three forest cantons of Uri, Schwyz, and Unterwald. Over time these were joined by a number of other cantons (13 by the eighteenth century) and subject regions, whose co-existence was impressive because of their diversity in religion (Protestant and Catholic), region (urban and rural), language (German, French, Romanch, and Italian), and government (five different forms of government, primarily oligarchic). For a brief outline, see Pierre Cordey, "The Historical Evolution," trans. Helmuth A. Lindemann, in *The Historical Evolution, Political Institutions*, volume 2 of *Focus on Switzerland* (Lausanne: Swiss Office for the Development of Trade, 1975), p. 48–49.

29. T. Rennie Warburton, "The Rise of Nationalism in Switzerland," *Canadian Review of Studies in Nationalism* 7 (1980):277.

30. Georg Thürer, *Free and Swiss: The Story of Switzerland*, trans. R. P. Heller and E. Long (Coral Gables: University of Miami Press, 1971), p. 97.

31. See Eric Hobsbawm, *The Age of Revolution 1789–1848* (London: Cardinal, 1988), p. 105.

32. Ernest Giddey, "1816: Switzerland and the Revival of the 'Grand Tour,' " *The Byron Society* 19 (1991):17–25.

33. On the popularity, even among the English, of Ramond's French translation of Coxe, Claire Eliane Engel explains "The original was dull; Ramond's translation was more lively and, on the whole, fairly accurate; his notes were masterly" (*A History of Mountaineering in the Alps* [London: George Allen and Unwin, 1950], p. 40).

34. See Max Wildi, "Wordsworth and the Simplon Pass," *English Studies* 40 (1959):225; and Duncan Wu, *Wordsworth's Reading* (Cambridge: Cambridge University Press, 1993), p. 40, 116.

35. Peter Barber, *Swiss 700: Treasures from the British Library and British Museum to Celebrate 700 Years of the Swiss Confederation* (London: British Library, 1991), p. 51.

36. Chris Jones, "Helen Maria Williams and Radical Sensibility," p. 15.

37. It was a common view among the French that "the Swiss would stage their own revolution." See R. R. Palmer, *The Age of the Democratic Revolution*, p. 410.

38. The *Memoirs* (1780) of Thomas Hollis (1720–74) are quoted by John Wraight, *The Swiss and the British* (Wilton: Michael Russell, 1987), p. 169.

39. William Coxe first travelled to Switzerland in 1776 and published an account of his journey in *Sketches of the Natural, Civil, and Political State of Swisser land* (1779), which was translated into French by Ramond de Carbonnière. After trips in 1785 and 1787, Coxe published an expanded edition under the new title *Travels in Switzerland, in a series of letters to William Melmoth*, 3 vols. (London: Cadell, 1789). All citations are from the 1789 edition. The first is from Coxe 1:4. His famous remark is often quoted. See for example, Gavin Rylands de Beer, *Early Travellers in the Alps* (London: Sidgwick & Jackson, 1930), p. 133.

40. Addison, who visited Switzerland in 1701, is quoted in Arnold Lunn, *Switzerland in English Prose and Poetry* (London: Eyre and Spottiswode, 1947), p. 14.

41. John Bernard Trotter, *Memoirs of the Latter Years of the Right Honourable Charles James Fox* (London: Richard Phillips, 1811), p. 255.

42. Rev. of Williams's *Tour*, in *Monthly Review* 27 (1798):144.

43. Helen Maria Williams, letter to Hester Thrale Piozzi, 10 August 1794, John Rylands University Library of Manchester.

44. John Murray III, *A Hand-book for Travellers in Switzerland* (London: John Murray, 1838).

45. The use of crampons was crucial to travel by foot in the regions of the glaciers. Discussing his journey across the ice fields at Chamounix near Mont Blanc, which Williams did not visit, William Coxe provides the following information (Coxe 1:421–22):

> we prepared for our adventure across the ice. We had each of us a long pole spiked with iron; and, in order to secure us as much as possible from slipping, the guides fastened to our shoes *crampons*, or small bars of iron, provided with four small spikes of the same metal. . . . One of our servants had the courage to follow us without *crampons*, and with no nails in his shoes; which was certainly dangerous, on account of the slipperiness of the leather when wetted.

46. Thomas Gray, letter to Mrs. Gray, 7 November 1739, in *Correspondence of Thomas Gray*, ed. Paget Toynbee and Leonard Whibley, 3 vols. (Oxford: Clarendon, 1935), 1:126.

47. She wrote, "O SWITZERLAND! how oft these eyes / Desire to view thy mountains," in "An Epistle to Dr. Moore, Author of A View of Society and Manners, in France, Switzerland, and Germany" (*Poems* 2:11).

48. Rev. of Williams's *Tour*, in *Analytical Review* 27 (June 1798):565.

49. Rev. of Williams's *Tour*, in *European Magazine* 31 (June 1798):391.

50. See *The Sublime: A Reader in Eighteenth-Century Aesthetic Theory*, ed. Andrew Ashfield and Peter de Bolla (Cambridge: Cambridge University Press, 1996), p. 300–306.

51. William Coxe, *Travels in Switzerland* 1:12.

52. Rev. of Williams's *Tour*, in *Monthly Review* 27 (1798):132–33.

53. Thomas Gray, letter to Richard West, 16 November 1739, in *Correspondence of Thomas Gray* 1:128.

54. William Wordsworth, letter to Dorothy Wordsworth, 6 and 16 September 1790, in *The Letters of William and Dorothy Wordsworth: The Early Years* 1:34.

55. Wordsworth, *The Prelude*, 1805: Book 6:617–57.

56. Wraight, *The Swiss and the British*, p. 54.

57. Basel was a center for the Swiss revolutionary movement, headed by the guildmaster Peter Ochs. Williams makes no mention of Ochs in her *Tour*, though she probably knew him by 1798, when he was something of a political rival to her friend La Harpe in Paris.

58. Wilhelm Oechsli, *History of Switzerland 1499–1914*, trans. Eden and Cedar Paul (Cambridge: Cambridge University Press, 1922), p. 265–66.

59. William Godwin, "On Property," in *Enquiry Concerning Political Justice*, ed. Isaac Kramnick (Harmondsworth: Penguin, 1985), p. 730–31.

60. Kate Silber, *Pestalozzi: The Man and His Work* (London: Routledge and Kegan Paul, 1969), p. 107–11.

61. Peter Kamber, "Enlightenment, Revolution, and the Libraries in Lucerne, 1787–1812," in *Libraries and Culture* 26 (Winter 1991):203.

62. Ibid., p. 204.

63. Ibid., p. 207–9.

64. Gavin Rylands de Beer, *Early Travellers in the Alps*, p. 133.

65. William Coxe, *Travels in Switzerland* 1:52–53.

66. Ibid., 1:52.

67. Chris Jones, "Helen Maria Williams and Radical Sensibility," p. 15–19.

68. Oechsli, *History of Switzerland*, p. 291–92.

69. William Coxe, *Travels in Switzerland* 2:77–78.

70. Burke, *Reflections*, p. 263.

71. Jacques Godechot, *The Counter-Revolution: Doctrine and Action 1789–1804*, trans. Salvator Attanasio (London: Routledge, 1972), p. 77–79. In her next book *Sketches* (1:62–73), Williams repudiates Mallet du Pan's well known essay on the French invasion of 1798, which he published in the first issue of the *Mercure Brittannique*, August 20, 1798, and which was translated into English the next year as *The History of the Destruction of the Helevetic Union and Liberty*. Mallet du Pan died May 10, 1801.

72. Another guide near Bellinzona had boasted of taking over St Gotthard Mountain the famous Duchess of Devonshire, whom Williams praises (2:190–91). In 1799 Georgiana Cavendish, Duchess of Devonshire (1757–1806) published "The Passage of the Mountain of St. Gothard" based on her trip to Italy and Switzerland in 1793, the year before Williams's tour. See *Eighteenth-Century Women Poets*, ed. Roger Lonsdale, p. 510–11.

73. Williams's conclusion is quoted in Walter Schmid, *Romantic Switzerland: Mirrored in the Literature and Graphic Art of the 18th and 19th Centuries* (Zurich: Swiss National Tourist Office, 1952), n. p. The same paragraph from Williams is also quoted by Arnold Lunn in *Switzerland in English Prose and Poetry*, p.xiii.

74. Announcement of Williams's *Tour*, in *Monthly Magazine* 5 (January 1798):131.

75. The *British Critic* implied that her relationship with Stone was an improper one: "Miss or Mrs. Williams consequently felt no compunction at attending Mr. S. on his excursion." Rev. of Williams's *Tour* in *British Critic* 12 (July 1798):24; and see "Misrepresentations," *Anti-Jacobin or, Weekly Examiner* 30 April 1798:233.

76. See "Misrepresentations," p. 233; p. 231.

77. Rev. of Williams's *Tour*, in *Monthly Review* 27 (1798):140; 139–40.

78. Rev. of Williams's *Tour*, in *European Magazine* (June 1798):390.

79. Rev. of Williams's *Tour*, in *European Magazine* (May 1798):324.

80. Rev. of Williams's *Tour*, in *Monthly Magazine* 5 (1798):492 (Supplement).

81. J. B. Say, Preface, *Nouveau Voyage en Suisse*, by Helen Maria Williams (Paris: Charles Pougens, AN VI [1798]), p. xi–xiii.

82. The French edition lists bookstores across Europe where the book was on sale.

83. John Hurford Stone, letter to Joseph Priestley, 12 February 1798, in *Copies of Original Letters Written by Persons in Paris to Dr. Priestley in America, Taken on Board a Neutral Vessel*, 2nd. ed. (London: J. Wright, 1798), p. 15–16.

84. The anonymous Preface in *Copies of Original Letters* is dated 14 May 1798. William Cobbett reprinted the letters in the August 1798 issue of his *Gazette* in Philadelphia; and he attacked Priestley, Stone, and Williams again in the September 1798 issue. The whole affair was very troublesome for Priestley, especially since the Alien and Sedition Acts had been passed in the United States Congress in June and July 1798, and "A foreigner suspected of being 'dangerous to the peace and safety of the United States' could now be deported by Presidential decree, without the right of redress or appeal." See Jenny Graham, *Revolutionary in Exile: The Emigration of Joseph Priestley to America 1794–1804* (Philadelphia: American Philosophical Society, 1995), p. 107.

85. Joseph Priestley, letter to Theophilus Lindsey, 6 September 1798, in *The Theological and Miscellaneous Works of Joseph Priestley* 1:407. It was not long before Priestley was again corresponding with Stone and recommending him to the new President Thomas Jefferson. See Joseph Priestley, letter to Thomas Jefferson, 29 October 1802, in Jenny Graham, *Revolutionary in Exile*, p. 185.

86. John Hurford Stone, letter to Benjamin Vaughan, 12 February 1798, in *Copies of Original Letters*, p. 29–30.

87. Cecilia Coquerel, in *Copies of Original Letters*, p. 36; and Helen Maria Williams, in *Copies of Original Letters*, p.36.

88. Announcement of Williams's *Tour*, in *Monthly Magazine* 5 (January 1798):131.

CHAPTER 5. THE NAPOLEONIC ERA

1. Bartoszewski, "La Famille Coquerel."

2. Helen Maria Williams, *Sketches of the State of Manners and Opinions in the French Republic, towards the Close of the Eighteenth Century. In a Series of Letters*, 2 vols. (London: G. G. and J. Robinson, 1801), 1:28–29. Subsequent quotations from this work are cited parenthetically in the text.

3. John Goldworth Alger, "English Witnesses of the French Revolution," *Edinburgh Review* 168 (July 1888):158.

4. Rev. of Williams's *Sketches*, in *Critical Review* 31 (February 1801):183.

5. Rev. of Williams's *Sketches*, in *Monthly Review* 35 (May 1801):82.

6. J. Mallet du Pan, *The History of the Destruction of the Helvetic Union and Liberty* (Boston: Manning and Loring, 1799), p. 217.

7. La Harpe, who escaped after being arrested for plotting against Bonaparte, lived in retirement till 1814, when he again became actively involved in Swiss politics. See Stephen Davies, "La Harpe, Frédéric César de, in *Biographical Dictionary of Modern European Radicals and Socialists*, volume 1: 1780–1815, ed. David Nicholls and Peter Marsh (New York: St. Martin's Press, 1988), p. 151–54.

8. Her poem was entitled "Peace and Shepherd." See William McCarthy and Elizabeth Kraft, ed. *The Poems of Anna Letitia Barbauld* (Athens: University of Georgia Press, 1994), note p. 299.

9. William James MacNevin, M. D., *A Ramble Through Swisserland in the Summer and Autumn of 1802* (Dublin: J. Stockdale, 1803), p. 176, note.

10. MacNevin, *A Ramble Through Swisserland*, p. 14.

11. Cornelia Knight, who lived with the Hamiltons in 1799, observed that "The common people generally agreed with the Court, but many of the young nobles were infected with the revolutionary spirit" (Ellis Cornelia Knight, *Autobiography of Miss Cornelia Knight, Lady Companion to the Princess Charlotte of Wales*, 3rd. ed., 2 vols. [London: W. H. Allen, 1861], p. 107).

12. Harry Hearder, *Italy in the Age of the Risorgimento 1790–1870* (London: Longman, 1983), p. 128.

13. Benedetto Croce, *History of the Kingdom of Naples*, ed. H. Stuart Hughes and trans. Frances Frenaye (Chicago: University of Chicago Press, 1970), p. 205.

14. Sir Nicholas Harris Nicolas, *The Dispatches and Letters of Vice-Admiral Lord Viscount Nelson. With Notes by Sir Nicholas Harris Nicolas*, vol. 3 (London: Henry Colburn, 1845), p. 499.

15. Ibid. 3:502.

16. Ibid. 3:504.

17. Robert Southey, *The Life of Nelson*, intro. R. D. Madison, Classics of Naval Literature (Annapolis, Maryland: Naval Institute Press, 1990), p. 166.

18. Charles James Fox is cited by Roy Hattersley in *Nelson* (London: Weidenfeld and Nicolson, 1974), p. 107.

19. See Nicolas, *The Dispatches and Letters of Vice-Admiral Lord Viscount Nelson* 3:504.

20. For a complete acquittal of Emma Hamilton, see Mollie Hardwick, *Emma Lady Hamilton* (London: Cassell, 1969), p. 59; and Norah Lofts, *Emma Hamilton* (London: Michael Joseph, 1978), p. 80–81.

21. Emiliana P. Noether, "Eleonora De Fonseca Pimentel and the Neapolitan Revolution of 1799," *Consortium on Revolutionary Europe* (1989):76–88; 77.

22. Ibid., p. 80.

23. See the entry in the *British Museum Catalogue*.

24. E. W. Pitcher, "Changes in Short Fiction in Britain, 1785–1810: Philosophic

Tales, Gothic Tales, and Fragments and Visions," *Studies in Short Fiction* 13 (Summer 1976):342.

25. Ibid., p. 340–41.

26. On the plebiscite for the Constitution of 1800, see William Doyle, *The Oxford History of the French Revolution*, p. 378.

27. See *Spectator* Numbers 57 and 81, in Richard Steele and Joseph Addison, *Selections from The Tatler and The Spectator*, ed. Angus Ross (Harmondsworth: Penguin, 1988), p. 250–54; 440–43.

28. Mary Astell, *A Serious Proposal to the Ladies*, ed. Katherine Rogers and William McCarthy, *The Meridian Anthology of Early Women Writers* (New York: New American Library, 1987), p. 118.

29. Ibid., p. 121.

30. Virginia Woolf, *A Room of One's Own* (1929; London: Granada, 1981), p.7; p.9.

31. Hannah More, from chapter thirteen and chapter one, *Strictures on the Modern System of Female Education* (1799), in *Women in the Eighteenth Century*, ed. Vivien Jones (New York: Routledge, 1990), p. 138; p. 131.

32. Mary Wollstonecraft, Chapter Nine, "On the Pernicious Effects which Arise form the Unnatural Distinctions Established in Society," *A Vindication of the Rights of Woman*, ed. Carol H. Poston (New York: Norton, 1988), p. 148–49.

33. See Peter Staffel, "Recovering Thalestris: Intragender Conflict in *The Rape of the Lock*," in *Pope, Swift, and Women Writers*, ed. Donald C. Mell (Newark: University of Delaware Press, 1996), p. 98.

34. Proctor, *Women, Equality, and the French Revolution*, p. 177–78.

35. Rev. of Williams's *Sketches*, in *Critical Review* 31 (February 1801):188.

36. David Chandler explains that "In March 1796 Napoleon Bonaparte was known only to comparatively restricted circles within France, but a year later his name had become a household word throughout Europe"(*The Campaigns of Napoleon* [London: Weidenfeld and Nicolson, 1967], p. 130).

37. "Original Anecdotes on Eminent Persons—Buonaparte," *Monthly Magazine* 4 (May 1797):377.

38. Simon Bainbridge cites a long list of famous historical personages to whom Bonaparte is compared. See Simon Bainbridge, *Napoleon and English Romanticism* (Cambridge: Cambridge University Press, 1995), p. 13.

39. Richard Brinsley Sheridan, *The Speeches of the Right Honourable Richard Brinsley Sheridan*, vol. 3 (New York: Russell & Russell, 1969), p. 382.

40. Coleridge's comment is from a letter to Southey dated 15 October 1799, quoted in Simon Bainbridge, *Napoleon and English Romanticism*, p. 22.

41. Hélèna-Maria Williams, *Aperçu de l'état des moeurs et des opinions dans la République française vers la fin du xviiie siècle*, traduit par Mme [Sophie] Grandchamp (Paris: Levrault, 1801). Sophie Grandchamp wrote a memoir of Madame Roland in 1806, which was published as "Souvenirs de Sophie Grandchamp," in *Mémoires de Madame Roland*, ed. C. Perroud, 2 vols, (Paris: Plon, 1905), 2:461–97.

42. The treaty of Luneville alienated Kosciuszko from Bonaparte in 1801. From 1809 to 1814 Kosciuszko lived under police supervision in a French country retreat. See Monica M. Gardner, *Kosciuszko: A Biography* (London: George Allen, 1920), p. 190.

43. Lafayette broke with Bonaparte when he became Consul for Life. See Lloyd Kramer, *Lafayette in Two Worlds: Public Cultures and Personal Identities in an Age of Revolutions* (Chapel-Hill: University of North Caroline Press, 1996), p. 57.

44. Louis Bergeron, *France under Napoleon*, trans. R. R. Palmer (1972; Princeton: Princeton University Press, 1981), p. 8.

45. Bertie Greatheed, *An Englishman in Paris: 1803*, ed. J. P. T. Bury and J. C. Barry (London: Geoffrey Bles, 1953), p. 43.

46. Ernest Lavisse, *Histoire de France Contemporaine depuis la révolution jusqu'à la paix de 1919,* vol. 3 (Paris: Librairie Hachette, 1921), p. 152.

47. Thomas Poole, *Thomas Poole and His Friends,* ed. Mrs. Henry Sandford, 2 vols. (London: Macmillan, 1888), 2:90.

48. Joseph Farington, entry for 5 October 1802, *The Diary of Joseph Farington,* p. 1902.

49. "Miss Williams," *Notes and Queries* 5 December 1968: 533–34.

50. Catherine Wilmot, *An Irish Peer on the Continent (1801–1803): Being a Narrative of the Tour of Stephen, 2nd Earl Mount Cashell, Through France, Italy, etc., as Related by Catherine Wilmot,* ed. Thomas U. Sadleir (London: Williams and Norgate, 1920), p. 40.

51. "Miss Williams," p. 533.

52. Gary Kelly, *Women, Writing, and Revolution 1790–1827* (Oxford: Clarendon, 1993), p. 200–203.

53. Wilmot (1774–1824) was an heiress and the eldest daughter of Captain Edward Wilmot, a resident of Cork. See Wilmot, *An Irish Peer,* p. viii–xiii.

54. Helen Maria Williams, letter to Penelope Pennington, 1803, in Piozzi-Pennington letters, Princeton University Library.

55. Wilmot, *An Irish Peer,* p. 38–39.

56. Helen Maria Williams, letter to Penelope Pennington, 1803, in Piozzi-Pennington letters, Princeton University Library.

57. Ibid., 26 June 1819, in Piozzi-Pennington letters, Princeton University Library.

58. Wilmot, *An Irish Peer,* p. 52.

59. Ibid., p. 40; p. 52; p. 77.

60. In her entry of 31 January 1802, recounting the party at Smith's two weeks earlier, Wilmot writes that "We were introduced to Madame de Stael-Holstein, Necker's daughter . . . We also were introduced to Helen Maria Williams" (Wilmot, *An Irish Peer,* p. 38). William Loughton Smith is mentioned in an article by Rosemarie Zagarri where she quotes from a speech he made in support of the rights of women. See Rosemarie Zagarri, "The Rights of Man and Woman in Post-Revolutionary America," *William and Mary Quarterly* 55 (April 1998):223.

61. Barlow is quoted in *Life and Letters of Joel Barlow,* ed. Charles Burr Todd (New York: G. P. Putnam), p. 195.

62. Greatheed, *An Englishman in Paris: 1803,* p. 150.

63. Helen Maria Williams, letter to Penelope Pennington 26 June 1819, in Piozzi-Pennington letters, Princeton University Library.

64. See Luc de Nanteuil, *Jacques-Louis David* (New York: Harry N. Abrams, 1985), p. 144–45. A portrait of Français de Nantes, painted in 1811, is regarded as one of David's masterpieces. For information on Antoine Français de Nantes, see *Dictionnaire de Biographie Française,* ed. M. Prevost, Roman D'Amat, and H. Tribout de Morembert (Paris: Librairie Letouzey et Ané, 1979), 4:944–45. See Woodward 69.

65. William Shepherd, *Paris, in 1802 and 1814,* 3rd. ed. (London: Longman, Hurst, Rees, Orme and Brown, 1814), p. 77–78.

66. For information on Caroline von Wolzogen, see Elke Frederiksen, ed., *Women Writers of Germany, Austria, and Switzerland: An Annotated Bio-Bibliographical Guide* (New York: Greenwood Press, 1989), p. 259.

67. This passage is quoted in "Miss Williams," p. 533. See also Ludwig von Urlichs, *Charlotte Von Schiller und ihre Freunde* (Stuttgart, 1862), p. 75–85.

68. Barlow is quoted in *Life and Letters of Joel Barlow,* p. 195.

69. Joel Barlow, letter to Ruth Barlow, 30 July 1802, in James Woodress, *A Yankee's Odyssey: The Life of Joel Barlow* (Philadelphia: J. B. Lippincott, 1958), p. 222.

70. Reichardt, J. F., *Un hiver à Paris sous le consulat 1802–1803*, ed. A. Laquiante (Paris: Plon, 1896), p. 80–85.

71. Poole, *Thomas Poole and His Friends* 2:90.

72. "Miss Williams," p. 533–34.

73. Maria Edgeworth, letter to Sophy Ruxton, 8 December 1802, in *Maria Edgeworth in France and Switzerland: Selections from the Edgeworth Family Letters*, ed. Christina Colvin (Oxford: Clarendon, 1979), p. 53.

74. Fox's secretary John B. Trotter gives an account of this incident:

[In September 1802] an invitation was sent to Mr. Fox, from Miss Helen Maria Williams. She requested the pleasure of his company to an evening party, and to express how much this honour would gratify her, wrote that it would be "a white day," thus distinguished. Some of Mr. Fox's friends wished him to decline this invitation altogether, from apprehension of giving a handle to ill-nature and calumny. He, however, always the same, disdaining the *fear of suspicion*, and unwilling ungraciously to refuse an invitation earnestly pressed, did not agree with them, and went for a short time. I mention this circumstance because it proves how unwilling he was to give offence or pain, as also, how much he soared above common party views. He was aware that he might be misrepresented and blackened by going to Miss Williams's *conversazione*, as much as he had been for admitting Mr. A. O'Connor to his presence; but he despised slander, was not anxious for place, and was too benignant to slight, with contempt and scorn, the request of an accomplished female, whose vanity, as well as a natural admiration of so great a man, were deeply concerned that he should grant it.

See Trotter, *Memoirs*, p. 287–88.

75. Farington, *The Diary of Joseph Farington*, p. 1902.

76. Jacobine Menzies-Wilson and Helen Lloyd, *Amelia: the Tale of a Plain Friend* (London: Oxford University Press, 1937), p. 113.

77. Ibid., p. 114.

78. "In 1801 came the Treaty of Luneville with Napoleon's bitter deception of Poland's hopes. . . . Henceforth Kosciuszko would have nothing further to say to Bonaparte" (Monica M. Gardner, *Kosciuszko: A Biography*, p. 187).

79. Helen Maria Williams, letter to Lord Holland, 22 July 1802, British Library. This material is published with the permission of the British Library Board.

80. E. Tangye Lean, *The Napoleonists: A Study in Political Disaffection 1760–1960* (London: Oxford University Press, 1970), p. 137–38.

81. Farington, *The Diary of Joseph Farington*, p. 1835.

82. Martyn Lyons, *Napoleon Bonaparte and the Legacy of the French Revolution* (London: Macmillan, 1994), p. 117.

83. George Lefebvre, *Napoleon: From 18 Brumaire to Tilsit 1799–1807*, trans. Henry F. Stockhold (1935; New York: Columbia University Press, 1969), p. 141.

84. Joel Barlow is quoted in Woodress, *A Yankee's Odyssey*, p. 223–24.

85. Poole, *Thomas Poole and His Friends* 2:86.

86. Coleridge is quoted in Bainbridge, *Napoleon and English Romanticism*, p. 17.

87. Felix Markham, *Napoleon* (London: Weidenfeld and Nicolson, 1963), p. 86. See also Lefebvre, *Napoleon: From 18 Brumaire to Tilsit 1799–1807*, p. 89–90.

88. On 27 September 1803, all books had to be approved before they were released for sale. See Lavisse, *Histoire de France*, p. 349. British detractors made frequent mention of these policies of censorship in order to contrast France unfavourably with Britain. For example, in 1809, one author wrote that "the freedom of the press, likewise, that bulwark of English liberty . . . is wholly unknown in France" (P. Coxe, *The Exposé; or Napoleone Bunoaparte Unmasked* [London: W. Miller, 1809], p. 160). Louis Bergeron comments that "As for liberty, there is no doubt that Bonaparte considered freedom of

the press a public scourge. The press existed in his eyes only for service to the State and as an instrument of propaganda" (Bergeron, *France Under Napoleon*, p. 8; p. 9).

89. Markham, *Napoleon*, p. 86.

90. See Markham, *Napoleon*, p. 93. As Conrad Gill states, "various measures were taken in France to silence the outspoken British press." See Conrad Gill, "The Relations Between England and France in 1802," *English Historical Review* 24 (1909):64.

91. Michael Polowetzky, *A Bond Never Broken: The Relations between Napoleon and the Authors of France* (London: Associated University Presses, 1993), p. 73.

92. According to Woodward (p. 146), the Ode was translated into French and published in *Decade Philosophique* on 31 December 1801.

93. Germaine de Staël, *Considerations on the Main Events of the French Revolution* (1818), in *An Extraordinary Woman: Selected Writings of Germaine de Staël*, trans. Vivian Folkenflik (New York: Columbia University Press, 1987), p. 371.

94. "Bonaparte, confident of his power within France, followed a lenient policy towards his opponents and left them alone as long as they proved to be ineffective. The few whom he regarded as potentially dangerous, such as Mme de Staël, were sent into exile" (Ruth F. Necheles, *The Abbé Grégoire 1787–1831: The Odyssey of an Egalitarian* [Westport, Connecticut:Greenwood, 1971], p. 181).

95. Henry James Pye, "Ode for the New Year, 1802," *Morning Chronicle*, 18 January 1802, p. 2.

96. Helen Maria Williams, *A Narrative of the Events Which Have Taken Place in France from the Landing of Napoleon Bonaparte on the First of March, 1815, till the Restoration of Louis XVIII* (Cleveland: Burrows, 1894), p. 193–94. Subsequent quotations from this work are cited parenthetically in the text. The first edition of *Narrative* was published in London in 1815 by John Murray.

97. Greatheed noted of one author that "Bonaparte does not like him on account of a late publication." See Greatheed, *An Englishman in Paris: 1803*, p. 21.

98. Ibid., p. 22.

99. Ibid., p. 43.

100. Ibid., p. 37.

101. Ibid., p. 128.

102. Ibid., p. 154.

103. Ibid., p. 183.

104. Michael Lewis, *Napoleon and His British Captives* (London: George Allen & Unwin, 1962), p. 23.

105. Bonaparte, letter to Cambacérès, 7 July 1803, in *Correspondence de Napoleon 1er*, vol. 8 (Paris: Henri Plon, 1861), p. 387.

106. Lewis, *Napoleon and His British Captives*, p. 183; J. David Markham, "Prisoners and Writers: Napoleon's British Captives and Their Stories," *Consortium on Revolutionary Europe* (1996):121–22.

107. A. F. Bertrand de Moleville, *A Refutation of the Libel on the Memory of the Late King of France, published by Helen Maria Williams, under the title of Political and Confidential Correspondence of Louis the Sixteenth*, trans. R. C. Dallas (London: Cadell and Davies, 1804), p. 27; p. 5.

108. Babié de Bercenay admitted, in a letter of 10 October 1822, to forging the letters of Louis XVI (Woodward, p. 234).

109. Theatres were required to submit their plays to the minister of police. See Polowetzky, *A Bond Never Broken*, p. 34.

110. Bonaparte, letter to Citoyen Regnier, 7 July 1803, in *Correspondence de Napoléon 1er*, p. 388.

111. Susan P. Conner cites this quotation in "The Merveilleuse and the Coquette:

Women during the Directory and the First Empire," *Consortium on Revolutionary Europe* (1980):53.

112. From 1804 to 1814 the only things that Williams published were a poem to her nephews and translations of books by Humboldt.

113. Herbert Richardson, *A Dictionary of Napoleon* (London: Cassell, 1920), p. 236.

114. Simon Burrows, "The Struggle for European Opinion in the Napoleonic Wars:British Francophone Propaganda, 1803–14," *French History* 11 (March 1997):41.

115. Polowetzky, *A Bond Never Broken*, p. 74.

116. Lyons, *Napoleon Bonaparte and the Legacy of the French Revolution*, p. 116–17.

117. Necheles, *The Abbé Grégoire*, p. 171.

118. Albert Leon Guérard, *Reflections on the Napoleonic Legend* (New York: Charles Scribner, 1924), p. 138.

119. Pieter Geyl, *Napoleon: For and Against* (1949; Harmondsworth: Penguin, 1982).

120. Anne Plumptre, *A Narrative of A Three Year's Residence in France, . . . 1802 to 1805*, 3 vols. (London: J. Mawman, et., 1810), 3:325.

121. Plumptre, *A Narrative of a Three Years' Residence in France* 3:382.

122. *Relation des évènemens qui se sont passés en France depuis le débarquement de Napoléon Buonaparte, au 1er Mars 1815, jusqu'au traité du 20 novembre*, par Miss Helen-Maria WILLIAMS, traduit de l'angalis par M. Breton de La Martinière (Paris: J. G. Dentu, 1816).

123. Barry O'Meara, *Napoleon in Exile; or a Voice from St. Helena*, 6th ed., 2 vols. (London: Jones, 1829), 1:24.

CHAPTER 6. VENERABLE WOMAN OF LETTERS

1. See Charles Pougens, *Memoires et Souvenirs de Charles Pougens*, ed. Louise B. de Saint-Leon (Paris: Fournier Jeune, 1834), p. 214–15. See Williams, *Recueil de Poésies, extraites des ouvrages d'Helena-Maria Williams*, trad. M. Stanislas de Boufflers et M. Esménard (Paris: F. Cocheris, 1808).

2. Helen Maria Williams, *Verses Addressed by Helen Maria Williams to Her Two Nephews, on Saint Helen's Day* (Paris, 1809).

3. See Robert Southey, third-person letter to Helen Maria Williams, c. May 1817, in Piozzi-Pennington letters, Princeton University Library.

4. Rev. of Williams's *Narrative*, in *Monthly Review* 78 (November 1815):301, quoted in Woodward, p. 252.; and Rev. of Williams's *Poems* 1823, in *Monthly Review* 102 (September 1823):21.

5. On Stone's work with Humboldt's French publishers see Woodward, p. 171–72.

6. Alexander von Humboldt, letter to Helen Maria Williams, 10 May 1810, in Ulrike Leitner, "Die englischen Ubersetzungen Humboldtscher Werke" *Acta historica Leopoldina* 27 (1997):67; translation mine.

7. Helen Maria Williams, Preface, *Personal Narrative of Travels to the Equinoctial Regions of the New Continent, during the Years 1799–1804 by Alexander de Humboldt, and Aimé Bonpland*, by Alexander de Humboldt, vols. 1 and 2. (London: Longman, Hurst, Rees, Orme, and Brown, 1818; New York: AMS, 1966), p. v.

8. Jason Wilson, Introduction, *Personal Narrative*, by Alexander von Humboldt (Harmondsworth: Penguin, 1995), p. xlix.

9. Humboldt had "a middle position" that enabled him to "work for the Prussian King and hold on to his youthful revolutionary fervours in Paris" (Jason Wilson, Introduction, p. xlvi).

10. Jason Wilson, Introduction, p. xlvi.

11. Douglas Botting, *Humboldt and the Cosmos* (New York: Harper & Row, 1973), p. 201.

12. On the publication history of Humboldt's work see Jason Wilson, Introduction, p. lv–lvi; lxiii.

13. Alexander de Humboldt, *Researches Concerning the Institutions and Monuments of the Ancient Inhabitants of America, with Descriptions and Views of Some of the Most Striking Scenes in the Cordilleras!*, trans. Helen Maria Williams (London: Longman, 1814; Amsterdam: Theatrum Orbis Terrarum, 1971).

14. Helmut de Terra, *Humboldt: The Life and Times of Alexander von Humboldt 1769–1859* (New York: Alfred A. Knopf, 1955), p. 380.

15. Malcolm Nicolson, Introduction, *Personal Narrative*, by Alexander von Humboldt (Harmondsworth: Penguin, 1995), p. xxxi.

16. Janet Browne, *Charles Darwin*, vol. 1 (London: Jonathan Cape, 1995), p. 135. In his autobiography, Darwin stated that the *Personal Narrative* was one of the two books that influenced him most. See Charles Darwin, *Autobiography of Charles Darwin and Selected Letters*, ed. Francis Darwin (New York: Dover, 1958), p. 24.

17. Alexander von Humboldt, letter to Helen Maria Williams, n. d., quoted by Leitner, "Die englischen," p. 3; translation mine.

18. Quoted in Jason Wilson, Introduction, p. lvi.

19. Helen Maria Williams, letter to Penelope Pennington, c. 1817, in Piozzi-Pennington letters, Princeton University Library.

20. Helen Maria Williams, letter to Henry Crabb Robinson, 25 March 1819, in Woodward, p. 184.

21. Ibid.

22. See Helen Maria Williams, letter to Mary Jane Godwin, 8 August 1817, Abinger Collection, Bodleian Library, Dep. C. 526.

23. See the records of the Koninklijk Huisarchief in The Hague.

24. Rev. of Williams's *Narrative*, in *Quarterly Review* 14 (October 1815):73.

25. Rev. of Williams's *Narrative*, in *Augustan Review* 1 (November 1815):808.

26. Rev. of Williams's *Narrative*, in *Quarterly Review* 14 (October 1815):69.

27. Helen Maria Williams, letter to Penelope Pennington, 10 June 1816, Piozzi-Pennington letters, Princeton University Library.

28. Ibid., and see Helen Maria Williams, letter to Penelope Pennington, 28 October 1822, both in Piozzi-Pennington letters, Princeton University Library.

29. Helen Maria Williams, letter to Ruth Barlow, 16 June 1815, Huntington Library, BN 454. This item is reproduced by permission of The Huntington Library, San Marino, California.

30. Helen Maria Williams, *On the Late Persecution of the Protestants in the South of France* (London: T. and G. Underwood, 1816), p. 24. Subsequent quotations from this work are cited parenthetically in the text.

31. See Roger Magraw, *France 1815–1914: The Bourgeois Century* (Oxford: Fontana, 1983), p. 37; and Thomas D. Beck, *French Legislators, 1800–1834: A Study in Quantitative History* (Berkeley: University of California Press, 1974), p. 57.

32. She refers to this incident in her *Letters* of 1819 as well, where she notes that M. Juillera "is now one of our protestant ministers at Paris" (*Restoration* 57, note).

33. Williams's and Stone's naturalization papers are held in the Archives Nationales, Cote BB 11/125/1.

34. Recent interest in the eighteenth-century actress Dorothy Jordan (1761–1816) has brought to light a document falsely said to have been written by Helen Maria Williams. The document, entitled "Miss Helen Maria Williams and Mrs. Jordan," is com-

posed of four interviews between Williams and Jordan, purported to have been recorded by Williams herself, when Jordan, the former mistress of the Duke of Clarence, spent her final days in Paris. It is appended to an anonymous biography of Jordan, entitled *The Great Illegitimates!!: Public and Private Life of that Celebrated Actress Miss Bland, Otherwise Mrs. Ford, or, Mrs. Jordan; the late Mistress of the Duke of Clarence; now King William IV* (London, c. 1832, p. 198–239). However, both internal and external evidence suggests the book is a literary hoax fabricated by the anonymous author. It casts both women in a negative light, and Williams cannot have written it.

35. Mary Campbell, *Lady Morgan: The Life and Times of Sydney Owenson* (London: Pandora, 1988), p. 141.

36. Lady Morgan is quoted in Lionel Stevenson, *The Wild Irish Girl: The Life of Sydney Owenson, Lady Morgan (1776–1859)* (London: Chapman and Hall, 1936), p. 169–70.

37. Campbell, *Lady Morgan*, p. 142.

38. Lady Morgan, *France*, 2nd. ed., 2 vols. (London: Colburn, 1817), 2:397, note. Though a very popular book, it was given a notoriously scathing review in the *Quarterly Review*, not unlike the anti-Jacobin attacks previously levelled at Morgan's hostess. In a later work, Lady Morgan venerated Williams as a celebrated writer of "ardent feelings and brilliant talents." See Lady Morgan, *France in 1829–30*, 2nd. ed., 2 vols. (London: Saunders and Otley, 1831), 1:363.

39. George Ticknor, *Life, Letters, and Journals of George Ticknor*, 8th ed., vol. 1 (Boston: James R. Osgood, 1877), p. 130.

40. See St. Clair, *The Godwins and the Shelleys*, p. 291–92.

41. On Mary Jane Godwin and her step-children, see Harriet Devine Jump, " 'A Meritorious Wife': or, Mrs. Godwin and the Donkey," in *The Charles Lamb Bulletin* 90 (April 1995):73–84. On the Coquerel boys, see Helen Maria Williams, letter to Mary Jane Godwin, 8 August 1817, Abinger Collection, Bodleian Library, Dep. C. 526.

42. Helen Maria Williams to Mary Jane Godwin, 8 August 1817, Abinger Collection, Bodleian Library, Dep. C. 526.

43. Helen Maria Williams, letter to Mary Jane Godwin, 28 November 1817, Abinger Collection, Bodleian Library, Dep. C. 526.

44. Ibid.

45. Stone's burial record cannot be located, but his gravestone is next to that of Williams and her mother. Mrs. Williams was buried on 14 April 1812 "dans la concession No. 130 PP 1812 située 39ème division 15/38 7/28." Helen Maria Williams was buried at "la concession No. 965 P de 1827, située dans la 39ème division, 11ème ligne face à la 38ème division et 1ère tombe à partir de la 40ème division" (The Conservator, private correspondence, 30 June 1998; 28 May 1998). John Hurford Stone's epitaph is described by Oswald G. Knapp, in *The Intimate Letters of Hester Piozzi and Penelope Pennington 1788–1821* (London: John Lane, 1913), p. 61.

46. I am gratefully indebted to Susan Lanser who visited Père Lachaise in 1999 and provided me with descriptions of the gravestones of Stone, Williams, and Williams's mother.

47. Helen Maria Williams, letter to William Shepherd, c. 1818, Harris Manchester College, Oxford. This material is published with the permission of the Library, Harris Manchester College, Oxford.

48. Helen Maria Williams, letter to Penelope Pennington, 26 June 1819, Piozzi-Pennington letters, Princeton University Library.

49. Helen Maria Williams, letter to Mary Jane Godwin, 17 September 1819 and 1 October 1819, Abinger Collection, Bodleian Library, Dep. C. 526.

50. Thomas Raffles, *Letters During a Tour Through Some Parts of France, Savoy, Switzerland, Germany, and the Netherlands: The Summer of 1817*, 2nd. ed. (Liverpool: Thomas Taylor, 1819), p.116.

51. Helen Maria Williams, letter to Henry Crabb Robinson, 21 June 1819, in Woodward, p. 188.

52. Ibid.

53. Helen Maria Williams, letter to Henry Crabb Robinson, 25 March 1819, in Woodward, p. 185.

54. Henry Crabb Robinson, *Henry Crabb Robinson on Books and Their Writers*, ed. Edith J. Morley, vol. 1 (London: Dent, 1938), p. 232.

55. Ibid., p. 230–31.

56. Ibid., p. 232.

57. Helen Maria Williams, letter to Henry Crabb Robinson, 25 October 1820, in Woodward, p. 191.

58. The translation appeared in the same year: *Évenements arrivés en France depuis la Restauration de 1815*, par Helen-Marie Williams, traduit de l'Anglais [par M. Moreau père] (Paris 1819). See F. Funck-Brentano, ed. *La Règne de Robespierre*, par Maria-Hélèna Williams (Paris: Arthème Fayard, 1909), p. 154.

59. Adrien Dansette, *Religious History of Modern France*, vol. 1, trans. John Dingle (1948; Edinburgh: Nelson, 1961), p. 177–78.

60. Magraw, *France 1815–1914: The Bourgeois Century*, p. 30; p. 39.

61. Beck, *French Legislators, 1800–1834*, p. 51.

62. Rev. of Williams's *Narrative*, in *Monthly Review* 78 (November 1815): 301.

63. Benjamin Constant is quoted in Beck, *French Legislators, 1800–1834*, p. 101.

64. Rev. of Williams's *Restoration*, in *British Critic* 12 (October 1819):392.

65. Janet Todd discusses attacks on sensibility in *Sensibility*, p. 129–32.

66. Janet Todd, *Sensibility*, p. 131.

67. Rev. of Williams's *Restoration*, in *British Critic* 12 (October 1819):399.

68. Rev. of Williams's *Restoration*, in *Monthly Magazine* 47 (July 1819):624.

69. Helen Maria Williams, letter to Henry Crabb Robinson, 25 October 1820, in Woodward, p. 190–91.

70. See Mary Moorman, *William Wordsworth, A Biography: The Early Years 1770–1803* (Oxford: Clarendon, 1957), p. 290.

71. Two short letters from Williams to Wordsworth (one dated Wednesday October 11, 1820, the other undated) are held in Dove Cottage by the Wordsworth Trust.

72. Dorothy Wordsworth, letter to Catherine Clarkson, 15 October 1820, in Woodward, p. 193.

73. "Miss Wordsworth has a desire to read my last little volume—your protegé. Will you obtain a copy for her of the second edition from Mr. Baldwin?" See Helen Maria Williams, letter to Henry Crabb Robinson, 25 October 1820, in Woodward, p. 190–91.

74. Lady Morgan, *France* 2:339.

75. Henry Crabb Robinson, *The Diary of Henry Crabb Robinson*, ed. Derek Hudson (London: Oxford University Press, 1967), p. 43.

76. The Rydal Mount catalogue shows that Williams's *Poems* 1823 were in William Wordsworth's library. See *The Letters of William and Dorothy Wordsworth: The Later Years*, 2nd. ed., vol. 5, ed. Alan G. Hill (Oxford: Clarendon, 1979), p. 260 note.

77. Helen Maria Williams, letter to Penelope Pennington, 28 October 1822, in Piozzi-Pennington letters, Princeton University Library.

78. Helen Maria Williams, letter to John Bowring, 24 June 1822, Huntington Library.

79. Rev. of Williams's *Poems* 1823, in *European Magazine* 83 (April 1823):355.

80. Rev. of Williams's *Poems* 1823, in *Monthly Review* 102 (September 1823):21.

81. Rev. of Williams's *Poems* 1823, in *Monthly Review* 102 (September 1823):20.

82. Rev. of Williams's *Poems* 1823, in *European Magazine* 83 (April 1823):355.

83. Helen Maria Williams, letter to Henry Crabbe Robinson, 25 October 1820, in Woodward, p. 190–91.

84. See "To the Baron De Humboldt, on his bringing me some Flowers in March," "To James Forbes, Esq. Author of 'The Oriental Memoirs," and "To James Forbes, Esq. on his bringing me Flowers from Vaucluse," in *Poems* 1823, 255; 251; 262.

85. Williams's poem on Bréguet is held in the Huntington Library.

86. Helen Maria Williams, letter to Henry Crabb Robinson, 5 October 1814, in Woodward, p. 180. On Catherine (Buck) Clarkson's support of the French Revolution, see Ellen Gibson Wilson, *Thomas Clarkson*, p. 92–94.

87. Thomas Clarkson is quoted in Ellen Gibson Wilson, *Thomas Clarkson*, p. 127.

88. Necheles, *The Abbé Grégoire 1787–1831*, p. 200.

89. On 4 February 1799, the Société des Amis des Noirs met to celebrate "the fifth anniversary of Negro emancipation . . . Say spoke, as did another member, on the 'usefulness of admitting women into philanthropic societies.' " The quotation is cited from the *Chronique universelle* 29 Pluvoise year 7 (17 Feb. 1799), in Necheles, *The Abbé Grégoire 1787–1831*, p. 162; p. 168, note.

90. Charles Wadstrom's letter to Grégoire was kindly brought to my attention by the librarians at the Société de Port-Royal, Paris where it is held. See Helen Maria Williams, "Memoirs of the Life of Charles Berns Wadstrom," *Monthly Magazine* 7 (July 1799):462–65; and William Dickson's reply, "Strictures on Miss Williams's Memoirs of Wadstrom," *Monthly Magazine* 7 (December 1799):862–69.

91. Thomas Clarkson, letter to Catherine Clarkson, 20 September 1815, Huntington Library, CN 45.

92. Williams's notes for Clarkson on the Rodeur are held at the Huntington Library. For further information see *The History of the Slave Trade, Ancient and Modern*, ed. William O. Blake (1857; New York: Haskell House, 1969), p. 287–89.

93. See Honour, *The Image of the Black in Western Art* 4:129–30.

94. Charles Coquerel, *La Législation anglaise relative a la traite des noirs, et sur l'État des Nègres affranchis*, reprinted in *Extrait de la Revue Encyclopédique* Aout 1820. See Athanase Coquerel fils, "Charles Coquerel," *Le Lien* 2:7 (15 fevrier 1851), p. 240.

95. Helen Maria Williams, letter to Penelope Pennington, 1803, Piozzi-Pennington letters, Princeton University Library.

96. *Poems* 1823 is dedicated to her nephews, "Inscribed, by their affectionate Aunt, Helen Maria Williams." Williams writes of the death of Bibi in a letter to Ruth Barlow:

> Amidst evils of great magnitude, we have sustained what you will perhaps term a very slight domestic misfortune, but which I assure you we felt very painfully—the death of poor old *Bibi*, but perhaps you have not forgotten all his good qualities, his tender and long-tried fidelity—you may recollect also the extreme urbanity of his manners, and the caresses he lavished on our friends, and on yourself in particular—he received all sorts of funeral honors—his skin is stuffed—his heart was preserved by the Chemist Charles, and I wrote for him a little elegy of which I enclose you a copy.

See Helen Maria Williams, letter to Ruth Barlow, 16 June 1815, Huntington Library, BN 454.

97. Athanase graduated with his degree in theology from Montauban in 1816; Charles returned to Paris to pursue studies in science and literature. See Stroehlin, *Athanase Coquerel fils*, p. 11.

98. Charles Coquerel, *Histoire Abregée de la litterature anglaise, depuis son origine jusqu'a nos jours* (Paris: Louis Janet Librairie, 1828), p. 503; translation mine.

99. Athanase Coquerel, Preface, *Christianity*, p. viii–ix.

100. John Bowring describes Nancy Rattier's father, as "a Swiss gentleman, the only person I have ever known on the continent to adopt the dress and profess the opinions of the English Quaker" (*Autobiographical Recollections of Sir John Bowring*, ed. Lewin B. Bowring [London: Henry S. King, 1877], p. 354). See also Stroehlin, *Athanase Coquerel fils*, p. 28.

101. Nancy Coquerel left three children, two others (Jean-Pierre and Helena) having died in infancy: Athanase fils (1820–75); Jean Charles (1822–67); and Cécile (1824–8?). On 25 October 1827 Coquerel married his second wife, Sophie-Gabrielle-Elisabeth Mollet (1802–91), with whom he had three children. See Marie Bartoszewski, "La Famille Coquerel."

102. Married in 1846 to a Protestant businessman in Reims, Cécile Gay published a number of children's books, using the pseudonym Saygé. See Bartoszewski, "La Famille Coquerel." Cécile Gay's books are listed in the catalogue for the *Bibliothèque Nationale*, including the novel *Maurice le Parisien* (Paris 1875). Cécile Gay's brother Athanase Coquerel, Jr., was staying at her country house in Fismes near Reims, recuperating from an illness, when he died in 1875. He had asked to be buried in the Catholic cemetery to "make a public declaration of the equality before the law of French Protestants and French Catholics." See Albert Réville, "A Memoir," in Athanase Coquerel fils, *Conscience and Faith*, trans. J. Edwin Odgers (London: British and Foreign Unitarian Association, 1878), p. xxiii.

103. See Albert L. Guérard, *French Prophets of Yesterday* (New York: Appleton, 1920), p. 82–83. For a discussion of this from Coquerel's point of view, see his nephew's comments in Albert Réville, "A Memoir," p. xvii.

104. Réville, "A Memoir," p. xix–xxi.

105. See Richard Chevenix, Rev. of *Tableau Historique* and *Fragment*, by Marie-Joseph Chenier, in *Edinburgh Review* 35 (March 1821):158–90. Chevenix wrote at least two other articles on France in the *Edinburgh Review* in 1819 and 1820.

106. Helen Maria Williams, letter to Mary Jane Godwin, 10 June 1821, Abinger Collection, Bodleian Library, Dep. b. 214/2.

107. See Beck, *French Legislators, 1800–1834*, p. 67.

108. On the electoral victories of the Ultras and the "massive victory of the Right" in 1824, see Beck, *French Legislators, 1800–1834*, p. 72–93; p. 84.

109. See Athanase Coquerel fils, "Charles Coquerel," p. 240.

110. Thomas Moore, *The Journal of Thomas Moore*, vol. 2, ed. Wilfred S. Dowden (Newark: University of Delaware Press, 1983), p. 428.

111. Helen Maria Williams, letter to Mary Jane Godwin, 10 June 1821, Abinger Collection, Bodleian Library, Dep. b. 214/2.

112. Helen Maria Williams, letter to John Bowring, 24 June 1822, Huntington Library.

113. See Janis Bergman-Carton, *The Woman of Ideas in French Art, 1830–1848* (New Haven: Yale University Press, 1995).

114. See *Dictionnaire des Lettres Françaises*: Le Dix-Neuvième Siècle, A-K (Paris: Librairie Artheme Fayard, 1971), p. 62.

115. For information on Dufrénoy, see *Biographie Universelle*, vol. 11, p. 435–38.

116. Elizabeth Colwill, describes the journal as "a leading scholarly revue edited by moderate republicans." See Colwill, "Laws of Nature / Rights of Genius: The *Drame* of Constance de Salm," in *Going Public: Women and Publishing in Early Modern France*, ed. Elizabeth C. Goldsmith and Dena Goodman (Ithaca: Cornell University Press, 1995), p. 225; 241.

117. Colwill, "Laws of Nature," p. 226.

118. Geneviève Fraisse, *Reason's Muse*, trans. Jane Marie Todd (Chicago: Chicago University Press, 1994), p. 125.

119. Williams writes of visits from Théremin in her letters to Mary Jane Godwin, 8 August 1817 and 28 November 1817, Abinger Collection, Bodleian Library, Dep. c. 526.

120. Colwill, "Laws of Nature," p. 236.

121. Ibid.

122. The term "beautiful literary crown" was applied to Salm by her friend Melanie Waldor in a letter, quoted in Colwill, "Laws of Nature," p. 240.

123. Reference to a "recent portrait" can be found in an obituary in *Gentleman's Magazine* 98 (April 1828): 373. I am grateful to Madeleine de Terris for discovering an undated late portrait of Williams in the René Laruelle collection, Bibliothèque nationale de France. Helen Maria Williams, letter to Samuel Rogers, 24 April 1825, Sharpe Papers, University College London.

124. Ibid.

125. Helen Maria Williams, letter to Benjamin Constant, 10 May 1827, Bibliothèque cantonale et universitaire, Lausanne.

126. Marilyn Yalom, *Blood Sisters: The French Revolution in Women's Memory* (New York: BasicBooks, 1993), p. 2.

127. Ibid., p. 9.

128. Ibid., p. 4.

129. Charlotte Hogsett, *The Literary Existence of Germaine de Staël* (Carbondale: Southern Illinois University Press, 1987), p. 141–42.

130. Yalom, *Blood Sisters*, p. 92.

131. Ibid., p. 286.

132. Gary Kates, *The "Cercle Social," the Girondins, and the French Revolution* (Princeton: Princeton University Press, 1985), p. 191.

133. On Genlis and Napoleon, see Violet Wyndham, *Madame de Genlis: A Biography* (New York: Roy, 1958), p. 200–203.

134. Christopher Herold, *Mistress to an Age: The Life of Madame de Staël* (London: Hamish Hamilton, 1958), p. 108; Gita May, *Madame Roland and the Age of Revolution* (New York: Columbia University Press, 1970), p. 146.

135. The manuscript is described in John Bowring, rev. of *Memoirs de Brissot*, *The Westminster Review* 14 (April 1831):332–33.

136. Athanase Coquerel, Preface, *Christianity*, p. viii–ix.

Bibliography

Adams, M. Ray. "Helen Maria Williams and the French Revolution." *Wordsworth and Coleridge: Studies in Honor of George McLean Harper*. Edited by Earl Leslie Griggs, 87–117. New York: Russell, 1967.

Adolphus, John. *The History of France from the Year 1790 to the Peace Concluded at Amiens in 1802*. 3 vols. London: George Kearsley, 1803.

Alger, John Goldworth. "English Eyewitnesses of the French Revolution." *Edinburgh Review* 168 (July 1888):137–70.

Analytical Review, 1790–98.

Arasse, Daniel. *The Guillotine and the Terror*. Translated by Christopher Miller. Harmondsworth: Penguin, 1991.

Armstrong, Nancy. *Desire and Domestic Fiction: A Political History of the Novel*. Oxford: Oxford University Press, 1987.

Arnaud, Claude. *Chamfort: A Biography*. Translated by Deke Dusinberre. Chicago: University of Chicago Press, 1992.

Ashfield, Andrew, and Peter de Bolla, eds. *The Sublime: A Reader in Eighteenth-Century Aesthetic Theory*. Cambridge: Cambridge University Press, 1996.

Ashmun, Margaret. *The Singing Swan*. New Haven: Yale University Press, 1931.

Astell, Mary. A Serious Proposal to the Ladies. In *The Meridian Anthology of Early Women Writers*. Edited by Katharine M. Rogers and William McCarthy. New York: New American Library, 1987.

Augustan Review, 1815.

Averill, James. *Wordsworth and the Poetry of Human Suffering*. Ithaca: Cornell University Press, 1980.

Bainbridge, Simon. *Napoleon and English Romanticism*. Cambridge: Cambridge University Press, 1995.

Barbauld, Anna Laetitia. Address to the Opposers of the Repeal of the Corporation and Test Acts. In *The Meridian Anthology of Early Women Writers*. Edited by Katharine M. Rogers and William McCarthy. New York: New American Library, 1987.

———. *Memoirs, Letters, and A Selection from the Poems and Prose Writings of Anna Laetitia Barbauld*. Edited by Grace A. Oliver. Boston: J. R. Osgood, 1874.

———. *The Poems of Anna Letitia Barbauld*. Edited by William McCarthy and Elizabeth Kraft. Athens: University of Georgia Press, 1994.

Barber, Peter. *Swiss 700: Treasures from the British Library and British Museum to Celebrate 700 Years of the Swiss Confederation*. London: British Library, 1991.

Barker-Benfield, G. J. *The Culture of Sensibility: Sex and Society in Eighteenth-Century Britain*. Chicago: University of Chicago Press, 1992.

Barlow, Joel. *Life and Letters of Joel Barlow*. Edited by Charles Burr Todd. New York: Da Capo Press, 1970.

Bartoszewski, Marie. *La Famille Coquerel*, 1983. Société de l'Histoire du Protestantisme Français, Paris.

Basker, James G. "Dancing Dogs, Women Preachers and the Myth of Johnson's Misogyny." *The Age of Johnson* 3 (1990):63–90.

Beck, Thomas D. *French Legislators, 1800–1834: A Study in Quantitative History*. Berkeley: University of California Press, 1974.

Bergeron, Louis. *France under Napoleon*. Translated by R. R. Palmer. Princeton: Princeton University Press, 1981.

Beer, Gavin Rylands de. *Early Travellers in the Alps*. London: Sidgwick & Jackson, 1930.

Ben-Israel, Hedva. *English Historians on the French Revolution*. Cambridge: Cambridge University Press, 1968.

Bergman-Carton, Janis. *The Woman of Ideas in French Art, 1830–1848*. New Haven: Yale University Press, 1995.

Bertrand de Moleville, A. F. *A Refutation of the Libel on the Memory of the Late King of France, published by Helen Maria Williams, under the title of Political and Confidential Correspondence of Louis the Sixteenth*. Translated by R. C. Dallas. London: Cadell & Davies, 1804.

Bindman, David. *The Shadow of the Guillotine: Britain and the French Revolution*. London: British Museum, 1989.

Blake, William O. ed. *The History of the Slave Trade, Ancient and Modern*. New York: Haskell House, 1969.

Blakemore, Steven. "Revolution and the French Disease: Laetitia Matilda Hawkins's *Letters* to Helen Maria Williams." *Studies in English Literature* 36 (1996):673–91.

Bloom, Edward, and Lillian D. Bloom, eds., *The Piozzi Letters: Correspondence of Hester Lynch Piozzi, 1784–1821*. Vols. 1–3. Newark: University of Delaware Press, 1989–93.

Bohls, Elizabeth. *Women Travel Writers and the Language of Aesthetics, 1716–1818*. Cambridge: Cambridge University Press, 1995.

Bonaparte, Napoleon. *Correspondence de Napoléon 1er*. Vol. 8. Paris: Plon, 1861.

Boswell, James. *The Life of Samuel Johnson*. 3 vols. Dublin: R. Cross, et al., 1792.

———. *The Life of Samuel Johnson*. 2 vols. London: J. M. Dent, 1906.

Botting, Douglas. *Humboldt and the Cosmos*. New York: Harper & Row, 1973.

Bowring, John. *Autobiographical Recollections of Sir John Bowring*. Edited by Lewin B. Bowring. London: Henry S. King, 1877.

———. Rev. of *Memoirs de Brissot*. *Westminster Review* 14 (April 1831):332–58.

Breen, Jennifer, ed. *Women Romantics 1785–1832: Writing in Prose*. London: Everyman, 1996.

British Critic, 1793–1819.

Brive, Marie-France, ed. *Les Femmes et la Révolution française*. Vol. 2. Toulouse: Presses universitaires du Mirail, 1990.

Browne, Janet. *Charles Darwin*. Vol. 1. London: Jonathan Cape, 1995.

Burke, Edmund. *The Correspondence of Edmund Burke*. 10 vols. Edited by Thomas W. Copeland. Cambridge: Cambridge University Press, 1958–78.

———. *Reflections on the Revolution in France*. Edited by Conor Cruise O'Brien. Harmondsworth: Penguin, 1987.

Burney, Charlotte. *The Early Diary of Frances Burney 1768–1778 with a Selection from Her Correspondence, and from the Journals of Her Sisters Susan and Charlotte Burney*. Edited by Annie Raine Ellis. 2 vols. London: George Bell and Sons, 1889.

Burns, Robert. *The Letters of Robert Burns*. Edited by J. De Lancey Ferguson. Vol. 1. Oxford: Clarendon, 1931.

— — —. *The Letters of Robert Burns*. 2nd. ed. Vol. 1. Edited by J. De Lancey Ferguson and G. Ross Roy. Oxford: Clarendon, 1985.

Burrows, Simon. "The Struggle for European Opinion in the Napoleonic Wars: British Francophone Propaganda, 1803–1814," *French History* 11 (March 1997):29–53.

Campbell, Mary. *Lady Morgan: The Life and Times of Sydney Owenson*. London: Pandora, 1988.

Carlyle, Thomas. *The French Revolution*. Edited by K. J. Fielding and David Sorensen. Oxford: Oxford University Press, 1989.

Chandler, David. *The Campaigns of Napoleon*. London: Weidenfeld and Nicolson, 1967.

Clayden, P. W. *The Early Life of Samuel Rogers*. London: Smith, Elder, 1887.

Colley, Linda. *Britons: Forging the Nation 1707–1837*. New Haven: Yale University Press, 1992.

Colwill, Elizabeth. "Laws of Nature / Rights of Genius: The *Drame* of Constance de Salm." In *Going Public: Women and Publishing in Early Modern France*. Edited by Elizabeth C. Goldsmith and Dena Goodman, 224–42. Ithaca: Cornell University Press, 1995.

A Complete Collection of State Trials and Proceedings for High Treason and Other Crimes and Misdemeanours. Edited by T. B. Howell and Thomas Jones Howell. Volume 25 (1794–96). London: Longman, Hunt, Rees, Orme, and Brown, 1818.

Cone, Carl B. *The English Jacobins: Reformers in Late 18th Century England*. New York: Charles Scribner's Sons, 1968.

Conner, Susan P. "The Merveilleuse and the Coquette: Women during the Directory and the First Empire." *Consortium on Revolutionary Europe* (1980):49–57.

Copies of Original Letters Written by Persons in Paris to Dr. Priestley in America, Taken on Board a Neutral Vessel. 2nd. ed. London: J. Wright, 1798.

Coquerel, Athanase. Preface to *Christianity: Its Perfect Adaptation to the Mental, Moral, and Spiritual Nature of Man*. Translated by Rev. D. Davison. London: Longman, 1847.

— — —. "Reply to Dr. Strauss's Book 'The Life of Jesus.' " In *Voices of the Church, in Reply to Dr. D. F. Strauss*. Edited by Rev. J. R. Beard, 27–66. London: Simpkin, Marshall, 1845.

Coquerel, Athanase, fils. "Charles Coquerel." *Le Lien, Journal des églises réformées de France*, Second Series, vol. 7, no. 4 (15 février 1851):239–44.

Coquerel, Charles. *Histoire Abregée de la litterature anglaise, depuis son origine jusqu'a nos jours*. Paris: Louis Janet Librairie, 1828.

Cordey, Pierre. "The Historical Evolution." Translated by Helmuth A. Lindemann. In *The Historical Evolution, Political Institutions*. Vol. 2 of *Focus on Switzerland*. Lausanne: Swiss Office for the Development of Trade, 1975. 7–77.

Cowper, William. *The Task and Selected Other Poems*. Edited by James Sambrook. London: Longman, 1994.

Cox, Stephen. "Sensibility as Argument." In *Sensibility in Transformation: Creative Resistance of Sentiment from the Augustans to the Romantics: Essays in Honor of Jean H. Hagstrum*. Edited by Syndy McMillen Conger, 63–82. Rutherford: Fairleigh Dickinson University Press, 1990.

Coxe, P. *The Exposé; or Napoleone Bunoaparte Unmasked*. London: W. Miller, 1809.

Coxe, William. *Travels in Switzerland. In a Series of Letters to William Melmoth.* 3 vols. London: Cadell, 1789.

Crawford, Thomas. *Boswell, Burns and the French Revolution.* Edinburgh: Saltire Society, 1990.

Critical Review, 1790–1801.

Croce, Benedetto. *History of the Kingdom of Naples.* Edited by H. Stuart Hughes; translated by Frances Frenaye. Chicago: University of Chicago Press, 1970.

Cummings, William H. "No Riches from his Little Store." *Notes and Queries* 28 July 1906:75.

Curran, Stuart. "Romantic Poetry: The I Altered." In *Romanticism and Feminism.* Edited by Anne K. Mellor, 185–207. Bloomington: Indiana University Press, 1988.

Currie, James. *The Life of Robert Burns.* Edinburgh: Chambers, 1838.

Dansette, Adrien. *Religious History of Modern France.* Vol. 1. Translated by John Dingle. Edinburgh: Nelson, 1961.

Darwin, Charles. *Autobiography of Charles Darwin and Selected Letters.* Edited by Francis Darwin. New York: Dover, 1958.

Davies, Stephen. "La Harpe, Frédéric César de." *Biographical Dictionary of Modern European Radicals and Socialists.* Volume 1: 1780–1815. Edited by David Nicholls and Peter Marsh. New York: St. Martin's Press, 1988.

Davis, Michael T., ed. *Radicalism and Revolution in Britain, 1775–1848.* London: Macmillan, 2000.

Davis, Richard W. *Dissent in Politics 1780–1830: The Political Life of William Smith, MP.* London: Epworth, 1971.

Delaney, Mary. *The Autobiography and Correspondence of Mary Granville, Mrs. Delaney.* Edited by Lady Llanover. 3 vols. London: Richard Bentley, 1862.

Dèveze, Jules. *Athanase Coquerel fils sa vie et ses oeuvres.* Paris: Librairie Fischbacher, 1884.

Dickens, Charles. *A Tale of Two Cities.* Edited by George Woodcock. Harmondsworth: Penguin, 1986.

Dickinson, H. T. *British Radicalism and the French Revolution.* Oxford: Basil Blackwell, 1985.

Dickson, William. "Strictures on Miss Williams's Memoirs of Wadstrom." *Monthly Magazine* 7 (December 1799):862–69.

Donald, Diana. *The Age of Caricature: Satirical Prints in the Reign of George III.* New Haven: Yale University Press, 1996.

Doody, Margaret Anne. "Women Poets of the Eighteenth Century." In *Women and Literature in Britain 1700–1800.* Edited by Vivien Jones, 217–37. Cambridge: Cambridge University Press, 2000.

Doyle, William. *The Oxford History of the French Revolution.* Oxford: Oxford University Press, 1989.

Dyer, George. *Poems.* London: J. Johnson, 1792.

Edgeworth, Maria. *Maria Edgeworth in France and Switzerland: Selections from the Edgeworth Family Letters.* Edited by Christina Colvin. Oxford: Clarendon, 1979.

Eliza [psued.]. "To Miss Helen Maria Williams on her Poem of Peru." *Gentleman's Magazine* (July 1784):532.

Ellison, Julie. "Redoubled Feeling: Politics, Sentiment, and the Sublime in Williams and Wollstonecraft." *Studies in Eighteenth-Century Culture* 20 (1990):197–215.

Elson Roessler, Shirley. *Out of the Shadows: Women and Politics in the French Revolution, 1789–95*. New York: Peter Lang, 1996.

Engel, Claire Eliane. *A History of Mountaineering in the Alps*. London: George Allen and Unwin, 1950.

English Review, 1792.

Equiano, Olaudah. *The Interesting Narrative and Other Writings*. Edited by Vincent Carretta. Harmondsworth: Penguin, 1995.

Erdman, David. *Commerce des Lumières: John Oswald and the British in Paris, 1790–1793*. Columbia: University of Missouri Press, 1986.

European Magazine, 1786–1823.

Fairer, David and Christine Gerrard, eds. *Eighteenth-Century Poetry: An Annotated Anthology*. Oxford: Blackwell, 1999.

Farington, Joseph. *The Diary of Joseph Farington*. Edited by Kenneth Garlick and Angus MacIntyre. Vol. 5. New Haven: Yale University Press, 1979.

Favret, Mary A. *Romantic Correspondences: Women, Politics, and the Fiction of Letters*. Cambridge: Cambridge University Press, 1993.

Ferguson, Moira. *Subject to Others: British Women Writers and Colonial Slavery, 1670–1834*. New York: Routledge, 1992.

Fielding, Henry. *Tom Jones*. Edited by John Bender and Simon Stern. Oxford: Oxford University Press, 1996.

Fraisse, Geneviève. *Reason's Muse*. Translated by Jane Marie Todd. Chicago: Chicago University Press, 1994.

"Français de Nantes, Antoine." *Dictionnaire de Biographie Française*. Vol. 4. Edited by M. Prevost, Roman D'Amat, and H. Tribout de Morembert. Paris: Librairie Letouzey et Ané, 1979.

Frederiksen, Elke, ed. *Women Writers of Germany, Austria, and Switzerland: An Annotated Bio-Bibliographical Guide*. New York: Greenwood Press, 1989.

Fruchtman, Jack, Jr., ed. *An Eye-Witness Account of the French Revolution by Helen Maria Williams*. New York: Peter Lang, 1997.

— — —. "Public Loathing, Private Thoughts: Historical Representation in Helen Maria Williams' *Letters from France*." *Prose Studies* 18 (December 1995):223–43.

— — —. *Thomas Paine: Apostle of Freedom*. New York: Four Walls Eight Windows, 1994.

Fullard, Joyce, ed. *British Women Poets 1660–1800: An Anthology*. Troy: Whitson, 1990.

Fulton, Henry L. "Disillusionment with the French Revolution: The Case of the Scottish Physician John Moore." *Studies in Scottish Literature* 23 (1988):46–63.

Funck-Brentano, F., ed. *La Règne de Robespierre*, par Maria-Hélèna Williams. Paris: Arthème Fayard, 1909.

Gardner, Monica M. *Kosciuszko: A Biography*. London: George Allen, 1920.

Gentleman's Magazine, 1784–1828.

George, Dorothy. *Catalogue of Political and Personal Satires Preserved in the Department of Prints and Drawings in the British Museum*. Vol. 6. London: British Museum, 1978.

Geyl, Pieter. *Napoleon: For and Against*. Harmondsworth: Penguin, 1982.

Giddey, Ernest. "1816: Switzerland and the Revival of the 'Grand Tour.' " *The Byron Society* 19 (1991):17–25.

Gill, Conrad. "The Relations Between England and France in 1802." *English Historical Review* 24 (1909):61–78.

Godechot, Jacques. *The Counter-Revolution: Doctrine and Action 1789–1804*. Translated by Salvator Attanasio. London: Routledge, 1972.

Godineau, Dominique. *The Women of Paris and Their French Revolution*. Translated by Katherine Streip. Berkeley: University of California Press, 1998.

Godwin, William. *Enquiry Concerning Political Justice*. Edited by Isaac Kramnick. Harmondsworth: Penguin, 1985.

Goldsmith, Lewis. *Female Revolutionary Plutarch*. Vol. 3. London: John Murray, 1806.

Goodwin, Albert. *The Friends of Liberty: The English Democratic Movement in the Age of the French Revolution*. Cambridge: Harvard University Press, 1979.

Graham, Jenny. *Revolutionary in Exile: The Emigration of Joseph Priestley to America 1794–1804*. Philadelphia: American Philosophical Society, 1995.

Graham, Ruth. "Loaves and Liberty: Women in the French Revolution." In *Becoming Visible: Women in European History*. Edited by Renate Bridenthal and Claudia Koonz, 236–254. Boston: Houghton Mifflin, 1977.

Grandchamp, Sophie. "Souvenirs de Sophie Grandchamp." In *Mémoires de Madame Roland*. 2 vols. Edited by C. Perroud. Paris: Plon, 1905.

Gray, Thomas. *Correspondence of Thomas Gray*. 3 vols. Edited by Paget Toynbee and Leonard Whibley. Oxford: Clarendon, 1935.

———. *Thomas Gray and William Collins: Poetical Works*. Edited by Roger Lonsdale. Oxford: Oxford University Press, 1977.

Greatheed, Bertie. *An Englishman in Paris: 1803: The Journal of Bertie Greatheed*. Edited by J. P. T. Bury and J. C. Barry. London: Geoffrey Bles, 1953.

Greer, Donald. *The Incidence of the Terror during the French Revolution: A Statistical Interpretation*. Cambridge: Harvard University Press, 1935.

Gregory, Desmond. *Minorca, The Illusory Prize: A History of the British Occupation of Minorca between 1708 and 1802*. Rutherford: Fairleigh Dickinson University Press, 1990.

Greville, Frances. "A Prayer for Indifference." In *Eighteenth-Century Women Poets: An Oxford Anthology*. Edited by Roger Lonsdale. Oxford: Oxford University Press, 1989.

Grundy, Isobel. "Samuel Johnson as a Patron of Women." *The Age of Johnson* 1 (1987):59–77.

Guérard, Albert Leon. *French Prophets of Yesterday*. New York: Appleton, 1920.

———. *Reflections on the Napoleonic Legend*. New York: Charles Scribner, 1924.

Gutwirth, Madelyn. *The Twilight of the Goddesses: Women and Representation in the French Revolutionary Era*. New Brunswick: Rutgers University Press, 1992.

Hamilton, Mary. *Mary Hamilton Afterwards Mrs. John Dickenson at Court and at Home. From Letters and Diaries 1756–1816*. Edited by Elizabeth and Florence Anson. London: John Murray, 1925.

Hardwick, Mollie. *Emma Lady Hamilton*. London: Cassell, 1969.

Harrison, Gary. *Wordsworth's Vagrant Muse: Poetry, Poverty, and Power*. Detroit: Wayne State University Press, 1994.

Hattersley, Roy. *Nelson*. London: Weidenfeld and Nicolson, 1974.

Hawkins, Laetitia Matilda. *Letters on the Female Mind, Its Powers and Pursuits. Addressed to Miss H. M. Williams, with Particular Reference to Her Letters from France*. 2 vols. London: Hookham and Carpenter, 1793.

Hayley, William. *Memoirs of the Life and Writings of William Hayley*. 2 vols. Edited by John Johnson. London: Colburn, 1823.

Hazlitt, William. *The Life of Napoleon Bonaparte*. 6 vols. Paris: Napoleon Society, 1895.

Hearder, Harry. *Italy in the Age of the Risorgimento 1790–1870*. London: Longman, 1983.

Hemans, Felicia. *Poetical Works*. Philadelphia: Lippincott, 1855.

Herold, Christopher. *Mistress to an Age: The Life of Madame de Staël*. London: Hamish Hamilton, 1958.

Hibbert, Christopher. *The French Revolution*. Harmondsworth: Penguin, 1980.

Hill, Bridget. *The Republican Virago: The Life and Times of Catharine Macaulay, Historian*. Oxford: Clarendon, 1992.

"Historical Retrospect of Presbyterian Churches and their Ministers." *Weekly Review* (1872), n. p.

Hobsbawm, Eric. *The Age of Revolution 1789–1848*. London: Cardinal, 1988.

Honour, Hugh. *The Image of the Black in Western Art*. Vol. 4. *From the American Revolution to World War I*. Cambridge: Harvard University Press, 1989.

Humboldt, Alexander von. Letters. Koninklijk Huisarchief, The Hague.

Hunt, Lynn. *The Family Romance of the French Revolution*. Berkeley: University of California Press, 1992.

— — —. *Politics, Culture, and Class in the French Revolution*. Berkeley: University of California Press, 1986.

Jacobus, Mary. "Incorruptible Milk: Breast-feeding and the French Revolution." In *Rebel Daughters: Women and the French Revolution*. Edited by Sara E. Melzer and Leslie W. Rabine, 54–75. Oxford: Oxford University Press, 1992.

Janes, Regina. "Beheadings," *Representations* 35 (1991):21–51.

Jennings, Judith. *The Business of Abolishing the Slave Trade 1783–1807*. London: Frank Cass, 1997.

Jerningham, Edward. "On Reading 'Letters written from France in the summer of 1790, to a Friend in England, by Helen Maria Williams.'" *Universal Magazine* 18(December 1790):472.

Jones, Chris. "Helen Maria Williams and Radical Sensibility." *Prose Studies* 12 (1989):3–24.

Jones, Vivien. "Women Writing Revolution: Narratives of History and Sexuality in Wollstonecraft and Williams." In *Beyond Romanticism*. Edited by Stephen Copley and John Whale, 178–99. London: Routledge, 1992.

Jump, Harriet Devine. "'A Meritorious Wife': or, Mrs. Godwin and the Donkey." *The Charles Lamb Bulletin* 90 (April 1995):73–84.

Kamber, Peter. "Enlightenment, Revolution, and the Libraries in Lucerne, 1787–1812." *Libraries and Culture* 26 (Winter 1991):199–218.

Kates, Gary. *The "Cercle Social," the Girondins, and the French Revolution*. Princeton: Princeton University Press, 1985.

Kegan Paul, Charles. *William Godwin: His Friends and Contemporaries*. 2 vols. New York: AMS, 1970.

Kelly, Gary. *Revolutionary Feminism: The Mind and Career of Mary Wollstonecraft*. London: Macmillan, 1992.

— — —. *Women, Writing, and Revolution: 1790–1827*. Oxford: Clarendon, 1993.

Kelly, Linda. *Richard Brinsley Sheridan: A Life*. London: Sinclair-Stevenson, 1997.

— — —. *Women of the French Revolution*. London: Hamish Hamilton, 1987.

Kemmerer, Kathleen Nulton. *"A Neutral being between the sexes": Samuel Johnson's Sexual Politics.* Lewisburg: Bucknell University Press, 1998.

Kennedy, Deborah. "Benevolent Historian: Helen Maria Williams and Her British Readers." In *Rebellious Hearts: British Women Writers and the French Revolution.* Edited by Adriana Craciun and Kari Lokke, 317–36. New York: State University of New York Press, 2001.

— — —. "Responding to the French Revolution: Williams's *Julia* and Burney's *The Wanderer.*" In *Jane Austen and Mary Shelley and Their Sisters.* Edited by Laura Dabundo, 5–17. Lanham: University Press of America, 2000.

— — —. "Revolutionary Tales: Helen Maria Williams's *Letters from France* and Wordsworth's "Vaudracour and Julia." *The Wordsworth Circle* 21 (1990):110–15.

— — —. "Revolutionizing Switzerland: Helen Maria Williams and 1798." *Republikanische Tugend.* Edited by Michael Böhler et al., 547–55. Geneva: Slatkine, 2000.

— — —. "Spectacle of the Guillotine." *Philological Quarterly* 73 (1994): 95–113.

— — —. " 'Storms of Sorrow': The Poetry of Helen Maria Williams." *Man and Nature* 10 (1991):77–91.

Kippis, Andrew. Advertisement. *Edwin and Eltruda. A Legendary Tale.* By a Young Lady. London: Cadell, 1782.

— — —. Letter to James Boswell. 12 July 1791. Yale University Library.

"Kippis, Andrew." *Dictionary of National Biography.*

Knapp, Oswald G. *The Intimate Letters of Hester Piozzi and Penelope Pennington 1788–1821.* London: John Lane, 1913.

Knight, Ellis Cornelia. *Autobiography of Miss Cornelia Knight, Lady Companion to the Princess Charlotte of Wales.* 3rd. ed. 2 vols. London: W. H. Allen, 1861.

Kramer, Lloyd. *Lafayette in Two Worlds: Public Cultures and Personal Identities in an Age of Revolutions.* Chapel-Hill: University of North Caroline Press, 1996.

Kramnick, Isaac, ed. *The Portable Enlightenment Reader.* Harmondsworth: Penguin, 1995.

Landes, Joan B. *Women and the Public Sphere in the Age of the French Revolution.* Ithaca: Cornell University Press, 1988.

Lavisse, Ernest. *Histoire de France Contemporaine depuis la révolution jusqu'à la paix de 1919.* Vol. 3. Paris: Librairie Hachette, 1921.

Lean, E. Tangye. *The Napoleonists: A Study in Political Disaffection 1760–1960.* London: Oxford University Press, 1970.

LeBlanc, Jacqueline. "Politics and Commercial Sensibility in Helen Maria Williams's *Letters from France.*" *Eighteenth-Century Life* 21 (February 1997):26–44.

Lefebvre, Georges. *The French Revolution from 1793 to 1799.* Translated by John Hall Stewart and James Friguglietti. London, Routledge & Kegan Paul, 1967.

— — —. *Napoleon: From 18 Brumaire to Tilsit 1799–1807.* Translated by Henry F. Stockhold. New York: Columbia University Press, 1969.

Leitner, Ulrike. "Die englischen Ubersetzungen Humboldtscher Werke." *Acta historica Leopoldina* 27 (1997):63–74.

Levy, Darline Gay and Harriet B. Applewhite. "Women and Militant Citizenship in Revolutionary Paris." In *Rebel Daughters: Women and the French Revolution.* Edited by Sara E. Melzer and Leslie W. Rabine, 79–101. New York: Oxford University Press, 1992.

Levy, Darline Gay, Harriet Bronson Applewhite, and Mary Durham Johnson, eds.

Women in Revolutionary Paris, 1789–95: Selected Documents Translated with Notes and Commentary. Chicago: University of Illinois Press, 1979.

Lewis, Michael. *Napoleon and His British Captives*. London: George Allen & Unwin, 1962.

List of the General and Field-Officers to September 1758. London: Millan, n. d.

Lofland, John. "The Dramaturgy of State Executions." In *State Executions Viewed Historically and Sociologically*. Montclair: Patterson Smith, 1977.

Lofts, Nora. *Emma Hamilton*. London: Michael Joseph, 1978.

Lonsdale, Roger, ed. *Eighteenth-Century Women Poets: An Oxford Anthology*. Oxford: Oxford University Press, 1989.

Lowenthal, Cynthia. "The Veil of Romance: Lady Mary's Embassy Letters." *Eighteenth-Century Life* 14 (1990):66–82.

Lunn, Arnold. *Switzerland in English Prose and Poetry*. London: Eyre and Spottiswode, 1947.

Lyons, Martyn. *Napoleon Bonaparte and the Legacy of the French Revolution*. London: Macmillan, 1994.

Macaulay, Catharine. *Observations on the Reflections of the Right Hon. Edmund Burke, on the Revolution in France, In a Letter to the Right Hon. Earl of Stanhope*. London: C. Dilly in the Poultry, 1790.

MacNevin, William James. *A Ramble Through Swisserland in the Summer and Autumn of 1802*. Dublin: J. Stockdale, 1803.

Magraw, Roger. *France 1815–1914: The Bourgeois Century*. Oxford: Fontana, 1983.

Mallet du Pan, Jacques. *Considerations on the Nature of the French Revolution and on the Causes Which Prolong Its Duration*. Introduction by Paul H. Beik. New York: Howard Fertig, 1974.

———. *The History of the Destruction of the Helvetic Union and Liberty*. Boston: Manning and Loring, 1799.

Marand-Fouquet, Catherine. *La Femme au temps de La Révolution*. Paris: Stock/Laurence Pernoud, 1989.

Markham, Felix. *Napoleon*. London: Weidenfeld and Nicolson, 1963.

Markham, J. David. "Prisoners and Writers: Napoleon's British Captives and their Stories." *Consortium on Revolutionary Europe* (1996): 121–34.

May, Gita. *Madame Roland and the Age of Revolution*. New York: Columbia University Press, 1970.

Mayo, Robert D. *The English Novel in the Magazines*. Evanston: Northwestern University Press, 1962.

McCarthy, William. *Hester Thrale Piozzi: Portrait of a Literary Woman*. Chapel Hill: University of North Carolina Press, 1985.

Mège, Francisque. *Le Conventionnel Bancal des Issarts*. Paris: H. Champion, 1887.

Menzies-Wilson, Jacobine and Helen Lloyd. *Amelia: the Tale of a Plain Friend*. London: Oxford University Press, 1937.

Midgley, Clare. *Women against Slavery: The British Campaigns, 1780–1870*. London: Routledge, 1992.

"Miss Williams." *Notes and Queries* 5 December 1968: 533–34.

Monthly Magazine, 1797–1819.

Monthly Review, 1783–1823.

Moore, John. *A Journal during a Residence in France, from the Beginning of August, to the*

Middle of December, 1792. To Which is Added, An Account of the Most Remarkable Events that Happened at Paris from that Time to the Death of the Late King of France. 2 vols. London: Robinson, 1793.

Moore, Thomas. *The Journal of Thomas Moore.* Vol. 2. Edited by Wilfred S. Dowden. Newark: University of Delaware Press, 1983.

Moorman, Mary. *William Wordsworth, A Biography: The Early Years 1770–1803.* Oxford: Clarendon, 1957.

More, Hannah. *The Works of Hannah More. A New Edition in Eighteen Volumes.* London: T. Cadell and W. Davies, 1816.

— — —. Strictures on the Modern System of Female Education. In *Women in the Eighteenth Century.* Edited by Vivien Jones. New York: Routledge, 1990.

Morgan, Lady. *France.* 2nd. ed. 2 vols. London: Colburn, 1817.

— — —. *France in 1829–30.* 2nd. ed. 2 vols. London: Saunders and Otley, 1831.

Murray, Craig C. *Benjamin Vaughan (1751–1835): The Life of an Anglo-American Intellectual.* New York: Arno Press, 1982.

Murray, John, III. *A Hand-book for Travellers in Switzerland.* London: John Murray, 1838.

Myers, Sylvia Harcstark. *The Bluestocking Circle: Women, Friendship, and the Life of the Mind in Eighteenth-Century England.* Oxford: Oxford University Press, 1990.

Nanteuil, Luc de. *Jacques-Louis David.* New York: Harry N. Abrams, 1985.

Necheles, Ruth F. *The Abbé Grégoire 1787–1831: The Odyssey of an Egalitarian.* Westport: Greenwood, 1971.

New Annual Register, 1782–95.

Nichols, John. *Illustrations of the Literary History of the Eighteenth Century.* Vol. 3. London: Nichols, Son, and Bentley, 1818.

Nicolas, Sir Nicholas Harris. *The Dispatches and Letters of Vice-Admiral Lord Viscount Nelson. With Notes by Sir Nicholas Harris Nicolas.* Vol. 3. London: Henry Colburn, 1845.

Nicolson, Malcolm. Introduction to *Personal Narrative,* by Alexander von Humboldt. Harmondsworth: Penguin, 1995.

Noether, Emiliana P. "Eleonora De Fonseca Pimentel and the Neapolitan Revolution of 1799." *Consortium on Revolutionary Europe* (1989):76–88.

Oechsli, Wilhelm. *History of Switzerland 1499–1914.* Translated by Eden Paul and Cedar Paul. Cambridge: Cambridge University Press, 1922.

Oldfield, J. R. *Popular Politics and British Anti-Slavery: The Mobilisation of Public Opinion against the Slave Trade 1787–1807.* Manchester: Manchester University Press, 1995.

Oman, Carola. *Sir John Moore.* London: Hodder and Stoughton, 1953.

O'Meara, Barry. *Napoleon in Exile; or a Voice from St. Helena.* 6th ed. 2 vols. London: Jones, 1829.

Outram, Dorinda. *The Body and the French Revolution: Sex, Class, and Political Culture.* New Haven: Yale University Press, 1989.

Ovid. *Tristia.* Translated by Arthur Leslie Wheeler. Cambridge: Harvard University Press, 1975.

Ozouf, Mona. *Festivals and the French Revolution.* Translated by Alan Sheridan. Cambridge: Harvard University Press, 1988.

Palmer, R. R. *The Age of the Democratic Revolution.* Vol. 2. Princeton: Princeton University Press, 1964.

Parker, Harold T. *The Cult of Antiquity and the French Revolutionaries: A Study in the Development of the Revolutionary Spirit.* New York: Octagon, 1965.

Parra-Pérez, C. *Miranda et la Révolution Française.* Paris: Librairie Pierre Roger, 1925.

Paulson, Ronald. *Representations of Revolution 1789–1820.* New Haven: Yale University Press, 1983.

Peltier, Jean. *The Late Picture of Paris, or Narrative of the Revolution of the Tenth of August.* Vol. 1. London, 1792.

Piozzi, Hester Thrale. *The Piozzi Letters: Correspondence of Hester Lynch Piozzi, 1784–1821.* Vol. 1–3. Edited by Edward Bloom and Lillian D. Bloom. Newark: University of Delaware Press, 1989–93.

— — —. *Thraliana: The Diary of Hester Lynch Thrale.* 2 vols. Edited by Katharine C. Balderston. Oxford: Clarendon, 1951.

Pitcher, E. W. "Changes in Short Fiction in Britain 1785–1810: Philosophic Tales, Gothic Tales, and Fragments and Visions." *Studies in Short Fiction* 13 (1976):331–54.

Plumptre, Anne. *A Narrative of A Three Year's Residence in France, particulary in the Southern Departments, from the Year 1802 to 1805: including Some Authentic Particulars Respecting the early Life of the French Emperor, and a General Inquiry into His Character.* 3 vols. London: J. Mawman, 1810.

Poland, Burdette C. *French Protestantism and the French Revolution: A Study in Church and State, Thought and Religion, 1685–1815.* Princeton: Princeton University Press, 1957.

Polowetzky, Michael. *A Bond Never Broken: The Relations between Napoleon and the Authors of France.* London: Associated University Presses, 1993.

Polwhele, Richard. *The Unsex'd Females.* New York: Garland, 1974.

Poole, Thomas. *Thomas Poole and His Friends.* Edited by Mrs. Henry Sandford. 2 vols. London: Macmillan, 1888.

Porter, Dale H. *The Abolition of the Slave Trade in England, 1784–1807.* New York: Archon Books, 1970.

Pougens, Charles. *Memoires et Souvenirs de Charles Pougens.* Edited by Louise B. de Saint-Leon. Paris: Fournier Jeune, 1834.

Price, Cecil. *The Dramatic Works of Richard Brinsley Sheridan.* Vol. 2. Oxford: Clarendon Press, 1973.

Price, Richard. *Richard Price: Political Writings.* Edited by D. O. Thomas. Cambridge: Cambridge University Press, 1991.

Priestley, Joseph. *The Theological and Miscellaneous Works of Joseph Priestley.* Edited by John Towill Rutt. 25 vols. New York: Kraus Reprint, 1972.

Proctor, Candice E. *Women, Equality, and the French Revolution.* New York: Greenwood, 1990.

Pye, Henry James. "Ode for the New Year, 1802." *Morning Chronicle*, 18 January 1802:2.

Quarterly Review, 1815.

Quinault, Roland. "Westminster and the Victorian Constitution." *Transactions of the Royal Historical Society* 6.2 London: Butler and Tanner, 1992. 79–104.

Raffles, Thomas. *Letters During a Tour Through Some Parts of France, Savoy, Switzerland, Germany, and the Netherlands: The Summer of 1817.* 2nd. ed. Liverpool: Thomas Taylor, 1819.

Reichardt, J. F. *Un hiver à Paris sous le consulat 1802–1803.* Edited by A. Laquiante. Paris: Plon, 1896.

Renwick, W. L. Introduction to *Mordaunt*, by John Moore. London: Oxford University Press, 1965.

Réville, Albert. "A Memoir." In *Conscience and Faith*, by Athanase Coquerel fils. Translated by J. Edwin Odgers, iii–xxviii. London: British and Foreign Unitarian Association, 1878.

Richardson, Herbert. *A Dictionary of Napoleon*. London: Cassell, 1920.

Rigby, Brian. "Radical Spectators of the Revolution: the Case of the *Analytical Review*. In *The French Revolution and British Culture*. Edited by Ceri Crossley and Ian Small, 63–83. Oxford: Oxford University Press, 1989.

Rigney, Ann. *The Rhetoric of Historical Representation: Three Narratives of the French Revolution*. Cambridge: Cambridge University Press, 1990.

"Robinson, George." *Dictionary of National Biography*.

Robinson, Henry Crabb. *The Diary of Henry Crabb Robinson*. Edited by Derek Hudson. London: Oxford University Press, 1967.

———. *Henry Crabb Robinson on Books and Their Writers*. Edited by Edith J. Morley. Vol. 1. London: Dent, 1938.

Robinson, Nicholas K. *Edmund Burke: A Life in Caricature*. New Haven: Yale University Press, 1996.

Robinson, Philip. "Traduction ou Trahison de *Paul et Virginie*? L'exemple de Helen Maria Williams." *Revue d'Histoire Littéraire de la France* 89 (September–October 1989):843–55.

Roland, Marie-Jeanne Phlipon. *Lettres autographes de Madame Roland, addressées a Bancal-des-Issarts*. Edited by Henriette Bancal-des-Issarts. Paris: Eugène Renduel, 1835.

———. *Memoirs of Madame Roland: A Heroine of the French Revolution*. Edited and translated by Evelyn Shuckburgh. London: Barrie and Jenkins, 1989.

Romilly, Samuel. *Memoirs of The Life of Sir Samuel Romilly*. 3 vols. London: John Murray, 1840.

Roscoe, William. *The Life, Death, and Wonderful Atchievements of Edmund Burke: A New Ballad*. In *William Roscoe of Liverpool*, by George Chandler. London: Batsford, 1953.

Roudinesco, Elisabeth. *Madness and Revolution: The Lives and Legends of Théroigne de Méricourt*. Translated by Martin Thom. London: Verso, 1991.

St. Clair, William. *The Godwins and the Shelleys: The Biography of a Family*. London: Faber, 1989.

Say, J. B. Preface to *Nouveau Voyage en Suisse*, by Helen Maria Williams. Paris: Charles Pougens, AN VI [1798].

Scheffler, Judith. "Romantic Women Writing on Imprisonment and Prison Reform." *The Wordsworth Circle* 19 (1988):99–103.

Schmid, Walter. *Romantic Switzerland: Mirrored in the Literature and Graphic Art of the 18th and 19th Centuries*. Zurich: Swiss National Tourist Office, 1952.

Schnorrenberg, Barbara Brandon. "An Opportunity Missed: Catharine Macaulay on the Revolution of 1688." *Studies in Eighteenth-Century Culture* 20 (1990):231–40.

Schor Esther. *Bearing the Dead: The British Culture of Mourning: from the Enlightenment to Victoria*. Princeton: Princeton University Press, 1994.

Seward, Anna. *Letters of Anna Seward*. 6 vols. Edinburgh: Constable, 1811.

———. "Sonnet to Miss Williams, On her Epic Poem PERU." *London Magazine* 4 (February 1785):113–14.

Sha, Richard C. "Expanding the Limits of Feminine Writing: The Prose Sketches of

Sydney Owenson (Lady Morgan) and Helen Maria Williams. In *Romantic Women Writers: Voices and Countervoices*. Edited by Paula R. Feldman and Theresa M. Kelley, 194–206. Hanover: University Press of New England, 1995.

Shepherd, William. *Paris, in 1802 and 1814*. 3rd. ed. London: Longman, Hurst, Rees, Orme and Brown, 1814.

Sheridan, Richard Brinsley. *The Speeches of the Right Honourable Richard Brinsley Sheridan*. Vol. 3. New York: Russell & Russell, 1969.

Shuter, Jane, ed. *Helen Williams and the French Revolution*. History Eyewitness Series. Austin: Raintree Steck-Vaughn, 1996.

Silber, Kate. *Pestalozzi: The Man and His Work*. London: Routledge and Kegan Paul, 1969.

Southey, Robert. *New Letters of Robert Southey*. Edited by Kenneth Curry. Vol. 1. New York: Columbia University Press, 1965.

— — —. *The Life of Nelson*. Annapolis: Naval Institute Press, 1990.

Staël, Germaine de. *An Extraordinary Woman: Selected Writings of Germaine de Staël*. Edited and translated by Vivian Folkenflik. New York: Columbia University Press, 1987.

Staffel, Peter. "Recovering Thalestris: Intragender Conflict in *The Rape of the Lock*". In *Pope, Swift, and Women Writers*. Edited by Donald C. Mell, 86–104. Newark: University of Delaware Press, 1996.

Stanhope, Charles. A Letter from Earl Stanhope, to the Right Honourable Edmund Burke; Containing a Short Answer to His Late Speech on the French Revolution. In *Political Writings of the 1790s*. Edited by Gregory Claeys. 8 vols. London: Pickering, 1995.

Steele, Richard and Joseph Addison. *Selections from The Tatler and The Spectator*. Edited by Angus Ross. Harmondsworth: Penguin, 1988.

Stevenson, Lionel. *The Wild Irish Girl: The Life of Sydney Owenson, Lady Morgan (1776–1859)*. London: Chapman and Hall, 1936.

Stockdale, Percival. *The Memoirs of the Life, and Writings of Percival Stockdale; containing many interesting anecdotes of the illustrious men with whom he was connected*. 2 vols. London: Longman, Hurst, Rees, and Orme, 1809.

"Stone, John Hurford." *Dictionary of National Biography*.

Stroehlin, Ernest. *Athanase Coquerel fils*. Paris: Librairie Fischbacher, 1886.

Terra, Helmut de. *Humboldt: The Life and Times of Alexander von Humboldt 1769–1859*. New York: Alfred A. Knopf, 1955.

Thiébault, Baron. *Mémoires du Général Baron Thiébault*. Vol. 1. Edited by Fernand Calmettes. Paris: Plon, 1894.

Thomas, Chantal. "Heroism in the Feminine: The Examples of Charlotte Corday and Madame Roland." In *The French Revolution 1789–1989: Two Hundred Years of Rethinking*. Edited by Sandy Petrey, 67–82. Lubbock, Texas: Texas Tech University Press, 1989.

Thomas, P. D. G. *The House of Commons in the Eighteenth Century*. Oxford: Clarendon, 1971.

Thompson, J. M. *English Witnesses of the French Revolution*. Oxford: Basil Blackwell, 1938.

Thomson, James. *The Seasons*. Edited by J. Logie Robertson. London: Oxford University Press, 1965.

Thorne, R. G. *The History of Parliament: The House of Commons 1790–1820*. London: Secker and Warburg, 1986.

Thürer, Georg. *Free and Swiss: The Story of Switzerland*. Translated by R. P. Heller and E. Long. Coral Gables: University of Miami Press, 1971.

Ticknor, George. *Life, Letters, and Journals of George Ticknor*. 8th ed. Vol. 1. Boston: James R. Osgood, 1877.

Tillotson, Geoffrey, Paul Fussell, Jr., Marshall Waingrow, and Brewster Rogerson, eds. *Eighteenth-Century English Literature*. San Diego: Harcourt, Brace, Jovanovich, 1969.

"To Miss Helen Maria Williams, on Reading Her Novel of Julia." *Gentleman's Magazine* (April 1790):355.

Todd, F. M. "Wordsworth, Helen Maria Williams and France." *Modern Language Review* 43 (1948):456–64.

Todd, Janet. *Mary Wollstonecraft: A Revolutionary Life*. London: Weidenfeld and Nicolson, 2000.

———. *Sensibility: An Introduction*. London: Methuen, 1986.

Tomalin, Claire. *The Life and Death of Mary Wollstonecraft*. New York: Meridian, 1974.

Trotter, John Bernard. *Memoirs of the Latter Years of the Right Honourable Charles James Fox*. London: Richard Phillips, 1811.

Trouille, Mary Seidman. *Sexual Politics in the Enlightenment: Women Writers Read Rousseau*. New York: State University of New York Press, 1997.

Ty, Eleanor. *Unsex'd Revolutionaries: Five Women Novelists of the 1790s*. Toronto: University of Toronto Press, 1993.

Urlichs, Ludwig von. *Charlotte Von Schiller und ihre Freunde*. Vol. 2. Stuttgart: Cotta, 1862.

Vance, John A. *Joseph and Thomas Warton*. Boston: Twayne Publishers, 1983.

Vickery, Amanda. *The Gentleman's Daughter: Women's Lives in Georgian England*. New Haven: Yale University Press, 1998.

Walker, John. "Maria Cosway: An Undervalued Artist." *Apollo* (May 1986):318–24.

Wallace, William. *Robert Burns and Mrs. Dunlop*. London: Hodder and Stoughton, 1898.

Walpole, Horace. *The Yale Edition of Horace Walpole's Correspondence*. 48 vols. Edited by W. S. Lewis. New Haven: Yale University Press, 1937–83.

Warburton, T. Rennie. "The Rise of Nationalism in Switzerland." *Canadian Review of Studies in Nationalism* 7 (1980):274–98.

Wildi, Max. "Wordsworth and the Simplon Pass." *English Studies* 40 (1959):224–32.

Williams, Helen Maria. *Aperçu de l'état des moeurs et des opinions dans la République française vers la fin du xviiie siècle*. Traduit de l'anglais par Mme [Sophie] Grandchamp. Paris: Levrault, 1801.

———. *The Charter, Lines Addressed by Helen Maria Williams, to her Nephew Athanase C. Coquerel, on His Wedding Day*. Paris, 1819.

———. *Edwin and Eltruda. A Legendary Tale*. By a Young Lady. London: Cadell, 1782.

———. *Évenements arrivés en France depuis la Restauration de 1815*, par Helen-Marie Williams. Traduit de l'anglais par M. Moreau père. Paris, 1819.

———. *A Farewell, for Two Years, to England. A Poem*. London: Cadell, 1791.

———. *Julia, A Novel; Interspersed with Poetical Pieces*. 2 vols. Intro. Gina Luria. New York: Garland, 1974.

— — —. *Julia, A Novel*. Edited by Peter Garside. London: Routledge / Thoemmes Press, 1995.

— — —, trans. *The Leper of the City of Aoste. A Narrative*, [by Xavier de Maistre]. London: George Cowie, 1817.

— — —. Letter to Colonel Barry. 17 November 1790. British Library.

— — —. Letter to Robert Burns. 20 June 1787. *The Edinburgh Magazine, and Literary Miscellany; a New Series of the Scots Magazine* 1 (September 1817):109.

— — —. Letter to Benjamin Constant. 10 May 1827. Bibliothèque cantonale et universitaire, Lausanne.

— — —. Letter to Lord Holland. 22 July 1802. British Library.

— — —. Letter to Samuel Rogers. 24 April 1825. Sharpe Papers, University College London.

— — —. Letter to William Shepherd. [1818]. Harris Manchester College, Oxford.

— — —. Letters. Abinger Collection. Bodleian Library, Oxford.

— — —. Letters. Piozzi-Pennington Collection. Princeton University Library.

— — —. Letters. Huntington Library, San Marino, California.

— — —. Letters. John Rylands University Library of Manchester.

— — —. *Letters from France*. Eight volumes in two. Intro. Janet Todd. Delmar, New York: Scholars' Facsimiles & Reprints, 1975.

— — —. *Letters on the Events Which Have Passed in France Since the Restoration in 1815*. London: Baldwin, 1819.

— — —. *Letters written in France, in the Summer 1790*. Spelsbury: Woodstock, 1990.

— — —. *Letters written in France, in the Summer 1790*. Edited by Neil Fraistat and Susan S. Lanser. Peterborough: Broadview Press, 2001.

— — —. *Lettres écrites de France à une amie en Angleterre pendant l'été 1790*. Traduit de l'Anglais par M. de la Montagné. Paris, 1791.

— — —. *Lettres sur les Évenemens qui se sont passés en France, depuis le 31 mai 1793 jusqu'au 10 Thermidor*. Traduites de Langlois. Paris, 1795.

— — —. "Memoirs of the Life of Charles Berns Wadstrom." *Monthly Magazine* 7 (July 1799):462–65.

— — —. "The Morai." In *The Life of Captain James Cook*, by Andrew Kippis. London: Robinson, 1788; Chiswick: Whittingham, 1822.

— — —. *A Narrative of the Events Which Have Taken Place in France from the Landing of Napoleon Bonaparte on the First of March, 1815, till the Restoration of Louis XVIII*. Cleveland: Burrows, 1894.

— — —. *Nouveau Voyage en Suisse*. Traduit par J. B. Say. Paris: Charles Pougens, AN VI [1798].

— — —. *An Ode on the Peace*. By the author of Edwin and Eltruda. London: Cadell, 1783.

— — —. "Ode to Peace." *Morning Chronicle* 17 November 1801.

— — —. "On the Death of the Rev. Dr. Kippis." *Gentleman's Magazine* 66 (1796):66.

— — —. *On the Late Persecution of the Protestants in the South of France*. London: T. and G. Underwood, 1816.

— — —, trans. *Paul and Virginia*, by J. H. Bernardin de St.-Pierre. Oxford: Woodstock, 1989.

— — —. *Peru, a Poem*. In Six Cantos. London: Cadell, 1784.

— — —. *A Poem on the Bill Lately Passed for Regulating the Slave Trade*. London: Cadell, 1788.

— — —. *Poems*. 2 vols. London: Cadell, 1786.

— — —. *Poems*. 2nd. ed. 2 vols. London: Cadell, 1791.

— — —. *Poems on Various Subjects. With Introductory Remarks on the Present State of Science and Literature in France*. London: Whittaker, 1823.

— — —. *Poems. Moral, Elegant and Pathetic, viz. Essay on Man, by Pope; The Monk of La Trappe, by Jerningham; The Grave, by Blair; An Elegy in a Country Churchyard, by Gray; The Hermit of Warkworth, by Percy; and Original Sonnets, by Helen Maria Williams*. London: Vernor and Hood, 1796.

— — —. *The Political and Confidential Correspondence of Lewis the Sixteenth; with Observations on Each Letter*. 3 vols. London: G. and J. Robinson, 1803.

— — —. Preface to *Personal Narrative of Travels to the Equinoctial Regions of the New Continent, during the Years 1799–1804 by Alexander de Humboldt, and Aimé Bonpland*, by Alexander de Humboldt. Vols. 1 and 2. Translated by Helen Maria Williams. London: Longman, Hurst, Rees, Orme, and Brown, 1818; New York: AMS, 1966.

— — —. Preface à la deuxième èdition. *Nouveau Voyage en Suisse*. 2nd. ed. 2 vols. Traduit par J. B. Say. Paris: Charles Pougens, 1802.

— — —. *Recueil de Poésies, extraites des ouvrages d'Helena-Maria Williams*. Traduit de l'angalis par M. Stanislas de Boufflers et M. Esménard. Paris: F. Cocheris, 1808.

— — —. *Relation des Évènemens qui se sont passés en France depuis le débarquement de Napoléon Buonaparte, au 1er Mars 1815, jusqu'au traité du 20 Novembre*, par Miss Helen-Maria Williams. Traduit de l'anglais par M. Breton de La Martinère. Paris: J. G. Dentu, 1816.

— — —, trans. *Researches Concerning the Institutions and Monuments of the Ancient Inhabitants of America, with Descriptions and Views of Some of the Most Striking Scenes in the Cordilleras!*, by Alexander de Humboldt. London: Longman, 1814; Amsterdam: Theatrum Orbis Terrarum, 1971.

— — —. *Sketches of the State of Manners and Opinions in the French Republic, towards the Close of the Eighteenth Century. In a Series of Letters*. 2 vols. London: G. G. and J. Robinson, 1801.

— — —. *Souvenirs de la révolution française*. Traduit de l'anglais par Charles Coquerel. Paris: Dondey-Dupré, 1827.

— — —. *A Tour in Switzerland; or, A View of the Present State of the Governments and Manners of those Cantons: with Comparative Sketches of the Present State of Paris*. 2 vols. London: G. G. and J. Robinson, 1798.

— — —. *Verses Addressed by Helen Maria Williams to Her Two Nephews, on Saint Helen's Day*. Paris, 1809.

Wilmot, Catherine. *An Irish Peer on the Continent (1801–1803): Being a Narrative of the Tour of Stephen, 2nd Earl Mount Cashell, Through France, Italy, etc., as Related by Catherine Wilmot*. Edited by Thomas U. Sadleir. London: Williams and Norgate, 1920.

Wilson, Ellen Gibson. *Thomas Clarkson: A Biography*. New York: St. Martin's Press, 1990.

Wilson, Jason. Introduction to *Personal Narrative* by Alexander von Humboldt. Harmondsworth: Penguin, 1995.

Wollstonecraft, Mary. *Collected Letters of Mary Wollstonecraft*. Edited by Ralph M. Wardle. Ithaca: Cornell University Press, 1979.

— — —. *Mary Wollstonecraft: Political Writings*. Edited by Janet Todd. Toronto: University of Toronto Press, 1993.

268 BIBLIOGRAPHY

— — —. *A Vindication of the Rights of Woman*. 2nd ed. Edited by Carol H. Poston. New York: Norton, 1988.

Woodress, James. *A Yankee's Odyssey: The Life of Joel Barlow*. Philadelphia: J. B. Lippincott, 1958.

Woodward, Lionel. *Une Anglaise Amie de la Révolution française: Hélène-Maria Williams et ses Amis*. Paris: Librairie Ancienne Honoré Champion, 1930. Geneva: Slatkine Reprints, 1977.

Woof, Robert, Stephen Hebron, and Claire Tomalin. *Hyenas in Petticoats: Mary Wollstonecraft and Mary Shelley*. Kendal: Wordsworth Trust, 1997.

Woolf, Virginia. *A Room of One's Own*. London: Granada, 1981.

Wordsworth, Jonathan. Introduction. *Paul and Virginia*, by J. H. Bernardin de St-Pierre. Oxford: Woodstock, 1989.

Wordsworth, William. *The Letters of William and Dorothy Wordsworth: The Early Years 1787–1805*. Edited by Ernest de Selincourt; 2nd. ed. rev. Chester L. Shaver. Oxford: Clarendon, 1967.

— — —. *The Letters of William and Dorothy Wordsworth: The Later Years*. 2nd. ed. 5 vols. Edited by Alan G. Hill. Oxford: Clarendon, 1979.

— — —. *Poetical Works*. Edited by Thomas Hutchinson. Revised by Ernest de Selincourt. Oxford: Oxford University Press, 1969.

— — —. *The Prelude: 1799, 1805, 1850*. Edited by Jonathan Wordsworth, M. H. Abrams, and Stephen Gill. New York: Norton, 1979.

Wraight, John. *The Swiss and the British*. Wilton: Michael Russell, 1987.

Wu, Duncan. *Romantic Women Poets: An Anthology*. Oxford: Blackwell, 1997.

— — —. *Wordsworth's Reading*. Cambridge: Cambridge University Press, 1993.

Wyndham, Violet. *Madame de Genlis: A Biography*. New York: Roy, 1958.

Yalom, Marilyn. *Blood Sisters: The French Revolution in Women's Memory*. New York: Basic Books, 1993.

Zagarri, Rosemarie. "The Rights of Man and Woman in Post-Revolutionary America." *William and Mary Quarterly* 55 (April 1998):203–30.

Index